VOID

Library of
Davidson College

PUBLIC SCHOOLS AND BRITISH OPINION

PUBLIC SCHOOLS
AND
BRITISH OPINION
1780 to 1860

An Examination of the Relationship Between Contemporary Ideas and the Evolution of an English Institution

by

EDWARD C. MACK, Ph.D.

GREENWOOD PRESS, PUBLISHERS
WESTPORT, CONNECTICUT

The Library of Congress has catalogued this publication as follows:

Library of Congress Cataloging in Publication Data

Mack, Edward Clarence, 1904–
    Public schools and British opinion, 1780–1860.

    Originally presented as the author's thesis, Columbia University, 1938.
    Bibliography: p.
    1. Public schools (Endowed)—England. 2. Education—England—History. I. Title.
LA634.M27   1973   373.42   72-11740
ISBN 0-8371-6703-5

First published in 1938
by Methuen & Co. Ltd., London

Reprinted with the permission
of Edward C. Mack

First Greenwood Reprinting 1973

Library of Congress Catalogue Card Number 72-11740

ISBN 0-8371-6703-5

Printed in the United States of America

TO
R.P.M.

PREFACE

THIS book has grown out of a suggestion by the late Professor Ashley N. Thorndike in regard to the peculiar attachment of Englishmen to their schools. During the more than three years that have been required for this idea to germinate into a book I have received aid and encouragement from many sources in both England and America. In particular I owe a debt of gratitude to Professor Emery Neff, under whose direct and painstaking guidance this work has been undertaken, and to Professors Hoxie N. Fairchild and Dr. Henry W. Wells, who have carefully read the manuscript and given invaluable help. I also wish to express my thanks to Professors Ernest Hunter Wright, Harry Morgan Ayres, G. C. D. Odell, Ralph L. Rusk, Frank A. Patterson, Rodger S. Loomis, Samuel L. Wolff, Susanne Howe Nobbe, Frederick William J. Heuser, Clarence Manning, Arthur Livingston, and Jefferson B. Fletcher, for useful suggestions which they have offered.

To Dr. Louis Ginzberg, Sir Philip Hartog, and Mr. H. W. Llewellyn-Smith I am especially grateful for having opened doors to me in England that might otherwise have remained closed. Within these doors I found gracious hospitality and unfailing assistance, for which I am indebted to the Rev. H. Costley White, formerly head master of Westminster School, Mr. Hugh Lyon, head master of Rugby School, and to Messrs. Cyril Robinson, A. W. Siddons, Stewart Mason, Patrick Hunter, and A. W. Sparling, masters at Winchester, Harrow, Stowe, and Rugby schools.

Finally, I want to thank my friends Professor Karl N. Llewellyn, Dr. Millard Meiss, Professor Garrett Mattingly, Dr. John C. Thirlwall, and above all my wife, Ruth Prince Mack, for the kind of criticism and encouragement to which no words of appreciation can do justice.

E.C.M.

CONTENTS

	PAGE
PREFACE	vii
INTRODUCTION	xv

PART I. PROLOGUE: 1382–1780

CHAPTER I: THE LATE EIGHTEENTH CENTURY PUBLIC SCHOOL	3
A. POLITICAL ORGANIZATION AND GENERAL STRUCTURE	4
B. MEMBERSHIP	16
C. INTELLECTUAL EDUCATION	25
D. MORAL EDUCATION—THE MASTERS	30
E. MORAL EDUCATION—THE BOYS	35
CHAPTER II: EARLY OPINION	47
A. APPROVAL	47
B. CRITICISM	55
C. GENERAL TENDENCIES	65

PART II. FROM COWPER TO ARNOLD

INTRODUCTION	71
CHAPTER I: CHANGES IN THE PUBLIC SCHOOLS, 1780–1830	73
A. CHANGES IN MEMBERSHIP AND THEIR RESULTS—BOY LIFE	73
B. CHANGES BY MASTERS—STRONG MASTERS OF THE OLD TYPE	85
CHAPTER II: FORCES AND PHILOSOPHIES	91
A. CONSERVATISM	91
1. INDIVIDUAL MOTIVES	92
2. THE UPPER CLASSES	103
3. THE MASTERS	106
4. ROMANTIC ATTACHMENT	107

Contents

	PAGE
B. LIBERALISM AND REACTION	116
1. INDIVIDUAL MOTIVES	116
2. REACTION	118
3. LIBERALISM	121
CHAPTER III: CRITICISM AND DEFENCE, 1780–1830	132
A. CONTROL AND MEMBERSHIP	132
B. THE ATTACK ON PUBLIC SCHOOL EDUCATION	143
1. INTELLECTUAL EDUCATION	143
2. MORAL EDUCATION	151
(*a*) BOY LIFE	151
(*b*) THE MASTERS	160
(*c*) REMEDIES	166
C. THE DEFENCE OF PUBLIC SCHOOL EDUCATION	170
1. INTELLECTUAL EDUCATION	172
2. HAPPINESS AND MORAL TRAINING	179
CHAPTER IV: THE EARLY THIRTIES	192
A. THE VICTORIAN COMPROMISE	192
B. CRITICISM: 1830–1835	199
1. CARLYLE	199
2. CONTROL	203
3. SCHOOLS AS SOCIAL INSTITUTIONS	206
4. INTELLECTUAL EDUCATION	207
5. MORAL EDUCATION	213

PART III. THREE REFORMERS

CHAPTER I: RUSSELL AND BUTLER	223
(*a*) RUSSELL	224
(*b*) BUTLER	228
CHAPTER II: ARNOLD	236
A. SUCCESS AND INFLUENCE	236
B. CHARACTER, BACKGROUND, AND EARLY STRUGGLES	242
C. ARNOLD'S EDUCATIONAL PURPOSES	248
D. ARNOLD'S EDUCATIONAL METHODS	261
E. THE FRUITS OF ARNOLD'S DOCTRINES	275

PART IV. FROM ARNOLD TO THE PUBLIC SCHOOL COMMISSION

	PAGE
CHAPTER I: ARNOLDIANISM	285
A. INTRODUCTION	285
B. THE CRITICAL REACTION TO ARNOLD	292
C. ARNOLD'S DISCIPLES—THE TRUE FAITH	300
D. ARNOLD'S DISCIPLES—THE PRACTICAL FAITH	323
CHAPTER II: THE PUBLIC SCHOOLS: 1840–1860	334
A. RUGBY	338
B. HARROW	341
C. THE NEW SCHOOLS—MARLBOROUGH	346
D. SHREWSBURY	352
E. WINCHESTER	355
F. THE CITY SCHOOLS—CHARTERHOUSE, WESTMINSTER	360
G. ETON	362
CHAPTER III. DEFENCE AND CRITICISM: 1840–1860	372
A. CONTROL	373
B. MEMBERSHIP	376
C. SOCIAL LIFE AND MORAL TRAINING	377
D. THE CURRICULUM	390
CONCLUSION	399
BIBLIOGRAPHY	405
INDEX	423

INTRODUCTION

PROBABLY no English institution has been more copiously criticized and less fruitfully studied than those non-local endowed boarding-schools for the upper classes which are termed Public Schools. Many volumes have been written in praise or dispraise of the Public School system and in exposition of its characteristics, but comparatively little has been attempted by way of a critical understanding of the nature of its evolution, of the forces which have governed its development at various periods, and of the manner in which these pressures have translated themselves into Public School ideals and practices.

Yet an appreciation of the character of Public School growth is of vital importance for the student of British civilization. Most directly it throws light on the present nature of that school system which still educates a majority of England's upper-class youth. It thus helps to explain both the peculiar relationship of the Englishman to his school and the effect on his outlook and character which has so often resulted from Public School training. More indirectly, it enhances one's understanding of the psychological, social, economic, and political forces which have governed British history. For, since the Public School system is a class institution of national scope, its growth has been inextricably linked with the development of British civilization. Influences other than those of a purely educational nature have governed its evolution more directly and obviously than they have most other educational systems. Indeed, one can view Public School history as a case study of British psychology and of the economic and other pressures to which it has been subjected in the last two hundred years. Finally, the evolution of the Public School is a prototype of the evolution of all British institutions. Like Parliament or the Church, the Public School has been, through most of its history, independent of outside interferences as well as of conscious theory. It has grown by a process of seemingly haphazard modifications of original structure to suit new circumstances, a method which lovers of the system have called organic growth. An understanding of the way in which this has occurred in regard to Public Schools should prove valuable to those who are interested in the general problem of institutional change.

It has seemed to me that a fruitful approach to a comprehension of the nature of Public School development would be through a critical analysis of the copious body of prose fiction, reminiscence, history, poetry, and pamphlet literature which has in the past centuries grown up in exposition, praise, or censure around the institution of the Public School.[1] I have, therefore, attempted in this work, of which the present book is the first volume, to write what is primarily a history of opinion in regard to Public Schools. I have recorded, in historical periods, the ideas of a large proportion of those who have expressed themselves on the subject of Public School education, and have classified these ideas into significant groups. Further, I have attempted to understand the quality of the emotional relationship of the writer to the system, particularly of the very prevalent, unique, and important relationship of romantic attachment with its tendency to personalize and humanize its object. Finally, I have tried to analyse the more obvious psychological, economic, or other motives that underlay the ideas and attitudes expressed by various writers.

A history of opinion, interesting enough in itself, is obviously of only limited significance unless set against the background of actual fact. I have, therefore, paralleled the discussion of ideas with a history of the Public Schools, of

---

[1] Of all those who have written about Public Schools, only Mr. W. R. Hicks, in *The School in English and German Fiction*, London, 1933, has seen the value of this approach. He has, however, dealt with only one aspect of the subject, the novel, and has had a point of view very different from mine. His interest has been less in the development of the Public School as studied through literature, than in the character of the novel in relation to all schools, German as well as English. I am, nevertheless, extremely indebted to Mr. Hicks, particularly for much of my bibliography. Two German works, *Die Reform des englischen höheren Schulwesens im 19 Jahrhundert*, Leipzig, 1929, by Paul Meissner, and *Geschichte der englischen Erziehung*, Leipzig, 1928, by Bruno Dressler, have dealt briefly with the relationship between ideas and practice in Public School history.

their condition at various periods, and of the modifications accomplished by reformers. For this purpose I have confined myself, with some exceptions, to the seven schools which before 1840 were the only ones that answered to the definition of a Public School as a non-local endowed boarding-school for the upper classes. The preoccupation with these seven—to wit, Eton, Harrow, Rugby, Shrewsbury, Winchester, Westminster, and Charterhouse—proceeds, it must be admitted, more from convenience than from logic: before 1780 such schools as Rugby and Shrewsbury and even Harrow were of doubtful status; to-day there are many rivals of the old Public Schools. But, since these seven schools were Public Schools by 1815, were *the* Public Schools until 1840, and have illustrated the system ever since, it serves my purpose to deal chiefly with them.[1]

This study, then, will be in reality an examination of the relationship between the evolution of the Public Schools and the reaction of various Englishmen to these schools. Such an analysis can shed considerable light on the important problems connected with upper-class educational development. In the first place it illuminates the response of the Public Schools to new ideas. Literature presents a panorama of the dominant points of view of each age; by comparing the written word with the condition of schools at various

[1] When speaking of any of the seven schools at the time of their foundations, it is inaccurate to call them Public Schools as I have defined the term; the fifteenth-century history of Eton is, for example, technically the history of a school that later became a Public School.

Englishmen have never been very consistent at any period in their use of the word Public School. In the eighteenth century some writers limited it to mean only Eton and Westminster, excluding even Charterhouse and Winchester. In the early nineteenth century Rugby and Shrewsbury and even Harrow were often omitted (cf. Oscar Browning, *Aspects of Education*, p. 169, Monographs of the Industrial Education Association, Vol. I, No. 5, New York, September 1888) and day schools like St. Paul's and Merchant Taylors and the semi-charitable Christ's Hospital included. (R. Ackermann, *The History of the Colleges of Winchester, Eton, etc.*, London, 1816.) As late as 1861, though Cheltenham and Marlborough had long been great upper-class schools, the Public School Commission could designate as the Public Schools the seven old boarding-schools and the two day schools mentioned above. To-day, with every school that has the slightest pretension of serving the upper classes calling itself a Public School, there is complete confusion. The Headmasters' Conference has been reduced to limiting the term to those schools that have governing bodies. On this tenuous basis, it excluded Sheffield School from the Conference in 1927 (the Labour Party, having gained control of Sheffield, dispensed with the school's governors). (*The Times*, October 13th 1927, p. 15.)

times and with the actions of reformers one can observe the way in which some ideas have been absorbed speedily, some slowly, and some not at all.

In the second place, it gives us a good deal of insight into the forces working for acceptance or rejection of new ideas. These forces, particularly the psychological traits that produced romantic attachment and social motives like class pride, are implicit in innumerable writings about schools. Moreover, at least one kind of secondary force, the mere power of writing, is explicit in literature. Sydney Smith's *Edinburgh* article and Hughes' *Tom Brown's Schooldays* might have had little influence had they not crystallized dominant ideas, but it is surely arguable that had these particular works not appeared, the ideas which they embodied might have remained for long, or indefinitely, sterile. At the same time, it is certainly true that a great many motives cannot be uncovered merely through a reading of Public School criticism. For example, to discover those economic interests which so often motivated writers one must as a rule study their lives. Moreover, there are without doubt some kinds of forces, like mere inertia, which find no implicit or explicit expression in literature about schools or anywhere else. Finally, it must be admitted that the existence of all motives is, in the last analysis, a matter of inference not proof.

Lastly, if it be asked what light a study of this kind casts directly upon the actual causes of specific Public School changes or resistance to change, the answer is a much less satisfactory one. An inquiry into causes involves the measurement of the effectiveness of various complicated forces, and is therefore a quantitative study. Literature provides much of the material for such a study, which must proceed through an analysis of opinion. But to transform criticism into significant scientific data is at best a long process, involving calculations in regard to the frequency with which an idea finds expression, and the accessibility of its author to the sources of effective action. This book can pretend to be no more than a qualitative examination of forces. It thus aims to suggest rather than to define the

Introduction

relationship between ideas and the development of the English Public School.

There is one important limitation upon a study of Public Schools through an examination of critical opinion: before 1780 relatively little was written about English upper-class schools. The end of the eighteenth century witnessed the beginnings of a growing self-consciousness among Englishmen with regard to their schools. From the last decades of the eighteenth century to the present day, there has been a continuous war between rival philosophies for control of upper-class education. The heat of this conflict is in marked contrast to the comparative indifference with which earlier generations viewed the system. Consequently, any review of opinion about the institution of the Public School must be virtually a nineteenth-century study.

It cannot be so entirely, however. There was enough important discussion of schools before 1780 to warrant treatment, especially since the beginnings of attitudes that were later to ripen and expand can be found in the early eighteenth and occasionally in the sixteenth century. More important, a study of Public School development that began with the nineteenth century would be virtually meaningless. The schools had a long evolution before they became the subjects of intense critical scrutiny or self-conscious adoration. The actual origin of some of the seven schools and many of their characteristics can be traced back as far as the fourteenth and fifteenth centuries. It will be necessary, therefore, even though literary material is scanty, to devote Part I of this volume to an attempt to trace in broad outline the growth of the Public School system prior to 1780. It will then be possible to give meaning to the story of later changes and their relationship to the history of opinion.

Part II will deal with the late eighteenth and early nineteenth century battle of opinion, which culminated in the reforms of the thirties and forties. Part III will discuss the work of three Public School masters, Russell, Butler, and Arnold, who, in various ways, embodied in action the forces of the previous period. In Part IV we shall proceed to the period that ended with the Public School Commission in the early sixties. The chapters in this section will be devoted to an account of the early Victorian reaction to the teachings of Arnold, the changes in the schools affected by Arnold and others, and the renewed battle over the Public School system in the forties and fifties. It is expected that Volume II will continue the story of Public School development up to the present day, and will relate the history of the struggle surrounding the Public School Commission in the sixties, the reaction to the system in its greatest days in the seventies and eighties, and finally, the story of the renewed struggles to change the Public Schools in the period just preceding, during, and after the War.

In concluding this introduction, I feel that a word of apology is in order. No one is more conscious than I am of the shortcomings in this book that have resulted from my being neither a Public School man nor an Englishman. If, however, I have secured a certain amount of objectivity and perspective as a result of distance, there may be some compensations for deficiencies in the direction of emotional penetration. Particularly is this true since what I have attempted is analysis and interpretation rather than evaluation.

PART I
PROLOGUE: 1382–1780

CHAPTER I

THE LATE EIGHTEENTH-CENTURY PUBLIC SCHOOL

IF by a system one means a group of institutions controlled by a central authority and displaying as a consequence practically identical traits, the English Public Schools at the end of the eighteenth century could hardly be said to deserve that appellation. The seven Public Schools[1] were virtually independent both of one another and of outside management, they were in no sense cut to pattern. Nevertheless, in the broad sense that they were marked by fundamentally similar characteristics, the Public Schools did form a system.

To begin with, they all showed several of what one might call spiritual resemblances. The most important of these was, paradoxically, the very independence and self-sufficiency which prevented the schools from being, strictly speaking, a system at all. The seven schools possessed, as their proudest boast, that quality of unique individuality which one associates with biologically distinct organisms. Closely related to this characteristic was traditionalism. In all the Public Schools, past experiences or customs served as the models for present action. This did not mean, however, that the schools were totally impervious to change—despite reverence for collective wisdom they had been influenced more or less by every important social and educational force of the day. It did mean that they had not and probably would not allow a direct, reasoned application of new ideas. Rather were they wedded—their third general characteristic—to the principle of organic growth: change ought to occur only through chance influence gradually modifying original structure.

These three spiritual traits, whose significance will become

[1] Though I have included Rugby and Shrewsbury in the following discussion, they became Public Schools, in the sense in which I have used the term, only after 1780, Rugby in the eighties and Shrewsbury in the early years of the nineteenth century.

clearer as we proceed, permeated all aspects of school life. But the eighteenth-century Public School system was also characterized by common features of a more specific nature. Indeed, though there were important differences which ought not to be minimized, the Public Schools exhibited a remarkable sameness in their entire political and social organization as well as in the education which they imparted.

POLITICAL ORGANIZATION AND GENERAL STRUCTURE

If one considers the diverse origins of the various eighteenth-century Public Schools, their basic resemblance to one another seems at first sight surprising. Winchester, the oldest of the schools, was founded in 1382 by a bishop, William of Wykeham.[1] Its purpose was a strictly medieval one. Wykeham, who had endowed New College at Oxford for the training of seventy scholars in theology, canon and civil law, and the arts, discovered that his candidates were pitiably poor and woefully ignorant of Latin. In order to remedy this deficiency and to secure a choice selection of students from all over the country, he established Winchester College,[2] a boarding-school for prospective secular priests. Eton and Westminster, the second and third of the Public Schools, though, like Winchester, endowed for religious purposes, came into being under very different circumstances. Eton, a product of the politically chaotic fifteenth century, owed its existence, not to a cleric, but to a king, the unhappy Henry VI. Westminster was founded a century after Eton, at the time of the Henrician reformation. Henry VIII established it as one of the twelve grammar schools which he endowed or re-endowed as part of the cathedrals 'of the new foundation'.[3] Elizabeth, who is considered by Westminsters as the real founder, re-established

[1] Arthur F. Leach, *A History of Winchester College*, New York, 1899, p. 65.
[2] The word college refers, in England, to the buildings, the living-quarters, the background of corporate life, and is used in connexion with other than educational institutions.
[3] Arthur F. Leach, *The Schools of Medieval England*, London, 1915, pp. 277, 310. A school controlled by the abbey had existed previously near Westminster.

The Late Eighteenth-Century Public School 5

it in 1559 after Mary had undone Henry's work by turning Westminster Abbey back into a monastery. The other four schools were all products of the late sixteenth and seventeenth centuries, and were founded, not by bishops and kings for religious purposes but by relatively inconspicuous laymen in order to bring to the poor and to the middle classes the benefits of the new classical culture of the Renaissance. The sixteenth century, though a time of great national prosperity, was woefully lacking in schools for both rich and poor. To make up for this deficiency, newly rich business men, inspired partly by a desire for fame and partly by a philanthropic interest in education, began to take it upon themselves to endow schools. Harrow, Rugby, and Charterhouse were founded in this manner. Harrow owed its existence to John Lyon, a yeoman landowner of moderate importance,[1] and Rugby to Lawrence Sheriffe, a grocer who had ingratiated himself with Elizabeth;[2] both were country grammar schools for the local poor. Charterhouse, established for the benefit of the sons of poor gentlemen who had served Her Majesty on land and sea, was founded by Thomas Sutton, a gentleman commoner and captain in Elizabeth's service.[3] Shrewsbury, on the other hand, differed from all the other Public Schools in being essentially a municipal undertaking, started at the instigation of the bailiffs and burgesses of Shrewsbury; it was, in other words, a town grammar school.[4]

---

[1] Percy M. Thornton, *Harrow School and its Surroundings*, London, 1885, p. vi.
[2] W. H. D. Rouse, *A History of Rugby School*, New York, 1898, pp. 1 ff.
[3] George Warren Gignilliat, Jr., *The Author of Sandford and Merton*, New York, 1932, p. 19, and Gerald S. Davies, *Charterhouse in London*, London, 1921, pp. 168 ff. The Charterhouse had a long and interesting history before it became a school. It was started as a burial-ground during the plague in 1349. In 1371 it became the Carthusian monastery celebrated by Froude in his great history. At the time of the dissolution of the monasteries the monks martyred themselves rather than accept Henry as their head. Then, from 1545 to 1611 it was owned by various courtiers, the most famous of whom was Thomas Howard, Duke of Norfolk and father of Surrey, the poet. The Howards became implicated in the Ridophi plot against Elizabeth, and for a while the history of the Charterhouse became the history of England. Thomas Sutton bought it from Thomas Howard, Surrey's son. It is memories like these that permeate the very air that English schoolboys breathe. (Cf. Davies, op. cit., pp. 91 ff., pp. 114 ff.)
[4] *A History of Shrewsbury School*, from the Blakeway MSS. and many other sources, Shrewsbury, 1889, pp. 27, 99.

This seeming diversity in origin was not, however, as fatal to Public School unity as one might suppose. To begin with, the various schools with their varying aims were influenced by the same general political ideas, in particular by the individualistic antagonism to both State and Church which, emanating from the middle classes, made itself a dominant characteristic of English life by the sixteenth century. Moreover, the schools borrowed constantly from one another. William of Wykeham was a genuine innovator, though he had indirect precedents for his foundation in monasteries and hospitals housing the poor, and in educational colleges at Oxford, particularly Merton. Winchester was the first semi-independent collegiate foundation whose primary object was a school;[1] moreover, her size, wealth, and exceptional education features were unusual. All the other founders were, in essential respects, mere imitators of Wykeham. Henry VI modelled Eton entirely on Winchester: indeed, when 'The King's College of Our Lady of Eton beside Windsor' opened in 1442 it boasted the possession of William Waynflete, Master of Winchester from 1429 to 1442, as head master.[2] Similarly, Henry VIII looked to Winchester for guidance, and Thomas Sutton to Eton, to which he had gone as a boy. The other three schools were all more or less indebted to their predecessors from the beginning. Moreover, in the eighteenth century Harrow and Rugby were remodelled on Eton lines, and in the nineteenth Shrewsbury developed in imitation of Rugby, and Rugby, under Arnold, in imitation of Winchester.

As a consequence of these circumstances the seven eighteenth-century Public Schools exhibited two political and structural similarities of far-reaching importance. In the first place, they were all more or less free from the State,

---

[1] Before Wykeham's time schools had seldom been either independent or colleges. The latter had existed for the purposes of charity, religion or higher education, not secondary education; if grammar schools existed in connexion with colleges, they were usually of relatively minor importance. (Cf. Leach, *History of Winchester College*, pp. 88 ff., and A. W. Parry, *Education in England in the Middle Ages*, London, 1920, pp. 188 ff.)

[2] H. C. Maxwell-Lyte, *A History of Eton College, 1440–1875*, London, 1875, p. 16.

The Late Eighteenth-Century Public School 7

and—with the exception of Westminster—at least semi-independent of Church control.[1] From the very beginning even the two oldest schools were independent of direct episcopal jurisdiction, and from Elizabethan times on all the schools—again excepting Westminster—were relatively self-sufficient educational endowments administered by their own rulers and, in educational matters, by semi-autonomous head masters. Winchester and Eton were governed respectively by a Warden who had to be a fellow of New College, Oxford, and by a Provost who had to be a fellow of King's College, Cambridge. The ten fellows or chantry priests, which each school possessed, were appointed by the Warden or Provost, who in turn selected the head master.[2] Westminster, the least autonomous of the schools, was administered by the Dean and Chapter of Westminster Abbey, which had been endowed by Elizabeth with lands for the support of the school; the masters, of which there were two, were to be chosen by the Dean of Christ Church and the Master of Trinity, alternately, with the consent of the Dean of Westminster.[3] Rugby, Harrow, and Charterhouse were ruled by self-perpetuating trustees who were originally appointed by the founder. Shrewsbury, which had been given a charter and endowed with the tithes of dissolved colleges and other income by Edward VI, was governed by the mayor, aldermen, and burgesses of Shrewsbury, though later St. John's College, Cambridge, won the right to nominate the head master.[4]

This political independence of the Public Schools was in a sense their most important attribute. For not only did it inevitably condition various specific features of schools but

[1] English education in general, having been in ecclesiastical hands throughout the Middle Ages—those of the regular clergy in the eleventh century, and the secular in the twelfth—had been virtually free from State control since the Conquest, when Church and State became separate and distinct institutions. (Parry, op. cit., p. 59.) By the thirteenth century it was, especially among the rising *bourgeoisie*, rapidly emerging from ecclesiastical control as well, and was beginning to be provided by civic and trade organizations, by partially independent institutions like Oxford and Cambridge, and by towns and individual men, who endowed schools under the guise of chantries.
[2] Leach, *History of Winchester College*, pp. 60 ff.; Lyte, op. cit., pp. 7 ff.
[3] Frederic H. Forshall, *Westminster School. Past and Present*, London, 1884, pp. 87 ff.
[4] *History of Shrewsbury*, pp. 27, 99.

it was largely responsible for their general spiritual traits. To find an ultimate cause one probably has to trace these traits to psychological preferences of the English people—to love of individuality, of tradition, of practicability as opposed to theory—and possibly even deeper to the economic and social conditions which may have conditioned these preferences. But for practical purposes, it was the fact that schools were, and had been from the beginning, practically independent endowments that was responsible for their quality of unique individuality. Similarly, it was in good part because Public Schools were relatively uncontrolled by external authority that they developed an ancestor worship which permitted growth, when it permitted it at all, only in terms of original structure and ideas. Founders' intentions and traditional practices came naturally to serve as guides to action where no other signposts existed.

In the second place, the seven Public Schools had important common stipulations in regard to educational facilities. On the one hand, they all had foundations on which the poor were to receive a free education.[1] Winchester and Eton made provision for seventy scholars, Westminster for forty, called King's scholars (or Queen's, as the case might be);[2] Charterhouse had a college of free students or gownboys;[2] Rugby, Shrewsbury, and Charterhouse were open to the poor of their respective communities. On the other hand, all the schools permitted the head master to receive money for instructing a certain number of paying students. These students, called commoners at Winchester, oppidans at Eton, and variously townboys, boarders, and foreigners[3] at other schools, were, in the minds of founders, merely an extra source of income for the masters, not an essential part of the school population. As we shall see in the next section,

---

[1] The term public, according to Parry (op. cit., p. 63), probably meant open to all, though it might have meant without pay. Of all the schools only Shrewsbury provided in its statutes for even a nominal entrance fee from the foundationers.

[2] Charterhouse and Eton also had provisions for boarding and lodging impoverished old men. At the former school these old men, all aged Army and Navy officers, were the 'cods' of Thackeray's *The Newcomes*.

[3] Westminster had three classes of these boys, *pensionarii*, or boarders with the Dean, Head, and Prebendaries, *oppidani*, or day boys, and *peregrini*, or ordinary boarders. (Forshall, op. cit., p. 96.)

this had become by no means the actual case by the eighteenth century.

Within this common framework, Public Schools showed marked structural dissimilarities. Particularly were there two important sets of contrasts between the three earlier schools (and to some extent Charterhouse) and the four (or three) later ones. The first of these sets of contrasts had to do with the relative wealth of the two groups of institutions, the extent of the educational facilities which they offered, and the variety of the groups to which their foundations catered.

A great many people have contended that Eton, Westminster, Winchester, and Charterhouse differed fundamentally from Rugby, Harrow, and Shrewsbury in that they were not really meant for the lower classes.[1] A. F. Leach, the painstaking historian of Winchester and of medieval education in England, has, for example, claimed that by '*pauperes et indigentes*' Wykeham meant the less well off of the professional and upper middle classes;[2] Oscar Browning has asserted that Harrow and Rugby in becoming upper-class schools were the only schools that very definitely have been lifted above the intentions of their founders.[3] It is possible that these writers are correct. With respect to Charterhouse, which was frankly meant for poor gentlemen, they assuredly were, and it is undoubtedly true that in the less democratic sixteenth century, whatever the intention of the founders, Eton, Winchester, and Westminster were serving a clientele very different from that which patronized the foundations of Rugby, Harrow, and

---

[1] Over this question English scholars, apologists, and critics of the Public Schools have been arguing for over a hundred years. Nothing better illustrates the hold of tradition over the most radical critics than the necessity that they have felt to find a founder's justification for democratizing the modern Public School.

[2] Leach, *History of Winchester*, pp. 96 ff. Leach's chief arguments are: (1) labourers were not educated in the fourteenth century; (2) the sum of 3s. 6d. that a student was allowed to have was a considerable amount; (3) there was a provision made for commoners. Leach argues that nobles would not have been asked to associate with labourers.

[3] Browning, *Aspects of Education*, p. 170. Even with regard to Harrow, however, Thornton can claim immunity from the accusation that they were meant for the poor on the grounds that the statutes ordered parents to buy paper, ink, pens, and books. (Op. cit., p. 45.)

Shrewsbury. But it does not seem to me that the case has really been proved. Many scholars have argued convincingly that the three older schools were meant for the poor,[1] and, in view of the democratic character of the medieval Church and the fact that even Westminster, founded in the earliest years of the English Renaissance, provided that no one could be a candidate for King's College whose father had independent property of more than ten pounds a year,[2] I am, on the whole, inclined to agree with them. In any case, by the eighteenth century, though for the very different reason that few poor went to any of the schools, there was little to choose between Eton and Harrow in the matter of the strata of the population that attended them.[3]

Whatever the intentions of the various founders of the schools in regard to social classes, there is no doubt that they had considerably different ideas as to the extent of the geographical areas which they wished their schools to serve. Wykeham, the two royal Henrys, and Thomas Sutton meant

[1] Cf., for example, Harold T. Wilkins, *Great English Schools*, London, 1925, and Parry, op. cit., pp. 197 ff. Parry maintains (1) that neither the middle classes nor the nobles went to the schools; (2) that there were no professional classes; (3) that *'pauperes et indigentes'* is plain enough language; (4) that Henry VI associated an almshouse with his college; (5) that 3s. 6d. as a top sum was not very much; and (6) that the ten commoners had nothing to do with the college.

[2] Cf. Forshall, op. cit., pp. 93 ff. In this connexion John Thynne's evidence before the Public School Commissioners in 1862 to the effect that Elizabeth refused to confirm the statutes because of this provision is extremely interesting. If it could be proved—it is a fact that Elizabeth never confirmed the statutes—it would be additional testimony to the growing anti-democratic sentiment in the Renaissance.

[3] There was one school at least that was founded for the poor and continued to serve them. Though Ackermann in his *History of Public Schools* classes Christ's Hospital as a Public School, it differs from, say Eton, in more respects than it resembles it. The differences are instructive. Founded during Edward VI's reign in 1553 out of a dissolved monastery, it served as an orphanage as well as a school. It never accepted any but foundation scholars, and these were to be either children of poor clergymen or of Londoners without means of educating their children. The foundation fed, clothed, and lodged its boys from the age of seven on. Only ten or twelve of a possible 1,156 children were normally expected to proceed to the universities. The school kept its semi-charitable aspect well into the nineteenth century, accepting not only tradesmen and small gentry but servants as well. 'It is, in a word,' wrote Charles Lamb in 1813, 'an Institution to keep those who have yet held up their heads in the world from sinking,' half-way between a charity school and a Public School. (Cf. Ackermann, *History of Public Schools*, Christ's Hospital, pp. 4 ff.; Leigh Hunt, *Autobiography*, 2 Vols., New York, 1903; Charles Lamb in *Gentleman's Magazine*, June, 1813, p. 541.)

The Late Eighteenth-Century Public School 11

their institutions to be national schools drawing scholars from all over England. As a consequence they endowed their foundations heavily and made them colleges. Moreover, they provided their scholars with the opportunity to proceed to the universities: Westminster maintained from its endowments twenty scholars at Oxford and Cambridge; Winchester, which possessed exclusive control of scholarships and fellowships at New College, and Eton, which had the same control at King's College, sent virtually all their foundationers to the universities. Rugby, Harrow, and Shrewsbury, on the other hand, were meagrely financed day schools for the local residents,[1] and offered little opportunity for their foundationers to proceed to a higher education.[2] They were, indeed, not different from other grammar schools of the sixteenth century, and could not—with the exception of Shrewsbury in the late sixteenth century—be considered Public Schools at all until the eighteenth century, since that term implies national scope as part of its essential meaning. And if they did eventually become national schools, it was not through means of their foundations, which remained local in character.

The second set of contrasts concerned questions of internal governmental flexibility and external affiliation and control. Rugby, Harrow, Shrewsbury, and Charterhouse were entirely free from either ecclesiastical, State, or outside educational authority; within the schools the masters were, relatively at least, independent of trustees who, having little vested interest in the small[3] endowments, were willing to allow the head masters a comparatively free hand in administration.[4] None of these statements are applicable, without

[1] Cf. Edward Graham, *The Harrow Life of Henry Montague Butler, D.D.*, London, 1920, p. 195, and Rouse, op. cit., pp. 1 ff. For almost a hundred years Rugby was in danger of disappearing entirely through the sale of its endowments by grasping trustees.

[2] Cf. Rouse, op. cit., pp. 1 ff. It was forty-five years after its foundation that Rugby sent its first student to Cambridge. Shrewsbury, on the other hand, because it possessed an exceptional master, sent a hundred students to the universities in 1583.

[3] Less true, as already indicated, of Charterhouse.

[4] Nevertheless, all the great reformers of Harrow, Rugby, and Shrewsbury had to struggle against relatively conservative and recalcitrant trustees. Dr. Arnold at Rugby was exceedingly hampered by the trustees' right to appoint assistant masters. (Rouse, op. cit., p. 123.)

considerable qualification, to the older schools. To begin with, the head masters of Eton, Winchester, and Westminster (though at the last of these schools the powerful Richard Busby did for a time win independence of the governing body) were so little autonomous that they dared make no important reforms in the face of opposition from the ruling powers. In the second place, the three earlier schools, though they had won their independence by the eighteenth century, were up to that time in constant danger of being devoured by the secular authorities. Until well into the seventeenth century, Eton, though it was not technically a royal school, was directly controlled by the English kings through their right to appoint the Provost. Winchester and Eton had to struggle for centuries against the attempt by the State to destroy them. As early as 1463 Edward IV almost abolished Eton by taking away the alien priories which it had received as land endowments;[1] when Henry VIII dissolved the monasteries, both schools narrowly escaped liquidation by being included with the universities as educational institutions rather than with the grammar schools as Church property; Edward VI, though he exempted them from Henry's Chantries Act, almost destroyed them himself; they were threatened for the last time in 1649 when Parliament ordered the sale of estates of religious corporations.[2] Finally, throughout Henry VIII's reign all three schools were virtually State schools. For, though Henry never contemplated administering educational institutions himself, he founded Westminster and re-established Eton and Winchester under the control of the English Church, which was entirely his tool. When royal power waned, however, the schools emerged freer than ever from the authority of the secular government.

Of much more importance than either of the above considerations was the relative dependence of the three older schools on the Church. Westminster was directly governed by the English Church, and Winchester and Eton were from the beginning and remained in the eighteenth century,

[1] Lyte, op. cit., pp. 9, 66.
[2] Leach, *History of Winchester*, pp. 246, 258, and Lyte, op. cit., pp. 107, 121, 126.

semi-ecclesiastical schools. The fellows and masters of both institutions as well as the Warden of Winchester and the Provost of Eton were priests. The statutes of both institutions provided for as many religious services as did those of a collegiate church,[1] and endowed ten fellows with good livings for the almost exclusive purpose of seeing that these services were performed. Since these fellows were part of the governing body of their respective institutions, the fact that they had a financial stake in those institutions became, later on, of great significance.

Finally, the three ecclesiastical schools, as we can now call them, were partially dependent on university colleges. This was true of Westminster only to the extent that the Master of Trinity had the alternate right to appoint the two head masters; the other two schools had much more vital university affiliations. As we have seen, Winchester and Eton had certain exclusive rights at Oxford and Cambridge colleges. In return New College and King's College exercised the right of supervision or 'visitation' over Winchester and Eton respectively. This did not, it may be added, amount to a great deal by way of control because school and college were so closely associated as to make this a mere brotherly gesture. Much more important was the monopoly of positions of importance at Winchester and Eton exercised by the university colleges. The schools were virtually committed to recruiting their head masters, fellows, Wardens, and Provosts from New and King's Colleges.

It might appear at first sight that most of these differences were to the advantage of the older schools. And indeed to a large extent they were. Eton, Winchester, Westminster, and probably Charterhouse offered more appealing educational opportunities to their scholars than did the other schools. Moreover, they could, because of their wealth and prestige, maintain themselves in the face of temporary internal setbacks and hostile external authorities; Rugby and Harrow, with their small endowments, were virtually dependent for their very existence on the chance of having a strong master.

[1] Parry, op. cit., pp. 188 ff. Only six of the forty-six chapters of the Winchester statutes deal with learning.

But Winchester, Eton, and Westminster suffered from serious disabilities as the result of their political structure.

To begin with, they were afflicted with inordinate conservatism. Their wealth and prestige, which allowed them to fight off disaster, also permitted them to scorn agitation for reform and to develop tenacious traditions. They were administered by governing bodies who, since they continued to have Church affiliations, long after education had become secularized, and, furthermore, had a vested interest in the *status quo*, were usually opposed to change. Their head masters, comparatively powerless in any case, were, particularly at Eton and Winchester, just as little interested in or capable of remodelling the established order as were the fellows. Eton and Winchester head masters were, as we have seen, recruited exclusively from King's and New Colleges; since they had previously all been foundationers at Eton or Winchester, they brought to the schools which they were to administer no fresh idea garnered in the outside world. As the *Edinburgh Review* stated the matter in 1830 with respect to Eton, where the system was still in vogue, 'Bred in the routine of Eton education, young men are sent to a college, inhabited solely by Etonians, where all, or nearly all, study is voluntary; and after a few years return to their old school to teach the things they were themselves taught, in the place, and in the manner, they had learnt them'.[1] At Rugby or Harrow, on the other hand, head masters, more often than not outsiders, and working with institutions comparatively unwedded to the *status quo*,[2] had at most times a virtually free hand in reforming their schools.[3] It is not surprising, therefore, that reformation of the Public School system in the late eighteenth and nineteenth centuries should have come through Rugby, Harrow, Charterhouse, and Shrewsbury, and not through the older schools. In this connexion it is worth noting that, with the growth of tradition and the creation of house masters with vested interests, Harrow and

---

[1] *Edinburgh Review*, April 1830, p. 67.
[2] Dr. James was given a new constitution to work with at Rugby in 1777. It is not without significance in this connexion that by 1783 not a single building of the original foundation existed at Rugby. (Rouse, op. cit., pp. 111, 112.)
[3] But cf. note 4, p. 11.

Rugby also became, later on, wedded to their pasts and less willing to borrow. Reform programmes have always been launched in each age by new schools, by Uppingham in the eighteen-sixties and by Oundle in the eighteen-nineties.

A second and allied evil to which the ecclesiastical schools were subject was the sort of corruption which seems inevitably to develop where there are vested interests whose usefulness is no longer very apparent. This corruption took three forms: theft of money due the scholars, insistence that foundationers pay for their education, and favouritism in admissions. Though the governing bodies of the three schools did not, in most cases, openly disobey the letter of the statutes in these respects, they certainly violated their spirit. Thus, technically, they could at least contend that the surplus revenues which prosperity caused endowments to yield did not belong to the scholars; but school founders surely did not intend that the money earmarked for the colleges should remain a comparatively fixed sum in the face of a rising standard of living. Again, though governing bodies found some justification for favouritism in appointments to the foundations in statutory provisions for preference to founders' kin, they unquestionably abused these provisions; assuredly the originators of the three schools would have been shocked to find that a whole host of people, most of whom could only by the greatest stretch of the imagination prove themselves founders' kin, were entering Eton or Winchester and eventually New or King's Colleges with merely farcical examinations.[1] Most of these people were, indeed, by no means poor, and it was but the shabbiest quibble to contend, as did the Winchester authorities in 1818, that the fathers of the boys, not the boys, had the money.[2] Finally, though Provost Goodall insisted that, if a boy pleaded poverty, he received a free education, it was notoriously the fact that no boy dared so insist.[3]

Corruption in all these respects existed at Winchester as

[1] Some writers contend that the examination to New College, at any rate, was not a farce. (Cf. Old Wykehamists, *Winchester College 1393–1893*, London, 1893, p. 91.)
[2] *Third Report from the Select Committee on the Education of the Lower Orders, 1818*, Minutes of Evidence, pp. 65, 69, 135.
[3] Ibid., p. 71.

early as 1414,[1] became prevalent at Eton and Winchester after the Reformation had taken away the religious importance of the fellows,[2] and was, by the eighteenth century, a crying scandal at all the schools.[3] That it existed at Eton and Winchester as late as 1818 is borne out by the testimony given before the House of Commons by the Reverend Peter Hinde, Fellow of King's, Provost Goodall of Eton, and David Williams, Second Master of Winchester to the effect that scholars did not receive a free education, that favouritism ruled in admissions, and that surplus money derived from the increase in value of property was divided among the fellows.[4] At Westminster conditions were in one respect less bad than at the other schools: collegers were and continued to be elected by a difficult competitive examination from among those who had been in the school a year. But here, also, the foundation, 'though nominally open to free competition, had been—it may be assumed from the earlier times—really a matter more or less of patronage on the part of the electors', who usually chose sons of Westminster or Christ Church families. Moreover, since the surplus of the Chapter went to the governing body, King's scholars received neither free board (until 1864) nor free education.[5]

MEMBERSHIP

None of the characteristics so far discussed, neither independence nor national scope nor provisions for both scholars and paying students, would alone or in combination have entitled eighteenth-century Eton and Westminster to the designation Public School. The reason that they were so

[1] Leach, *History of Winchester College*, p. 139.
[2] A. K. Cook, *About Winchester College*, London, 1917, p. 216; Leach, *History of Winchester College*, p. 326. By the reign of James I the close corporate life was beginning to break up: the fellows began to live out of college and marry.
[3] Though there is evidence in 1569 and in 1605 that the wealthy were receiving a gratuitous education at Winchester, it was only in 1710, 1712, and 1776 that we have direct testimony to the fact that the poor were, because of robbery by the fellows, paying as high as sixty pounds for an education. (Wilkins, op. cit., pp. 88, 121 ff.)
[4] *Third Report from the Select Committee*, Minutes of Evidence, pp. 65, 69, 130.
[5] (W. L. Collins) *The Public Schools*, Edinburgh, 1867, pp. 180-81.

designated, and that Christ's Hospital, despite many resemblances to Eton, was not,[1] is that the former had become by 1780 essentially upper-class schools. The poor, for the most part, no longer patronized their foundations. More important, the foundations had become of secondary importance; at Eton, for example, though the seventy scholars remained, they were lost in a school of four or five hundred young bloods from the ruling classes.

The seven Public Schools did not all earn their titles to that term at the same time, and—as one would have expected among independent institutions—varied greatly at different periods in their relative popularity among the upper orders. Eton, because of her large resources, her situation, and the favour of kings, was, despite frequent inefficient administration, the most continuously popular of the schools. As early as 1534, when Nicholas Udall was head master, it was widely famous, and, except for a brief loss of prestige around 1721, when it carried the stigma of Jacobite sympathies, it gained steadily in importance.[2] After 1760, through the partiality shown it by George III, it wrested the leadership from Westminster and, if numbers are any criterion—Eton has had, except at infrequent intervals, over twice as many students as any other school—it has never lost that leadership. Winchester had no such prosperous history. Steeped in medievalism,[3] it would have needed to change considerably at the time of the Renaissance in order to preserve a leadership which it had previously shared with Eton. Having failed to do so, it became a home of lost causes, and was, from the sixteenth to the nineteenth century, always exceeded in numbers by at least two other schools. Even its seventeenth-century record enrolment of eighty-six commoners, reached during the reign of Charles II, and its eighteenth-century high-water mark of 123 in 1734 were less than a quarter of Eton's top figures.[4] Moreover, it experienced such a decadence in mid-century that it virtually

[1] Some early writers, like Ackermann, do call it a Public School.
[2] Cf. Lyte, op. cit., pp. 114, 227, 243. Another famous early master was Sir Henry Savile, who reigned during James I's kingship.
[3] For a full description of Winchester's medievalism in the eighteenth century cf. W. Thomas, *Le Poète Edward Young, 1683–1765*, Paris, 1901, pp. 10–12.
[4] Leach, *History of Winchester College*, p. 372.

ceased to be an upper-class school. At that time the number of its commoners dropped to ten, a figure seldom greatly exceeded until the reign of Dr. Goddard in the nineties.[1]

Westminster had both the most glorious and the most tragic career. Under the leadership of Richard Busby, probably the greatest schoolmaster before Arnold, it became, at the Restoration, England's foremost school, and educated a large percentage of the English aristocracy as well as men like Dryden, Locke, Christopher Wren, Prior, Jeffreys, and Atterbury.[2] After Busby's day his school continued to flourish, and attained another period of greatness under John Nicoll (1733–53); after mid-century, however, it began to decline before Eton's and Harrow's rising stars, and has never since recovered its early prestige. Charterhouse, in contrast to Westminster, had no period of greatness; nor did it, like Winchester, suffer any catastrophic decline; always a reasonably good school, it existed through most of the seventeenth and eighteenth centuries on an even and undistinguished keel, having neither many more nor many less than a hundred students.[3]

The histories of the other three schools were, because of their almost complete dependence on the skill of their head masters, full of violent reversals of fortune. Harrow remained, except for a brief influx of paying students under Dr. Horne in 1669, virtually a local grammar school until 1721.[4] At this time a combination of circumstances—the patronage of the Hanoverian Duke of Chandos, the Jacobitism of Eton and Winchester, and the possession of a strong head master, Dr. Brian—suddenly elevated it into a Public School with 144 foreigners.[5] This glory was eclipsed in the forties, but after mid-century Harrow began again to rise steadily to fame under a series of great masters, Dr. Thackeray, Dr.

---

[1] *A Cyclopedia of Education*, edited by Paul Monroe, 1913, Vol. V, p. 784.
[2] John Sargeaunt, *Annals of Westminster School*, London, 1898, p. 80; G. F. Russell Barker, *Memoir of Richard Busby*, London, 1895, p. 24. Busby reigned for nearly sixty years, from 1638 to 1695.
[3] Davies, *Charterhouse in London*, pp. 247 ff.
[4] Thornton, *Harrow School*, pp. 91 ff.
[5] Ibid., p. 109–12. The number of foundationers, on the other hand, had dropped to four.

The Late Eighteenth-Century Public School 19

Sumner, Dr. Heath, and Dr. Drury. By 1780 the obscure grammar school had become the educator of 250 of England's future rulers. Rugby's growth was slower. Though it made two early attempts to become a Public School, one in 1675, when half of its members were foreigners, and one at the end of the century under Dr. Holyoake, who succeeded in drawing a hundred students to the school, of whom four-fifths were non-foundationers, its real rise came after Dr. James took over the school in 1777.[1] Shrewsbury's pre-nineteenth-century development was the exact opposite of Rugby's and Harrow's. In the first seven years of its existence it admitted 875 scholars, some from the best families in the neighbourhood. In 1581 there were 360 scholars at Shrewsbury, and the school continued to flourish, with some setbacks, until 1688.[2] After that, incompetence and the rise of other schools caused a decline, which continued until, when Samuel Butler took over the school in 1798, it had almost ceased to exist.

If the various schools exhibited different degrees of popularity, they also presented striking and fairly permanent contrasts in respect to the character of the foreigners who patronized them. Eton, because of its royal connexions, was, from the Restoration on, the school of the Tory aristocracy, a fact which accounts for its prestige during the last half of the eighteenth century. Westminster, on the other hand, was attended in its early eighteenth-century days of glory by the sons of the politically ascendant Whig oligarchy. Unlike Eton, however, Westminster did not retain its distinguished patronage into the nineteenth century. The aristocratic Whig rival of Eton at the end of the eighteenth century was Harrow, which drew to itself the titled gentry who were sympathetic to the Prince Regent and hostile to Farmer George. Though such men as Thackeray and Sumner developed Harrow in imitation of Eton, they imparted to it the rather different spirit of Whig liberalism, which proved, some years later, so congenial to Byron.[3] The Eton-Harrow rivalry has seldom been an entirely

---

[1] Rouse, op. cit., pp. 86, 90, 129. [2] *History of Shrewsbury*, pp. 60, 104.
[3] Thornton, op. cit., pp. 121 ff.

friendly one: to many Etonians the school on the Hill has always seemed a *nouveau riche* upstart. None of the other schools were aristocratic schools at all, though Winchester always and Shrewsbury for a time in the sixteenth century were attended by some of the titled nobility. All of them were schools for the professional and upper middle classes and the small gentry.

Though these contrasts are important, they are of far less significance than the general fact that by 1780 five of the seven schools and by the early nineteenth century all of them had become permanently institutions attended almost entirely by members of the English ruling classes. To state this circumstance is a far simpler matter than to explain it. None of the schools were founded for the upper classes; some of them did not receive upper-class patronage till the eighteenth century; and none of them procured aristocratic support until the Restoration. What caused the nobility and the upper middle classes to send their sons to the Public Schools? What happened to the poor for whose benefit the schools were established?

The answer to the first of these questions is, in part, very simple. The Public Schools were the best schools, they had provisions in their charters for paying students, and, though they were not ecclesiastical schools, they all had connexions with the Church of England, to which most of the upper classes belonged. By the eighteenth century, when Public School education had become both useless and ineffective, it had become the 'thing to do' to go to a Public School. Snobbery and conservatism preserved what merit had won.

But these considerations neglect one vital fact. They assume that the upper classes were in the habit of sending their sons to school, which was by no means the case. During the Middle Ages gentlemen were practically never educated in an institution of learning. The change that overspread England in this respect from 1500 to 1700 was of twofold character. In the first place, the Renaissance created a new type of gentleman. In the Middle Ages, though certain moral and intellectual qualities were also necessary, a man had initially to be well born to be considered a gentleman. The sixteenth century broke down this exclusive use of the term: the professions and the *bourgeoisie*, who were rapidly rising to a position of political and social equality with the older ruling class, laid claim to the title of gentleman by virtue of wealth and education. It was this new upper class that—together with sons of clergymen and of a few country squires—peopled Eton and Winchester in the sixteenth and seventeenth centuries in order to compensate by education for a deficiency in birth. And to a great extent it succeeded, for, as David Nutt says,[1] 'when, from the sixteenth century, scholastic knowledge became of great and ever-increasing value, the esteem in which the scholars and all professional men were held, increased too'. The idea had gained general currency by the end of the seventeenth century. Addison and Steele, the great defenders of the upper middle class, would naturally insist on the superior status of that class. Defoe wrote *The Compleat English Gentleman* partly, at least, to proclaim to the world that education and wealth made gentlemen.

In the second place, some of the schools were beginning to attract the born gentlemen, who had previously not gone to schools at all. This was a much slower process, however, than the winning of the *bourgeoisie*. The pressure of respect for education affected the aristocracy, but not rapidly. Swift, in his *Essay on Education*, says that the gentry and the nobility think Public School education useless, and 'that to dance, fence, speak French, and know how to behave yourself among great persons of both sexes, comprehends the whole duty of a gentleman'. The Army was the school for gentlemen; as one officer said to Swift, 'Do you think my Lord Marlborough beat the French with Greek and Latin.'[2] The older sons had tutors and learned little except vice; many travelled abroad. In regard to Westminster, Russell Barker writes,[3] 'Before 1650 the sons of the nobility were

[1] David Nutt, Introduction to Daniel Defoe, *The Compleat English Gentleman*, edited by Karl D. Bülbring, London, 1890, p. xxxv.
[2] Jonathan Swift, *An Essay on Modern Education, Prose Works*, Temple Scott Edition, London, 1907, Vol. XI, p. 52. Originally, when it appeared in *The Intelligencer* in 1729, this essay was called 'The foolish Methods of Education Among the Nobility'.
[3] Barker, *Busby*, p. 121.

usually taught at home by tutors, and, if they went to the University, went there young. The boarders were sons of country gentlemen and clergymen, the day boys were largely sons of professional men, and of residents in London and Westminster.' The nobility sent only their younger sons intended for trade or the professions to the Public Schools.[1]

In his *Compleat English Gentleman* Defoe endeavoured to combat the idea that the nobility did not need an education. He criticized the English idea 'that to be a good sportsman is the perfection of education, and to speak good dog language and good horse language is far above Greek and Latin'.[2] 'An untaught, unpolished gentleman is one of the most deplorable objects in the world.'[3] Similarly, Swift wrote his *Essay on Modern Education* to 'prove that some proportion of human knowledge appears requisite to those, who by their birth or fortune are called to the making of laws'.[4] For, since 'education is always the worse in proportion to the wealth and grandeur of the parents', younger sons and men of ignoble birth are usurping the great offices of State'.[5]

What gradually brought the change in the attitude of the nobility towards the Public School is not easy to see. Locke, the chief writer on education, was against the schools. But even had he been in favour of them, his influence would not, any more than that of most writers on education in England, have been great. Probably one important cause was the fact that many of the seventeenth-century nobility were, a generation earlier, members of the middle class, and thus accustomed to the idea of schools. A more inclusive factor was the hatred of the dissoluteness which the hereditary politicians felt that their sons learned abroad. This opinion received support from the Puritan nobles who hated the French Catholics.[6] Moreover, the growing upper-class aspect of the schools must have made them more congenial places for the aristocracy. Swift had given as one of his reasons for the refusal of the aristocracy to go to schools that 'public schools, by

---

[1] Though, as Locke pointed out, Latin was useless for one going into trade. (John Locke, *Some Thoughts Concerning Education*, with Introduction and Notes by Rev. Canon Daniel, M.A., London, *c*. 1895, p. 287.)
[2] Defoe, *Compleat English Gentleman*, p. 38.   [3] Ibid., p. 60.
[4] Swift, *Essay on Modern Education* in *Prose Works*, Vol. XI, p. 56.
[5] Ibid., p. 49.   [6] Sargeaunt, *Annals of Westminster*, p. 109.

mingling the sons of noblemen with those of the vulgar, engage the former in bad company'.[1] Again, probably the Renaissance idea of the importance of education was permeating the English upper-class mind. Undoubtedly the most important single influence, however, was the reputation of Busby at Westminster. 'Some time before the Restoration the great families began to send their sons to Busby.'[2] 'By the end of Busby's time Westminster was become a nursery of statesmen.'[3] From Westminster the idea spread to Eton and later on to Harrow.

Theoretically, there was no reason why the coming of the upper classes to the Public Schools should have been paralleled by the virtual disappearance of the lower orders. In the sixteenth century there was considerable intermingling of classes at Shrewsbury, where gentlemen like Sir Philip Sydney were sent to school with the burghers,[4] and even at Harrow and Winchester. As late as 1542 Cranmer fought against educational stratification at King's School, Canterbury, to which a large group of people wished to admit only sons of gentlemen.[5] But social conditions in the late sixteenth and seventeenth centuries precluded the continued democracy of the schools. The Renaissance, though a period of liberation for the middle classes, widened the gap between those classes and the poor; Disraeli's two nations sprang originally not out of the industrial revolution but out of the breach between peasant and squirearchy.[6] The *bourgeois* Cecils who ruled Elizabethan England were anything but democratic in their sympathies, and seventeenth-century Puritanism, with its reverence for the attainment of riches, was, despite its original egalitarian character, equally contemptuous of the poor.[7] The virtual exclusion of the poor from the Public Schools, already appropriated by the upper classes, was, by the Restoration, a foregone conclusion. Indeed, the consciousness of class distinctions had

---

[1] Cf. Swift, *Essay on Modern Education*, p. 52.   [2] Barker, *Busby*, p. 12.
[3] Sargeaunt, *Annals of Westminster*, p. 105.
[4] *History of Shrewsbury*, p. 183; Thornton, *Harrow School*, p. 28.
[5] Ernest Barker, *National Character and the Factors in its Formation*, New York, 1927, p. 246.
[6] Ibid., p. 249.
[7] Cf. R. H. Tawney, *Religion and the Rise of Capitalism*, London, 1926, p. 267.

grown so great that, even after the poor no longer frequented the foundations, to be a foundationer—except at Westminster where the collegers were recruited from the school—carried a stigma with it.

The exclusion of the under-privileged was brought about by various means, though only one, the Act of Uniformity of 1664, which forbade Nonconformists to teach at Anglican schools,[1] and thus seriously discouraged Dissenters, who were, on the whole, members of the lower classes, from attending those schools, was of general applicability. At the ecclesiastical schools, the chief methods were the practices, already alluded to, of nominating as foundationers only those with influence, and of making collegers pay for their board and education. As a result of these practices, the poor, who were by definition those without influence, could seldom gain admission to school foundations; when they did, they were unable to support themselves there. At schools without colleges, there were no such direct means by which the poor were excluded. A free education was always offered at Harrow, Rugby, and Shrewsbury, and the local poor had only to establish residence in order to be eligible for their foundations. Nevertheless the poor ceased to frequent these schools, whose free education came to be offered chiefly to sons of gentlemen like Matthew Arnold who established residence at Harrow in order to benefit by John Lyon's charity. The reason for this was that, as the parishioners of Harrow stated before a Court of Chancery in 1809, the poor received no benefit from the foundations.[2] The classical education provided by John Lyon was of little use to tradesman or farmer. To the professional man it was still important, to the rich man it was at least decorative, but to the inhabitants of Harrow, Rugby, and Shrewsbury, it was totally worthless.[3] And if by chance a parishioner wanted to make his son a professional man, he was barred by poverty, since Rugby and Harrow provided no means

[1] Ernest Barker, op. cit., p. 249. Also cf. Cyril Norwood and Arthur H. Hope, *The Higher Education of Boys in England*, London, 1909, p. 17.
[2] *Vesey's Chancery Reports*, Vol. XVII, p. 498, quoted in Ackermann, *History of Public Schools*, Harrow, p. 11.
[3] Cf. Ackermann, *History of Public Schools*, Harrow, p. 11; also Graham, *Life of Montague Butler*, p. 196.

of support for students at the universities. Finally, even if he benefited by the education offered, the poor man was likely to find a Public School of more ultimate harm than good to him. As the people of Harrow asserted, the rich majority ill-treated their sons and initiated them into expensive habits.[1]

INTELLECTUAL EDUCATION

The system of intellectual education in practice in all the eighteenth-century Public Schools owed its origin, for the most part, to the sixteenth century. Winchester and Eton in the fifteenth century, though, like all the schools down to the present day, they made Latin the staple of the education they offered, had as their aims such medieval objectives as training for the priesthood and the salvation of the soul,[2] and used as their means authors seldom read later on, like Prudentius, Juvencus, Augustine, Donatus, and various other early Christian and late Roman writers.[3] Renaissance Humanism, the first and last great intellectual movement to touch the schools until the nineteenth century, revolutionized both the means and ends of education as they had been understood in the Public Schools during the Middle Ages. Through the agency—direct or indirect—of such men as Lily,[4] Mulcaster,[5] and Udall,[6] it substituted Horace, Juvenal, Cicero, and other classical Roman writers for

[1] Anthony Trollope, who was on the foundation at Harrow, bears convincing testimony to this. (Cf. Anthony Trollope, *An Autobiography*, The World's Classics Edition, London, 1928, p. 11.)
[2] Cf. Parry, *Education in England in the Middle Ages*, p. 232.
[3] Cf. Leach, *Schools of Medieval England*, pp. 44 ff. Parry (op. cit., p. 67) defines a medieval grammar school as a place where Donatus' fourth-century Latin grammar was taught.
[4] William Lily was a teacher of Greek and the first high master of St. Paul's (1509–22). (Cf. Michael F. J. McDonnell, *History of St. Paul's School*, London, 1909, p. 69.)
[5] Mulcaster was an Etonian and high master of St. Paul's from 1596 to 1608. (McDonnell, op. cit., p. 144.) As head master of Merchant Taylors from 1561 to 1586 he helped introduce sense realism into English education. (Paul Monroe, *A Textbook in the History of Education*, New York, 1918, pp. 442 ff.)
[6] Nicholas Udall, who wrote *Ralph Roister Doister*, was head master of Eton in 1534. Later, after a period of obscurity caused by the confession of scandalous immorality, he became, in 1554, head master of Westminster. (Cf. Lyte, *History of Eton*, p. 114.)

those previously studied, added Greek to the curriculum,[1] and made the aim of education the worldly one, in the broad sense of the term, of disciplining the mind and enlarging the spirit. The classics thus became the basis of Public School education; they continued, until well into the nineteenth century, to be virtually the only education offered at those institutions.[2]

At their best the classics were a fruitful method of education. For in the sixteenth century they were the door not only to the professions—worldly as well as clerkly—but to civilization and mental stimulation. If they seemed to the Renaissance a more universal panacea for ignorance than they do to us, it is true that they did offer a newer and finer culture. In order to profit by this culture, it was necessary, however, for the student to read and absorb large quantities of Roman and Greek literature. But such was not the conception of classical education which prevailed at the Public Schools either in the sixteenth or in the eighteenth centuries.[3] This education consisted solely in learning Latin and Greek grammar rules by heart, in memorizing portions of Horace, Sallust, Ovid, Cicero, Virgil, Terence, and Aesop, and the names and dates of generals out of ancient history,[4]

---

[1] As Leach says (*Schools of Medieval England*, p. 246), the teaching of Greek in Public Schools, which occurred before 1500, was an effect, not a cause, of the Renaissance. McDonnell (*History of St. Paul's*, p. 46) claims that Lily was the first to introduce the subject.

[2] Occasionally other studies such as mathematics (at Eton in 1635 and at Rugby in the eighteenth century) and Hebrew were taught. (Lyte, op. cit., p. 227; Rouse, op. cit., p. 123.) Often one could learn mathematics or French as extras, for which additional money was paid. Teachers of other subjects than the classics were of inferior rank.

[3] According to Oscar Browning it was John Sturm of Strasbourg who 'must be regarded, more than any one else, as the creator for Protestants of the classical system of English public school education as it is remembered by many who are still living'. Sturm, who lived from 1507 to 1589, was rector of the gymnasium in Strasbourg. According to his plan seven years were to be devoted to grammar, two to style. Robert Quick, *Essays on Educational Reformers*, London, 1890, p. 29; Oscar Browning, *Aspects of Education*, p. 135.)

[4] Quick and Browning, in characteristic English fashion, blame the Jesuits for much of this undue emphasis on memory work. Since, according to them, the Jesuits frowned on originality, independence, and love of truth, they encouraged a brilliant display from memory, the trappings not the reality of learning. (Cf. Quick, op. cit., p. 36, Browning, *Aspects of Education*, p. 135, and *Introduction to the History of Educational Theories*, New York, 1886, pp. 118 ff.

The Late Eighteenth-Century Public School 27

and in writing Latin verses.[1] As Browning puts the matter, boys learn Latin grammar before English and do Latin verses before prose. And the Latin they learned was the ornate and artificial diction of Horace, Virgil, and Cicero. 'To know Horace and Virgil by heart became the first duty of an English gentleman.'[2]

Even this education had, ideally, the virtue of compactness, and could have been a discipline for the mind. The manner in which it was taught, however, seriously detracted from its usefulness. The school books, under the influence of the over-dissection and over-classification typical of the sixteenth century, were full of hair-splittings, of distinctions without differences.[3] Classroom procedure was formal, strict, and dull: the master sat in glowering majesty, rod in hand, high above his students, and listened to their droning recitations of incompletely mastered rules of grammar or passages from Latin literature, ready to mete out punishment for the slightest error. Of other than classroom (or form) teaching there was so little that in the eighteenth century many rich boys brought their own tutors with them to school.[4] Later on a tutorial system grew up at Eton, Harrow, and Rugby, but it proved, at Eton in particular, wasteful, inefficient, and uneducative: since the tutor's business was to correct exercises before they reached the master, the boys had no stimulus to work and the tutor no time for the real business of education. Emulation there was none: as late as the nineteenth century there were no examinations at Harrow, the forms moving up in a body;[5] until 1820 the same was

---

[1] The best contemporary accounts of the curriculum in the sixteenth and seventeenth centuries are contained in two documents in Latin verse, a *Consuetudinariun* of Eton in the sixteenth century when Malim was head master (paraphrased in Sir Edward Creasy, *Memoirs of Eminent Etonians*, London, 1876, p. 87 ff), and a poem called *De Collegio Seu Potius Collegiata Schola Wicchamica Wintoniensi*, probably written by one Robert Mathew in 1647, when he was a senior at Winchester. (Cf. A. K. Cook, *About Winchester College*, pp. 1, 2.) Leach, and others, believed that it was written by Christopher Johnson in the sixteenth century. [2] Oscar Browning, *Aspects of Education*, p. 135.

[3] Sir Henry Savile introduced Camden's Westminster Grammar into Eton in 1650; it became the Eton Latin Grammar over which there was such a conflict as late as the nineteenth century. (Cf. Lyte, op. cit., p. 209.)

[4] Cf. Tobias Smollett, *The Adventures of Peregrine Pickle*, p. 103, from the *Works of Tobias Smollett*, edited by George Saintsbury, London, n.d.

[5] Cf. *Autobiography of Dean Merivale*, edited by Judith Anne Merivale, London, 1899, p. 24.

true of Eton, where the only incentive to work was the possibility of 'being sent up for good', which meant—not as an American might suppose, to be incarcerated—but to have your verses read aloud by the master.[1] So little was this incentive effective that it became, as Gladstone said, an 'insufferable solecism' to do any work.[2]

The limitations and positive defects of Public School intellectual education were manifest as early as the sixteenth century, but it was not until the eighteenth century that their worst effects were felt. At the beginning a classical education had at least been a novel idea, and had had some utilitarian and cultural justification. As the years went by, however, changed times demanded a changed curriculum: a classical education became an outmoded and unreal form of training to those who did not need it for their professions. Moreover, its purveyors had become for the most part apathetic and indifferent. Safe in their positions because of the closed character of Public School organization and the fact that parents sent boys to school less for educational than for social reasons, they lost interest in the business of teaching. Possibly, also, in rare instances, they realized the futility of classical training as conceived in the eighteenth century. Finally, even had masters been concerned over mental training, there were not enough of them to take care of the hordes of upper-class boys who invaded the schools after the Restoration.

As a consequence of these circumstances, Public School education became, by the eighteenth century, an exceedingly dreary process, an artificial game that was more likely to depress than to stimulate the mind. Few boys profited by this education even to the extent of acquiring a smattering of classical learning; if they carried away anything as a result of their labours, it was a permanent aversion to any form of intellectual endeavour. By 1750, at any rate, Fowler's comment[3] that the English 'public school education of those

---

[1] (William Hill Tucker) *Eton of Old*, London, 1892, pp. 12 ff. and 79 ff.
[2] John Morley, *The Life of William Ewart Gladstone*, 3 vols., New York, 1911, Vol. I, p. 29. Cf. also Sir Francis Hastings Doyle, *Reminiscences and Opinions*, London, 1886, pp. 29 ff.
[3] Thomas Fowler, *Shaftesbury and Hutcheson*, New York, 1883, p. 6.

days probably left fewer traces of culture, and inspired boys less with the love of letters, than it does even in our own' was probably fully justified.

Despite these considerations, it was unquestionably true that, as we shall see in Chapter II, some boys did learn the classics at a Public School in the eighteenth century. All the schools produced some scholars, though they differed considerably in the amount of education that they were able to impart. At aristocratic Eton, where learning was despised, good masters had less success in instilling the classics into youthful heads than did masters of equal capacity—not to mention exceptional men like Busby and Nicoll— at Winchester or Westminster, where learning was, on the whole, more respected. College at the two latter schools had, until recent times, a far better reputation than it had at Eton. This was particularly true of Westminster, where it was an honour not a disgrace to be a foundationer.

If, finally, one asks what permanent effects the classics had on those who learned them, only the most tentative sort of an answer can be given. Undoubtedly, the influence on literary style was great, though often superficial, and was not confined to real students of the Latin writers. As Oscar Browning says: 'Speeches in parliament were considered incomplete if they did not contain at least one Latin quotation. . . . A false quantity was held to be a greater crime than a slip in logical argument.'[1] But to carry the matter farther, to claim that Cicero was largely responsible for 'the continual reference to what is dignified and becoming, coupled with a high-minded devotion to duty and a strong if somewhat romantic patriotism . . . [which] distinguished English statesmen in the eighteenth century',[2] or to contend that Virgil and Horace helped considerably to impart human sympathy and noble emotions to the members of the House of Commons,[3] is to tread on dangerous ground. There are so many sources from which these ideas could have come that one ought to be wary about claiming the direct influence of schooling in the classics as their source. It is just as

[1] *Aspects of Education*, p. 135. [2] Ibid.
[3] Cf. R. L. Archer, *Secondary Education in the Nineteenth Century*, Cambridge, 1921, p. 22.

reasonable to assume, as was undoubtedly in part the case, that English character was responsible for a love of the classics as to insist on the reverse. The probable fact of the matter is that the Latin writers influenced English conduct because the English discovered in them what they already felt to be true.

MORAL EDUCATION—THE MASTERS

From the very beginning character has seemed, on the whole, more important to the English than learning. Wykeham's belief that manners or character make the man was probably less an axiom of Public School education when it was first formulated than it is to-day, but masters, parents, and boys have cared, all through Public School history, as much if not more about character than about anything else. John Lyon made religious and moral teaching the basis of the education he provided at Harrow in the sixteenth century,[1] and Arnold, Thring, and Cyril Norwood[2] have but modified the content of the words.[3]

Just as widespread and of as long duration as the belief in the special importance of character training was the conception of education as a mental and moral discipline. In reality, as illustrated throughout Public School history, this is not one but two distinct conceptions, which are united only in their opposition to the modernist theory of self-development in a friendly environment. The first of these two ideas, which I will here term for convenience education by coercion, has been the more fundamental of the two. It arose from medieval religion with its belief in the importance of an ethical code derived from God and its suspicion of natural instincts. Since these ideas were reinforced by Puritanism, and accepted by such enlightened seventeenth-century

---

[1] Cf. Thornton, *Harrow School*, pp. 46, 77. Lyon very specifically denounced such things as 'swearing, lying, kicking, stealing, filthiness, or wantonness of speech'.

[2] Cf. *The English Tradition of Education*, London, 1929.

[3] Here as well as elsewhere, unless otherwise specified, I have used the term moral or character training in its broadest sense of education of the will in contrast to education of the intellect, rather than in its more restricted meaning of the teaching of altruism or other socially desirable behaviour.

The Late Eighteenth-Century Public School 31

writers as Milton, Defoe, and Locke,[1] they formed the background for at least formal Public School educational theory throughout most of school history. In essence they meant that education was to consist in the inculcation of an absolute and authoritarian morality by authoritarian means. Man, naturally sinful, was to have his evil instincts extirpated and to be socialized and moulded into a pattern of behaviour by pressure from without. In other words, strict discipline and exhortation were to be the methods for producing obedient and virtuous Christians. The other meaning of education as a discipline was a later development and stemmed consciously from Humanism and more particularly from Locke. In reality, however, it was more a rationalization of actual procedure than an idea which created practice, since the classics and the miniature world of a Public School were existent facts before masters and parents ever heard of a disciplinary theory of education. According to this theory, external pressures served the purpose less of moulding than of testing. They were obstacles against which a boy was to struggle; by overcoming them he sharpened his faculties and strengthened his character. From Rousseau to Spencer, and from Spencer to Bertrand Russell, modern educational theory has, it will be noted, found much of value in this conception of education.

In attempting to train boys' minds, Public School masters availed themselves of both these theories. They coerced boys into learning the classics and then justified this procedure by insisting that the classics were educative just because they were difficult. The moral training which, in accordance with Church doctrines, Public School masters felt it their duty to give, proceeded, however, almost entirely in accordance with the medieval idea of discipline. Boys were to be endowed with obedience and Christian humility through the agency of frequent floggings leavened by occasional exhortations in chapel and in private. From the boys'

[1] The end of education is to repair the ruins of our first parents by virtue, wrote Milton. There is more depravity in human nature than believers in 'natural religion' will admit, said Defoe, in answer to the growing rationalism and Deism of the age. Locke supported the idea of evil and recalcitrant instinct. (John Milton, *On Education*, in *Prose Works of John Milton*, London, 1835, p. 98; Defoe, *Compleat English Gentleman*, p. 112.)

point of view, these methods had at least the virtue of simplicity. Moreover, since, either from indifference or principle, masters scorned any further surveillance such as spying on boys, they meant that the British schoolboy was given a quite considerable amount of freedom.

Flogging and later caning and whopping or tunding, the monitorial counterpart of the masters' prerogative, have been one of the most persistent traditions of British schools. To those who came under the rod of a Mulcaster, the recent excitement in *The Times* and elsewhere over the suicide of a boy who disliked caning and fagging would have had a familiar ring.[1] In the *History of Shrewsbury*[2] it is recorded that in the sixteenth century one boarder hanged himself, but that, in the words of a contemporary account, 'he was an idle boye and hated the school'. There was long a rumour that a seventeenth-century head master of Eton had to resign for beating a boy to death.[3] A tradition of discipline, whether it be army toughening or that of the Public School, is almost bound to preserve severe methods.[4]

The scanty records of schooldays from Ascham to Locke and Hoole[5] and Steele give the same impression of discipline that we get in Tusser's poem:

> For fault but small, or none at all
> It came to pass, thus beat I was.[6]

And the greatest offenders were the greatest masters: Nicholas Udall's reputation was based equally on his scholarship and his flogging ability;[7] Malim at Eton, as reported in the *Consuetudinarium*, was a severe disciplinarian, as was Mulcaster at St. Paul's;[8] much of Busby's reputation was

---

[1] *The Times*, May 10th, 1930, p. 10; *Nation and Athenaeum*, November 1st, 1930; *New Statesman*, May 17th, 1930.
[2] p. 76.   [3] Lyte, op. cit., p. 275.
[4] In the beginning at all the schools only the master could flog. John Lyon was, however, unique in urging that the rod be used sparingly; the ferule was to be used for slight offences. (Thornton, *Harrow School*, p. 74.) Wykeham provided one day, Friday, for the flogging of those reported by the monitors as being rowdy or wanton. Friday was also the day for punishments at Eton. (Leach, *History of Winchester*, p. 278; Cook, *About Winchester College*, p. 23.)
[5] Charles Hoole, *A New Discovery of the Old Art of Teaching School*, Syracuse, N.Y., 1912 (1660).
[6] John Timbs, *Schooldays of Eminent Men*, London, n.d., p. 127.
[7] Lyte, op. cit., p. 114.
[8] David Nutt, Introduction to Defoe, *Compleat English Gentleman*, p. lx.

The Late Eighteenth-Century Public School 33

made through the terror of his rod: only the older boys ever discovered that he could be a friend as well as a judge. Thus the idea of the awesome schoolmaster has descended through Busby to Keate and Arnold down almost to our own day. Even Thring and Sanderson, the most enlightened later nineteenth-century masters, were often accused of brutality in discipline.

Despite its severity, flogging did not produce either order or virtue in the eighteenth-century school: it was, like Public School methods for training the intellect, an outworn instrument wielded by too few hands.[1] Its only real effect, indeed, was a negative and unfortunate one: it increased the hatred of learning implicit in efforts to force the classics into unwilling heads,[2] and produced a tradition of enmity between master and boy, which later caused the outbreak of open rebellion, and which has not been entirely eradicated to-day.

The story of religious teaching is an even less edifying one. Henry VI and Wykeham provided—in fact, they over-provided—for religious services of various kinds. At Eton there were prayers during dressing at 5 a.m., again in school at 6, and a third time during the morning at 10. At 8 p.m. the boys went to bed chanting prayers.[3] At Winchester there were two chapel services before 6 a.m., and another in the evening. Sundays, of course, meant services a good part of the time.[4] Most of the holidays were holy days, though sport was allowed on some of them. Each had its own peculiar religious custom: on Shrove Tuesday, for example, a live bird was tormented;[5] at both Winchester and Eton on St. Nicholas Eve a divine service was read by a boy-bishop chosen for the occasion.[6]

---

[1] When one sees what happened at Westminster under the relaxation of discipline in Nicoll's time, one is inclined to concede that, given the paucity of masters in comparison with the turbulent young aristocrats who peopled the schools in the eighteenth century, harshness may have been necessary. (Sargeaunt, *Annals of Westminster*, pp. 165 ff.)

[2] Obviously, boys do not take to study naturally; however, any love that they might have had was discouraged, not encouraged.

[3] Lyte, op. cit., pp. 142 ff.   [4] Leach, *History of Winchester*, p. 266.

[5] Lyte, op. cit., pp. 142 ff.

[6] Obviously such customs are not peculiar to Public Schools. This one probably goes back, as Frazer indicates in the *Golden Bough*, to the custom of sacrificing a human scapegoat in place of a king or priest at certain festivals. The meaning disappeared; the custom remained.

The Reformation, which saw the break-up of the communal life shared by fellows and scholars, witnessed the gradual degeneration of the religious life at Eton and Winchester and the other schools as well, and the general religious apathy of the eighteenth century finished the process. The directly ecclesiastical schools suffered, as we have seen, from corruption and neglect of religious duties by the fellows. Schools like Harrow and Rugby were Anglican chiefly in externals, religious services being purely formal. The churchman, as the rather prejudiced Cowper said, cared only for wages: 'The parson knows enough who knows a duke.' Religion is dead, and only heathen morality is taught.[1] By the middle of the eighteenth century the masters in most schools tacitly ceased to concern themselves with anything but instruction, and permitted the moral character of the boys to develop by itself.

Thus, by the middle of the eighteenth century, the formal system of Public School education, intellectual and moral, had almost entirely broken down. There was, moreover, little prospect of the sort of sweeping changes that might have given it renewed life. From the end of the seventeenth until late in the eighteenth century there were few new educational or religious ideas from which the schools could draw invigoration. But if there had been, masters and governing bodies, wedded as they were to tradition, would probably not have gone to them for help. Masters loved the old methods, which were the only ones they knew. To have procured teachers who were acquainted with fresh ideas would have required—at the ecclesiastical schools at any rate—a radical change in the system of selecting masters. Finally, there was not even much likelihood that masters would willingly increase their numbers: since the foreigners paid the masters, the fewer of the latter that there were, the more money each one received.

Despite this condition of affairs, Public Schools in the eighteenth century were by no means decadent and

---

[1] Cowper, *Tirocinium*, Aldine Edition of the British Poets, Vol. II, London, 1843, pp. 211, 217, 231.

The Late Eighteenth-Century Public School

educationally worthless institutions. For, starting in the seventeenth century there occurred a silent and undirected revolution which, in a way wholly unanticipated by masters and governors, revitalized Public School life. This revolution, in part a result and in part a cause of the ineffectiveness of masters, was the virtual conquest of the Public Schools by those who attended them. By the middle of the eighteenth century, though the older rulers were still nominally in command, a Public School had, in all essential respects, become what the student body made it. It had become, in other words, a place dominated by very different ideals and practices from those which had previously guided its life. Moreover, it had not only been transformed but it had been regenerated. For boys brought with them from home ways of thought and action that, unlike those of the masters, were in touch with the living reality of eighteenth-century life. Thus, in that unconscious and unpremeditated way which was so typical of them, Public Schools had evolved to meet new conditions.

MORAL EDUCATION—THE BOYS

The education that boys gave to boys was, like that imparted by the masters, disciplinary in both senses of the term: a boy was coerced by his fellows and given the opportunity to struggle against obstacles. But neither the aims nor the methods of the training that a boy received from his companions in any sense resembled those of formal Public School training. Indeed, the words themselves are hardly applicable to the former: boys were not trying to develop one another's characters, and consequently they had no conscious educational methods. What happened was that certain kinds of boys lived together under certain conditions and that the development of certain character traits resulted.

The boys came, to begin with, from a more or less homogeneous social group. This fact, alone, is of incalculable importance, for it meant that they possessed an *esprit de corps*, a powerful group unity, which was the chief educational and disciplinary instrument that existed in Public Schools. Group unity brought order and pattern to school life and prevented the chaos that was all too likely to occur where so many boys were thrown together. Even more important, it acted as the primary agent in forming the individual's character according to prescribed standards, since a homogeneous group almost inevitably forces newcomers or outsiders to conform to its own patterns of behaviour.

Moreover, the boys who went to Public Schools were not from any but from a particular social group: they were the sons of upper-class Englishmen. As such, they brought with them the ideals of English gentlemen, ideals considerably at variance with the earlier aims of Public Schools. The ruling classes had acquired their purposes and modes of behaviour not from the clerkly but from the chivalric tradition. Their ancestors had gone, not as scholars to the schools, but as pages to the houses of nobles, where they had learned that bravery, loyalty, and the ability to lead were more important than the knowledge or the Christian humility taught at the Public Schools.[1] Their descendants, therefore, when they overran the Public Schools in the eighteenth century, revolutionized those institutions. In one respect, however, they reinforced rather than destroyed older practice. The ruling classes, like school founders and masters, were traditionalists. This meant that, even more than before, schools would rely on past practice as a basis for action, and would be increasingly difficult to change in the future. Moreover, it meant that worship of the past would become an important educational instrument: boys and masters alike were bound, consciously or unconsciously, to utilize reverence for tradition as a means of securing conformity to patterns of behaviour on which they wished the majority to model themselves.

The school's contribution to informal education, though enormously important, consisted entirely in the fact that the Public Schools were boarding-schools whose existence was continuous.

As one would expect, no one realized, at the time when Schools were founded, the moral value of having boys live together. The Public Schools became boarding-schools for

---

[1] Cf. Parry, op. cit., pp. 117 ff.

The Late Eighteenth-Century Public School 37

reasons quite other than educational ones. Wykeham and Henry made their foundations colleges merely because they wanted to gather the best talent from all over the country for the benefit of Mother Church. The part of the school outside of the colleges, which later became the essence of a Public School, came to consist of a number of boarders for equally simple reasons. When good schools were few, and the upper classes decided to send their boys to school at all, they would naturally send them to the best institution of learning, wherever it was. Sir Philip Sydney was sent miles to Shrewsbury because that was the only good school in the West Country. And, since communications were not too good, the boy would be unable to come home every day, and would stay at school. Because of the medieval custom of sending boys away to private houses, the upper classes were, and still are, quite accustomed to dispense with the presence of their sons at an early age, so that this aspect of the matter did not bother them.[1] If, as at Shrewsbury at first, there was no boarding accommodation in the school, the boy would live in town. Masters soon saw, however, the advantages of having the boys under their direct control. Such control gave the head masters at ecclesiastical schools prestige, as they had complete charge of the oppidans, which, because of the governing bodies, they did not have of collegers. At Eton the Dames' houses were not completely superseded until the nineteenth century, but they gradually came more and more under the authority of the school.[2] At Winchester, Commoner's College was erected by Dr. Burton in the middle of the eighteenth century.[3] When Rugby and Harrow began to grow, the foreigners were closely connected with the school, though Harrow borrowed the Eton system of Dames' houses.

However incidental to educational considerations were its causes, the fact that Public Schools were boarding-schools proved of anything but incidental educational import;

[1] Cf. Parry, op. cit., p. 117.
[2] A Dame's house is a boarding-house run by some one not officially connected with the school. Later those houses were called Dames' houses that were not presided over by a classical master. It was late in the nineteenth century before non-classical masters had the status of house-master and tutor.
[3] A. K. Cook, *About Winchester College*, p. 52.

indeed, so essential a characteristic was it that St. Paul's and Merchant Taylors cannot be considered Public Schools simply because they were essentially day schools. Being places where boys lived, the Public Schools became tiny worlds, miniature societies, and thus offered to those who went to them direct experience of social life. On the small stage of a Public School a boy was able to train for and rehearse the part he was later to play amid the realities of upper-class life.

Of only less significance than their boarding-school character was the long history and the continuing existence of the Public Schools. For, since they were enduring institutions, they became the preservers of customs and patterns of behaviour inherited from the past, both from the far past of founders and early generations of boys and masters and the more recent past of upper-class usurpation. The schools embodied tradition and thus made traditionalism possible.

Many late eighteenth-century school traditions, particularly certain specific practices, were so trivial or had so obviously outlived their usefulness that their rigid observance is explicable only in terms of the excessive reverence for concrete ritual which characterizes the English. Relatively modern customs like special slang and enforced differences in dress have at least symbolic value as evidences of youthful solidarity and of hierarchy of rank. But such traditional Eton practices as shirking[1] or refusing to eat a good dinner because scrags of mutton were considered *infra dig.*[2] were absurdities unjustifiable—by the end of the eighteenth century at any rate—in rational terms; Eton Montem was an elaborate pageant, the colour and gaiety of which did little to conceal its essential meaninglessness.[3]

[1] Hiding when out of bounds so that a master would not be under the necessity of reporting you. Bounds were realized to be absurdly limited; instead of changing the rule, the authorities countenanced and encouraged shirking.

[2] Tucker, *Eton of Old*, pp. 34–35. Scrags of mutton were probably at one time inedible.

[3] Montem had originally a very practical purpose, which was to send the head boy in college through the university. It was this purpose which gave meaning to the collection of 'salt' or money from passers-by and the ensuing triumphal march to Salt Hill. But, though the original intention remained, it came to have little relation to the spectacle of five hundred young aristocrats begging money from the gaping populace.

Some of the bequests from the past were, on the other hand, the very basis of late eighteenth-century and subsequent school life: such, above all, unless one includes ideals of conduct, were the tradition of freedom from control by the masters, athletics, and the prefect-fagging system. To a certain extent, Wykeham and other founders encouraged the freedom of the boys, but they exercised a strict control over it. The tradition of almost complete independence developed later as a result of the lack of masters, the decay in the system of formal education, and the undisciplined arrogance of the eighteenth-century student body. By 1700 the conception of a world of boys living in virtual obliviousness of the presence of masters, an idea that would have been abhorrent to Wykeham, had become the basic meaning of the term Public School. Later on, by a process of rationalization, Englishmen began to imagine that the tradition of freedom, in actuality so largely the chance result of a breakdown in the system of control, had been the product of the spirit of the race. As such it must necessarily embody educational wisdom. The belief became virtually indestructible that the best way to educate a boy was to leave him alone.

The tradition of sport at schools was produced by the love of games among normal boys, especially English boys, and by the free atmosphere which made their practice possible. Even masters contributed. Wykeham believed in the value of recreation for boys, though he probably had no theories about its educative value. John Lyon provided for games, especially for the Harrow sport of archery. Even in the early days there was plenty of spare time for play, though not as much as in the eighteenth century: there was an hour allowed for recreation on regular days, and there were whole and half holidays. The boys amply availed themselves of these opportunities. Robert Mathews' seventeenth-century poem about Winchester mentions quoits, hand-ball, bat-ball, tennis, football (not described) as games indulged in by the boys.[1] Earlier than that there were such amusements as fishing, shooting, and keeping dogs. The modern traditional

[1] A. K. Cook, op. cit., p. 21.

games were, however, slow in developing. Rowing was sufficiently developed at Westminster in the forties of the eighteenth century for Warren Hastings to distinguish himself at it;[1] but cricket, Harrow's great game, did not become popular until the sixties,[2] and football was a product of the nineteenth century.

So much nonsense has been written about the prefect-fagging system that it is difficult to treat it impartially. It has been applauded as the greatest discovery for training boys ever made; it has been denounced as legalized slavery. Without necessarily subscribing to either of these opinions, one can readily agree that without it Public School education would lose its most basic and unique feature.[3] The prefect-fagging system was, though still in a formative state, already fairly well established as far as its primary structure was concerned by the latter part of the eighteenth century. In the last years of the eighteenth century the system was legalized and thus made a regular part of formal Public School discipline by such masters as Dr. Goddard at Winchester[4] and Dr. Heath and Dr. Drury at Harrow,[5] but they were merely sanctioning a *fait accompli*: monitorial privileges, had, as Cook says, been 'exercised, probably or certainly, before they were conferred'.[6] By the second quarter of the nineteenth century Dr. Arnold found the forms of the system so well established, so sanctified by tradition, that he preferred or was forced, in order to achieve his moral ends, to leave the externals, the tangible ceremonials, as they were, and to transform their spirit and meaning.

The eighteenth-century prefect-fagging system was the political manifestation of control of the schools by the student bodies: it was a government of boys functioning in almost complete independence of supervision by the masters. The older and stronger boys, supported by the sanction of custom, ruled the schools like feudal oligarchs under the titles, at

[1] Colonel G. B. Malleson, *The Life of Warren Hastings*, London, 1894.
[2] Thornton, *Harrow School*, p. 148.
[3] And this is true even though technically the prefect system does not exist, except in college, at as important a school as Eton; for the general social structure at Eton is similar to that at schools which have such a system.
[4] Cook, op. cit., pp. 119 ff.   [5] Thornton, op. cit., pp. 164 ff.
[6] Cook, op. cit., p. 119.

The Late Eighteenth-Century Public School 41

different institutions, of prefect, monitor, or praepostor. In the eighteenth century and for a long time afterwards a prefect was very much of an autocrat. He had almost unlimited power to inflict physical punishment, called variously tunding or whopping, on the younger boys, and was virtually unimpeded in the exercise of his right to extract services from certain subordinates, called fags, who ran his errands, made his bed, blacked his boots, and performed other menial tasks for him. Indeed, the system was likely to be an extremely harsh and tyrannical one, as many who experienced it have amply proved. A prefect's treatment of his subjects, though less indiscriminate because more or less ordered and regularized by custom, was often not very different from ordinary bullying.

Like other aspects of Public School life, the eighteenth-century prefect-fagging system was not really planned by anybody. William of Wykeham gave it its initial impetus when he provided that there should be eighteen seniors to maintain discipline by example and precept and to report to the master for a flogging those who had been disorderly.[1] But these prefects, like those which Henry VI established at Eton[2] and John Lyon placed at Harrow,[3] were reporting policemen, not feudal administrators, their duties being to take the roll and watch others at play, at work, and at meals.[4] They had, as far as we know, no fags, and, if we can judge by Robert Mathew's failure to mention them in his account of Winchester, they continued to have none as late as 1647. The later forms of the prefect system were the inevitable and unpremeditated result of social conditions in the late seventeenth and eighteenth centuries. When the schools were overrun by the upper classes, and when, partly as a result, formal discipline broke down, control passed insensibly into the hands of the strongest boys, who transformed

---

[1] A. K. Cook, *About Winchester College*, p. 13.
[2] At Eton there were also eighteen praepostors or praepositors, four in the schoolroom, four in the college dormitory, four in the playing-fields, two in church, one in the dining-room or 'hall', two for commensals, and one to enforce cleanliness. (Cf. Lyte, op. cit., p. 142.)
[3] At Harrow there were two monitors to report offences and a third to watch the other two. (Thornton, op. cit., p. 74.)
[4] Leach, *History of Winchester College*, p. 174.

Wykeham's system of dependent advisors into an autonomous government. Similarly, when, during the same period, there was a scarcity of food and servants, the all-powerful older boys made up for this deficiency by employing the younger to procure eatables for them and to keep their rooms in order.[1]

The life at an English Public School in the eighteenth century was, then, the resultant of a group of unpremeditated factors: a number of upper-class boys lived together in virtual freedom from any guidance beyond that which was derived from sedulously worshipped past custom and group ideals like loyalty, honourableness, and respect for physical strength and self-reliance. This life—the nature of which subsequent sections will make increasingly clear—was anything but a mild or gentle one. These were not the qualities of adult existence in the eighteenth century, much less of an existence dominated by boys. Public School society, like a society of primitive savages, was a world of brutal compulsions and taboos, in which happiness and freedom could be won, if at all, only after much hardship and struggle.

The average individual suffered cruelly. To begin with he was—particularly at closely organized schools like Winchester, Westminster, and Charterhouse—under constant pressure to obey the meticulously exact customs and laws of his school. Often these laws had their justification in preventing disorder or helping to develop desirable character traits; equally often they were merely the expression of the will of the strong, and were, from an ethical point of view, of highly questionable value. In either case strict obedience to them, enforced by a harsh and often unjust public opinion, meant loss of moral independence. But these compulsions were at least more or less legitimate and regularized. The individual in the relatively unorganized eighteenth-century schools was, however, also subjected to the capricious orders

---

[1] Cf. Cook, op. cit., p. 126 Cook is probably right in considering far-fetched Professor Freeman's idea that fagging was an outgrowth of the comitatus. That there is a parallel caused by somewhat parallel conditions is quite a different story. The medieval idea of service and vassalage has also a probable connexion with fagging; at least the young aristocrat was used to the idea.

and brutality of the strong. High-handed tyranny and cruel bullying were almost universal occurrences at all the schools.[1] As in a primitive society—or for that matter, in the economic sphere, under the *laissez-faire* industrial system of England and America—lack of rigid governmental protection of the rights of individuals spelled unhappiness and servitude for the less strong among those individuals.

Public School life was not, however, all repression. If one was among the chosen few, there were the joys of leadership, of which Horace Walpole wrote glowingly, 'Alexander at the head of the world never tasted the true pleasure that boys of his own age have enjoyed at the head of a school. Little intrigues, little schemes, and policies, engage their thoughts, and at the same time they are laying the foundation for their middle age of life.'[2] But even for the average boy, if he survived his early years at school and accepted group standards, there was much pleasure and freedom. Indeed, from the point of view of masters, parents, and moralists there was a good deal too much. For, though boys would countenance no sort of revolt against their own standards,[3] they condoned and encouraged revolt against masters and a general defiance of middle-class morality. To be a hero at Winchester, according to Smollett, meant to defy the 'laws and regulations of the place', and to become involved in sanguinary adventures.[4] Locke wrote that 'waggeries or cheats practiced amongst schoolboys' were common occurrences at Westminster, and that a general unruliness was the prevailing state of affairs.[5] Cowper, writing of Westminster at a later date, said that boxing, driving coaches, bilking

[1] Thomas Day, for example, described his life at Charterhouse as a combination of submission to rules, bullying and toadying, and clashes with authority. (Gignilliat, *The Author of Sandford and Merton*, p. 16.)

[2] *The Letters of Horace Walpole*, edited by Mrs. Paget Toynbee, 16 vols., Oxford, 1903, Vol. I, p. 12.

[3] Thus, certainly for no general ethical reasons, they found reprehensible in the extreme Charles James Fox's spending a year on the continent as a member of fashionable society, and made his life miserable when he returned to school; similarly, the boys were the first to demand that Tate Wilkinson be flogged for having run away from school, though they applauded when he took his flogging without a whimper. (Cf. *Memorials and Correspondence of Charles James Fox*, edited by Lord John Russell, London, 1853, p. 12; Tate Wilkinson, *Memoirs of his Own Life*, 4 vols., New York, 1790, Vol. I, pp. 39 ff.)

[4] Cf. *Peregrine Pickle*, Vol. I, pp. 108, 112.

[5] *Some Thoughts Concerning Education*, p. 144.

tavern bills, and getting out of scrapes were the 'frolics' of the day, which mingled often with whoring, drinking, and gambling.[1] Discipline was, indeed, so bad at Westminster that, according to tradition, Lord Rockingham once visited the school dressed as a lady, and Cowper's favourite master, Vincent Bourne, had his ears boxed in order to extinguish a fire in his locks, which the boys had lighted.[2]

Finally, there was, even for the weak, occasional opportunity for freedom in the relatively unorganized eighteenth-century school. Particularly at Eton, where, because of its size and genteel traditions, there was a certain spaciousness of life among the oppidans, and, to a lesser extent at Harrow, with its Whig-liberal principles, the eccentrics might escape the ordinary tyrannies of a Public School and lead their own lives. Thus the poet Gray was free at Eton to follow where his fancy led, even though this meant—despite his praise of chasing 'the rolling circle's speed'—studying, an occupation abhorred by the average boy.[3]

To have experienced four to six years of the kind of existence suggested in the preceding paragraphs could not but have had a profound influence on the average boy. Yet it is dangerous to dogmatize in regard to the effect of Public School moral training. Even less than in the case of intellectual education can one be sure that the traits of the English upper classes that one cites as evidence of the effects of that training were not either inherited, produced at home, or acquired in later life.[4] For, since the machinery of

---

[1] *Tirocinium*, p. 210.
[2] Sargeaunt, *Annals of Westminster*, p. 173. These descriptions hardly tally with Cumberland's assertion that 'Dr. Nichols had the art of making his scholars gentlemen', unless one is willing to give a very broad meaning to the term gentleman. Cumberland also seems partially to contradict prevailing opinion when he says that 'there was a court of honor in that school, to whose unwritten laws every member of our community was amenable, and which, to transgress by any act of meanness that exposed the offender to public contempt, was a degree of punishment, compared to which the being sentenced to the rod would have been considered as an acquittal or reprieve'. (Richard Cumberland, *Memoirs*, written by himself, Philadelphia, 1856, pp. 42, 43.)
[3] Cf. Thomas Gray, *Ode on a Distant Prospect of Eton College*, and Edmund Gosse, *Gray*, London, 1906, p. 6.
[4] Many over-enthusiastic alumni in the nineteenth century have made extravagant claims for the influence of their schools on various great individuals, but the evidence that they bring forth for their contentions is pitifully meagre. Later writers who have purported to trace the relationship between boys and

The Late Eighteenth-Century Public School 45

Public School moral education had been itself the creation of upper-class boys, one often suspects that the qualities it produced were those which might have resulted in any case. It may well be that frequently schools did little more than not to inhibit the development of the English gentleman.

Nevertheless, it was certainly true that the life at a Public School was admirably suited to create various moral traits, that often it turned out boys marked by these traits, and that in many instances it was responsible for the traits which these boys possessed. In the first place, the very struggle against obstacles, which was the first necessity of existence at school, was likely to leave its mark on those who succeeded in fighting their way to the higher forms. At its worst it occasionally produced among the strong, as Cowper said, arrogance, pride, and effrontery; more often it taught self-reliance, poise, and a sense of proportion: a boy had the conceit knocked out of him, his ambitions aroused, his powers of leadership and responsibility tested, and in general learned to know his capabilities and shortcomings in the world he was to inhabit. In the second place, the influence of group *mores* and the direct coercion of his fellows usually endowed a boy with certain fixed beliefs and indestructible moral qualities. Negatively, they probably destroyed any respect he might have had for orginality or the ordinary Christian virtues such as humility, chastity, industry, and love of noble and commoner alike. Positively, they taught a boy loyalty to his fellows, and, through that, loyalty to his school and to his nation, circumstances welcomed later on by self-conscious imperialists, who saw the uses both of the virtue itself and of the corporate life of the Public School as a means of producing it. Moreover, they

schools have been more careful, but as a result their books are not very illuminating. Neither Arthur Benson's long *Fasti Etonenses* (Eton, 1899) nor Timbs' *Schooldays of Eminent Men*, nor J. G. Cotton Minchin's *Our Public Schools* (London, 1901) tells us anything except facts about the social life of boys. The most interesting conjectures as to influence are Courthope's remarks on Harrow in Edmund W. Howson's and George Townsend Warner's *Harrow School* (London, 1898). But even he, in such statements as the following about Byron, 'in his rebelliousness, his turbulence, his ardent passion for political liberty, he seems to be an embodiment of the traditional spirit, which for fifty years before his entrance into the school had characterized the life of the place' (op. cit., p. 187) is careful not to imply that the school was chiefly responsible for these qualities of character.

produced such virtues as courage and honourableness, qualities which boys usually admire and which English boys of the upper classes had always been taught. Finally, if they instilled undue respect for physical prowess, in compensation they made it clear to a boy that money and rank were not, at school at any rate, very important, and that, within relatively narrow social limits, one ought to have a democratic respect for talent as the highest of human attributes.

CHAPTER II
EARLY OPINION[1]

APPROVAL

EVEN before 1700 the Public Schools had become prominent enough to elicit published statements as to their merits and defects. By the middle of the eighteenth century such comment had attained sufficient volume to make it, with reservations, a cross-section of English opinion. One can discover from it what in general seventeenth- and eighteenth-century Englishmen believed about their schools; in a more tentative way one can begin to discern, particularly in the criticism, certain group attitudes and opinions which have an important bearing on later school history. However, even in the eighteenth century the battle to preserve or change the Public Schools was only beginning, and there were comparatively few self-advertised critics or advocates. An account of opinion in this early period, unlike such an account later on, can, therefore, be only very tentatively an analysis of various systems of adverse and favourable ideas.

Much favourable comment in both the seventeenth and eighteenth centuries centred around intellectual education. Many alumni praised their schools because they felt that they had learned the classics there; a lesser number—since some, like Gray, Walpole, Warton, and Collins, garnered an education without magisterial assistance—expressed admiration for those who taught them. If it seems surprising, in view of the general state of decay that existed in the schools, that there should have been widespread praise of Public

[1] Because we are interested in criticism and praise as evidence of psychological and social forces at work during a period we will discuss throughout this book writings chiefly of the age under discussion. Where material outside of the epoch is used as corroboration or contradiction of facts given by a critic, it will be differentiated from the latter. Reminiscences written after the fact must be used with care. Where there is good reason to believe that opinions expressed in them are of long standing they may be cited as characteristic attitudes of an earlier time. They cannot be used as evidence of an active critical movement, since, obviously, opinions must be expressed to be influential.

School classical training, it must be remembered that much of this comment came from exceptional people, that any school at any time might have one or two good masters, and that, finally, some writers, lacking a standard of comparison or a good memory, may have exaggerated the merits of their schools. It is notable that only such propagandists as Defoe made the statement that the masters at Eton and Winchester were good as a group.

Since praise had reference to particular situations, it naturally was unevenly distributed, clustering around outstanding schools under outstanding masters. Thus in the seventeenth century, though Milton[1] and Pepys[2] could praise St. Paul's, and Cowley had kind words for Westminster early in the century,[3] it was the latter school under Busby which drew forth most eulogy. Busby earned not only gratitude from such as Dryden,[4] but recognition from important outsiders like Steele, who wrote in the *Lover*: 'His scholars were the finest Gentlemen, or the greatest Pedants in the age. The soil which he manured always grew fertile, but it is not in the Planter to make Flowers of Weeds, but whatever it was under Busby's eye, it was sure to get forward towards the Use for which nature designed it.'[5]

Similarly, in the eighteenth century it was Westminster, this time under Nicoll, which seems to have been the centre of Public School culture, though men such as Pitt and

---

[1] Milton studied hard under Alexander Gill at St. Paul's (1620 to 1624–5), and was much helped by his masters, for whom he had great respect. (David Masson, *The Life of John Milton*, Vol. I, London, 1881, pp. 83–5, 272.)

[2] Pepys, at St. Paul's a good deal later than Milton (1644–50), acquired there habits of serious industry and regularity, and a good knowledge of tongues. Moreover, St. Paul's, a staunch Puritan school, taught him both Puritanism and republicanism. Drinkwater says that Pepys probably got more learning than a Public School man does to-day. (John Drinkwater, *Pepys, His Life and Character*, London, 1930, pp. 21 ff.) Pepys often spoke of his old master, whom he considered learned though conceited; once, after Pepys had been talking of St. Paul's, 'he did upon my declaring my value of it, give me one of Lilly's grammars of a very old impression'. (*The Diary of Samuel Pepys*, by Henry V. Wheatley, 8 vols., London, 1893, Vol. IV, p. 345.)

[3] Cowley claimed that he was soaked in classical literature; fortunately he had masters who recognized his talent and allowed him to dispense with grammar rules.

[4] Cf. Dryden, *The Dramatic Works*, Edited by Montague Summers, London, 1931, Vol. I, pp. xxi–xxii; also cf. Timbs, *Schooldays of Eminent Men*, p. 135.

[5] Quoted from Barker, *Busby*, p. 24.

Fielding[1] wrote in praise of their education at other schools. Even Cowper and Chesterfield, surely neither of them staunch advocates of Public Schools, had words of admiration for the London school. In 1776 Cowper advised Joseph Hill to follow the Westminster method of teaching Greek and Latin, it being 'the best upon the whole that I have had an opportunity of observing'.[2] Chesterfield sent his son to Westminster under Nicoll in the forties,[3] and urged A. C. Stanhope to do the same, because the boy 'will get a tolerable share at least of classical learning . . . which he is never supposed to have, unless he has been at a great school'.[4] George Colman the elder, Richard Cumberland, and Warren Hastings, all at Westminster in the forties, paid tribute to the eminence of the school at the time.[5] Finally, it was Westminster, to which Gibbon went for a short time in 1749 and 1750, that inspired the following comment in his autobiography: 'these schools may assume the merit of

[1] Pitt, though he had no love for Eton otherwise, admitted learning the classics there: he used his Latin for quotations, his Greek for examples and analogies. Fielding, a friend and schoolmate of Pitt, not only learned but adored the classics. He imbibed his love of ancient learning from the two assistants of Henry Bland, the head; the memorizing, which most boys hated, helped him to make the authors he read his own. (Albert von Ruville, *William Pitt, Earl of Chatham*, 3 vols., New York, 1907, Vol. I, p. 73; Wilbur Cross, *The History of Henry Fielding*, 3 vols., New Haven, 1918, Vol. I, pp. 42, 43, 47.)

[2] Cowper adored his careless, indolent master, Vincent Bourne, who wrote Latin poetry and had his locks set on fire by the boys. From him Cowper learned to write Latin verse, to be a classical scholar, and to have reverence for classic form. (The *Letters of William Cowper*, Edited by J. G. Frazer, 2 vols., London, 1912, Vol. I, pp. 116–17; Sargeaunt, *Annals of Westminster*, p. 173; Goldwin Smith, *Cowper*, London [1880], pp. 10–11.)

[3] The Earl of Chesterfield, *Letters to His Son*, 2 vols., New York, 1925, Vol. I, p. 247.

[4] *The Letters of Philip Dormer Stanhope*, Edited by Bonamy Dobrée, 6 vols., 1932. To A. C. Stanhope, February 16, 1765, p. 2646.

[5] Richard Brinsley Peake, *Memoirs of the Colman Family*, 2 vols., London, 1841, Vol. I, p. 33. Richard Cumberland was enthusiastic about the stimuli to work provided by the approbation of masters such as Kinsman and Bourne; he praised Westminster for its taste in verse composition and for being the cradle of the Muses. (Richard Cumberland, *Memoirs*, pp. 42, 45.) Warren Hastings was enthusiastic about Nicoll, who took such a personal interest in him that he offered to pay for the boy's education rather than have him sent to India. 'I hazard the imputation of vanity,' Hastings wrote, 'in yielding to the sense of gratitude and justice which is due to the memory of my revered master, Dr. Nicholls, to relate that, when I waited upon him to inform him of that purpose of my guardian [to send him to India] he, in the most delicate manner, remonstrated against it, adding that if the necessity of my circumstances was the only cause requiring my removal, and I should continue at school, he would undertake that it should be at no expense to me.' (Malleson, *Life of Warren Hastings*, pp. 5–6.)

teaching all that they pretend to teach; the Latin and Greek languages: they deposit in the hands of a disciple the keys of two valuable chests; nor can he complain if they are afterwards lost or neglected by his own fault.'[1]

It is important to note, in connexion with this subject of intellectual education, that in these days very few of those who applauded the teaching facilities of their schools felt it necessary to justify a classical education in itself. Swift, early in the century, had written that 'the books read at school and college are full of incitements to virtue, and discouragements from vice'; but he was engaged in the special mission of inducing the aristocracy to frequent schools, and is an exception to the general rule that defenders took the virtues of the classics much for granted.[2] One can see from comments by Chesterfield and Locke that one cause of this was that, since Latin was the fashion, it was not necessary to find solid reasons for defending it. Chesterfield found that the classics were very necessary for a young man of quality;[3] Locke, who was very sceptical about the time spent on Latin, could still say, 'Latin I look upon as absolutely necessary to a gentleman.'[4] Later on, society learned to dispense with the classics, and, though custom still acted to keep it in fashion, better reasons for its retention had to be found.

Though many boys had pleasant relations with masters, this did not mean that they approved of ordinary Public School disciplinary methods, but that they had either escaped these methods or liked their masters in spite of floggings. Amusingly enough, only the kindly old Tory bear, Dr. Johnson—and he possibly with his tongue in his cheek—had praise for the extreme severity of masters. 'There is', he wrote, 'now less flogging in our great schools than formerly, but then less is learned there; so that what the

[1] Edward Gibbon, *The Autobiography*, Everyman's Edition, 1923, p. 31.
[2] Swift, *Essay on Modern Education, Works*, Vol. XI, p. 55. If Swift discovered that the classics could teach truth, honour, justice, temperance, courage and good sense, others like Budgell found that most masters at Public Schools were not availing themselves of the opportunities offered by Greek and Roman literature.
[3] *Letters to His Son*, Vol. I, p. 54.
[4] *Some Thoughts Concerning Education*, p. 286.

boys get at one end they lose at the other.'[1] Though he sarcastically deprecated crippling children, he thought that boys could be educated only by fear.[2] Johnson was, it may be added, a staunch defender of Public Schools in general, and successfully urged Boswell to send his sons to Eton and Westminster.[3] For reformers like Milton and Locke he had no use: Milton was impractical, and Locke had been tried and found wanting because he underrated a literary (that is, a classical) education.[4]

If there were many to applaud the intellectual education given at schools, there were an equal if not greater number who found virtues in the social life led by the boys. As Cowper said[5]—and as others like Bulwer Lytton were to repeat later on—many parents sent boys to school merely from habit or in order that the boys might mix with the titled. But there were also some who, even in those days, undoubtedly favoured a Public School education because of the manliness which they believed boys were taught. This manliness of the Public School product has always been the chief justification for an Eton or Westminster training.

That manliness existed and was a good thing has been asserted by even the most irreconcilable enemies of schools. Locke wrote admiringly that a school would make a boy hustle and shift for himself, and, through the emulation of his fellows, would put life and industry into him.[6] Budgell, in his attack on Public School morals in the *Spectator*,[7] admitted that schools produced manly assurance and imparted knowledge of the way of the world: according to him, the youth who could rob an orchard learned caution, secrecy, and circumspection. Fielding—with a certain amount of sarcasm, however—said that Public Schools taught more than private. Sir Thomas Booby 'used to say,' wrote Fielding, 'the school itself initiated him a great way (I remember that was his very expression), for great schools are little societies, where a boy of any observation may see

[1] James Boswell, *Life of Samuel Johnson*, edited by Augustine Birrell, 6 Vols., New York, 1906, Vol. III, p. 249.
[2] Ibid., p. 41.   [3] Ibid., Vol. IV, p. 22.
[4] Ibid., Vol. V, p. 62.   [5] *Tirocinium*, p. 215.
[6] *Some Thoughts Concerning Education*, pp. 138 ff.
[7] Boston, 1872, 8 vols., No. 313, Vol. V, p. 21.

in epitome what he will afterwards find in the world at large.'[1] Finally, Gibbon, despite his own failure at school and his misgivings about Public School education, was fully aware of the virtues of a Public School. 'I shall always be ready to join in the common opinion, that our public schools, which have produced so many eminent characters, are the best adapted to the genius and constitution of the English people. A boy of spirit may acquire a previous and practical experience of the world; and his playfellows may be the future friends of his heart or his interest. In a free intercourse with his equals, the habits of truth, fortitude, and prudence will insensibly be matured. Birth and riches are measured by the standard of personal merit; and the mimic scene of a rebellion has displayed in their true colours the ministers and patriots of the rising generation.'[2]

Finally, we come to a much more intangible but none the less important set of reasons for liking schools. As we have seen, though the organization of school life was such that the weak were likely to suffer from the tyranny of the strong, many individuals—and these often gentle dreamers who would never be 'ministers and patriots'—managed to achieve actual leisure and freedom as a result of the comparative casualness of eighteenth-century Public School organization. Such boys liked Eton and Harrow, not because they were educationally beneficial, but because they were pleasant spots in which to spend youthful days and make friendships. In short, they defended schools as places in which they had been happy.

In this connexion a number of things should be noticed. To begin with, comparatively few students in the eighteenth century *were* happy at school. Even fewer wrote of their happiness or their friendships: poets like Otway, Collins, and the Wartons were probably not unhappy at Winchester. The two latter formed one of those romantic friendships that schools are traditionally supposed to foster.[3] We know that

[1] Henry Fielding, *The Adventures of Joseph Andrews*, Vol. I of the *Works of Henry Fielding*, Edited by G. Maynadier, Boston, n.d., Vol. II, Book 3, p. 97.
[2] Gibbon, *Autobiography*, p. 31.
[3] Cf. *The Poems of William Collins*, Edited with an Introductory Study by Edmund Blunden, London, 1929, p. 7. Cowper, who was sceptical about most things in regard to school, said that friendships there were not lasting, and

Early Opinion 53

Addison and Steele formed their great friendship at Charterhouse.[1] Pepys and Fielding could express pleasure at the recollection of school. Yet only the Eton quartet, made up of Gray, Walpole, West, and Ashton, have left accounts of schooldays or friendships.[2]

In the second place, those who did base their defence of schools on happiness were usually expressing an attitude very different from that of mere defenders of curriculum or social life. They were expressing love, not liking, as one can see from Gray's famous lines:

> Ye distant spires, ye antique towers,
> That crown the watery glade,
> Where grateful Science still adores
> Her Henry's holy shade,[3]

warned those who cultivated the rich and noble that mature life, which showed the reality of dispositions, would sever relationships formed with advancement in mind. George Colman the younger, who had no axe to grind in the way that Cowper had, wrote, of a school friendship of his, 'as one instance, among many, that school connexions are not lasting, I have never seen Cranstoun from the time of our leaving Westminster'. (Cf. Cowper, *Tirocinium*, p. 216; Peake, *Memoirs of the Colman Family*, Vol. I, p. 312.)

[1] Thackeray, a loyal Carthusian, as well as a brother writer, tried to make up for the deficiency of knowledge in regard to Addison's and Steele's friendship by a lovely piece of fiction. He pictured their relationship, quite unjustifiably, as that of a fag to an adored older boy. 'Dick Steele, the Charterhouse gown-boy, contracted such an admiration in the years of his childhood, and retained it faithfully through his life. Through the school and through the world, whithersoever his strange fortune led this erring, wayward, affectionate creature, Joseph Addison was always his head boy. Addison wrote his exercises. Addison did his best themes. He ran on Addison's messages: fagged for him and blacked his shoes: to be in Joe's company was Dick's greatest pleasure; and he took a sermon or a caning from his monitor with the most boundless reverence, acquiescence, and affection.' (William Makepeace Thackeray, *The English Humourists of the Eighteenth Century*, Edited by George Saintsbury, London, n.d., p. 551.)

[2] Gray, Walpole, West, and Ashton were at Eton from 1727 to 1734. Since, as Gwynn says, 'the separation of youth into groups according to the income of their parents was much less exactly carried out in the eighteenth century than in our democratic age', the relatively poor Gray and Ashton could associate on a plane of equality with the aristocratic Walpole. (Stephen Gwynn, *The Life of Horace Walpole*, Boston, 1932, p. 23.) Neither Walpole nor Gray were typical schoolboys. Walpole enjoyed neither cricket nor expeditions against bargemen and suffered no reproaches for being a slacker in these respects. Gray was a shy, studious lad, never quite a boy, but already the scholar and moralist 'moving somewhat gravely and precociously through the classes of that venerable college which has since adopted him as her typical child, and which now [1882] presents to each emerging pupil a handsome selection from the works of the Etonian *par excellence*, Thomas Gray'. (Gosse, *Gray*, p. 7.) He and Walpole and West talked in 'poets' walk' and shared the delights described in the *Ode*. When the four had left, they carried on a correspondence full of tender reminiscences.

[3] *Ode on a Distant Prospect of Eton College.*

or from Walpole's lighter tribute, 'I have not forgotten my Almae Nutrices, wet or dry, I mean Eton and King's. I have laid aside for them, and left them in my will, as complete a set as I could of all I have printed.'[1] Moreover, the love which appeared in their writing was of a particular kind, which we characterize as 'romantic', and usually developed not at school but through the agency of time after a boy had left his *alma mater*. Romantic attachment became, later on, an attitude typical of great numbers of alumni, and was not confined to those who had been actually happy at school. We shall study it in more detail in the next chapter.

Finally, this liking for the school had very little to do with the institution as an active agent in promoting happiness. Occasionally, Eton or Winchester served as a direct, though passive, influence on such as Otway or Warton or Walpole or Young, to whom its medievalism was a poetic inspiration. Young's biographer, for example, has written: '*Qui dira que ces dispositions originales et ces phrases latines tranchantes et concises sont restées sans influence aucune sur de jeunes intelligences auxquelles elles s'offraient sans cesse au cours de l'éducation? La recherche de la pointe et le désir d'être spirituel qui se trahissent si souvent chez Young n'ont-ils pas été au moins encouragés par les préceptes laconiques du Collège?*'[2] Usually, however, even as a passive background, the school was more often a mere symbol for friendship or for lost youth than an objectively seen reality.

Cowper wisely saw that it was the desire to be young again that made men return in fancy to their schools: they liked the old initials and the old games as reminders of a boyhood which they regretted having lost.[3] Cowper himself, when thirty years distant from them, could recall with pleasure his days in the sixth form at Westminster, 'a period of life in which, if I had never tasted true happiness,

[1] Walpole, *Letters*, Vol. XI, p. 328.
[2] Thomas, *Le Poète Edward Young*, p. 13. Thomas, indeed, seems to believe that '*l'influence occulte et persistante des localités*', by which he refers to the many Winchester burial-grounds with their reminders of the dead, was in part responsible for the melancholy of the graveyard school of poets. (Op. cit., p. 20.)
[3] *Tirocinium*, pp. 213-14.

I was at least equally unacquainted with its contrary'.¹ Surely, judging from his rational attitude, this sentiment was hardly based on anything in the school.

To the Quadruple Alliance, Eton was merely a background for friendship. West wrote that it was thought of Gray that 'tips my pen with poetry and brings Eton to my view'.² Walpole upbraided West for passing Eton without stopping because 'that dear scene of our Quadruple Alliance would furnish me with the most agreeable recollections. 'Tis the head of our genealogical table.'³ To Walpole, Eton's playing-fields had a far different meaning than they have to those who view them in the light of reality: 'Dear George, were not the playing fields of Eton food for all manner of flights? No old maid's gown, though it had been tormented into all the fashions from King James to King George, ever underwent so many transformations as those poor plains have in my idea.'⁴ Finally, if Walpole's memory and feelings fastened on minute details of Eton life, as memory and feeling always do, it was for their relationship to his schoolfellows and to his youth: 'By the way, the clock strikes the old cracked sound—I recollect so much, and remember so little, and want to play about, and am so afraid of my playfellows, and am ready to *shirk* Ashton [who is a fellow]. . . . In short, I should be *out* of all *bounds* if I was to tell you half I feel, how young again I am one minute, and how old the next. . . . If I don't compose myself a little before Sunday morning, when Ashton is to preach, I shall certainly *be in a bill for laughing at church.*'⁵

CRITICISM

Criticisms of the eighteenth-century schools were not, with some exceptions, attacks on the truth of statements made by defenders. Few doubted that a classical education or a

¹ *Letters*, Vol. II, p. 81.
² *The Correspondence of Gray, Walpole, West and Ashton, 1734-1771*, by Paget Toynbee, 2 vols., Oxford, 1915, Vol. I, p. 51.   ³ Ibid., p. 97.
⁴ Walpole, *Letters*, Vol. I, pp. 12-13. Walpole was a member of a triumvirate consisting of Charles Lyttelton, George Montagu, and himself, as well as of the Quadruple Alliance.
⁵ Walpole, *Letters*, Vol. II, pp. 227-28.

manly character might be obtained at a Public School. Critics were usually those who sought ends other than the mere acquisition of Latin grammar and the hardy virtues, or objected, on humanitarian or other grounds, to the means employed to bring about current ends. The faults of the schools, according to the critics, lay in their failure to envisage intellectual and moral purposes for the accomplishment of which neither the narrow conception of classical training which prevailed, nor the rod, nor the unhampered boy existence of a Public School were adequate instruments.

On the whole, it was the curriculum that found the most disfavour among the learned. But most of those who attacked the intellectual education of schools did so only indirectly: they objected to the classics as a method of learning but with no specific reference to schools. For most of the writers on education were theorists, not direct reformers. They were part of the great seventeenth-century educational movement known as realism, and this movement was not, except through Locke, directed towards reform of the Public Schools. That realism failed to touch the Public Schools until almost our own day, despite its general acceptance by educators and by schools, is, it may be added, eloquent proof of the tradition-rooted power of the older system.[1]

The actual references to schools by writers of various kinds are casual and fragmentary, but two lines of criticism can, nevertheless, be noted. In the first place, there was the attack on the classics by those who felt that learning should be directly useful. Early in the century 'the current

[1] Realism is a product of the growth of science. In reaction against the Renaissance personal, literary, aesthetic ideal, it was impersonal and objective. Its end was utilitarian—to fit one for life in society. Its method was Bacon's inductive one. Bacon taught that one learned through the concrete, through experiment and sense experience. Ratich, and especially Comenius, the spiritual ancestor of Pestalozzi, worked out the method of teaching through following nature, through dealing with things concretely. In the seventeenth century he taught what only the nineteenth century began fully to appreciate, that the school should be made for the child, not vice versa. Locke is, of course, the great English realist, though, as we shall see, he deviated in important ways from the line of development that led to the naturalism of Rousseau, in which unhindered self-development became the ideal. For discussion of seventeenth-century educational writers, cf. F. P. Graves, *Great Educators of Three Centuries*, New York, 1912, pp. 15 ff; Monroe, *Education*, pp. 442 ff.; O. Browning, *Aspects of Education*, pp. 131 ff.

opinion' among the aristocracy was that 'the study of Greek and Latin is loss of time'.[1] The rising middle classes agreed with this idea, though for different reasons, and their criticism was more persistent than that of the aristocrats, who learned to accept classical education when it grew fashionable. The *bourgeoisie* wanted studies that would give a practical training for business and the professions. One of the first champions of this doctrine, so closely related to the theory of the realists, was Defoe, who had the temerity to suggest that, since things, not words, made the man of learning, Latin was not necessary even for the scholar.[2] Somewhat later—about 1740—an anonymous gentleman wrote a pamphlet which referred more directly to schools than had Defoe. While English gentlemen, he wrote, were kept at the dead languages and useless pedantry in the Public Schools, Jews were getting ahead by learning modern languages and principles of business; Latin and Greek made men mere idle ornaments. Even these studies, he added, were not taught very well, since the clergy, who were interested only in preferment, neglected their pupils.[3] But it was Locke who, more than any one else, was important in this connexion. To class him as a mere utilitarian is, however, unfair. His was a many-faceted criticism, which saw and commented on all sides of the education problem. His specific recommendations must be viewed in the light of his whole theory, which, both in his *Thoughts* and in *The Conduct of the Understanding*, arose out of his epistemology.

Since, to Locke, the mind was a *tabula rasa*, which must gain its experience through sense impressions, he was necessarily a realist in educational method. Moreover, his object was the realist one of making useful human beings, not scholars. From these premises Locke developed several different ideas. The first of these was the desirability of making work pleasant and useful: the child should be led gradually, in accordance with his capacity, from sense impression to sense impression, and then to abstractions.

[1] Swift, *Essay on Modern Education*, p. 52.
[2] Defoe, *Compleat English Gentleman*, pp. 212, 215.
[3] *An Enquiry into the Melancholy Circumstances of Great Britain*, London, 1740(?), pp. 41 ff.

Books were less important than things; an appeal should be made to love and respect, not merely to fear.[1] In the light of this idea, Locke severely criticized the intellectual training given in the Public Schools. The 'ado' made to no purpose over a little Latin and Greek seemed to him absurd. Parents must still fear the rod 'which they look on as the only instrument of education; as a language or two to be its whole business'.[2] Otherwise, why this seven to ten years spent on learning a language? Latin might be necessary for the gentlemen, but 'it is silly for a man going into trade to have it', and it ought not to be the chief business of education for any one. There was, according to Locke, endless knowledge of practical use in the world to be learned. Even more, there were habits of study and love of knowledge to be acquired: a tutor's business was not so much to teach a boy 'all that is knowable, as to raise in him a love and esteem of knowledge, and to put him in the right way of knowing and improving himself'.[3] The end was preparation for life, not the ability to dispute.

There was, however, another side to Locke, which was even more important for Public Schools, and which in many ways directly opposed what would seem to follow from the ideas already stated. From Locke's theory of sense impressions, Rousseau derived quite logically his idea of unhampered self-development from within. But Locke, more English and in a sense less consistent, came instead to a belief that education consisted in forming good habits by discipline. Since the mind was a blank, he wished to paint on it correct habits and ideas. This was to be achieved not by self-development, but by strenuous denial. As Locke states his theory, one perceives behind the modern scientist, the old Puritan moralist, who implies the very evil natural tendencies which in another breath he attempts to deny. 'The great thing to be minded in education is what habits you settle.'[4] 'As the strength of the body lies chiefly in being able to endure hardships, so also does that of the mind. And

---

[1] Cf. F. P. Graves, *Great Educators*, pp. 52 ff.; Locke, *Some Thoughts Concerning Education*, pp. 154 ff.
[2] *Some Thoughts Concerning Education*, p. 269.
[3] Ibid., p. 341.   [4] *Some Thoughts Concerning Education*, p. 82.

the great principle and foundation of all virtue and worth is placed in this, that a man is able to deny himself his own desires, cross his own inclinations, and purely follow what reason directs as best, though the appetite lean the other way.'[1] Applied to intellectual education, this meant that studies were to be used in great part to exercise the faculties, to provide a formal discipline, to train the mind to perceive reality.

In a sense this side of Locke's belief had always been the unconscious aim of Public School education, so that it did not in any sense conflict with school procedure. Indeed, it now provided a new theory to sanction an apparently senseless practice. Latin (and later mathematics) were now justified even if (or just because) the student hated the subject and learned nothing useful or even nothing at all from it. For education was a discipline, and the process of learning was more important than the thing learned.

The other line of criticism in regard to intellectual education held that the classics ought to educate boys morally as well as mentally, and blamed Public School methods of teaching the classics for their failure to do so. Though this point of view was at no time very popular, since most critics, including Locke,[2] preferred to place virtue ahead of the classics and to disregard their possible relationship or to attack the classics as pagan,[3] it found several important defenders. Milton, a staunch Humanist, mercilessly attacked the logic-chopping and the excessive emphasis on grammar, themes, and verses of which the schools were guilty. For, believing that education ought to fit 'a man to perform justly, skilfully, and magnanimously all the offices, both private and public, of peace and war', he wanted the soul of a culture taught, so that, by the examples of Plato and Cicero no less than by that of the Scriptures, virtue might be produced.[4] Budgell, writing in the *Spectator*, had much the same idea: finding that 'nothing is more wanting to our public schools, than that the masters of them should use the same care in fashioning the manners of their scholars, as in

[1] Ibid., p. 96.   [2] Ibid., p. 138.
[3] Cowper, *Tirocinium*, p. 210.   [4] *On Education, Prose Works*, p. 99.

forming their tongues to the learned languages', he suggested the use of Greek and Roman writers as examples of vice and virtue.[1] Cowper, the most passionate of eighteenth-century critics, also severely castigated the methods of schools on moral grounds. Schools provided, he wrote, no nourishment

> But conjugated verbs and nouns declined.
>
> . . . . .
>
> For such is all the mental food purvey'd
> By public hackneys in the schooling trade;
> Who feed a pupil's intellect with store
> Of syntax, truly, but with little more;
> Dismiss their cares when they dismiss their flock.[2]

This was reprehensible, Cowper felt, chiefly because it meant the neglect or corruption of morals. He was, however, so fearful of sacrificing morals to learning that, unlike Milton or Budgell, he saw no solution of the problem through study, and even attacked the encouragement of emulation because, though it might incite to scholarship, it made 'less for improvement than to tickle spite', destroyed the heart, and aroused hate.[3]

Against the disciplinary methods used by the masters there was considerable straightforward protest. Swift claimed that one of the aristocratic objections to sending boys to school was that 'whipping breaks the spirit of lads wellborn'.[4] On grounds of efficiency as well as of humanity, flogging was condemned by a whole host of people, most of whom had no particular theories of education.

As early as the sixteenth century Roger Ascham, that gentlest and most progressive of early humanists, said, in simple language, almost all that needed saying on the subject of flogging. The learning of the day, he wrote, dulled the wits and took away love of study: 'For, the scholer, is commonlie beat for the making, when the master were more worthie to be beat for the mending, or rather, marring of the same.'[5] In place of flogging, he advised

---

[1] *Spectator*, No. 337, Vol. V, p. 163. Budgell said that he had never seen the subject treated before.
[2] *Tirocinium*, p. 224.   [3] Ibid., pp. 219, 220.
[4] Swift, *Essay on Modern Education*, p. 52.
[5] Roger Ascham, *The Scholemaster*, Edited by John E. B. Mayor, London, 1911, p. 71.

kindness: 'I assure you, there is no such whetstone, to sharpen a good witte and encourage a will to learninge, as is praise.' Do not, said Ascham, chide mistakes if there has been effort. 'For I know by good experience, that a childe shall take more profit of two fautes, ientlie warned of, than of foure thinges, rightly hitt';[1] 'Loue is fitter than feare, ientleness better than beating', since the object is to mend, not break the wicked.[2] In the seventeenth century Locke repeated much that Ascham had said a century earlier. But Locke's position was a peculiar one: on the one hand, he could criticize parents for seeing no other instrument of education than the rod, and advise love and leniency;[3] on the other—following his disciplinary concepts—he clung to the idea of fear as a necessary means of education and the rod as the last pedagogical resource.[4]

In the eighteenth century numbers of critics, including Thomas Day, Tate Wilkinson, Gibbon, Fielding, Pitt, Smollett, and Steele, protested against the severe discipline at the Public Schools. Only the last two, however, need be more than mentioned. Steele, who was, significantly enough, the accepted mouthpiece of awakening middle-class sentimentality, delivered the most scorching denunciation of flogging that the century produced. 'The boasted liberty we talk of,' he wrote, 'is but a mean reward for the long servitude, the many heartaches and terrors, to which our childhood is exposed in going through a grammar school. Many of these stupid tyrants exercise their cruelty without any manner of distinction of the capacities of children, or the intention of parents in their behalf.' Many boys were, according to Steele, simply incapable of learning the classics, and then nothing could be done. Usually, however, innocent children could be trained by appealing to their sense of shame and honour, and it was the master's fault if they were not: no matter, said Steele, 'the sufferings of the scholar's body are to rectify the mistakes of his mind'. 'I am confident,' he added, 'that no boy, who will not be allured to letters without blows will ever be brought to anything

[1] Ibid., p. 73. [2] Ibid., p. 78.
[3] *Some Thoughts Concerning Education*, p. 269. [4] Ibid., p. 96.

with them.' A great or good mind would necessarily be worse for such indignities; the less good would be made saucy and hard. 'Picture', Steele concluded, 'an ingenuous creature expiring with shame, with pale looks, beseeching sorrow, and silent tears, throw up its honest eyes, and kneel on its tender knees to an inexorable blockhead to be forgiven the false quantity of a word in making a Latin verse.'[1] Smollett is notable for having not only denounced but offered constructive suggestions. As a contrast to Winchester, he pictured as his ideal a small boarding-school with a body of laws 'suited to the age and comprehension of every individual; and each transgressor was fairly tried by his peers, and punished according to the verdict of the jury. No boy was scourged for want of apprehension, but a spirit of emulation was raised by well-timed praise and artful comparison, and maintained by a distribution of small prizes, which were adjudged to those who signalized themselves either by their industry, sobriety, or genius.'[2]

If there was a good deal of criticism of masters' disciplinary methods, this did not mean that opinion favoured laxity. On the contrary, it was against laxity that most attacks were launched; the implied, if not stated, desire of all critics was for more, not less, surveillance. Flogging was deplored, not because it inhibited boy independence, but because it was ineffective in limiting that independence. As Fielding put it, 'because one man scourges twenty or thirty boys more in a morning than another, is he therefore a better disciplinarian?'[3] Most of the critics of the eighteenth-century Public School were either humanitarians or moralists or both. They felt that, though schools might produce manliness and self-reliance, they also—and this was far more important—allowed and indeed encouraged cruelty and tyranny and immorality. Therefore, the purpose of any

[1] *Spectator*, No. 157, Vol. III, pp. 54–5. Steele's article stirred up, for the moment, a good deal of excitement. One supporter of Steele recounted in lurid terms the terror of undeserved floggings at Eton. The victim's hands, once kissed by his mother, he wrote, were covered with blood, 'perhaps for smiling, or for going a yard and a half out of a gate'. Another letter to the *Spectator* stated that 'many a brave and noble spirit had been there broken'. (*Spectator*, No. 168, Vol. III, p. 109.)
[2] Smollett, *Peregrine Pickle*, Vol. I, p. 76.
[3] Fielding, *Joseph Andrews*, Vol. II, Book III, p. 98.

sane person ought to be to put shackles on the free life of the boys, to end the chaos and roughness of Eton's and Westminster's miniature world by means of a wise surveillance.

The immorality and tyranny of schools were roundly denounced by a whole host of Carthusian, Wykehamist, and Etonian critics, including Thomas Day, Steele, Smollett, Fielding, and Pitt. Fielding, for example, asserted that 'public schools are the nurseries of all vice and immorality', and asked rhetorically, 'what is all the learning in the world compared to his [a boy's] immortal soul?' about which masters concern themselves not at all.[1] The great Lord Chatham insisted even more vehemently 'that he had hardly known a boy whose spirit had not been broken at Eton; and that while a public school might be an excellent thing for a youth of hot and violent character, it was not the place for a tender or docile disposition'.[2] It was, however, Westminster School—and during its great periods under Busby and Nicoll at that—which produced the severest and most voluble critics: Locke, Chesterfield, Gibbon, and Cowper.

Locke was the leading critic of seventeenth-century Public School life. Judging chiefly by his own experiences at Westminster under Busby, he came to the conclusion that at school boldness and spirit became rudeness, courage and steadiness, roughness and ill-breeding. Vice and corruption, he felt, were growing in society, and they started at school.[3] Locke therefore urged parents not to send their children to Public Schools, but to keep them at home and, by a regime of discipline and denial, teach them correct moral habits. Locke's doctrine, meant for home use, subsequently proved, ironically enough, to be, like his intellectual theory, a justification rather than a criticism of Public School methods. For fagging and magisterial severity were, when effectively controlled, a fulfilment of Locke's intention that education should be, not a leading out, but a moulding and chastening through struggle. Moreover, Locke, in his emphasis on training of the body—treated again as a hardening process—

[1] Fielding, *Joseph Andrews*, Vol. II, Book III, pp. 95–6.
[2] Ruville, *Life of Pitt*, Vol. I, p. 73.
[3] Locke, *Some Thoughts Concerning Education*, pp. 138 ff.

gave theoretical justification for the games that boys had always enjoyed, and which later were found to be a method for training character.

The puritanical and rather prejudiced Cowper,[1] writing almost a hundred years later, echoed Locke's sentiments in even more vigorous terms. If you train your boy with a mob, he wrote in *Tirocinium*, he will be, in infidelity and lewdness a man, in mischief and noise a child. At a Public School the rich imbibe a scorn for all delights but earthly ones and a love of profuse and lewd expense; the middle classes learn to cater to the rich. A virtuous schoolboy is the exception that shows how dark are the rest. The whole corrupt world is made as it is by schools—greater offices are disgraced and Churchmen are Christians in name only.[2] In his letters, Cowper was equally severe. Schools 'are so negligent in the article of morals,' he asserted, 'that boys are debauched in general the moment they are capable of being so.' A 'scandalous relaxation of discipline . . . obtains in almost all schools universally, but especially in the largest'.[3] The tall captain whose pride is called courage, whose effrontery is wit, and whose wild excursions are a favourite theme, is the hero. This will always happen, as Cowper wrote in *Tirocinium*, when boys of eighteen mingle with younger boys and are not disciplined.[4]

Chesterfield, though much less caustic, expressed in gentlemanly and dignified tones much the same sentiments as did Cowper and Locke. 'Westminster School is,' he said, 'undoubtedly, the seat of illiberal manners and brutal behaviour,'[5] a place where a boy 'may learn more things than he should learn'.[6] Finally, Gibbon supplemented the opinions of his schoolmates by comments of a more personal nature. 'My timid reserve,' he wrote in his autobiography, 'was astonished by the crowd and tumult of the school; the

---

[1] Cowper was prejudiced less by personal experience than by his religious convictions. Most of the bullying from which he suffered as a boy did not take place at Westminster, which Cowper did not hate, but at the private school of Dr. Pitman.
[2] *Tirocinium*, pp. 211 ff. [3] Cowper, *Letters*, Vol. I, p. 326.
[4] *Tirocinium*, p. 210.
[5] *The Letters of Philip Dormer Stanhope*, January 18, 1750, p. 1494.
[6] Ibid., February 16, 1765, p. 2646.

want of strength and activity disqualified me for the sports of the play field.'[1] He secretly rejoiced in these infirmities, which 'delivered me from the exercises of the school and the society of my equals',[2] and protested against the 'lavish praise of the happiness of our boyish years, which is echoed with so much affection in the world. That happiness I have never known, that time I have never regretted.'[3] Indeed, 'there is not, in the course of life, a more remarkable change than the removal of a child from the luxury and freedom of a wealthy house to the frugal diet and strict subordination of a school; for the tenderness of parents, and the obsequiousness of servants, to the rude familiarity of his equals, the insolent tyranny of his seniors, and the rod, perhaps, of a cruel and capricious pedagogue.'[4]

GENERAL TENDENCIES

The most obvious fact about eighteenth-century criticisms and defences of the Public Schools is their limited quantity, intensity, and scope. The time for heated debate over the virtues and defects of Eton and Winchester was, as late as 1780, still in the future. The Public Schools were not yet thought of as national institutions of a special and uniquely British kind, to be attacked and defended as if their existence involved by implication the continuance of the whole social and political organization of the British Isles. Before this could occur, the comparatively comfortable, static, eighteenth-century world had to be split asunder by the French and the Industrial Revolutions. On the one hand, new purposes had to be created or old ones crystallized by economic and social circumstances. A new desire for education and abhorrence of old ways had to emerge from these purposes. On the other hand, a conscious reaction to change and revolution had to develop, and a new philosophy and attitude towards old institutions to emerge from the questionings to which all things established were subjected.

In the meantime, in the eighteenth century, criticism and

[1] Gibbon, *Autobiography*, p. 26. [2] Ibid., p. 34.
[3] Ibid., p. 36. [4] Ibid., p. 26.

defence were infrequent and casual: there were the merest suggestions of consistently held philosophic viewpoints. Moreover, discussion did not cut very deep. One did not feel he was involving himself in an attack on the British Empire or even on the British system of education when he preferred say private to public education, as did Locke. And, indeed, he was not. For criticism, and thus vindication, confined themselves to discussion of personal enjoyment of schooldays or of educational matters. The all-embracing social and economic attack which fought closed and corrupted trusts and the class aspect of education was entirely silent until Adam Smith's attack in 1776, and Cowper's objection to the snobbery that drove the *nouveau riche* to go to aristocratic schools. And Cowper and Smith were, until the nineteenth century, almost lone voices. Partly as a consequence, sentimentality—an uncommon enough phenomenon in any case among the aristocracy in the rational eighteenth century—did not include the Public Schools *qua* venerable class institutions among the objects of its love.

Nevertheless, certain tendencies of importance later on were already partly present in the eighteenth-century reaction to schools. The emotions of Walpole and Gray were only too similar to those felt by 'old boys' ever since, even though additional objects more directly connected with the school may have been found for them. In this connexion it is important to note that both Walpole and Gray were literary forerunners of the new sentimentalism that was making itself felt in England. Their feeling for their school was but part of a larger feeling of yearning for the past, whether personal or national, that was to be echoed by a whole nation a few years later. In the second place, most of the defences that were to be typical until 1830, and in many cases, until our own day, were already there. The men who liked schools were, allowing for certain changes, not so very different from the men who founded the schools; moreover, they admired much the same aspects of the schools in 1600, in 1750, and in 1935. Finally, much of the particular criticism of the schools voiced by Locke, Cowper, and others was but a forerunner of more concentrated attack along the same lines. In particular, the utilitarian attack on the classics and the moral and humanitarian denunciation of boy life were to prosper as the new century advanced. The leaders of this attack, Steele and Locke and Cowper, were, it will be observed, the spokesmen of the increasingly powerful middle classes. For long in the eighteenth century most of the members of these classes were Dissenters whose influence was felt more in the Nonconformist academies than in the Public Schools. But as the century progressed, the business classes grew in size and importance, and added to their ranks many who either had gone or who wanted to go to Public Schools, thus increasing the pressure on those bodies.

Finally, it must be said that the criticism so far discussed had, by itself, no influence at all, and certainly no immediate effect. A greater charge of abuse was necessary to set in motion the machinery of reform. Once the wheels were turning, the special influence of all except possibly Locke and Cowper was lost in the general clamour of criticism. Cowper was looked back on, even late in the nineteenth century, as the father of moral criticism, as proved by the necessity that so many defenders have felt of answering his arguments. Locke became, because of his great name, the chief justifier, unwittingly as we have seen, of some of the very practices that he disliked. On the other hand, he was an inspiration for critics of both the moral and intellectual life of the Public Schools. But all this was long after the fact: like Adam Smith in economics, Cowper and Locke were influential because they unconsciously represented tendencies that happened to come to fruition years after they were dead.

PART II
FROM COWPER TO ARNOLD

INTRODUCTION

IF important changes in the general organization of Public Schools were the sole basis of historical classification in this book, there would be no great need to label the period from 1780 to 1835 a distinct era. For, with notable exceptions, the schools changed very little from Cowper to Arnold: though the world in general was experiencing not one but two revolutions, the English Public Schools continued to pursue their calm eighteenth-century way. They were, as in the previous hundred years, dominated by the forces of conservatism, pressures such as inertia, congenital hatred of change, vested interest and class prejudice, the meaning of which will be analysed later.

But conservatism was not unchallenged after 1780, and therein lies the distinctive feature of the succeeding fifty years. Social and political movements in the eighties and nineties created new groups or strengthened old ones with interests and desires at odds with those of the groups that had patronized the Public Schools in the eighteenth century. As a result, a struggle of far-reaching importance ensued, the object of which was to reform upper-class education. Various groups of critics, armed with various social and educational philosophies, attacked the schools from almost every possible angle in the years between 1780 and 1835.

In response, the average supporter of the schools, who had taken them very much for granted in the past, began to grow increasingly self-conscious in regard to their merits. He found them to be very vital institutions, indispensable to his welfare and to that of the nation, and worthy of the most passionate love. Romantic attachment grew in intensity and attached itself to new objects. Every aspect of the school found its defenders, who expressed themselves in print with increasing frequency and emotion. A whole philosophy of institutions and of education arose in justification of the Public School as it existed at the beginning of the nineteenth century.

For many years the conflict of opinion was, with notable exceptions, without fruit in practice. But in the thirties and forties a reform movement, led chiefly by Dr. Arnold of Rugby, swept over the Public Schools. This movement was the outcome of the struggle of the tens, twenties, and early thirties, and has meaning only when viewed as the successful reconciliation in practice of conflicting ideas from the past and as the resolution of opposed psychological and social forces. It is vitally important, therefore, in order to understand the nature of later Public School change, to study in some detail the battle of opinion which was waged in the first thirty years of the century.

CHAPTER I

CHANGES IN THE PUBLIC SCHOOLS
1780–1830

A. CHANGES IN MEMBERSHIP AND THEIR RESULTS—BOY LIFE

THOUGH schools were modified relatively little between 1780 and 1830, one important change did take place which, together with its manifold results of both a direct and indirect nature, demands some consideration before we can proceed further. By 1830 the number, quality, and homogeneity of those who patronized Public Schools showed marked differences when compared with conditions in these respects in 1780. To begin with, there were, by the early nineteenth century, a good many more students at all the schools except Westminster than there had been through the eighteenth century. Eton grew rapidly and steadily all through the period. Harrow had its greatest era at the eve of the century, as did Winchester under Goddard. Charterhouse had a rise to fame around 1815. Rugby and Shrewsbury were both born as Public Schools during this period. In the second place, the nature of the membership had changed. Though the group that accounted for this increase was still the ruling class, it was not made up chiefly of aristocrats. The social register had been widened to include some of the professional classes and many of the upper middle classes enriched by the industrial revolution and later by the war against the French. The large capitalists, together with those aristocrats who had only just been completely won over to sending their sons to schools made up the difference in numbers at many schools, particularly at Eton and Harrow. The newer Public Schools recruited their numbers chiefly from the professional classes and the gentry.

Though there was a general rise in the number of students at the Public Schools, all schools did not, it is important to add, share equally in this rise. Moreover, a good many schools lost what they had gained as the century progressed and were superseded in importance, for a time at least, by other institutions of learning, some of them new ones. Finally, several schools, as they degenerated lost an aristocratic membership which they had previously possessed. Of the older schools only Eton rose steadily in prestige. The patronage of George III raised her numbers to five hundred at the end of the century, and established her as England's semi-royal school. As a result, every Tory aristocrat and would-be aristocrat fought for the privilege of paying many times what a good education was worth for the honour of being beaten by Keate. Harrow, Eton's rival, on the other hand, after a half-century of greatness, began to decline after Dr. George Butler took control in 1805. By 1844, when Vaughan began to reform the school, she had lost most of her aristocratic membership. Similarly, Winchester, after a rise to fame in the nineties, slowly lost prestige during the tens and twenties, to be only momentarily revived by Moberly in the thirties. She never, it may be added, rose to as great heights as did Harrow; nor did she have aristocratic patronage to lose. Charterhouse, because of Russell's experiment with the Bell system, had an unprecedented popularity in the twenties; when the experiment was shown to be a failure, the school almost collapsed. Westminster's is the saddest story of all. From the glorious days of Nicoll almost to our own times, she has lost importance. By 1830 there was hardly a vestige of her former patrician glory. Rugby and Shrewsbury, on the other hand, experienced a rejuvenation which was an important counterweight balancing the decline of other schools. Though just before Arnold's day the mediocrity of Wooll, the head master, was beginning to cause a decline in numbers, Rugby remained all through the period a popular school for the Midland gentry. Samuel Butler virtually re-created Shrewsbury—when he took over the school in 1798 there were only eighteen boys there—and maintained it for over thirty years with an increasing prestige.

In general then, despite individual setbacks and a later more general decadence, the period saw a rise in the number of young upper-class boys in the schools. Principally from this fact emerges another important change—the greater importance of boys relative to masters. If the boys were the important factors in the school previously, now they virtually were the school. Masters did not change their methods or increase their numbers, and, as a result, lost in control and prestige. A Public School now referred almost exclusively to the group of boys who went to it. A strong man like Keate might thunder and flog, but boy life went on for the most part untouched by his efforts.

Without carrying the matter too far, a suggestive parallel might be drawn in this respect between school life and the world outside. For the late eighteenth- and early nineteenth-century English world saw the decay of traditional authorities parallel a vigorous economic and social rebirth. And as in the schools, so in the world outside, the failure of government to control the strong in the interests of the weak produced tyranny and chaos. Finally, in both society and school, *laissez-faire*, as far as the relationship between government and subject were concerned, became a fundamental doctrine with which even Arnold dared not fundamentally disagree.

The general result was the completion of the process of turning the loose group of eighteenth-century schools into a system of education and an important national institution without at the same time destroying the individuality of each school. To be more accurate, since such matters are partly subjective, a matter of attitude rather than fact, what boys' control really did was to give final objective justification for the current conception. Schools could be thought of as national institutions because the great part of the upper classes of the British nation now imbibed there standards of conduct that were a vital part of national polity. Schools thus could become the focus for political battle. They were definitely a system now, because the same kinds of boys went to them and upheld or created similar customs. As Mozley writes,[1] 'their whole idea, their composition, their formation and management, was traditional, prescriptive, almost

[1] Rev. T. Mozley, *Reminiscences, Chiefly of Towns, Villages, and Schools*, 2 vols., London, 1885, Vol. I, p. 380.

hereditary, and very select. A boy went to the school which his parents and relatives had gone to. The school in this way was a society continually replenished with like materials, and strong in social unity for good or for ill.'

Now, as already pointed out, many common factors in the past had already contributed to making schools into a national system. Time itself, hardening institutions, was exceedingly important. Moreover, even within our period there were such things as direct borrowing—Harrow and Rugby were revived by Etonians, Shrewsbury by a Rugbeian. Yet, the unity of the boys is the crucial factor.

Turning to internal conditions in the schools, we find that the most important change that occurred in the years after 1750 was an increased tendency to discipline and socialize the individual. Unquestionably the prime reason for this was the greater unity of which we have been speaking. For unity produced increased *esprit de corps*, greater loyalty and group spirit than there had been. As a result, the group moulded the individual boy much more than it had before, whether for social or anti-social purposes. But in socializing and disciplining, other factors besides unity contributed. First of all, there was the school as the embodiment of traditions and customs from an ever remoter past. The illustrious dead gave lessons in conduct to the living. Roundell Palmer writes that 'the *genius loci* was a powerful factor in my education'[1] at Winchester. The Byronic tradition pervaded Harrow life for years after Byron left and was a sore point to Victorian reformers.[2] Moreover, the dead left customs and ceremonies in the schools[3] which, since they were rigidly observed,[4] acted as powerful agents in preserving order and in moulding the individual.[5]

[1] Cf. *Memorials*, Vol. I, London, 1896, p. 87.
[2] Cf. Edmund Sheridan Purcell, *Life of Cardinal Manning*, 2 vols., London, 1896, Vol. I, p. 20.
[3] Customs may take, of course, only a few years to become traditional where a belief in tradition prevails. But time helps, if only in inspiring tradition lovers.
[4] Cf. Roundell Palmer, *Memorials*, p. 94. Speaking of Winchester, Palmer wrote: 'The traditions of the place were, on some points, as inflexible as the laws of the Medes and Persians.'
[5] Sargeaunt, *Annals of Westminster*, p. 236. Granting the virtues of traditionalism under normal circumstances, there are times when it is an unequivocal evil. Such was the case at Westminster from 1819 to 1846, when law became

On the whole the chief change in the schools was this greater moulding of the individual.[1] The particular ideals of character and the particular opinions which were forced on boys so much more effectively did not differ much from earlier ideals, nor did customs change much. But there were a few attitudes and ways of behaviour in the Regency Public School that were either not present in 1750 or differed considerably in importance in those days.

To begin with, there was more snobbery than there had been, and paradoxically, it grew greater as the democratic nineteenth century advanced. Mozley writes that the aristocratic society of schools was 'disposed to deal hardly with intruders, as they were deemed, from the mercantile or professional classes',[2] making the friendship of such as Gray, West, and Walpole more difficult. The historian, Merivale, says that he felt for years the 'social inferiority which was impressed upon me at Harrow'.[3]

As we have seen, there were many from the mercantile classes in the schools by 1810. Often their presence resulted from a snobbish desire to imitate the aristocracy. Long before 1800, Bentham had been sent to Westminster for social reasons,[4] and we have seen Cowper's comment on the subject. Colonel Newcome's father had been a weaver's apprentice; almost all of Thackeray's characters, who were from the *nouveau riche* middle class, went to Public Schools.[5] Such boys as young Newcome were accepted well enough at Charterhouse, though they might not have been at Eton.

Snobbery probably increased among the upper classes in direct proportion to the danger to their prestige from the

petty conservatism, routine, the letter without the spirit (and therefore all the more meticulously enforced). In adult society, it may be added, one of the touchstones of decadence is this transformation of law into dogma without meaning, to be enforced just because it is the law.

[1] To a certain extent Eton, the most conservative of the schools, held out longest against this change. She vigorously resisted the tendency to develop a perfect system and a closer group life. Through almost the whole of the nineteenth century she stood as the champion of the loose organization and free life of the eighteenth century.
[2] Mozley, *Reminiscences*, Vol. I, p. 380.
[3] Merivale, *Autobiography of Dean Merivale*, p. 35.
[4] Cf. Charles Warren Everett, *The Education of Jeremy Bentham*, New York, 1931, p. 4.
[5] Cf. *The Newcomes*, edited by George Saintsbury, London, n.d., pp. 17 ff.

influx of the new rich. These new rich, when they were accepted, were probably the most snobbish of all, since insecurity is the great producer of social contempt. Gradually the meaning of 'upper class' became extended in scope; as in the sixteenth century the gap between it and those designated as lower class was correspondingly broadened.

Between collegers and paying students[1] the social breach was the greatest. Day boys were never part of the school at Harrow and Rugby. Samuel Butler, the future head of Shrewsbury, was, according to Nimrod, contemptuously treated at Rugby: 'partly because he was the son of a small shopkeeper in the small but beautiful village of Kenilworth, and at Rugby as a foundation boy; and partly on account of his churlish temper, we of the same boarding-house voted him nothing better than a snob, and the meanness of his personal appearance gave a colour to our proceedings.[2] The Trollopes fared abominably at Harrow. At the older schools collegers were distinct from the rest until they reached the top of the school. At Winchester commoners and collegers had their own *esprit de corps*.[3] At Eton the separation was emphasized by differences in living conditions. The collegers were all crowded into the notorious Long Chamber and Carter's; the food was insufficient and abominable.[4] The Oppidans, on the other hand, had nice tidy rooms in a dame's or tutor's house and were treated as gentlemen.[5] As a result, the latter considered the former inferior; to collegers, oppidans were muffs; 'it was caste antipathy'.[6] This feeling, it may be added, was less marked at Winchester and Westminster, where there was greater respect for learning than at Eton.

The most noticeable changes involved the relationship between boys and masters. The increasingly solid and powerful public opinion of boys was more than ever hostile to masters. This manifested itself in several ways. In the first place, learning was even less admired than formerly. Juvenile opinion was strengthened in this behaviour pattern

---

[1] The collegers at the older schools had to pay, though not as much as others.
[2] *Fraser's*, August 1842, p. 170.   [3] Roundell Palmer, *Memorials*, p. 90.
[4] Tucker, *Eton of Old*, pp. 20 ff.   [5] Ibid., p. 73.   [6] Ibid., p. 97.

by parental approval. The rich, new and old, had not the incentive to learn that had the younger sons in the eighteenth century, for they were not going into professions. Parents cared more that a boy should have proper contacts and win athletic glory than that he should be a student. As we shall see, Hawtrey, head master of Eton, complained about this in the thirties.

If hate of learning was only negatively an indication of hostility to masters, the actual revolutions against master authority that were a distinctive feature of the period were not. All through the period a state of war was assumed. Francis Trench could write naïvely when at Harrow in 1820 that, although 'the general conduct and character of the boys is as good as can be expected at any school', 'there was a regular smash last night, and the monitors cannot prevent it entirely'. The boys had been breaking Butler's windows. Trench adds that 'every boy who has any sense must be angry at it'; he does not believe—in extenuation—that they throw stones more than most.[1] Smouldering revolt became, when masters tried to enforce discipline, actual rebellion. From one cause or another, and often inspired by the example of the French Revolution,[2] every school had at least one revolution during the period. Further, the greater group solidarity of boys often produced victory on the field, though seldom ultimate success. Such unusual conditions are worth a few pages of explanation and illustration, for they tell us much of the peculiar character of early nineteenth-century school life, with its two nations of boys and masters living side by side but having only a negative educational relationship to one another.

In general it may be said that the important revolts were caused by authority's attempt to interfere with the rights of boys. Though French revolutionary and radical influence

[1] Cf. Rev. Francis Trench, *A Few Notes from Past Life*, Oxford, 1862, pp. 40, 44.
[2] If it seems strange that young English conservatives should find inspiration in French radicalism, it must be remembered that boy philosophy and indeed English upper-class philosophy in general was, as we shall see, partly libertarian in nature. Further, to boys masters were an enemy nation, not a government to which they owed respect. Typically, boys did not revolt against what they considered to be recognized authority, boy leaders chosen by boys.

often inspired them, the revolts were typically English. The boys always fought to protect, not to gain rights, and it is beside the point that many of these sacred rights had not been granted, but usurped through the centuries. The English have always—in political life, notably in 1642 and in 1688—fought not to obtain something, but to preserve what was considered legally theirs because in the course of time it had become customary.

If the revolts were typically English, the same, one trusts, cannot be said for authority's fumbling attempts to stem them. Often it had to resort to trickery to win, and thus further helped to undermine respect for the powers that be. Occasionally a strong master could conquer with honour, but usually master victories no less than the revolts themselves indicated the overpowering need for reform at the top of the school system.

Winchester, the oldest school, led in the matter of rebellions. It had as many as four during Dr. Warton's reign —in 1770, 1774, 1778, and 1793—of which the last, known as the Great Rebellion, and probably suggested by doings across the Channel, was the most significant. Though the cause—a refusal by the warden to allow the boys leave to attend a concert of the Bucks militia—was trivial enough, the revolt reached such proportions that the warden had to give in. He promptly proceeded to go back on his word, demanding apologies or resignation.[1] Dr. Goddard, the next master, who trusted the boys, and was on the whole a good master, was not free from rebellions. He had to face a prefects' rebellion in 1808 when he tried to make a Saint's Day a schoolday without asking the prefects.[2] Under Dr. Gabell there was another rebellion in that great year of rebellions, 1818. It tells us much of the times in a number of ways. Its cause was a protest in the name of liberty against the spying methods used by Gabell. Its course was checked by the militia with bayonets. Its end was darkened, as was the revolt in 1793, by treachery on the part of a weak and false warden.[3] The second prefect in Commoner's, the

[1] Leach, *History of Winchester*, p. 402.
[2] Augustus J. C. Hare, *Memorials of a Quiet Life*, 2 vols., London, 1872, Vol. I, p. 163.   [3] Leach, *History of Winchester*, p. 419.

Changes in the Public Schools, 1780–1830

future Lord Hatherley, resigned when his comrades were expelled; the masters attributed his conduct to 'radical propensities' acquired by reading the mildly liberal *Morning Chronicle*.[1] Dr. Williams, the next master, reverted to Dr. Goddard's reliance on prefects rather than on spying. But in 1828, when W. G. Ward and other mere students (rather than athletes or boy leaders) were prefects, the Commoners revolted against them.[2] Unrecognized authority everywhere was suspect, whether it came from master or boy.

Eton also had more than its share of rebellions. As far back as 1768 her praeposters (the first seven collegers and the first ten oppidans) revolted because Dr. Foster would not recognize their privilege of punishing lower boys for going out of bounds. As early as this the revolt against masters took the form of a fight for self-government. Dr. Foster had to use terrorism to win, and even so, it may be added, was forced to resign. It is significant that because his father had been a tradesman, he was despised by the aristocrats whose sons were at the school.[3] Keate had many rebellions to cope with, the most serious being the one in 1818. If his harshness provoked them, he was strong enough to put them down, which may or may not be to his credit.[4] He probably was a bit annoyed at being thought an authority on rebellions.[5]

At Harrow, life was freer than at other schools, but not, for that reason, freer of rebellions. The boys got to feel that they had some rights in the election of head masters, and this was the cause of two revolts, one when Dr. Heath was appointed instead of Dr. Parr, and the other, of which Byron was the leader, when Dr. Butler won over Mark Drury.[6] Dr.

---

[1] W. R. W. Stephens, *A Memoir of the Rt. Hon. William Page Wood, Baron Hatherley*, 2 vols., London, 1883, Vol. I, pp. 11–14.
[2] Leach, *op. cit.*, pp. 424 ff.
[3] Lyte, *History of Eton*, pp. 333 ff.
[4] Cf. Tucker, *Eton of Old*, pp. 199 ff. For the rebellion on Keate's taking over power, cf. Arthur Milman, *Henry Hart Milman, D.D.*, London, 1900, pp. 13 ff.
[5] Cf. Samuel Butler, *The Life and Letters of Dr. Samuel Butler*, 2 vols., London, 1896, Vol. I, p. 158. Keate wrote Butler a letter urging him not to rescind the expulsions he had made after a Shrewsbury revolt.
[6] Thomas Moore, *The Life of Byron* from *The Works of Lord Byron with his Letters and Journals and His Life*, 17 vols., London, 1833, pp. 86 ff.; Rev. William Field, *Memoirs of the Life, Writings, and Opinions of the Rev. Samuel Parr*, 2 vols., London, 1828, Vol. I, pp. 61 ff.

Parr's defeat caused a secession of forty students to Stanmore with him. In 1808 Dr. Butler, who was no Keate or Gabell, nevertheless had to face a full-fledged revolt because he would not let the monitors flog. The boys paraded with banners inscribed 'Liberty and Rebellion', 'No Butler', and hissed and threw stones. Later, when Christopher Wordsworth was head master and had trouble with discipline, Butler admitted in a letter to him that he was always afraid of rebellions on Guy Fawkes Day.[1]

Charterhouse's most severe rebellion, in 1808, was again caused by the denying of an established privilege. Dr. Raine refused to allow the gownboys to have visitors in hall on Founder's Day; the result was a shower of brickbats.[2] At Rugby, Dr. James, with his sternness and his refusal to let the praeposters share in disciplining, was bound to have trouble.[3] But the two rebellions during his reign were nothing compared with the Great Rebellion of 1797, during which windows were broken, books burned, soldiers called out, and, for the first and only time, the Riot Act was read.[4]

Finally, Samuel Butler, the great head master of Shrewsbury, did not escape without trouble. The great revolt of 1818, though ostensibly caused by the poor food and the boiled beef, was in reality a general reaction, in the spirit of the times, to Butler's insistence on discipline. After some stone-throwing and threats of violence by the boys, Butler conquered, expelled a number, and was congratulated by the Master of St. John's for his firmness before the 'turbulence and self-will of foolish and presumptuous boys'.[5]

Evidently, the most important privilege for which the boys fought was the legal right of self-government. What they struggled for was recognition by the masters of those rights of prefects to govern and have fags, which had been existing unrecognized, as we have seen, for some time. And they won their struggle, though occasionally a strong master like James at Rugby held out. The most significant difference, indeed, between pre- and post-French revolutionary school

[1] Cf. Graham, *H. M. Butler*, pp. 13–16.   [2] Davies, *Charterhouse in London*, p. 264.
[3] Cf. Rouse, *History of Rugby*, pp. 129 ff.   [4] Ibid., p. 182.
[5] Butler, *Life of S. Butler*, Vol. I, pp. 156, 163; and *History of Shrewsbury*, pp. 137–39.

Changes in the Public Schools, 1780–1830   83

life is this legalizing and regularizing of the prefect-fagging system. By 1820 or so the system had become almost the basic means of government and education at a Public School. Even to-day no one who approves of the idea of a Public School as a whole would think of modifying radically this unique boy self-government.

Though the boys often had to struggle for recognition of their system, they were not always at odds with masters on the subject in general. Many of the latter by the end of the eighteenth century were beginning to acquiesce in the inevitable, and even to find certain virtues in legalized boy rule. Unconsciously admitting the bankruptcy of their own disciplinary methods, they began to count more and more on their older boys to keep order. They soon found out that recognizing the privileges of these older boys not only made them more useful disciplinary aids but also cut down indiscriminate usurpations of power. A regularized system, working within the limits of traditional practice, made for more order and less cruelty than the unchecked rule of the strong. Even those who disapprove of the whole system can see that its only alternative in early days was worse.[1] Unless intellectuals like Roundell Palmer and W. G. Ward were prefects—and except at Rugby under Arnold, who had full control of his system, this seldom occurred—order was kept and bullying reduced.[2] T. A. Trollope, who knew both, preferred the regularized system of Winchester to the freer and therefore more arbitrary system of Harrow. Merivale, the historian, records that even his cruel fagmaster at Harrow with his bitter taunts 'afforded me a sort of sublime protection'.[3] Further, there was something soothing to the tortured in the very regularity of the system even when the cruelty remained. Knowing what to expect helped one to bear it. Moreover, as Thackeray says, Thomas Newcome could black 'his master's shoes with perfect readiness', because he could wait 'till he rose in the school, and the time came when he should have a fag of his own'.[4] Masters,

---
[1] One can criticize the defenders of the system chiefly on the basis that they failed to recognize possible future alternatives.
[2] Cf. Roundell Palmer, *Memorials*, pp. 97 ff.
[3] Merivale, *Autobiography*, pp. 26 ff.   [4] *The Newcomes*, p. 26.

probably seeing these relative benefits of the system and conniving at the usurpation of authority, allowed boy government to gain a firm foothold in the years between Cowper and Arnold. By 1830 defenders of schools had found a number of positive virtues in the system as well, and were equipped to answer all arguments; the war over a well-established praefectorial government was on.

If the early nineteenth-century masters accepted the prefect system, they did not make it an instrument of government in the way that Arnold and later masters did. They accepted the *fait accompli* of boy privileges and trusted that the leaders would produce a semblance of order; if they did not, the master flogged. Only a few went further. Goddard at Winchester—and Arnold, be it noted, studied under him— tried to exercise influence over his leaders by trusting them. Russell at Charterhouse made an abortive attempt to have boys as educational lieutenants. Butler at Shrewsbury tried to inculcate a certain amount of moral responsibility. On the whole, however, prefects were thought of as privileged boys functioning under the independent laws of boy society. A master supported them; occasionally he checked them. Rarely did he raise boys to the further privilege of being his trusted lieutenants. Obviously, therefore, he seldom tried to fill them with moral responsibility or impose his ideals upon them. Indeed, when young prefects were themselves full of zeal to reform, they seldom found support from a master. Archdeacon Randall records that in 1807 he and A. J. C. Hare were 'full of speculative plans for the improvement of the republic in which we lived, and the constitution of which in the main we much approved and admired, though we were sensible of blemishes which we longed to remove'.[1] They realized that there was no use appealing to the master; he could rarely even get justice done. Twenty-two years later Williams, head master of Winchester, though he supported W. G. Ward on the basis that his was, as prefect, the legal authority, failed to make use of the religious earnestness of the future High-Churchman in the way that Arnold would have done.

[1] A. J. C. Hare, *Memorials of a Quiet Life*, Vol. I, p. 161.

Changes in the Public Schools, 1780–1830

Besides the revolts and the growth of the prefect system there was little in actual boy life to mark the late eighteenth and early nineteenth centuries as a distinct period. Only the tentative beginnings of organized athletics deserve mention, and then only because of the later importance of games. Games, as we have seen, existed in the eighteenth century, but even by Arnold's day they were still relatively unimportant. Their educational value was definitely perceived only in the fifties.

By the second decade of the century we begin to hear talk of organized games. As late as 1820, however, football was in a primitive state at the school that has become the most famous for it.[1] At Harrow in the twenties football was played, but it was not of absorbing interest.[2] An Etonian can write, as late as 1831, 'I cannot consider the game of football as being at all gentlemanly; after all, the Yorkshire common people play it.'[3] Cricket, on the other hand, was fast growing popular by the twenties. As early as James's day it was popular at Rugby,[4] and had been played at Harrow much earlier. In Charles Wordsworth's day cricketing was a career at Eton. Keate forbade an Eton-Harrow match in 1821, but in 1822 the long series began at Lord's.[5] The Eton-Winchester game also came into existence at this time. Wordsworth can speak of 'the distinction which success in them [games] among boys . . . never fails to bring with it', and the encouragement given by masters, though they do not yet put games on a par with intellectual achievements.[6]

B. CHANGES BY MASTERS—STRONG MASTERS OF THE OLD TYPE

If all-important general changes had reference chiefly to boy society, it is not altogether true that studies and master government were in all cases the same in 1750 and in 1830.

[1] Rouse, *History of Rugby*, p. 218.
[2] Cf. Charles Wordsworth, *Annals of My Early Life*, London, 1891, p. 19.
[3] An Etonian, *Reminiscences of Eton*, Chichester, 1831, p. 47.
[4] *Fraser's*, August 1842, p. 173, Nimrod, *My Life and Times*.
[5] Charles Wordsworth, *Early Life*, p. 10. Matches had, presumably, been played previously in 1805 and 1818.
[6] Charles Wordsworth, *Early Life*, p. 9.

To begin with there was inevitable decay in the effectiveness of both studies and master discipline. Masters were not to blame for this except in their failure to remedy the situation; the solidarity of the boys was the cause, as already indicated, of the relatively greater failure of both intellectual endeavour and of discipline in the early nineteenth-century schools; indeed, a statement of decay in these fields is but another way of stating facts already mentioned. On the other hand, there were some feeble attempts to remedy the deplorable state of affairs, either by new methods or more effective administration of old ones.

Of the new methods, Russell's introduction of boy monitors at Charterhouse and Samuel Butler's more important emulative system at Shrewsbury were the most thorough and the most radical, though even these reformers left the fundamentals of the system very much the same in most respects. While it is important to remember that the reforms of both fall within our period, they are best discussed in detail in the next chapter as forerunners of Arnold's more important contributions to change. For both were individual efforts outside the main stream of development when they occurred. Russell's practices were abortive and without fruit at any time; Butler's had an influence that extended beyond Shrewsbury only in the thirties. Besides the reforms of these two, there were only scattered efforts such as the greater relative importance given to mathematics at Rugby under James, the institution of the Newcastle at Eton in the twenties as a stimulation to emulation among the older boys, and, in the moral sphere, the trust of the boys by a Goddard of Winchester or a Parr at Harrow.

Such reforms were, however, mere pinpricks in the side of traditional educational and disciplinary practice. Old methods of education and of discipline ruled. The best that could be expected from even a good master was that he should more effectively administer the old system. And it must be admitted that there probably were more strong masters of the old Busby type, as well as more relatively enlightened men in this period than in the previous one. There were indeed enough to warrant the statement that it was the system,

Changes in the Public Schools, 1780–1830

not the men, that was chiefly at fault in the failure of education and discipline. At Harrow from 1750 to 1800 there were men such as Thackeray, Sumner, Heath, and Drury as head masters, who earned the praises of Samuel Parr, Sir William Jones, Sheridan, and Byron.[1] Coleridge found in the stern and narrow Bowyer at Christ's Hospital just the discipline he needed, at the same time that he hated the cruelty and ruthless suppression of instincts in which the man indulged. Lamb also testified to the power of the man whom they all feared.[2] The soldier-priest Havelock had praise for his tutor at Charterhouse, Dr. Raine.[3] Praed speaks of the kindness and careful tuition of J. F. Plumptre, his Eton tutor,[4] as does Metcalfe, of Indian Civil Service fame, of Goodall.[5] Gladstone was made into a studious youth by Hawtrey, whom he always described as 'the life of the school, the man to whom Eton owed more than to any of her sons during the century'.[6]

Of strong masters of the old type, Dr. James of Rugby and

---

[1] Cf. Field, *Life of Samuel Parr*, pp. 12 ff.; The Rt. Hon. Lord Teignmouth, *Memoirs of the Life, Writings, and Correspondence of Sir William Jones*, 2 vols., London, 1835, Vol. I, pp. 109 ff.; Moore, *Life of Byron*, p. 64; Thomas Moore, *Memoirs of the Life of Richard Brinsley Sheridan*, Philadelphia, 1825, p. 11. It was neither Sumner's nor Parr's fault if, as far as Sheridan was concerned, 'remonstrance and encouragement were equally thrown away, upon the good-humoured but immoveable indifference of their pupil'. (Moore, *Sheridan's Memoirs*, p. 11.) Similarly, it was not Drury's fault if Byron did not learn all that he might have. Drury appreciated his talent, was supremely tactful in the treatment of his pride, and encouraged his reading in modern literature. (Cf. Moore, *Life of Byron*, pp. 57–58.) Byron, who always loved Drury, calls him 'the best, the kindest (and yet strict, too) friend I ever had'. (Moore, *Life of Byron*, p. 64.)

[2] Samuel Taylor Coleridge (*Biographia Literaria*, 2 vols., New York, 1847, Vol. I, p. 145) wrote, 'At school . . . I enjoyed the inestimable advantage of a very sensible, though at the same time, a very severe master, the Reverend James Bowyer,' who improved his taste and disciplined his style, showing him that the loftiest poetry 'had a logic of its own, as severe as that of science'. In *Table Talk* (2 vols., New York, 1835, Vol. I, p. 108) he even admitted, 'I had one just flogging.' He had told Bowyer why he was an infidel. 'For this, without more ado, Bowyer flogged me,—wisely, as I think,—soundly, as I know.' Lamb wrote to Coleridge in 1802 (*Letters*, Vol. VI, of the *Works of Charles and Mary Lamb*, edited by E. V. Lucas, New York, 1905, p. 248) of the 'Hostel of our Christ wherein by the exceeding diligence of a relentless master I was in days gone by deeply imbued from top to bottom with polite learning'.

[3] Rev. William Brock, *A Biographical Sketch of Sir Henry Havelock*, London, 1859, pp. 13–47.
[4] Derwent Coleridge, *Memoir of Praed*, in Winthrop Mackworth Praed, *Poems*, 2 vols., London, 1864, Vol. I, p. xv.
[5] John William Kaye, *The Life and Correspondence of Charles, Lord Metcalfe*, 2 vols., London, 1858, Vol. I, p. 7. [6] Morley, *The Life of Gladstone*, Vol. I, p. 30.

Dr. Keate of Eton have been the most famous. James and particularly Keate went as far with the old methods as one could go. They represented the best in the old disciplinary type of master and thus illustrated its insufficiency. In a sense they were reformers, for they tried to halt the chaos of futility which was coming over the schools. But they had as administrative weapons only the old methods. James came from Eton in 1778 and reformed Rugby along Eton lines with praepostors, fags, dames' houses, and tutors. He was a stern but just master carrying on his school under the guidance of eternal principles of right and wrong with the aid of the rod. His severity and refusal to allow self-government produced rebellion. Many of his boys hated him.[1] Nimrod (James Apperley) claims that he was a little 'inclined to be mad', and since he was harsh and humorous at the wrong times, was neither respected nor loved.[2] On the other hand, Samuel Butler always maintained cordial relations with his old master, who guided him in his first years at Shrewsbury.[3] Butler—and his grandson as well—maintained that James was a more important man than Arnold, an interesting if prejudiced belief. The grandson wrote that 'no subsequent head master so completely re-created the school as Dr. James did during his fourteen years' tenure of office'.[4] Be this as it may, it was James who made Rugby into a great school, and he must be counted as one of the strongest men whom the old system developed to defend it by the power of example.

But it was Keate who was both the greatest and the most typical master of the period. More has been written about him than about any other master except possibly Arnold. As Gladstone says, 'Dr. Busby was the first of the race of schoolmasters of which Keate was the last.'[5] But though

[1] Cf. Rouse, *History of Rugby*, pp. 146, 182. Walter Savage Landor had personal troubles with James, which ended in his expulsion; the proceedings do not show the master in too amiable a light.

[2] *Fraser's*, August 1842, p. 168. Nimrod adds, 'Whoever loved a schoolmaster?' who has to flog one. Boys hate arbitrary power and never acknowledge intellectual benefit.

[3] Butler, *Life of Samuel Butler*, Vol. I, p. 14.

[4] Ibid., p. 9. Butler quotes James as maintaining that, while a lower boy is bound to fear his master, the upper boys have good relations with him. Much of Butler's own flogging propensities in the early days must have been derived from James. (Rouse, *History of Rugby*, p. 171.)

[5] Cf. Benson, *Fasti Etonenses*, p. 499.

one thinks of Keate as a symbol of what was passing away, it must be remembered that in the sense that he was a strong man attempting to stem the tide of disintegration, he represented a positive force. Since he found laxness and chaos when he took over the reins of government in 1809, he determined that he would have order at all costs.

By sternness and unprecedented flogging, he made the boys fear him to such an extent that his name has become a symbol of the tyrannical master. As early as 1809 Milman, who was at the school, could write, 'Keate talks in a very spirited manner, and I must say I think he will soon be more feared than Goodall, but he will never be so much beloved.'[1] Flogging was the 'head and tail' of his system;[2] he flogged regularly and for small reason, considering it to be a rather pleasant pastime.[3] 'He had such a complete command over his temper—I mean over his *good* temper, that he scarcely ever allowed it to appear: you could not put him out of humour—that is, out of the ill-humour which he thought to be fitting for a head-master.'[4] If Keate was severe, it was at least partly a matter of policy; his severity may have been necessary for a man who was not a genius in the understaffed Eton of the tens and twenties. There were indeed those who felt that

> Beneath his rough exterior there lurk'd
> A kindly heart

and that his severity was a consciously assumed false mask.[5] Unfortunately, Keate was also unjust and suspicious; for this there was little excuse beyond the deficient knowledge of psychology of the day. Gladstone says that his injustices dulled the moral sense: he acted like a 'graceless, senseless, cruel little martinet'.[6] He never believed that a boy was telling the truth, and consequently no boy ever did tell the truth; Keate but confirmed the deep-seated enmity of boy and master.[7] When, after the rebellion of 1818, Keate

[1] Milman, *Life of Milman*, p. 15.
[2] Rev. C. Allix Wilkinson, *Reminiscences of Eton*, London, 1888, p. 17.
[3] Tucker, *Eton of Old*, p. 84.
[4] Cf. A. W. Kinglake, *Eothen*, Edinburgh, 1896, p. 266.
[5] Cf. a poem called 'Old Long Chamber' in *The Legacy of an Etonian*, edited by Robert Nolands, Cambridge, 1846, p. 110.
[6] *Temple Bar*, February 1883, p. 201. [7] Cf. Tucker, *Eton of Old*, p. 179.

expelled a boy for crying 'Never!' after the master had said that the boys would now return to the old order, the sense of his unfairness reached dangerous heights among the boys[1]

In general, from almost every point of view, it must be admitted that the nineteenth-century Busby was a failure. He did keep better order than most of his contemporaries. Occasionally he educated a few boys—or, to be more precise, got credit from aged alumni for educating them.[2] On the whole, he educated neither morally nor intellectually; indeed the harm he did by lending his prestige to the conception of the cruel, suspicious master was of incalculable harm to future Public School education. If he kept order, it was at the price of rebellion,[3] fear, and hate. Allowing for Keate's personal deficiencies, which were many, we must still impute his failures to the deficient methods of discipline, instruction, and moral training that he inherited. A narrow classical curriculum administered by a master with a rod was all that he knew. And the old formula was insufficient in 1820. Yet, despite exceptions, most masters clung to the old ways. As a result the system nearly collapsed entirely.

[1] Cf. Tucker, *Eton of Old*, pp. 199–203.
[2] Bishop Selwyn, in a letter to Keate, gave the latter credit for giving purpose to his wandering and restless spirit by 'judicious forbearance, and sometimes by well-deserved castigation'. (H. M. Tucker, *Memoir of the Life and Episcopate of G. A. Selwyn*, Vol. I, New York, 1879, p. 297.) Many sentimentalists loved Keate just because he symbolized the old order and felt that Keate's days were the golden age after which decay began.
[3] Gladstone told Benson that the boys booed Keate because 'it gave us a sense of our national privilege of disagreeing with constituted authority'. (Cf. Benson, *Fasti Etonenses*, p. 499.)

CHAPTER II

FORCES AND PHILOSOPHIES

A. CONSERVATISM

THE criticisms and defences of the early nineteenth-century Public School were in no sense a mere chaos of ideas produced by individual whim. From the battle of opinion that began at the end of the eighteenth century there emerged in the course of the succeeding thirty years a number of more or less distinct, complete, and conflicting theories with regard to the ideal purposes of education and the adequacy of the Public Schools in fulfilling these purposes. It is these general ideas which give meaning to individual opinions, and it is to their detailed exposition and illustration that the chapter succeeding this one will be primarily devoted.

A comprehension of the full significance of ideas is not, however, possible without some understanding of the individual and group forces which conditioned these ideas. This chapter will, therefore, attempt to survey the psychological, economic, political, and social motivations which underlay criticisms and defence of the Public Schools, and to suggest briefly the connexion between motivations and ideas. And in the process of discovering the sources of ideas it is hoped that some light will also be shed indirectly on the motives of those who patronized Public Schools or tried to reform them. For the active agents in school evolution were, after all, but a fragment of that English public, a cross-section of whose opinions appears in criticisms and defences of the Public School.

Though an analysis of forces is a precarious undertaking, based often on doubtful inference, it is possible, with the help of contemporary opinions, understanding of the conditions of the time, and the evidence of critics and defenders, to make at least a general classification of pressures at work in society, and to indicate in broad outline the kinds of ideas which resulted from certain motives. To attempt to do much more than this would be presumptuous. On the one hand, to attach a specific source to a particular opinion is, except in rare instances, virtually impossible. Those who criticized or defended schools seldom, when they give them at all, give reasons for their opinions that one can entirely trust; and the possible motives for any idea are usually numerous. On the other hand, given a particular force, to predict confidently that it will result in a certain set of ideas is equally precarious.

Since most of the ideas of those who defended schools and the forces that produced these ideas existed, expressed or unexpressed, before the wave of early nineteenth-century criticism that washed over the schools, it is well to start with a consideration of conservative motives and doctrines.

I have used the word conservative throughout primarily as a term of reference for those who did not want change in some or all of the aspects of a Public School.[1] Secondarily, since conservatives developed certain doctrines, the word has, where the meaning is clear in the context, been used to refer to those who supported these doctrines. Obviously, after reform occurred in schools, a supporter of what were previously conservative ideas could no longer be considered a conservative in the primary sense of the term.

I. INDIVIDUAL MOTIVES

In general the *status quo* in the Public Schools was supported by two not mutually exclusive groups of people, the comparatively few but powerful rulers of the schools, which included fellows as well as masters in ecclesiastical schools, and, much more important, the ruling class of the British nation, the class to whom the schools chiefly catered. The most powerful forces actuating opinions were the interests and desires of these groups; the dominant theories of the merits of Public Schools emanated from them. But there

[1] My use is therefore both more and less inclusive than the use of the word as a description of a state of mind. Many individuals who were not temperamental conservatives fought change in the schools and vice versa. It ought to be added that, since many who desired change in Public Schools were in certain respects satisfied with the *status quo*, the word conservative is often used with reference to men who were not thoroughgoing conservatives.

Forces and Philosophies

were a number of psychological motives for defence of schools which, though shared by many individuals of these groups, were not specifically, exclusively, or even in some cases characteristically motives of the upper class or the masters. Though they are difficult to separate except in thought from class traits on the one hand, or from economic and other motives on the other, these forces were often of decisive importance.

To begin with, there was one important individual motive which, though not itself of psychological nature, had a psychological origin. This was the happiness experienced by boys at school. Whether there were more boys who actually enjoyed their schooldays than in the previous period is an open question, but it is certain that a greater number than in the eighteenth century have testified to their happiness and to the general fact that Public School life was a source of pleasure. As early as the eighties an editor of the *Microcosm* could say, 'Sadly I go . . . the truth my tears will tell . . . Sadly, dear Eton, take a long farewell.'[1] Forty years later a contributor to another Eton school magazine, *The Etonian*, wrote, 'I have heard from good authority, that few leave Eton without feeling real sorrow at their departure.'[2] Throughout the entire fifty years preceding Arnold's day the pages of literature have been cluttered with statements by illustrious figures in regard to the happiness of their schooldays.[3]

For the most part it was a matter of individual temperament whether one enjoyed school or not. To this statement

[1] Gregory Griffin, *The Microcosm*, A Periodical Work, Windsor, 1788, p. 198.
[2] *The Etonian*, 3 vols., London, 1823, Vol. II, p. 55.
[3] Charles Metcalfe, the Colonial leader, has written of his days at Eton: 'Ah—those were days of real happiness.' (Kaye, *Metcalfe*, p. 8.) Dean Milman says his father 'always looked back . . . what old Etonian does not?—with pleasure to the years of his school life'. Milman, (*Life of Milman*, p. 15.) Praed, Moultrie, Gaskell, Gladstone, and Hallam have all fond memories of Eton days. Gladstone calls his schooldays the happiest of his life, and Praed longs to be once again a 'happy boy, at Drury's'. (*Gladstone Papers*, London, 1930, p. 12; Praed, *Poems*, Vol. II, p. 232.) Byron at Harrow was no less happy than the Etonians, as were others like Manning, Charles Wordsworth, and Isaac Williams, whose testimony is doubly valuable since they came later to disapprove of their schools. Williams wrote: 'I enjoyed much freedom and happiness at Harrow.' (*Autobiography*, edited by the Ven. Sir George Prevost, London, 1892, p. 7.) Manning testified to the fact that 'Harrow was a pleasant place, and my life there a pleasant time'. (Purcell, *Life of Manning*, p. 19.) Wordsworth 'seemed to realize that I had been happier there [at Harrow] than I could ever hope to be again.' (*Early Life*, p. 24.)

one qualification must be made, however, for happiness was in part conditioned by a social element. Those poor who went to Eton or Harrow did not have the chance for enjoyment that the rich had. It is doubtful whether Anthony Trollope, had he been a presentable figure or even an outstanding leader, could have conquered completely the stigma of being a day boy. With this qualification in mind, one can confidently assert that it was those boys who were psychologically equipped to ride the turbulent waves of a Public School who were happy there. On the whole these were the healthy extroverts. Occasionally, as in the case of a Hallam or a Praed, exceptional circumstances made it possible for a gentler temperament to be happy through escape of the ordinary routine, but in general it was the Tom Browns, blunt, normal, unthinking young animals, or the Byrons who, though unusual, were able to lead, that made up the bulk of those who found schools enjoyable. These extroverts were able to forget the hardships of being a fag in the joys of being a fagmaster,[1] and thus in later years to sing in all sincerity the praises of institutions that they had found on the whole satisfactory.

Obviously, given the conditions in the pre-Arnoldian school and the varieties of human temperament, there were many individuals who were not happy at school. Some of these, like Shelley, hated their schools as a result. Others liked their schools because as Ackermann says, their early troubles were 'buried in the grateful sense of the advantages derived from' them.[2] One of the greatest defenders of Public Schools was the Duke of Wellington. He was a dreamy, idle, shy boy, who made few friends and entered into few sports. He was unhappy and seldom spoke of his youth.[3] Some, indeed, praised schools just because they were unpleasant. These, be it noted, were mostly masters, whose theory of education, differing fundamentally from that of the alumni, was the authoritarian disciplinary one derived from the Middle Ages.

None of these groups had much in common with those

[1] Charles Rowcroft, *Confessions of an Etonian*, 3 vols., London, 1852, Vol. I, p. 112.
[2] Ackermann, *History of Public Schools, Rugby*, p. 2.
[3] G. R. Gleig, *The Life of Arthur, Duke of Wellington*, London, 1865, p. 3.

who enjoyed their schooldays. But there were numbers of individuals, considerably more than in the previous period, who defended their schools for a reason indistinguishable in its manifestations from that of boys who had actually been happy at school. These people were sentimentalists in love with the idea of being young. They worshipped their schools, from the far distance of adult life, as the home of their lost youth. Since they were concerned with a sentimentally conceived time of happiness, which was contrasted with the actuality of later years, rather than with actual youth, their attitude was not dependent on whether or not they had been happy at school.[1] They could, since they saw life through a veil of memory, make the past seem pleasant even when it was not. Thus their writings are usually of much the same kind as those of men who had actually enjoyed their schooldays.

Thackeray provides both an illustration of youth-worship and a statement of its nature. In early days he hated and severely criticized the school at which he had been so unhappy. As he grew past middle age his whole attitude changed: criticism disappeared, and even the obviously unpleasant took on a new aspect when seen as part of that never to be recovered state of bliss: youth. In *The Newcomes* Thackeray wrote in explanation, 'to others than Cistercians, Grey Friars is a dreary place possibly. Nevertheless, the pupils educated there love to revisit it; and the oldest of us grow young again for an hour or two as we come back into those scenes of childhood.'[2] Years later he added, 'Men revisit the old school, though hateful to them, with ever so much kindliness and sentimental affection. There was the tree under which the bully licked you: here the ground where you had to fag out on holidays, and so forth.'[3]

Sentimentalism in regard to youth is a distinctly individual psychological phenomenon, though it has been so widespread in England that one can very nearly call it racial.

[1] One could, of course, be a worshipper of youth, indeed was more likely to be, if he had actually been happy at school. Even to the extroverts distance lent an enchantment to reality which it did not originally possess.

[2] Thackeray, *The Newcomes*, p. 951.

[3] William Makepeace Thackeray, *Roundabout Papers*, London, 1907, p. 72, 'On a joke I heard from the late Thomas Hood.'

It is part of that desire to return to childhood, to a simpler and more secure world, which is, as Freud has shown, almost universal among men. Half-way on the road back to non-existence lies youth, which, though often not without trouble, is less complex and more secure than the state of men in maturity.

In the hectic, difficult, and complicated world of the late eighteenth, nineteenth, and twentieth centuries men have increasingly been lured by this prospect of a safer world. As a result, Public School sentimentalism increased after 1800 at such a rate that it soon became a crucial force in Public School evolution.

Viewed broadly, regret for youth among Public School men was but one aspect of romanticism, that general revulsion against rationalism and materialism which overspread Europe at the end of the eighteenth century. It was as much a part of the romantic movement as was interest in Rousseau's noble savages and in Percy's ballad collection. Like these other interests, Public School sentimentality was an imaginative return to childhood, to the past of the individual or the race. As part of romanticism it found encouragement and justification in the writings of the romantic philosophers.

Long before Rousseau, Gray and other English sentimentalists had begun the idealization of nature and of childhood. That the Gray who wrote *The Bard* with its glorification of the ancient poets, and the *Elegy* with its praise of simple life should also have been the writer of the *Ode on a Distant Prospect of Eton College* with its eulogy of Public Schools is surely no mere chance. But sentimentalism did not become the dominant note in English literature or life until Rousseau gave it philosophic justification and Wordsworth gave English expression to Rousseau's ideas. It was the politically radical Rousseau and the equally radical younger Wordsworth who were indirectly behind the idealizations of Eton by generations of nineteenth-century Tories. What they did was to give currency to that interest in early days which provided Englishmen with an excuse to idealize those glorious institutions which harboured unspoiled youth.

To Rousseau youth, being close to nature, was an ideal

Forces and Philosophies

condition, a time to which one ought to look back with regret. Wordsworth transmitted Rousseau's philosophic idealization of youth to England, and by translating it into poetry, made it a vital part of English romanticism. In the famous *Ode on Intimations of Immortality*, Wordsworth gave a philosophic justification of his and of Rousseau's ideas. Youth was nearer to God than maturity and was therefore the ideal state. In the *Prelude* he re-created in poetry the story of a Rousseauistic education.[1] Though the Public School boy might be very different from Wordsworth and very far from external nature, he was, compared with the over-pampered or over-disciplined, a boy and free. He was similar enough to a Wordsworthian hero to make the comparison valid, and sentimentality needed only the slenderest thread of the actual on which to work.[2]

The happiness of schooldays or the belief, for sentimental reasons, in that happiness had certain peculiarities as a force working against change in the Public Schools. In the first place happiness was often less powerful as a motive for attitudes towards the Public School than other conflicting motives, and as a result many who were happy at school were conservatives only in part or not at all. Notably was this true of a number of boys whose middle-class religious backgrounds proved stronger than their love for school.

[1] *Prelude*, from *The Complete Poetical Works of William Wordsworth*, Cambridge Edition, Cambridge, 1904.

[2] As is hardly necessary to point out, few school supporters consciously approved either of Rousseau's political or of his educational theories. Nominal Public School educational ideals, based as they were on the wickedness of human nature, attempted to discipline and mould youth into maturity. Yet Arnold, who, though he subscribed to these doctrines, had at least the faith to believe that there was native good to be developed, and accordingly gave his older boys freedom and independence, was attacked by Tories with the Rousseauist plea that he would not let boys be boys. In part this can be explained on the basis that what these people objected to was that Arnold gave too much liberty; their conception of the joy of youth which Arnold denied to boys was the privilege of being dependent and subject to a flogging, as much as the freedom which Rousseau advocated. Public Schools as places of education were consciously run, whether under Keate or Arnold, along very different lines from any Rousseau would have approved. At the same time, it must be remembered that, as we shall see, in some ways alumni ideals were nearer to Rousseau's conception than to Arnold's. But more important, the sentimentalists were not thinking of education when they praised youthful days. In so far as they were dealing with actuality at all, it was with those aspects most remote from the educational process. As a result there is nothing really paradoxical about their relation to Rousseau.

Isaac Williams writes that 'Happy as my youth was at Harrow, and much pained as I was to leave it,' . . . 'I earnestly pray God that He will prolong my life for the education of my own children, that they may never go to any school.' Indeed, he deplores even the friendships he made: 'My great bane at Harrow was the very warm and strong attachments I formed with boys not in every case of the best principles.'[1] Charles Wordsworth claimed sadly that his happiness would not bear religious scrutiny: 'there was in it, I fear, no sufficient consciousness of Him to Whom I owed it.'[2] Manning wrote of his pleasant life at school, 'I look back on it with sadness,' because it 'was the least religious time of my life.'[3]

In the second place, when happiness did provoke defence of the schools, this defence concerned itself only with certain special features of the schools. For only certain aspects produced pleasure, and personal pleasure was the chief interest of extroverts and sentimentalists. Reminiscers spoke chiefly of friendships, escapades, the beauty of the schools, or learning derived from other than master sources. Direct master teaching was obviously no part of happiness. But further, it will be noted, freedom from masters was prized chiefly in so far as it meant freedom from group-pressure as well. Happiness was the result of individualistic activities or perceptions.[4]

Nevertheless, most sentimentalists and extroverts were upholders of the system as a whole, even though they wrote but about certain parts of it and were concerned only with personal happiness. Their happiness made them believe not only that all boys were happy but that most of those who went to schools were well educated there. And for this they gave credit to the school. As the radical *Westminster* remarked bitterly, 'Physical, animal delight' seen in memory is likely to 'cause the thoughtless to attribute to the system,

[1] Williams, *Autobiography*, p. 7.
[2] Wordsworth, *Early Life*, p. 24.
[3] Purcell, *Life of Manning*, Vol. I, p. 19.
[4] As has been pointed out, freedom from masters seldom meant the opportunity to be actually free, and certainly did not mean that exclusively. Thus writers about happiness were speaking not only of special results of special conditions, but of results that often did not occur at all.

Forces and Philosophies

to the public school or the college, to Latin and Greek, what would have existed under any system.'[1]

Other individual factors activating support of schools are even more difficult to separate from group motives or from one another than those which produced happiness or the belief in happiness. They cannot for that reason be neglected. To begin with, there is simple loyalty as a motive for defence. Though in many cases it was the mere offspring of happiness, in others the result of cultivation by the group life of the school,[2] and even more frequently a mere reflection of the consciousness of caste privilege, its existence assumes a nature suitable to its cultivation. Most, though not all boys, are susceptible to influences which produce loyalty, but some are not, and in any case, such susceptibility is an individual matter.[3]

Similarly with the governance by habit and its more positive counterpart, temperamental conservatism. Many individuals supported various school institutions simply because these institutions were familiar to them or merely because they existed. Both of these important motives, the willingness, conscious or unconscious, to allow the habitual to be the test of merit, and the preference for the established, have purely individual psychological causes. At the same time they have been so widespread among Englishmen as to be very nearly racial phenomena. They have most certainly been general boy characteristics, and have been further accentuated among Public School boys by the influence of the school. As Roundell Palmer says, speaking of Winchester reform, 'Even the boys for whose benefit improvements might have been made would have disliked and (as far as they could) resisted them, with the whole force of their

---

[1] *Westminster Review*, July 1825, p. 155.
[2] Moultrie, speaking of Eton, refers to 'the loyalty thou lov'st to cherish in thy sons'. (Moultrie, *Dream of Life*, p. 55.)
[3] Its workings are well illustrated by the example of Rowland Williams, though in his case loyalty did not entirely prevent a desire for change. Williams, whose 'recollection of Eton schooldays always seemed to be chequered with a sadness with which not overstrong health and "long chamber" hardships had no doubt much to do', still was 'greatly attached to and proud of Eton, and, while he recognized the imperfections in her system and welcomed all changes which tended to reform, he would always warmly defend the college against objectors'. (Mrs. E. Williams, *The Life and Letters of Rowland Williams, D.D.*, 2 vols., London, 1874, Vol. I, p. 10.)

strong, if irrational, conservative instincts.'[1] Arthur Duke Coleridge reports the same phenomenon in regard to Long Chamber at Eton in the forties.[2] Although in every group there are those who react 'no' until 'yes' is proved—the conservatives, and those who react 'yes' until 'no' is proved—the potential liberals, English men and boys draw heavily on the first category.

There was one powerful force opposing Public School change which was similar in a sense to temperamental conservatism, but which was not a human motivation at all and thus found no expression through literature. I refer to inertia. Even had those opposed to various aspects of schools been more powerful than those in favour of them, there might have been no change. For reform is positive, unchangingness negative; thus there is always, in any institution, an initial weight in favour of the maintenance of the *status quo*. This was particularly true in respect to Public Schools, that had remained unchanged so long. As generations passed and schools, guided by tradition and cut off from outside influence, remained the same, habits and ways of doing things hardened until they lost the spirit that originally caused them and thus indirectly the elasticity that would have made change from within possible. Along with age there were several other factors inherited from the past that furthered inertia. These were the wealth and inherited majesty built up through the generations. A wealthy institution has a prestige which solidly resists reform; an institution set apart by kings or prelates seems above the petty turmoils of the present. The mere weight of a proud, unchanged majesty, in other words, exerts a conservative force over and above the desires of those who approve of the established.

All the psychological motives so far discussed might have worked to preserve institutions very different from Public Schools. There were some psychological forces, however, which could have been called into play only by Public Schools. Or, to state the matter more concretely, some people defended schools because those people were constitu-

[1] Roundell Palmer, *Memorials*, p. 94.
[2] Cf. Arthur Duke Coleridge, *Eton in the Forties*, London, 1896, p. 7.

tionally in sympathy with the character of school life. They were temperamentally friendly towards a disciplinary and authoritarian system of education or a free life in beautiful surroundings. Above all there were many who loved agedness and traditionalism, those most general characteristics of schools.

From the Anglo-Saxon *Wanderer* of the seventh century to Noel Coward's *Cavalcade*, backward-looking sentiment with conservative implications has been probably the most persistent note in English literature. In one sense this sentiment is hardly distinguishable from love of the established; in another it is but one aspect of love of youth, in this case the youth of the race. Yet it is a distinct phenomenon, and in regard to Public Schools a most important one. For it fastened tenaciously to Eton's and Westminster's old walls and old customs, and, finding them good just because they were old, fought bitterly against change.

To justify itself, the love of the past evolved a philosophy of the merits that were supposed to reside in mere age. It contended that mouldering walls and practices consecrated by time ought to be preserved because they embalmed the spirit of the great dead, the experience and thus the wisdom of the race. Over and above specific merits or in spite of seeming defects, each Public School custom was justified as the embodiment of the wisdom of past experience. This philosophy, like that which justified love of youth, was one aspect of general European romantic thought. In England its great exponents were Burke and Scott, in whom romanticism became conservative and nationalistic. Burke was the theoretic expounder, Scott the literary illustrator of the virtues of the past.

Edmund Burke, who had for years fought for liberty, seemingly turned traitor to it in *Reflections on the French Revolution*. Though this was not the case—Burke approved of revolution which meant the preservation of rights long held, and disapproved of that which destroyed the established in the name of reason—the doctrines of the great Whig proved an intellectual bulwark for defiant conservatives. Against the revolutionary abstractions of reason

Burke set up experience and the feelings of the heart as guides, and gave them a conservative interpretation. Experience meant not experience but the collective knowledge of the past. Emotion meant not untutored individual feeling but the group prejudices of centuries. According to Burke, Englishmen rightly cherish their aged institutions, since, embodying as they do the group instincts of former times, they must contain wisdom.[1] Church and State, inseparable ideas, have proved their rightness, their ability to preserve learning, discipline, and morality, by their mere continued existence.[2] Though Burke admitted the idea of change at the behest of circumstances, it must be a modification in order to preserve, not a reform to destroy.[3] And, since he was writing to defend English institutions against a present terror, his emphasis was less on the need for some modification than on the contrast between preservation and destruction.

Scott's work was less distinct and obvious, but probably on the whole more powerful than Burke's. For he presented Burke's philosophy pictorially. Medievalism, which for most writers meant the love of a dream world of escape, signified for Scott the love of an actual if idealized world of the past. In novel after novel Scott described with meticulous detail the rich and colourful pageant of the vanished middle age of the English race. The upper-class Englishman could picture himself as the inheritor of this noble civilization and grow tearful over its beauties. He could feel himself chivalrous in defending those English institutions which were the heritage from a medieval past against the assaults of a brash and vulgar rationalism. His prejudices had been conveniently transformed into idealism.

In the foregoing discussion we have assumed that love of the antiquity of schools resulted solely from temperamental bias. This was, of course, by no means the case. Often temperamental factors were less important than conditioning by the school. And, it may be added, what was true of love of age in this respect was also true of other preferences. A

[1] *Reflections on the French Revolution*, Vol. III of the *Writings and Speeches of Edmund Burke*, Boston, 1901, pp. 346 ff.
[2] Ibid., p. 363.
[3] Ibid., p. 460.

Public School not only helped to turn a boy into a certain kind of man, but it encouraged him to be a defender of the education that aimed to produce the type that he had become. More often, traditionalism among conservatives was not the result of psychological factors at all, but of group motivations of a social and political nature. Attachment to oldness under these circumstances was but a cloak for more specific preferences.

In concluding a consideration of individual motives, it ought to be said that there were undoubtedly some whose defence of schools was based on a purely intellectual conviction in regard to their merits. Though such a motive is difficult to disentangle from others, and though it is certainly not the predominant one with most people, one ought not to assume that it did not play its part. As we shall see, there are grounds for believing that objective considerations are of great importance in the criticism of Public Schools; they are surely not absent as a motive for the defence of upper-class education.

2. THE UPPER CLASSES

The main body of defenders of the *status quo* in the Public Schools were the members of the classes who had for a century or more patronized them, the British ruling classes. The most important motives that actuated support of the *status quo* were class motives.[1]

Most upper-class motives for approval of schools existed before 1780. But there was then no need to develop or express opinions in defence of this approval. Through most of the eighteenth century the Tory squirearchy and the equally conservative Whig oligarchy had complacently ruled a complacent England. Royalty and Parliament, and indirectly

[1] Among the upper classes the most powerful group were parents, that is those who supported schools by their patronage as well as by their pens. As long as they continued to send their sons to Eton or Harrow, school authorities remained unmoved in the face of attack. They could, with some logic, assume that no change was needed so long as the schools were full. Many defenders of the Public Schools have used their popularity as a vindication of their aims and methods. (Cf. *Public Education*, London, 1817, p. 33. This consists of three Tracts reprinted from various periodicals. The article referred to above is from the *Classical Journal*, and is an answer to Sydney Smith's *Edinburgh* article.)

the Universities and the Public Schools were safely in their hands, and as a result they were at first impervious to manifestations of change such as the industrial revolution, the religious revival, and the ominous doings across the Channel. Only when, after 1792, the French Revolution became bloody and militant did the squirearchy on the back benches begin to manifest agitation. Politically, they planted their feet firmly on the ground of things as they were, and for thirty years fought every reform of even the most moderate character. Verbally, they set about finding reasons for their hatred of reform. Institutions that they had always taken for granted had now to be justified by some semblance of logic and defended in print against the attacks of enemies.

The upper classes were unwilling to permit even moderate reform of the Public Schools. For, in the first place, the schools belonged to these classes. Change of any kind, particularly if forced from without, thus seemed a symbol of the destruction of privilege, and its prevention was the duty of every loyal alumnus. In the second place, the schools had been developed consciously or unconsciously to satisfy class needs, and they still served those needs.

From the social point of view they were obviously ideal. The exclusive class nature of the Public Schools appealed to the snobbery of the privileged, particularly of those not too sure of their rank. The near aristocrat as much or more than the aristocrat wanted to preserve schools to which only the right people had been going for generations. Indeed, both of these groups patronized the schools often solely because their sons would mingle there only with their peers or with superiors who might be of value to them in later life.[1] Thus to some, snobbery proved a motive actuating defence of the *status quo* which needed no aid from educational considerations.

To many of the upper classes, however, the education afforded at a Public School was in itself appealing. But they were not interested equally in all of its aspects. For the most part they considered the classroom contribution to education

[1] The Rt. Hon. Lord Lytton (Edward Bulwer), *England and the English*, London, 1874 (1833), p. 134. The *Quarterly* in 1829 also mentions this fact.

of secondary importance. The classics were decorative and socially useful to acquire, but learning was in general of little value to men who would never have to work. Moreover, the aristocracy felt that its power in the past had been earned with relatively minor help from the intellect; undue knowledge in its offspring might be an impediment to the preservation of the existing order. Master discipline was necessary and religious instruction commendable, but neither won active upper-class support, for the learning, the moral virtue, and the religious feeling that were the purposes of these activities were not prime concerns of these classes. Until Victoria's day moral or religious enthusiasm was scorned by an aristocracy that inherited its ideas from the irreligious eighteenth century and whose representatives in high places were George IV and Lord Melbourne. Religion was mere social cement and virtue a middle-class attribute. Character traits such as self-reliance were more important than chastity or knowledge of the catechism. Finally, in so far as the upper classes approved of master teachings—and in their belief in obedience and respect for authority they did agree with formal Public School theory—they found the influence of boy on boy better training than any provided by the masters.

What the upper classes cared about was the social life led by boys, for it was the miniature world of a Public School that turned out the kind of boy that satisfied their requirements. The privileged orders needed boys trained to defend those orders against revolution at home and loss of prestige and power abroad, to fight the lower classes and the pestiferous French. As the century progressed, the use of the Public Schools in the creation of servants of imperial expansion began to assume a more and more important role among the motives for defence of upper-class education. But in the twenties and thirties consciousness of Empire was still in its infancy; moreover, the pre-Arnoldian school was not, in reality, a perfect instrument for the production of Colonial leaders.

The sort of boy who made a perfect servant of privilege was one who was at once obedient and self-reliant. He was one who, on the one hand, knew the proper distinctions, was full of patriotic fervour, and obeyed implicitly those who were his superiors, and who, on the other, could command an army or head a government. Upper-class psychology was thus, in contrast to master psychology, libertarian as well as authoritarian. It applauded the social life of schools because it combined freedom and authority and created a product that was both independent and dependent.

3. THE MASTERS

Masters and Fellows were no less interested in preserving the *status quo* and no less concerned over liberal and radical attacks than were the classes who merely patronized the schools. Often, indeed, their motives were similar. The Established Church, of which they were all members at the beginning of the nineteenth century, was in part made up of sons of the ruling classes. Further, the clergy had for long shared power with the aristocracy and professional classes. Snobbery and the sense of caste privilege were thus as much clerical as lay motives. Clerics, no less than the aristocracy, defended schools as bulwarks against the French.

Nevertheless master and alumni motivations were dissimilar in important respects. In the first place, the psychology of the Church differed considerably from that of the political rulers. Religion, learning, and morality were ostensibly at any rate, prime clerical desires. Churchmen conceived of a Public School as a place where medieval and Renaissance conceptions of moral and intellectual education were furthered. Thus, what they defended was not boy social life, but master education with its inculcation of classical learning and authoritarian morality with the aid of the rod.

In the second place, fellows and masters, as rulers of the schools, had motives not shared by either alumni or the members of the establishment in general. They had a vested interest in the *status quo*. Fellows supported the governmental structure of Public Schools because they derived pecuniary advantage from their positions as receivers of the founders' bounty. Masters defended the classics because knowledge of the Latin and Greek languages was all that they possessed as teachers. Further, they ignored the paucity of either moral or intellectual attainment because an admission that the system had broken down would have been a reflection on themselves. In this respect, as we shall see, they differed from more disinterested clerics who, desiring ends similar to those of masters, attacked Public Schools because these ends were not being secured.

4. ROMANTIC ATTACHMENT

Many conservative writings were polemics which attempted to justify the *status quo* in the Public Schools by logical argument. An equal, if not greater number, however, and sections of all books and articles by supporters of schools were mere records of the attachment which the author bore towards the institutions in question. This latter sort of writing has a twofold interest. In the first place, it was frequently considered by both the author and the public to be an important form of defence of Public Schools. The very fact that a man liked Eton or Harrow was believed to be a proof of the merits of those institutions. So widespread was this belief that criticism had to spend almost as much time refuting it as attacking specific evils. The English, especially the upper classes, are congenitally irrationalists, and the romantic movement gave added encouragement to the cult of unreason. Furthermore, Burke lent the weight of his authority to its justification. For he contended that only instinct and feeling could judge as to the merit of institutions which were the product of group prejudices.

In the second place, many books written merely to express satisfaction with schools reveal a particular form of attachment which has a vital importance in Public School history. I refer to that curious group of alumni sentiments which I have already designated by the term romantic love or attachment. Romantic love deserves a special consideration not accorded to ordinary preferences. To begin with, it was unique among attitudes towards the Public School from the point of view of the elements which composed it, the nature of the objects which inspired it, and above all the intensity with which it fought change.[1] As early as 1818 Brougham could allude to 'the romantic attachment of the English gentlemen to the scenes of their early instruction' as the the chief obstacle to his inquiry;[2] in 1825, the *Westminster* cited 'that party spirit and feeling, that mystical and masonic sentiment and language, which adhere for life to those who have been educated at our public institutions' as the greatest supporters of their abuses.[3] Even more important, romantic love was, unlike mere liking, more than a passive attitude. It was creative in the sense that it coloured or transformed the objects which inspired it. In so far as its creations seemed to be realities, romantic love became, no less than objects themselves, a conditioner of attitudes, and thus of extreme importance.

Though romantic attachment existed, as we have seen, in the eighteenth century, it was, before 1780, the attitude of only a few of that small group of alumni who had been happy at school. By the early nineteenth century, on the other hand, it was the habitual sentiment of most alumni who liked their schools, whether they had been happy there or not. It was in 1824, four years before Arnold came to Rugby, that an Old Etonian could write in the *New Monthly*:

'To forget, or be indifferent to the recollections of Eton, is a crime which can seldom or ever be laid to the charge of those who have grown up there. What Etonian was ever lukewarm in the panegyric of the scene of his boyish delights? or could ever admit the possibility of comparison between that school and any other? . . . To the latest period of existence, the grey-headed Etonian will catch a spark of lingering fire from the subject, and his eye will beam

---

[1] Nothing in the reactions of those who disapproved of schools parallels romantic love. The latter found fault, they disliked, or they hated—the differences between their attitudes seem to have been chiefly in matters of degree; but the distinction between those who merely approved and those who loved was, despite the seeming parallel between love and hate, a distinction of kind.
[2] *Vindication of the Enquiry into Charitable Abuses, etc.*, London, 1819, p. 35.
[3] *Westminster,* July 1825, p. 155.

with renovated lustre in reverting to the day when he "urged the flying ball" and "cleft the glassy wave", in those favourite haunts.'[1]

The rapid spread of adoration for schools can be accounted for by factors already mentioned. Fear of radicalism and of Napoleon was naturally conducive not only to self-conscious justification of institutions attacked but to passionate love of them as well. The philosophy of the romantic movement as stated by Rousseau and Burke gave encouragement not only to certain beliefs in regard to the virtues of childhood and aged institutions, but to the emotion which accompanied these beliefs.

Romantic love was a much more complicated phenomenon in the nineteenth than in the eighteenth century. Since it proceeded from groups with diverse motives, it came to consist of a number of different sentiments and was called forth by a variety of objects. It had as its instigator not only happiness and temperamental love of the past, but the psychological, political, and social motives of the English upper classes. As a result it was composed of all the sentiments which these motives created in the hearts of the privileged orders, and was aroused by all the ideals and aspects of school life which pleased these orders.

Early nineteenth-century romantic attachment was a sentiment compounded of love, regretful yearning, patriotism, and reverence. Its essence was softness, passivity, static uncreativeness, and humility, blended with bellicosity, passion, and mysticism. Though in different people it differed somewhat, these feelings and qualities of feelings usually entered into the total attitude. One can observe this in the expressions of love voiced by any of the great alumni of the pre-Arnoldian schools from Canning with his 'pious fondness and veneration'[2] to Gladstone and Thackeray. But it was in the writings of the poets that, as one would expect, one can best discern the characteristics of sentiment. Lines such as Byron's,

[1] *New Monthly*, XIII, 1824, p. 497, 'Recollections of Eton.'
[2] Cf. Creasy, *Eminent Etonians*, p. 492.

> Sweet scenes of my childhood! your blest recollection
> Has wrung from these eyelids to weeping long dead,
> In torrents the tears of my warmest affection,
> The last and the fondest I ever shall shed.[1]

or Praed's

> Oh still, through many chequered years,
> 'Mid anxious toils and hopes and fears,
> Still I have doted on thy fame,
> And only gloried in thy name.
> How I have loved thee! ...
>
> .   .   .   .   .
>
> I have always found thee kind, and thou
> Hast never seen me weep—till now.[2]

express the essence of romantic feeling.

Numerous features of school life inspired romantic feeling. The early nineteenth-century Public School man was, in contrast to his predecessor, intensely concerned over his school as a political and educational institution. As a result he could be aroused to expressions of love by thought of the antiquity and authority of schools or of the education given there no less than by those friendships and escapades which had contributed directly to his happiness. The Public School was no longer, to the romanticist, a mere symbol of happiness; it was the home of established authority, of the past glory of the English race, of great educational ideals. It was 'primitive habits', 'Grey antiquity', 'the customs of our forefathers', and the 'royal origin' of schools which aroused the 'enthusiastic veneration' of old Etonians and Westminsters just as frequently as youthful sports or rambles in the woods.[3] Often, indeed, it was not the antiquity alone

[1] *Hours of Idleness*, from the *Poetical Works of Lord Byron*, New York, 1868, p. 396, 'On a Distant View of the Village and School of Harrow-on-the-Hill.' These violent lines were not published originally in the poem. Since they were written in 1806 they represent the disillusioned weeping of an eighteen-year-old grandfather.

[2] Praed, *Poems*, Vol. II, p. 129, 'My Vale.'

[3] Cf. *New Monthly*, 1824, p. 497; *A Very Short Letter from One Old Westminster to Another, etc.*, London, 1829, p. 12; *The Eton System of Education Vindicated, etc.*, London, 1834, p. 66. The *Westminster Review*, attacking Romantic love, spoke of these sources of inspiration under one head, since it considered all attachment to be the result of habit. The public is 'led by usage, it venerates habitually that which it has been accustomed to connect with church and state, with remote antiquity, with recollections of its parentage and of parental authority, and with recollections of childhood'. (*Westminster*, July 1825, p. 155.)

but the memory of a valuable education received that inspired love. Thus, for example, the Marquis of Wellesley wrote the following to Lord Denman with reference to Eton: 'My whole fame, my whole character, whatever success has attended my life, . . . whatever I can hope to be hereafter, are all drawn from that (to me sacred and hallowed) spring.'[1] Wellesley, indeed, asked to be buried at Eton, and wrote the following epitaph for himself:

> If on my life some glory shine,
>   Some honours grace my name, the meed is thine;
> My boyhood's nurse, my aged dust receive,
>   And one last tear of kind remembrance give.[2]

There was, however, one important aspect of the school which was not, in the early nineteenth century, an inspiration for romantic love. This was master education and master ideals of conduct and learning: Wellesley was referring to the education that he had received through the social life of the school, and it will be noted that his ideal is neither disinterested learning nor virtue, but the knowledge and the character traits which lead to glory. Romantic love was an alumni phenomenon, and masters and their purposes were not, in the pre-Arnoldian school, an essential part of the alumni conception of a Public School. What Dr. Arnold did was to establish the place of the master and his values in the life of Eton and Harrow.

Though romantic love could be inspired by any feature of the school which was appealing to alumni, it was likely to attach itself more passionately to some aspects than to others. In the first place, it was aroused, as emotion typically is, by concrete objects, and more specifically by those which were pleasurable to the senses. Even where the feature loved was abstract, it was usually loved through its concrete embodiment. In this connexion it is worth noting that often the abstract reason was forgotten in preoccupation with the concrete. Only too often the beauty of an old chapel blinded its worshippers to the emptiness of the ideals

[1] Sir Joseph Arnould, *Life of Thomas, First Lord Denman*, 2 vols., New York, 1874, Vol. II, p. 101.
[2] A. D. Coleridge, *Eton in the Forties*, p. 140. The epitaph was written in Latin.

for which it stood. In the second place, those concrete objects were the most appealing which provided associations for sentiments connected with either the individual or the group past. The youth of the individual and of the race were the most potent of all inspirations for romantic sentiment.

The objects which aroused sentimentalists over lost youth were the many inconsequential people and places of which their memories were full, and which for them constituted a Public School. These objects did not need to be of any particular kind, or aesthetically appealing, or even pleasurable, since they were mere symbols and were seen veiled by years. Thus Lord Dalhousie's comment on his Harrow schooldays, written in 1850, was without reference to details of intrinsic merit:

> 'I have seldom seen the old place since we parted there in '27. Each time there was a change for the worse, and I felt more reluctant to return. One could bear up under the loss of even such a dignitary as "Peachy's devil"; but when on my last visit I found the studies burned down, and No. 1, Lower Row, among the things that had been, I gave it up, and have never been there since.'[1]

Thackeray's famous passage about Charterhouse[2] contains affectionate memories of many things that were anything but pleasant considered objectively:

> 'There he lies, Fundator Noster, in his ruff and gown, awaiting the great Examination Day. We oldsters, be we ever so old, become boys again as we look at that familiar old tomb, and think how the seats are altered since we were here, and how the doctor—not the present doctor, the doctor of *our* time—used to sit yonder, and his awful eye used to frighten us shuddering boys, on whom it

[1] Captain L. I. Trotter, *Life of the Marquis of Dalhousie*, London, 1889, p. 4.
[2] *The Newcomes*, p. 952. Thackeray's feelings have a touch of Victorianism perhaps not quite appropriate to the Regency, but they are the best expression of sentiments in regard to the pre-Arnoldian school.

lighted; and how the boy next us *would* kick our shins during service time, and how the monitor would cane us afterwards because our shins were kicked. Yonder sit forty cherry-cheeked boys, thinking about home and holidays to-morrow. Yonder sit some three-score old gentlemen pensioners of the hospital, listening to the prayers and the psalms. You hear them coughing feebly in the twilight—the old reverend blackgowns. Is Codd Ajax alive, you wonder?—the Cistercian lads called these old gentlemen Codds, I know not wherefore—I know not wherefore—but is old Codd Ajax alive, I wonder? or Codd Soldier? or kind old Codd Gentleman, or has the grave closed over them?'

At the same time aesthetic beauty might be an aid to sentiment for youth. A writer in the *New Monthly*, who claimed that he had been happy at Eton, and had 'departed with a feeling of attachment and regret, which years since past have confirmed and heightened', found beauty to be the chief source of love.

'But to breathe for years the atmosphere of that classic spot—to frolic in the ample bounds of those green meadows which stretch (in the schoolboy's estimation) into a boundless extent—to muse and meditate, if that gentler mood be his, under the shade at the front entrance, enjoying the delicious fragrance of the lime-trees; to do all this for successive years, is to invest the spot with such a deep-felt interest as no time can diminish, no events erase; and not to feel this interest, is to have a heart more torpid than ever belonged to a true Etonian.'[1]

For lovers of the group past, for those who were stirred by forsaken loyalties and impossible beliefs in contrast to sentimentalizers over youth, certain objective conditions were necessary. District School No. 342 could hardly have been romanticized by Burke. Reverence for age required old walls and old customs steeped in beauty and rich with

[1] *New Monthly*, 1824, p. 497.

suggestions of past generations of boys. This Eton had, as Moultrie, along with a good many others, has testified to:

> Fair art thou, with thy crown of ancient towers,
> Thy cloister'd dim arcades, thy spacious courts,
> Thy verdant fields and venerable trees,
> Reflected in the mirror broad and clear
> Of thy praeterfluent Thames.[1]

This Charterhouse possessed, as Thackeray's lines indicate:

> 'A plenty of candles lights up this chapel, and this scene of age and youth, and early memories, and pompous death. How solemn the well-remembered prayers are, here uttered again in the place where in childhood we used to hear them! How beautiful and decorous the rites; how noble the ancient words of the supplications which the priest utters, and to which generations of fresh children, and troops of bygone seniors have cried Amen under those arches!'[2]

Indeed, all the Public Schools, with the exception—so far as buildings were concerned—of Rugby, were picturesque symbols of ancient wisdom. Conservative sentimentalists have never tired of using them as texts for glorification of the wisdom of ancestral ways.

As already suggested, romantic love was not a mere reflector of the objects which inspired it: it was a transformer, a creator of new values and qualities. In general, love changed the Public Schools in three ways. It personified them, it idealized them, and it sanctified them.

Personification was the result of the tendency to fasten itself on to the concrete which, as we have seen, was a characteristic of romantic love. If objects were not concrete, it was desirable to make them so, and one of the simplest ways of doing this was to personify them. This is a common enough procedure, and can be observed in the treatment of ships, nations, or God. It was particularly feasible in regard to Public Schools, whose development seemed very similar

[1] John Moultrie, *The Dream of Life*, London, 1843, p. 55.
[2] Thackeray, *The Newcomes*, p. 952.

to that of organisms. As a result, for generations of boys the conception of a school as an organism, a personality, a living being, an adored mother has seemed perfectly natural and right. Wellesley's calling his school 'my boyhood's nurse',[1] and Praed's statement that Eton

> ... hast been
> my Hope, my Mistress, and my Queen[2]

have been echoed by many to whom the thought of poetic licence was very remote indeed. Once Public Schools were thought of as adored mistresses they became increasingly difficult to change. For such a conception not only further encouraged the love which had created it, but it blinded those who accepted it to obvious faults which might not have escaped them had they viewed their schools as a system of customs and practices.

Idealization was a no less natural and no less far-reaching process than personification. Love sees only the good. Romantic lovers, particularly those writing from memory, formed their conceptions of schools from a carefully censored selection of details. The result was, when taken as a whole, an idealization, even when, as was usually the case, there was no distortion involved. Though it is extremely hard to prove or even to show interaction, this ideal conception, which constantly paralleled the actuality, was a constant influence on that actuality. Had lovers of schools been conscious that their picture was an ideal one, this influence might have been in the direction of making the actuality conform to the ideal. Typically, however, they assumed that the ideal was identical with the real, so that idealization tended to preserve the *status quo*.

Consecration of schools was very similar to idealization. Not only does love omit the unpleasant, but it sets the loved object on a pedestal as well. School romanticists imparted to their portrait of a Public School glamour and majesty and mystery. Schools became 'sacred and hallowed'.[3] As a result, since to question is to deny sublimity, it was sacrilege

[1] A. D. Coleridge, *Eton in the Forties*, p. 140.
[2] Praed, *Poems*, Vol. II, p. 129, 'My Vale.'
[3] Arnould, *Life of Denman*, Vol. II, p. 101.

to touch them or to criticize them. The Public Schools were 'too large, sacred, and fundamental' to be reformed.[1] They were to be reverently and humbly worshipped by mere human beings whose feeble intellects could not possibly understand their mystic grandeur and perfection.

B. LIBERALISM AND REACTION

Conservatives were opposed by two general classes of critics: those who wanted to return to conditions that existed prior to the nineteenth century, the reactionaries, and those who advocated new ideas, the liberals. Like the conservatives, liberals and reactionaries developed fairly consistent bodies of doctrine, which I have designated by the terms liberalism and reaction.[2] The motives behind these doctrines fall into the same general classifications as do the motives behind defence. There were attacks dictated by individual temperament or by reason; there were those caused by group motivations of a psychological, social, political, or economic nature.

1. INDIVIDUAL MOTIVES

Individual motivations require little special treatment. Their general nature has already been made clear, and there is no special psychology like sentimentality over youth to claim attention. Further, and most important, no purely individual motive resulted in any special kind of relationship to the schools. Conservatives actuated solely by happiness concerned themselves, as we have seen, with only certain aspects of the schools and with their own happiness. Liberals whose attacks were based on personal grievance usually made war on the whole social and educational system which formed the subject-matter for less personal criticism. Moreover, they objectified their hate and personal unhappiness into a concern for the happiness, virtue, and learning of boys in general.

[1] (Holt) *A Letter to the Rt. Hon. Sir Wm. Scott, etc.*, London, 1818, p. 7.
[2] The terms liberal and reactionary have been used, even more often than the term conservative, to refer to holders of specific ideas.

Yet individual factors cannot be entirely neglected. In the first place, there were a number of boys who attacked schools chiefly because they were unhappy there,[1] and unhappiness usually had such personal temperamental sources as inability to face the world or aversion to conformity.[2] Introverts like Coleridge or Sydney Smith, slovenly misfits like Trollope, or boys like Shelley who passionately rebelled against fagging and coercion at the same time that they were 'not made to endure the rough and boisterous pastime', were the alumni who had been most unhappy while at school, and who most hated their alma maters afterwards.[3]

In the second place, individual temperamental bias undoubtedly actuated many critics who had no personal grievance at all. There must, for example, have been many who attacked aged class institutions in general because they were congenitally individualists, rebels, lovers of novelty, or democrats. There were without question some who objected to particular aspects of the schools such as authoritarian morality, intellectual narrowness, or prefectorial tyranny

[1] Many unhappy alumni were not, as has been pointed out, enemies of the schools. They might be sentimentalists or patriots or believers in a disciplinary system of education.

[2] Given the conditions prevalent in the early nineteenth-century school, one does not always have to posit an exceptional temperament in order to account for unhappiness. As a magazine journalist writing of Eton in 1836 says, Gray's *Ode* was mostly twaddle. Childhood was anything but a time of freedom from pain and carelessness. (*New Monthly*, October 1836, p. 155.) Nimrod, writing in the forties about Rugby at the turn of the century, says that boys were not happy there. He even believes that school friendships do not last because we do not want to be reminded of schooldays. (*Fraser's*, September 1842, p. 322.) Ackermann, whose *History of the Public Schools*, written in 1816, is on the whole a glorification of those institutions, does not believe many boys find their schooldays the happiest in their lives. 'A good education is one of the blessings of life, which seldom appears in that light to the immediate objects of it.' There are too many 'necessary restraints' and too much 'continual application'. (Ackermann, *History of Public Schools*, Rugby, p. 1.)

[3] Cf. Walter Edwin Peck, *Shelley, His Life and Work*, 2 vols., Boston, 1927, Vol. I, p. 27. Many of these boys have avoided speaking or writing about their unhappiness. Not so Trollope, who wrote that 'my boyhood was, I think, as unhappy as that of a young gentleman could well be' (*Autobiography*, p. 2); nor Theodore Hook, whose 'school life was not a happy one' (Theodore Hook, *Gilbert Gurney*, 3 vols., London, 1836, Vol. I, p. 10), nor Dean Hook, who wrote home from school, 'I hate this place more and more' (W. R. W. Stephens, *The Life and Letters of Walter Farquhar Hook*, 2 vols., London, 1879, Vol. I, p. 9); nor Thackeray who, in the days before Slaughterhouse became Greyfriars, called his schooldays 'years of infernal misery, tyranny, and annoyance'. (Lewis Melville, *William Makepeace Thackeray, A Biography*, 2 vols., London, 1910, Vol. I, p. 36.)

because, as individuals, they were libertarians, intellectuals, or humanitarians. To cite only one example, Darwin hated Shrewsbury, though he was not maladjusted there, solely because his temperament led him to love science and not the classics.

In the third place, rational motivations caused much criticism. These require no elucidation, but there are two points of interest in connexion with them that ought to be mentioned. In the first place, there were probably relatively more objective critics than there were objective defenders. Defenders were enlisted more from those intimately connected with schools as masters or boys than were critics; there was less chance for these to extricate themselves from temperamental or interested prejudice than for outsiders. Critics, on the other hand, might well be disinterested observers of the system, people who had no temperamental bias or social or economic interest. There were so many obvious faults in the Public Schools, from no matter what point of view that they were looked at, that there was plenty of occasion for destructive analysis. In the second place, rational argument, if not rational motivation, was of far greater frequency among critics than among defenders. Critics, in self-defence against the conservative contention that love was its own justification, made reason their battle-cry in the fight against abuse. Since they were attacking those who contended that their romantic love for their schools was a proof of the merits of those institutions, they were careful to buttress hate with logical proof.

2. REACTION

Reactionary and liberal criticism of the Public Schools was motivated chiefly by the desires and needs of various groups. It was these groups that for the most part dictated the extent and direction of the suggestions for change, and developed the dominant theories of Public School education which ran counter to conservatism.

The reactionary attack on the Public Schools came, in the early part of the nineteenth century, from groups within the schools, that is, from special sections of the ruling classes. It was led by those members of the upper middle class with whom interest in aping the aristocracy was not an all-absorbing motive, and by clergymen of the Establishment who were without a vested interest in the *status quo*.

Since it was an upper-class movement, reaction, in the hands of these groups, was in no sense a doctrine of violent change. With regard to Public Schools as a whole, it was in complete agreement with conservative theory. Like conservatism, and for the same reasons, it supported old class institutions. With regard to education, it was a staunch supporter of one half of conservative doctrine, that held by masters. Particularly did it uphold an authoritarian morality and the discipline and religious instruction that were to bring it about. Not only the clergy but the middle classes had always been greater believers in morality than the aristocracy.[1] The *bourgeoisie* had closed the theatres in 1642, and destroyed the worst excesses of Restoration drama in 1700. Steele and Richardson had fought for morality all through the early eighteenth century as champions of the middle class. Furthermore, those sections of the clergy and of the middle classes that helped form the ruling classes have always been moralists of an authoritarian stripe. Respect for authority was traditional with them; moreover, it had been and still was a great weapon against radicalism.

If reactionaries protested against any aspect of Public School life it was against alumni ideals. Even here there was no real objection, since aristocratic purposes at their best were respected. The basic quarrel of the reactionaries with the Public Schools was that alumni and not master ideals predominated. Master ends were the essential ends of a Public School, and these were being flouted not only by alumni, but, more serious, by masters themselves. In other words the Public Schools were unfaithful to the ideals that

[1] Though the love of virtue among the *bourgeoisie* may at one time have been caused by the necessities of middle-class family as well as business life, it had become by the end of the eighteenth century so essential a part of class psychology that one hardly thinks of it as economic in origin.

had animated their founders. Alumni ignored them and masters were half-hearted in carrying them out. Reactionaries wanted to turn back the hands of the clock. They wanted a revival of old-time discipline and religious teaching to the end that there should be a vigorous religious and moral renaissance. Thus reactionaries were authoritarian extremists in contrast not only to liberals but to alumni conservatives. And much more than the half-hearted masters were they the defenders of this doctrine against libertarian extremists. It was they more than the conservatives who stood as champions of the theories which, all through the early Victorian period, were to struggle for supremacy with liberalism and to be, to a certain extent, reconciled with it through the Victorian Compromise.

In their desire for a moral revival in the Public Schools the reactionaries were animated by several forces. In the first place, there was the negative factor of lack of vested interest. They were able to recognize and admit obvious deficiencies to which masters wilfully blinded themselves. In the second place, there was the growing fear of radicalism. The French doctrines of reason, democracy, and libertarianism aroused in the clergy and upper middle classes a passion seldom evinced by the aristocracy. The reactionaries felt that only a more living religious teaching and a stricter discipline than the Public Schools possessed could check these pernicious influences. The desire for moral revival was a direct answer to political liberalism. In the third place, there was a psychological factor. In the second half of the eighteenth century there was a renaissance of emotional interest in morality and religion which cannot be entirely accounted for by political factors. This renaissance, in a sense the coming to fruition of forces represented by Steele and Richardson, was one aspect of the romantic movement. Its spearhead was Wesley and its first manifestation was Methodism. It thus began as a lower middle-class movement, and was radical in that it appealed to the heart rather than to dogma. At first it gained adherents chiefly among those outside the Church, but later it spread, under the name of Evangelicalism, to the ruling classes, and in this way affected the Public Schools. Most of the reactionaries were Evangelicals.[1]

3. LIBERALISM

The liberal attack on the Public Schools was of far greater significance than was the reactionary one. It was of broader scope and cut deeper. Moreover, it was created and sponsored by a most powerful social group in early nineteenth-century Europe, and was but one phase of a general attack by this group on all institutions in England and abroad. The liberal movement was the child of the vast middle class that rose to economic and political power in the years between 1780 and 1832.

In England, as we have seen, a good portion of the middle class had become members of the ruling class long before 1780. The merchants more than the squires ruled Elizabeth's kingdom; the Puritan Revolution broadened the base of *bourgeois* power; the Revolution of 1688 confirmed upper middle-class importance. But it was not these ruling-class *bourgeoisie* who were the creators or chief supporters of early nineteenth-century liberalism. The industrial revolution at the end of the eighteenth century caused a further shifting of class alignments and the emergence of an enlarged and reconstituted middle class as rival to both the older middle class and the aristocracy. It was this class that led the political attack on the supremacy of the ruling orders, and that was the chief instigator and supporter of the liberal movement in Public School criticism.

The ideas which formed the basis of the liberal attack on the Public Schools between 1790 and 1830 were of middle-class origin. They were ultimately the product of the historic position of the *bourgeoisie* as the business class of the nation and as the political underdog excluded from the benefits of power and privilege. They emanated from the needs and interests of merchants and the psychological

[1] Though the whole movement was, from its lack of any real philosophic foundation, doomed to eventual stagnation, its vigour not only blew life into the religion of the time, but stimulated indirectly much of the later reform spirit in the Established Church.

characteristics imparted to them by centuries of fighting for recognition and prestige. As these ideas appeared in the writings of eighteenth-century philosophers, they had, however, become in good part divorced from any obvious economic and political origin. Specific middle-class needs shine through a number of liberal doctrines, but the philosophy of liberalism as a whole had become by 1800 a doctrine of universal scope and application.[1]

A number of general attitudes, purposes, and beliefs underlay liberal doctrine in all fields. Liberalism was essentially a revolutionary and Utopian theory, desiring radical change effecting the improvement of man and his institutions. Its ultimate ends were the freedom, the happiness, and the material, moral, and intellectual welfare of all men. It had a deep faith in experiment, reason, the mechanistic interpretation of the universe, the importance of the practical and the useful, freedom, equality, and the essential goodness and ultimate perfectibility of man. It was rationalistic, humane, materialistic, and libertarian, and it hated absolutism, dogmatism, obscurantism, authoritarianism, class divisions, the doctrine of original sin, guidance by tradition and prejudice.

Liberalism carried these ideas in one way or another into all fields. It fought for a naturalistic, rationalistic religion, a humanitarian, democratic, practical ethics sanctioned by an empirically discovered utility, and a materialistic associational psychology. In politics it was a staunch defender of democracy and in economics of *laissez-faire*. *Laissez-faire*, an outgrowth of the hatred of Tory governmental restrictions, was applicable to other fields than economics, and is of extreme importance, since it meant that liberalism deprived itself of the use of the government as an instrument for effecting general reforms.

The liberal theory of social change was diametrically opposed to Burkian ideas. To Burke old institutions were the results of an organic growth from a nucleus of instincts and prejudices; to liberals they were mechanisms created

[1] That political and economic needs were the source of liberal philosophy can be readily seen by the way in which the middle classes deserted many liberal tenets when they became members of the ruling orders.

by an original conscious compact. To Burke they were the sacred expression of a people's ideals; to liberals they were a collection of dead ideas hampering the present. Liberals wanted to destroy them and to manufacture new ones with the aid of reason and science.[1] In the field of education, which most directly concerns us, liberals kept in view not only the immediate ends of education, mental, moral, and physical improvement, but ultimate purposes such as the freedom, happiness, and prosperity of the individual man. Education was to be a chief instrument in changing society. Stated briefly, liberalism stood for a broad and practical intellectual education whose object was mental freedom and knowledge of life, both general and professional, and a moral training which should inculcate ethical principles dear to liberal hearts. On the whole it emphasized practical example rather than precept and encouragement rather than severity as methods of teaching. It was an enemy of formalism and authoritarianism and a friend to freedom, humanity, and utility.

Though liberalism arose first in England, and though its growth can be traced through English philosophers from Milton and Locke to Adam Smith and Hume, and from Bentham and Mill to John Morley, the spearhead of liberal doctrine at the end of the eighteenth century and the chief source of subsequent liberal movements were the French philosophers of the Enlightenment. It was the encyclopedists who elaborated and crystallized liberal thought in all fields and who developed a complete radical philosophy out of the ideas of natural goodness, natural rights to freedom, equality, and the power of reason to create perfect institutions and to bring about man's infinite progress. And it was they who provided the theories which gave intellectual justification to the dramatic triumph of the middle classes in France in 1789, and to the reform movements in England and elsewhere.

Though it would carry us too far afield to discuss in any detail here the general theories of any of the leading

[1] Liberals had a naïve faith in the power of manufactured mechanisms to change the world. To them institutions were something you could superimpose on man, not mere natural expressions and embodiments of his ideals.

encyclopedists, the educational ideas of the greatest of the French philosophers, Rousseau, deserve a moment's consideration. For not only were they the chief expression of the dominant theory opposed to that of Public Schools, but they were both directly and indirectly influential in guiding liberal attacks on those schools.

The first thing that strikes one about Rousseau's ideas is how similar they are to the boy practice, if not the master theory of the early nineteenth-century school. 'One would think . . . that, like Locke, he is depicting the English public-schoolboy; but he could not have known any such, and the country gentleman who favours such institutions would rather follow any counsel than that of a dreamy revolutionist'.[1] The essence of Rousseau's doctrine is that 'God makes all things good; man meddles with them and they become evil;'[2] from this belief follows the idea that the best education can do is to guide a boy's natural development and prevent him from coming under artificial influences.[3] He is to be disciplined by nature herself, by things, by consequences, until he learns that 'true happiness consists in decreasing the difference between our desires and our powers, establishing a perfect equilibrium between the power and the will'.[4] Now this is in a sense what happened to a boy when left to shift for himself in a Public School; a Public School's miniature world gave a boy the education of natural consequences and the physical toughening that Rousseau desired. It should be added, however, that Rousseau considered the tyranny of public opinion an artificial influence; dependence on man, in contra-distinction to dependence on nature is slavery.[5] In the second place, schools placed character-building ahead of intellectual education and acted on the

[1] Oscar Browning, *Aspects of Education*, p. 164.
[2] J. J. Rousseau, *Emile, or Education*, Everyman's Library, 1930, p. 5.
[3] Cf. Ernest Hunter Wright, *The Meaning of Rousseau*, London, 1929, p. 45. Since youth is bound to be subject to some human control, it is desirable to make that control as nearly an imitation of natural forces as possible.
[4] Ibid., p. 44. Also cf. Matthew Josephson, *Jean Jacques Rousseau*, New York, 1931, pp. 361 ff. Thus, as Wright says (*Meaning of Rousseau*, p. 66) Rousseau's object was by no means to produce a libertine. Self-control, renunciation of desire, submission are fundamental to the educated natural man. But they must be voluntary.
[5] Cf. *Emile*, p. 49.

Forces and Philosophies

belief that boys were boys, not hot-house plants, both of which things Rousseau would have approved.

But in most other respects Rousseau and Public Schools were diametrically opposed. Rousseau's whole purpose was to encourage self-development, not to train recalcitrant instincts.[1] He tried to study the child in order that education might fit him and not vice versa. He wanted to interest his pupils and stimulate them to self-exertion, though not to cajole or artificially entice them. The authority of the rod, the discipline and the superficial culture of Latin verses, the whole paraphernalia of tyranny whether from boys or masters was inimical to him.[2] He hated, moreover, the impracticality of Latin teaching. Experience, not words, ought to be the teacher. Fact, sense observation were the things to start with. Later on more abstract subjects might be taught, but experience was to be the means. Usefulness should be the test by which a choice of subjects was made; Rousseau carried this idea as far as to advocate the teaching of a trade.[3] Finally, he deprecated the teaching of religion until late in the educational process when a boy could comprehend it.[4] Rousseau's whole teaching was directed towards the education of a boy for a new and free society. The whole spirit of the *Emile* is of freedom and joy and self-expression. It was at the very opposite pole from an education planned to produce leaders in a conservative society, warriors in the battle to preserve Tory traditions.

Though English liberalism was tremendously influenced by French ideas, most of its leaders did not accept them *in toto*. National differences in temperament and national suspicion of the French militated against such acceptance. Immediately before and after the Revolution there was some unmodified transference of the theories of the Enlightenment to English soil. Tom Paine, Godwin, and Priestley preached

---

[1] Here he has also differed from Locke, whose psychology was the basis of his sensationalism. (Cf. Monroe, *Education*, p. 522.) Rousseau did not believe, however, that all that a boy did must be pleasant. The useful, about which Rousseau cared much, was often unpleasant. (Wright, *Meaning of Rousseau*, p. 52.)
[2] Cf. Josephson, *Rousseau*, pp. 361–76.
[3] Cf. *Emile*, pp. 128 ff.
[4] Cf. Graves, *Great Educators*, pp. 85 ff.

revolutionary political doctrines, Day and the Edgeworths the educational ideas of Rousseau. The French spirit of revolt penetrated even the Public Schools, as evidenced by the hoisting of the tricolour in at least one school rebellion. Advanced young Englishmen everywhere were flirting with Encyclopedist doctrines even while at school.[1] But from the mid-nineties to 1820 or later the war against the French stopped entirely the flow of revolutionary theories. When the ideas of the Enlightenment again penetrated English shores, it was in modified and disguised form.[2] Virtually no one in England championed directly the doctrines of Voltaire or Rousseau.[3] If English liberals borrowed from France,

[1] Coleridge and Southey, later to turn renegades to the Revolution, fed deeply on French literature in the eighties. Coleridge and his friends hailed the Continental upheaval in poems written at school; it gave encouragement to their fight against Bowyer (Alois Brandl, *Samuel Taylor Coleridge and the English Romantic School*, London, 1887, p. 29.) Southey early got in trouble with the tyrannical and illiberal authorities at school by reading Rousseau, Gibbon, and Voltaire, and abusing Burke. The same Southey who, in 1818, opposed the Whig principles in the Eton rebellion on the ground that only 'subordination' produces real liberty, was expelled from Westminster for attacking the 'divine right to flog'. (William Haller, *The Early Life of Robert Southey*, 1774–1803, New York, 1917, pp. 38–43.) Shelley, a rebel all his life, read Godwin's *Political Justice* at Eton in the darkest years of reaction in the first decade of the new century. (Peck, *Life of Shelley*, p. 25.)

[2] A few emotional revolutionists like Shelley and Byron accepted French ideas in their original form, but it is significant that they spent most of their mature years in a politically fruitless Italian exile.

[3] It is interesting to note that, in contrast to their treatment in England, Rousseau's educational ideas had a direct and important effect across the Rhine. Early nineteenth-century German education, though very different from anything that he would have admired, was based directly on Rousseau.

Already in his own day, Rousseau was imitated by two educators, Basedow and Campe. Basedow revolted against German schools, with their classical grammar unpleasantly taught, their strict discipline, their absence of physical training, their treatment of boys as miniature adults, and, with his friend Campe, who wrote the *Swiss Family Robinson* because Rousseau loved *Robinson Crusoe*, founded the Philanthropinum in 1771, in order to embody Rousseau's ideas of the direction of natural instincts. (Cf. Graves, *Great Educators*, pp. 112 ff.) More important than Basedow and Campe was Pestalozzi, probably the greatest educator of the century. He put Rousseauism into practice, and developed the negative naturalism of the *Emile* into a positive revolutionary system of education.

Beginning by taking twenty needy children into his home in 1774, he tried in one school after another to develop individuality by pleasurable practice rather than by painful precept. He attempted scientifically to study child psychology, in order to give a child just what he needed at each stage of his development. The ideal of 'harmonious development' according to nature, explained in *How Gertrude Teaches her Children* and illustrated at Pestalozzi's schools at Stanz in 1798 and at Yverdun in 1805, became the basis of modern progressive education. (Cf. Graves, *Great Educators*, pp. 122–44.) In *Leonard and Gertrude*, through the medium of a story of a mason's wife who educates

Forces and Philosophies

they borrowed piecemeal and changed foreign doctrines to suit English temperament. In accordance with this temperament, English liberalism was more conservative, more practical, and less Utopian than the French. Even in the hands of its most radical exponents, the Benthamites or philosophical radicals, it became a much more distinctly *bourgeois*, less passionately idealistic and revolutionary doctrine than when under French auspices. The Benthamites, though they used French deductic logic and aimed at radical change, talked little about logical truth or the rights of man or infinite perfectibility or violent revolution. They aimed at gradual progress, particularly in a materialistic sense, not perfection, and made usefulness, not abstract justice, their guide in effecting change.

In general it was the above doctrines either in the original English or French forms, or more frequently as readapted from France into England after 1815 which formed the basis of middle-class liberal criticism of royalty, Church, Parliament, the economic system, the Universities, and the Public Schools between 1780 and 1830. But to say this is not to imply that all liberals accepted completely all the tenets of liberalism. The new middle classes that formed the backbone of the liberal movement were composed of several groups, each of which had its own special relationship to liberalism.

The most important division in the *bourgeois* ranks was between the upper and lower middle classes, between the new capitalists, merchants, and professional men and the tradesmen and small shopkeepers. Among the former there

---

her children in a corrupt Swiss town, Pestalozzi set down his principles in popular form. The education she gives in order to develop to the fullest extent all the faculties of the child's nature is practical and ethical. (Cf. Pestalozzi's *Leonard and Gertrude*, Boston, 1885, p. 118.) 'Her verbal instruction seemed to vanish in the spirit of her real activity.' (Cf. Ibid., p. 130.) Being is more important than knowing. (Ibid., p. 152.) Each activity is in harmony with the inner nature of man. The whole process was as far from Public School education in spirit as an impoverished Swiss woman in a small town was from a dignified Public School master surrounded by Eton's aged pomp.

Pestalozzi's ideas did not lie fallow in Germany as did those of Rousseau's early followers in England. The philosopher Fichte made them the basis of his scheme to regenerate Germany. Transformed in Fichte's hands to serve new purposes, Pestalozzi's theories were the foundation of German State education.

were a few who early succeeded in becoming members of the ruling classes. These, since they had lost the political motive for desiring change, were liberals only in so far as their business needs conflicted with those of the older ruling classes. In respect to Public Schools, as we have seen, they were likely to be either conservatives or reactionaries; some of them, however, in whom financial interest was stronger than social snobbery, joined the liberal front in certain important attacks on Public School education.

The most important section of the upper middle-class liberals were those capitalists who were still struggling for power. They were, indeed, the most aggressive of all the liberals, for they were the most powerful and the most directly interested in reform. With regard to Public Schools they were the only group thrown up by the industrial revolution which had either the money or the social ambition to want to go to Public Schools and hence to make these institutions congenial to them.[1] The disenfranchised upper middle classes were not, however, thoroughgoing liberals. They were moderates, accepting liberal doctrines only up to a point. For they shared upper-class interests and psychology in many spheres and were as hostile to the lower classes as were the former. They were at one with the lower middle classes only in certain common needs and in a common exclusion from various institutions. Thus they adopted a semi-liberal philosophy which poised itself nicely between democracy, liberty, logic, humanity,[2] the swift and complete destruction of the old, and a faith in the class system, authority, feeling, and preservation of the established. Expediency —called induction by the apologist Macaulay—gradualness, and compromise became the *bourgeois* watchwards. Later on in the century, partly because they had attained their ends and partly because, as members of the ruling class their interests were different, they ceased to talk at all about liberty or democracy. In politics Whiggery became after 1832

[1] Many capitalists were not, of course, interested in sending their sons to Public Schools. On the other hand some lower middle-class merchants and tradesmen, like the inhabitants of Harrow, were.

[2] Middle-class humanitarianism seldom extended to the lower classes. The Tories in the thirties and forties took a leaf out of the middle-class book in this respect and read the Gradgrinds a lesson from it.

distinct from Toryism only on points where commercial and agricultural interests directly conflicted.[1]

The lower middle classes together with a number of *bourgeois* philosophers who supported them were the most persistent and thorough-going adherents of liberalism. The small business man was the individual for whom liberal tenets were best suited. Liberty, democracy, *laissez-faire*, a rational practical ethics, were more in keeping with lower middle-class psychology, interests, and political situation than they were with either those of the aristocracy, the capitalists, or the proletariat.

Liberals of all shades of opinion attacked the Public Schools. For these schools were both one of the symbols of upper-class privilege and one of the institutions that most failed to measure up to the political, economic, social, and educational desires of the middle classes. They were upper-class preserves and catered to upper-class needs: it was on this basis that the ruling orders supported them; on the same basis the middle classes criticized them.

The liberal attack proceeded on all fronts, aiming its blows at the government, social organization, and indeed at the whole idea of a Public School as much as at the education given there. In all these fields the nature of the attack was dictated by middle-class needs and middle-class psychology and illustrated the general principles of liberalism. It evidenced those ideas which proceeded from the historic position of the middle classes no less than it did those which were their heritage as a business class.

Except for specific educational features of schools there were three objects of liberal criticism, the traditional nature of the Public Schools as a whole, the monopolistic character of school government, and the undemocratic nature of the social system. These aspects of the upper-class educational system violated all the most sacred political and social ideals of liberals, their love of change and experiment, their faith in reason, and their belief in liberty and democracy.

[1] The lower classes profited as much by the fight between the agricultural and business interests as they did by the struggle of the latter for political power. Both the Whig-sponsored repeal of the Corn Laws and the Tory revenge of the Factory Act of 1847 were beneficial to them.

All the educational features of schools from boy government to master methods were the source of some attack. Occasionally, as in the case of discipline and formal religious instruction, objection was based on the methods themselves. Liberal lovers of the practical, the empirical, and the humanitarian found flogging cruel and religious teaching dull and outworn, and preferred more positive, interesting, and elastic methods of securing intellectual and moral ends. Usually, however, it was educational ends that concerned critics when they attacked the curriculum or master inefficiency or boy life. Liberals felt that schools were not living up to their own ideals. More important, liberals often disagreed fundamentally with those ideals. In the intellectual field they desired boys to possess more mental independence and elasticity and a broader and more useful knowledge of the world than schools gave them. In the moral field they desired more individual freedom and happiness for boys and the production of more virtuous characters than schools typically brought forth. Their conception of virtue, moreover, differed from that of either conservatives or reactionaries in that it was less authoritarian and more democratic, practical, and broadly humanitarian than theirs.

If liberal criticism of Public Schools illustrates the principles of liberalism, it also demonstrates the disagreements between the radicals and moderates among supporters of those principles. Thus, to begin with, there was a wide difference in the extent to which various critics wished to destroy traditionalism, trustee management, or the class nature of education. No one, it may be added, had any profound objection to the wisdom of the past as such: the most that was claimed was that no custom ought to be exempt from the test of reason merely because it was old or because it was loved. Few desired a thoroughly democratic educational system, and, as in politics, these became even fewer after 1832. Only a small minority advocated the substitution of *laissez-faire* as a principle of educational management for endowments. As a rule the tendency as far as government of schools was concerned was in the other direction, towards State control, though liberal fear of Parliament hindered this development.

As far as Public School education went, only the most radical were thoroughgoing liberals. In the intellectual field many, in reality false liberals, narrowed their desired ends to the merely practical, neglecting mental freedom. Even the demand for the practical, however, was in abeyance until the thirties, when the effects of the capitalistic system began to be more widespread. As far as means were concerned, critical ideas ranged all the way from a complete redrafting of the curriculum to a mere redirecting of the old system. In the moral field few cared chiefly about more individual freedom or less authoritarian and dogmatic ethics. Even fewer were willing to scrap the whole paraphernalia of prefects, flogging, and formal religious instruction and substitute a control by masters grounded in kindness, encouragement, and the power of example. Indeed, even the most radical reformers were at odds among themselves in this respect. They saw that *laissez-faire* in the relations of boys and masters was the root of Public School cruelty and immorality. Yet, as liberals, they feared giving the master too much power, just as in the political world they feared State control. The usual solution was, as in politics, a compromise. Boy self-government was to be preserved, but democratized.

CHAPTER III

CRITICISM AND DEFENCE
1780–1830

A. CONTROL AND MEMBERSHIP

BEFORE 1830 no attack on either the government or the class nature of schools was both concentrated and thoroughgoing. Direct concentrated criticism focused around Lord Brougham's parliamentary inquiry into the education of the lower orders in 1816 and 1818, but none of this criticism was very radical; not even the most liberal members of Brougham's committee or their supporters went so far as to suggest that the schools ought to have an essentially different system of control or be anything but upper-class institutions. Individuals who wanted to cut deeper were isolated phenomena.

It is appropriate that the most radical suggestion in regard to control came from the author of *The Wealth of Nations*, since his was, in general, the most radical philosophy expounded by an Englishman at the time. In characteristic fashion, Adam Smith's plea was for complete *laissez-faire*. Schools should be more, not less independent than they had been; they ought to be independent of endowment as well as of the Government. What Smith deplored was the deadening effect of security on Public School teachers, just as he deplored the effect of endowments of all kinds on those who profited by them. If 'the public schools are much less corrupted than the universities', it was just because the schoolmaster was partially dependent on the fees of his pupils, and had no exclusive monopoly.[1] Yet even the schools were endowed institutions, and thus did not respond to the needs of the age. They continued to teach Greek and Latin, not useful subjects. Smith offered as a solution to the problem of conservative refusal to meet new circumstances the destruction of endowments. This would force the teacher, if

[1] Adam Smith, *An Inquiry into the Nature and Causes of the Wealth of Nations*, Everyman's Library, 2 vols., 1931, Vol. II, p. 250.

he were to survive in a competitive world, to satisfy the needs of that world. He believed that 'were there no public institutions for education'[1] a gentleman would learn that which would be useful to him in life. Smith's *laissez-faire* solution of the problem of monopoly was, as we have seen, an extreme liberal position. But even those who did not want to do away with endowments shared Smith's views enough to prevent them from wanting State control as a means of correcting the faults of endowed institutions. To all radicals but the socialist, Robert Owen, the State was suspect.[2] As a result the Public Schools were long able to keep clear of any control; they still can to-day, while fees and revenues hold out, afford to disregard criticism from Downing Street.[3]

Between Smith's attack and that of Brougham's Commission there was virtually no one in England to voice criticism of educational monopolies. Occasionally the *enfant terrible*, Cobbett, expressed his hate of the 'close professional corporations' in the *Political Register*, but even he did not concern himself much about the matter. The last years of the eighteenth century and the early years of the nineteenth were a barren time for liberalism.[4]

If there was little radical attack on the control of schools until at least the thirties, there was even less objection to them as upper-class institutions. No one directly suggested, except the parishioners of Harrow who were fighting for their rights in Chancery,[5] that the Public Schools should actually be turned back to the poor. The most radical ideas were those of the English followers of Rousseau, who, though they did not directly suggest the destruction of aristocratic

[1] Ibid., p. 263.
[2] Cf. Robert Owen, *A New View of Society*, London, 1813.
[3] If this liberal attitude was harmful to upper-class education, it was disastrous for the education of the poor. For liberals like Brougham and James Mill, who wanted the poor to be educated, have fought the only means for bringing this about, the State. They rationalized their fear of the State into a belief that the poor were better off paying for that education which their self-interest would surely make them demand. (Cf. H. Brougham, *Practical Observations on Popular Education*, Boston, 1826, pp. 5, 33.) It is noteworthy that Smith himself favoured State education of the poor, for he was a humanitarian before he was a dogmatist. (For an interesting discussion of Smith as a social reformer rather than as an apologist for capitalism, cf. Eli Ginzberg, *The House of Adam Smith*, New York, 1934.)
[4] Cf. G. D. H. Cole, *The Life of William Cobbett*, London, 1924, p. 140.
[5] Ackermann, *History of Public Schools, Harrow*, p. 11.

institutions, avowed their dislike for them and proposed a contrary ideal of education. Thomas Day was violently opposed to the aristocratic manners taught at Eton or Harrow. In Day's *Sandford and Merton*, as well as in Brooke's *Fool of Quality*, the country-bred democrat is contrasted favourably with the snobbish follower of fashion. Day preached against the luxurious and effeminate 'gentleman', the Rousseauist caricature of a Public School boy, by contrasting the spoiled Merton with the farmer's son, the democratic savage, who has led a hardy and useful life close to nature.[1] Other democrats like Cobbett occasionally spoke of 'those frivolous idiots that are turned out from Winchester or Westminster School', but for the most part anti-aristocratic sentiment was not crystallized until much later.[2]

The questions of most vital interest at the time in regard to schools as political and social institutions cut less deeply than did Smith's and Day's ideas. Englishmen were chiefly perturbed over two seemingly minor points; were the schools offering to the poor that to which they were legally entitled?[3] Did Parliament have the right to see that the founders' statutes in regard to the poor were obeyed? But discussion of these two questions was an opening wedge in the long struggle against upper-class monopolies; by implication it brought up the whole problem of their right to existence.

The fight over the statutes concerning the poor centred

[1] Cf. Henry Brooke, *Fool of Quality*, 2 vols., New York, 1860, Vol. I, p. 51; Thomas Day, *The History of Sandford and Merton*, Corrected and Revised by Cecil Hartley, London, n.d., p. 261; Gignilliat, *The Author of Sandford and Merton*, pp. 262 ff.

[2] Cf. Charles Knight, *Passages of a Working Life*, 3 vols., London, 1864, Vol. I, p. 185.

[3] Curiously enough, until much later, there was little protest in regard to the treatment of those poor who did get in. There must, however, have been much bitterness among the snubbed and mistreated boys of the lower class. Anthony Trollope's comments, written long afterwards, surely reflected a good deal of early nineteenth-century feeling. 'The indignities I endured are not to be described. As I look back it seems to me that all hands were turned against me—those of masters as well as boys. I was allowed to join in no play. Nor did I learn anything—for I was taught nothing.' Thomas is even more explicit. 'What a pariah I was among these denizens of Mark's and other pupil rooms! For I was a "town-boy", "village boy" would have been a more correct designation; one of the very few, who by the terms of the founder's will, had any right to be there at all; and was in consequence an object of scorn and contumely on the part of all the paying pupils.' (A. Trollope, *Autobiography*, p. 11; T. A. Trollope, *What I Remember*, Vol. I, London, 1887, p. 77.)

around Lord Brougham's parliamentary investigation into the education of the lower orders in 1816 and 1818. As the industrial nineteenth century got under way, the English, particularly the radicals, with their faith in education as a panacea, began to feel responsible for giving some sort of instruction to the growing proletariat. The only important provisions for their education up to the beginning of the nineteenth century had been numerous grammar-school endowments, most of which dated back to the sixteenth century. The object of Brougham's committees of 1816 and 1818 was to find out what had happened to the income from these endowments. Since Public Schools were technically grammar schools, the Whig leader included them in his investigation. In 1816 the committee investigating the city schools looked into the workings of Charterhouse and Westminster. Two years later a second committee called before it the managements of Eton and Winchester. On the basis of the findings of these two committees Brougham proposed that supervision of Public Schools be included in the powers of the 'Commissioners to inquire into the Abuses of Charities connected with the Education of the Poor, in England and Wales'. The Tory outcry was instant and vehement, and Brougham and his followers were driven into passionately defending themselves; in so doing they gave the first historic expression to the moderate liberal position in regard to class schools and closed educational corporations.

Brougham's committees had in general discovered, as Carlisle wrote, that 'many of our numerous and ample Endowments have fallen to decay, by the negligence or cupidity of ignorant or unprincipled Trustees'.[1] The committee of 1818 had referred specifically to Public Schools. The result of their inquiry, they wrote, '. . . unquestionably shows, that considerable unauthorized deviations have been made, in both Eton and Winchester, from the original plans of the founders; that those deviations have been dictated more by a regard to the interests of the Fellows than of the Scholars, who were the main object of the foundations and

---

[1] Nicholas Carlisle, *A Concise Description of the Endowed Grammar Schools* London, 1818, p. xxxv.

of the founder's bounty'.[1] To the most moderate liberals this meant merely 'that the scholars are under various pretences deprived of their statutable allowances by the Fellows'.[2] But to the majority it meant also that these scholars did not come from the class of people from which the founders had wished to draw them, the *pauperes et indigentes*.[3] It was this that aroused liberal anger and was the basis of their desire to have Public Schools investigated. Brougham and his followers wanted to restore the rights of the poor, disregarded by the Fellows, and to do so they wished Parliament to intervene. The State has the right to correct 'established abuses' and 'undeserved power'.[4] They did not want to turn out the aristocrats,[5] nor did they advocate State control. Indeed they were doing no more than defending founders' intentions, and were horrified at the suggestion that they might be detracting from the 'high character' of the Public Schools or 'lessening their utility in the formation of the national character and habits of the upper classes of society'.[6]

Yet in their attacks they evidenced savage indignation not only against the fundamental assumptions on which schools were based, but also against the attitudes of conservatives. Brougham and his followers represented, they felt, the righteous tide of moderate liberalism, which, now that fear of revolutionary radicalism was quelled, would prove irresistible. Since their cause was just, resistance to it could be dictated only by blind fear and defended only by prejudice and unreasoning sentiment.[7] It was opposed by a swarm of 'opponents whose peculiar business it is to defend all usages that are ancient, all established power, to repress every liberal opinion, and to strengthen all the boundaries that separate the classes of mankind'.[8] The liberals were vindictive against schools which 'strive to do away with the stigma of being Charitable foundations, as a libel on their

[1] *Third Report from the Select Committee*, 1818, p. 58.
[2] *The Times*, September 11th 1818, p. 3.
[3] Cf. Henry Brougham, *A Letter to Sir Samuel Romilly upon the Abuse of Charities*, London, 1818, pp. 24 ff., 48 ff.
[4] *Edinburgh*, March 1819, pp. 497 ff.   [5] *Vindication of the Enquiry*, p. 94.
[6] Ibid., p. 105.   [7] *Edinburgh*, March 1819, pp. 497, ff., 536 ff.
[8] *Vindication of the Enquiry*, p. 3.

Criticism and Defence, 1780–1830

constitutions'.[1] They were even more angered by the plea of sacred immunity from parliamentary interference. Trustees have responsibility to the public,[2] and that responsibility is not fulfilled when visitors from an Oxford or Cambridge college inspect the schools, for visitors either cannot know abuses or, since they are part of the whole scheme of privilege, may be corrupt and allow masters to pervert charitable funds and reap profits without teaching.[3] Brougham argued vehemently in favour of the rights of Parliament in a speech before the House of Commons. 'I hear it said, that they [the proposed powers of the commissioners] are inconsistent with the rights of private property. Under the flimsy pretence of great tenderness for those sacred rights, I am well aware that the authors of the outcry conceal their own dread of being themselves dragged to light as robbers of the poor, and I will tell those shameless persons, that the doctrine which they promulge, of charitable funds in a trustee's hands being private property, is utterly repugnant to the whole law of England.'[4]

Despite liberal efforts, the practical outcome could not have been in doubt. Brougham had to exempt charities with 'visitors, governors, or overseers' from the power of his commissioners in order to get his Bill through at all.[5] Parliament was not to gain the right to interfere with schools until the sixties. The poor were never to have their right to education with the rich in Public Schools legally vindicated. Education in England had been definitely established on a class basis; the educations of the poor and of the rich were to follow such divergent lines that never again were they even to be discussed in common by a single committee as they were in 1818.[6]

---

[1] Ibid., p. 87.   [2] *Edinburgh*, September 1818, p. 486.
[3] Brougham, *Letter to Romilly*, pp. 24 ff., 48 ff.
[4] Henry Brougham, Speech in the House of Commons, May 8th 1818, on *The Education of the Poor, etc.*, London, 1818, p. 33.
[5] Brougham, Speech on *The Education of the Poor*, p. 37. Forty years later, in answer to a letter of Henry Reeve's in regard to the evidence of the 1818 committee, Brougham blamed Lord Eldon for causing the defeat of his proposal in 1818, and Sir Robert Peel for preventing the carrying out of a similar proposal in 1819. (Cf. John Knox Laughton, *Memoirs of the Life and Correspondence of Henry Reeve*, 2 vols, London, 1898, Vol. II, p. 66.)
[6] Because the education of the poor followed such a different direction from

For a time, indeed, the liberal attack on the constitution of the Public Schools almost ceased. In the twenties the philosophical radicals maintained a persistent attitude of hostility to 'these monopolizing establishments' which 'are entwined in a triple twist with Church and State' to such an extent 'that to "speak evil" of Westminster or Eton, of Oxford or Cambridge, is heresy, schism, and all manner of abomination'. They fiercely attacked the clergy, which 'esteems the head of its religion beyond the head of its Government', and would have liked to break its monopoly of education. But since they despaired of doing so, and since their chief interest was in intellectual education, they were content to educate the clergy and leave control in their

that of the rich, it is not necessary to discuss the organization of the former at great length in a book on Public Schools. Yet a brief note on this organization is illuminating and in a sense necessary. Though there was little actual borrowing by the Public Schools from the education of the lower orders—with the exception of such short-lived experiments as Russell's borrowing of Bell's system of mutual instruction—schools for the poor had an important indirect influence on those of the rich. Their whole organization and plan of education followed different lines from those of Public Schools, lines that were more in keeping with the tendencies of a new age. Tradition did not stand in the way of new ideas. As a result, the schools for the poor offered a competition, particularly in educational matters, which profoundly affected Public Schools. Of the education given in these schools brief mention will be made later. Here I shall give a very short outline of their organization as contrast and parallel to that of Public Schools.

The liberal forces that pushed Brougham's investigation began the agitation in regard to schools for the poor. Though there were many in England who believed that it was politically dangerous (they'd read revolutionary works—*Blackwood's*, May 1825, p. 542) as well as economically inadvisable to give the new industrial proletariat an education, and though even a radical like Cobbett could object to teaching the poor to read on the basis that they would find only unenlightening lies in a censored Press (cf. Cole, *Life of William Cobbett*, p. 192), the liberals received enough support to make their agitation more effective than it was in regard to Public Schools. A sense of guilt among the upper classes, Whig theories of the necessity of an educated nation for the material progress of which they dreamed, and Benthamite logic, which maintained that democracy was the best government and education a necessary corollary to democracy, combined to bring about the beginnings of national education.

But from the very beginning there was disagreement. The Tories wanted the Church to educate the poor in order to keep them morally under their thumb; their conception of education was one of philanthropy and paternalism. The Whigs and radicals, imbued with French anti-clerical ideas, and naturally suspicious of Tory institutions, fought this tooth and nail. They both agreed on one aspect of the matter, however. Both fought State education just as they did in regard to Public Schools.

Since the two parties could not agree, and since they both feared the State, the education of the poor began in the hands of two voluntary philanthropic societies, one non-religious, the British and Foreign Society, the other under

Criticism and Defence, 1780–1830   139

hands.¹ Agitation for interference with Public School government had to wait until the thirties, and more particularly the sixties.

To the upper classes the independence of the Public Schools from the Government was the most sacred of all their features. Even those of the ruling classes who, in the thirties, ceased to be thoroughgoing conservatives, were not willing to sanction Government interference. Public Schools have responsibility to a 'far higher tribunal than that of public opinion'. They must do their own reforming.²

The arguments which conservatives advanced in defending school autonomy were of two kinds. State interference would have dire consequences; moreover such interference was contrary to custom and indeed illegal.

The first of these arguments was based in good part on the assumption that Parliament was unable and unwilling to preserve the essential characteristics of schools. No outsider could possibly understand the peculiar nature of Public Schools; this was an insight reserved for masters who had been through them.³ Moreover, Parliament did not desire such understanding, since it was, in Tory eyes, made up, even in 1818, of fiery-eyed radicals. Brougham's object

the governance of the Church of England, The National Society for Promoting the Education of the Poor in the Principles of the Established Church. Both societies were interested in procuring the cheapest education possible. They therefore welcomed the monitorial systems of Lancaster and Bell, nearly the only English educational discoveries of the time.
    Though the two systems are very similar, they became rivals because Lancaster, who frowned on teaching religion, was taken up by the British and Foreign Society, while Bell, who favoured religious instruction, became the mentor of the Church organization. The two societies fought for years over which was the real originator of the monitorial system. The Tory Southey, in his long biography of Bell, defends the Madras system and claims that Lancaster admits in his *Improvement in Education* (1805) that he was aided by it, though his system was already started when he heard of Bell. (Cf. Robert Southey, *The Life of the Rev. Andrew Bell*, 3 vols., London, 1844, Vol. II, pp. 116 ff.) Bell and Lancaster were not so much theorists as practical Englishmen who worked out a cheap way of teaching a number of pupils: the pupils teach each other.
    Through mutual instruction it was possible to educate the poor at a time when government aid was grudgingly given. Even so, it was necessary to secure State assistance in the thirties. A State system of compulsory elementary education had to wait until 1870. State secondary education is a growth of the very end of the century, and is not a finished system even to-day.
    ¹ *Westminster*, July 1825, pp. 153, 169 ff.   ² *The Eton System Vindicated*, p. 7.
    ³ Cf. *Quarterly Review*, August 1834, p. 128.

was to disparage 'the most revered institutions of this country' 'those illustrious seminaries, which have for ages contributed to form the character of English gentlemen'.[1] He and his followers were motivated by a 'disposition to subvert and discredit' those established institutions 'familiar from custom, or venerable from antiquity'.[2] They, and later parliamentary Whigs, wished to root up, not to reform.[3]

Feeling as they did about their opponents, conservatives naturally believed that 'subversion of many of the established and most highly important institutions of the country' would follow from a parliamentary investigation.[4] Such an investigation would destroy property rights, an argument based on the highly dubious contention that endowments were the private property of trustees. It would destroy reverence for authority, since the schools, independent of outside censure, were symbols of such authority. 'What wilful boy would have been flogged, without seeking his revenge by an anonymous impeachment of the master?' if this power of the master were subject to parliamentary check?[5] Finally, it would destroy traditional religion, of which the schools were the chief mainstay. The *Quarterly* asserted vehemently that 'the ample revenues of our Royal and Christian foundations shall never (while we have life to struggle for them) go to the support of schools for the professors of no particular religion'.[6]

The conservative recital of the disastrous consequences of parliamentary interference was accompanied by various forms of insistence on the schools' immunity from such interference. In general it was contended that no one had the right to touch that which was sacred because of its great age. As the *Quarterly* stated the matter, 'it is not seemly that the venerable establishments for English education should be called to plead for their existence (an existence in many instances as old as that of Parliament, . . . in all perhaps as

---

[1] Cf. *Quarterly Review*, July 1818, p. 494.
[2] *Vindication of Enquiry*, p. 31; W. L. Bowles, *Vindiciae Wykehamicae, etc.*, London, 1818, p. 5.
[3] *Quarterly*, July 1818, p. 518; *Etonensis, a Few Words in Reply to Some Remarks, etc.*, London, 1834, p. 3.
[4] Rev. Liscombe Clarke, *A Letter to H. Brougham, etc.*, London, 1818, pp. 5, 6.
[5] *Quarterly*, July 1818, p. 565.   [6] Ibid., July 1818, p. 568.

Criticism and Defence, 1780–1830 141

deeply interwoven with the habits and interests of this country); and to stand an inquiry, not whether they answer the purposes of their institution, but whether those purposes might not be advantageously changed'.[1] More specifically, Tories contended that the regulation of private property was the business of the House of Lords.[2] 'We have stricter notions of property' than to believe that its revenues can be parcelled out by the House of Commons.[3] Finally, conservatives argued that founders—to whom defenders paid even more lip-service than did liberals[4]—explicitly intended schools to be independent of outside interference.[5] In proof of this they cited the oath, to which a Winchester boy had to swear, that he would not reveal to the outside world the nature of school statutes.[6]

Only less obnoxious to the upper classes than the idea of Government control was that of destruction of the class nature of schools. The Public Schools were primarily upper-class institutions and were to remain so. Starting with this premise there was considerable disagreement as to whether any of the less-favoured classes ought to be admitted. Some, like De Quincey and Hallam, contended that they ought. Furthermore, they believed, what was only partially true, that not only did many poor actually go to a Public School, but that they mixed on a plane of equality with the rich. De Quincey's chief praise of schools is that they allow rich and poor to mix, the one paying, the other not.[7] Hallam, Gladstone says, 'heartily acknowledged and habitually conformed to the republican equality long and happily established in the life of our English public schools'.[8] Commendable as this attitude may have been, it is certain that in actuality few poor went to schools, and that Halévy's statement that 'common membership of the same school, a source of pride to all the boys alike, levelled every distinction of wealth or rank' was true only a certain distance down the social

---

[1] Ibid., July 1818, p. 568.   [2] (Holt) *Letter to Sir William Scott*, p. 79.
[3] *Quarterly*, July 1818, p. 567.   [4] Clarke, *Letter to Brougham*, p. 6.
[5] *Quarterly*, July 1818, p. 517.
[6] *Third Report from Select Committee, Minutes*, pp. 131–33.
[7] Thomas De Quincey, *Autobiographic Sketches*, Vol. II of *Works*, New York, 1876, p. 62.
[8] William Ewart Gladstone, *Arthur Henry Hallam*, Boston, 1898, p. 17.

scale.¹ It is significant, nevertheless, that many Englishmen were proud of their schools because these institutions supposedly mixed the aristocratic and the democratic, just as they applauded them because they represented both freedom and authority.

A number of alumni violently opposed the contention that poor and rich ought to mix. There were diehards who found only evil in the 'temporizing spirit of indiscriminate concession' which would allow those below the professional classes into the Public Schools. These are not 'the doctrines from which, in our youth, Public Schools derived their vigour'.² 'Why should we bring into undue contact, and unnecessary collision, those between whom an almost impassable gulf is to be fixed as soon as they cease to be schoolboys,' a gulf created by the 'wise policy of civilization'.³

If there was disagreement among the upper classes as to the desirability of admission of the poor, there was very little as to the legal right of the dispossessed to go to these schools. Few conservatives, no matter how tolerant they might be, could admit the validity of Brougham's contention that Public Schools were charity schools, since such an admission would not only have hurt Tory pride but would have been tantamount to renouncing the whole claim of the upper classes to the control of Public Schools. Occasionally a very clear-headed conservative did make such an admission, taking the very realistic position that the statutes offering a free education ought to be changed, since they no longer conformed to the facts.⁴ Usually, however, defenders clung to founders' intentions, and tried to prove that *pauperes et indigentes* meant 'poor scholars', not the 'lowest orders', and that schools did educate the poor clergy and thus fulfil founders' aims.⁵ As one liberal wrote bitterly, conservatives 'have not contended that by the expressions of the *poor and indigent scholar* as used in these documents, [the statutes] the rich are obviously designated, but only that such terms,

---

[1] Élie Halévy, *History of the English People in 1815*, New York, 1924, p. 46.
[2] *Letter from one Old Westminster*, p. 12.
[3] Ibid., p. 7.   [4] *The Eton System Vindicated*, p. 45.
[5] Bowles, *Vindiciae Wykehamicae*, pp. 13 ff; (Holt) *Letter to Sir William Scott*, p. 62; *Quarterly*, July 1818, p. 510.

Criticism and Defence, 1780–1830   143

when interpreted by practice and explained by inference and construction, point at the powerful, the favoured, and the well connected.'[1]

B. THE ATTACK ON PUBLIC SCHOOL EDUCATION

The majority of criticism levelled at the Public Schools centred around those features which had directly to do with education: the curriculum, discipline, and religious training, the prefect system, and boy life in general. This attack took, roughly speaking, two main directions: it concentrated on the nature and effectiveness of the intellectual training which schools offered: it concerned itself with moral results, with the contribution of schools to freedom, happiness, and virtue.

I. INTELLECTUAL EDUCATION

The revolt against the mental training given by the schools was much slower in developing and required longer to make itself felt than the denunciation of the social and moral effects of the educational process. Neither an exclusively classical curriculum nor antiquated teaching methods, the chief instruments of intellectual training,[2] aroused very widespread dissatisfaction until the thirties.[3] In part this was due to admiration for the present system. For a number of reasons to be discussed later, most Englishmen interested in schools approved of the classical training that boys

---

[1] *Vindication of the Enquiry*, p. 3.
[2] They were, as we shall see, in part instruments for moral training as well.
[3] Many who did not voice dissatisfaction undoubtedly felt it, however. Occasionally, one of these expressed himself in later years. Darwin, for example, wrote long after leaving school: 'Nothing could have been worse for the development of my mind than Dr. Butler's school, as it was strictly classical, nothing else being taught, except a little ancient geography and history. The school as a means of education to me was simply a blank.' (*Charles Darwin, His Life told in an Autobiographical Chapter*, etc., New York, 1893, p. 9.) He 'learnt absolutely nothing except by amusing myself by reading and experimenting in chemistry'. (Reginald Farrar, *Life of Frederic William Farrar*, New York, 1904, p. 104.) The bitter Trollope wrote that he was not even helped to learn the classics. 'There were twelve years of tuition in which I do not remember that I ever knew a lesson!' 'During the whole of those twelve years no attempt had been made to teach me anything but Latin and Greek, and very little attempt to teach me those languages.' (Trollope, *Autobiography*, pp. 16–17.)

received, and assumed that they profited by it.[1] Of these Englishmen, the majority were unaffected by those forces of the age which motivated the desire for new subjects, since they neither belonged to the class which represented these forces nor were influenced as yet by the competition of that class. They therefore preferred other subjects than the classics to be taught outside of schools,[2] and echoed the dictum of Dr. James of Rugby that 'young people are narrow-necked vessels, into which you cannot pour much at a time without waste and running over.'[3] In part the feebleness of the attack on intellectual training was due—and this applies to defence of intellectual education as well—to the comparative lack of interest in the intellect felt by most Englishmen. The average John Bull, whether middle class or aristocrat, hardly cared whether a boy learned anything at a Public School or not.

The criticism of Public School intellectual education proceeded from the moderate liberals and radicals. The former, as a whole far less concerned over the problem than the latter, contented themselves for the most part with attacks on details of classical instruction, rather than with suggestions as to new studies. Sydney Smith, who had so much to say in moral affairs, confined himself in his remarks on mental training to criticism of the scarcity of masters with its resulting idleness and indifference to learning and to denunciations of excessive verse-making![4] In his own schooldays he made, as he says, ten thousand Latin verses, 'and no man in his senses would dream in after-life of ever making another. So much for life and time wasted.'[5] His positive suggestions were limited to a plea for quick translations with the help of cribs, and did not envisage additions to the curriculum. Similarly, the *Edinburgh* in 1812—and this is the last word

[1] A large assumption, in the face of later testimony to the effect that few boys actually learned even the classics at a Public School.
[2] Cf. *Letters from a Nobleman to his Son, etc.*, 2 vols, London, 1810, Vol. I, p. 6; Rev. William Barrow, *An Essay on Education*, 2 vols., London, 1802, Vol. I, pp. 115 ff.
[3] S. Butler, *Life of Butler*, Vol. I, p. 18.
[4] Cf. reprint of Sydney Smith's *Edinburgh* article in *Public Education*, pp. 15-17.
[5] Lady Saba Holland, *A Memoir of the Reverend Sydney Smith*, 2 vols., London, 1855, Vol. I, p. 7.

on the subject by the Whig journal until 1830—went no farther in its advocacy of change than the sponsoring of a voluntary system in respect to Latin verses. It found even verse making good in itself, but contended that having it compulsory produced merely flogging and cheating. 'Why, then, insist on wringing a few meagre lines from hard-bound brains, by efforts that would be far more usefully directed to the common business of translating the classics?'[1] Finally, the *New Monthly* was chiefly concerned over the fact that 'Of all the youths crowded into a public school,' few found learning anything but a most irksome and detested slavery'. This state of affairs was due, it felt, less to the limited curriculum, than to master neglect and inability to teach and to the fact that schools 'are too much an affair of routine'.[2]

If moderate liberals occasionally envisage curriculum changes, their ideas, in contrast to those of radicals, were tentative and fragmentary. Thus Brougham went no further than to voice the hope that some day a cheap scientific education on the plan of the Scotch day schools would be possible in a 'great public school'.[3] Thomas Campbell, influenced by radical ideas, contended that 'it is a vestige of barbarism in our language that learning only means, in its common acceptation, a knowledge of the dead languages and mathematics'.[4] But in regard to Public Schools he did little more than to suggest that habits of application can be learned from German as well as from the classics.[5] It is noteworthy that in his reason for wanting modern subjects Campbell shows himself to be a very undemocratic Whig. He protested against the cant of 'venerable institutions' because he wished to preserve those institutions. The upper classes must be educated so that the poor will not revolt in disgust at the ignorance of their masters.[6]

For a thoroughgoing criticism of the fundamental structure of Public School intellectual training backed by a

[1] *Edinburgh*, November 1812, p. 395. Even this mild suggestion brought forth scathing comments from the *Quarterly*.
[2] *New Monthly*, 1823, p. 566. Also cf. 1827, pp. 171 ff., 478 ff.
[3] Brougham, *Practical Observations*, p. 36.
[4] *New Monthly*, 1824, p. 406.
[5] Ibid., 1829, p. 190. [6] Ibid., 1827, p. 479.

consistent liberal philosophy, one must turn to the eighteenth-century radicals and to their nineteenth-century followers. The leading eighteenth-century educational radicals were the Rousseauists. They are important partly for their direct attacks on schools: Edgeworth, in particular, criticized Public School training; he felt that even when schools taught Latin and Greek well, they were on the wrong track, for it was futile to study one subject so long at the expense of a general improvement of the understanding.[1] Chiefly they are important, however, for their abstract statement of those liberal principles which were in such direct contrast to the principles of Public Schools. Day and the Edgeworths combined Rousseau's naturalism with his appeal to the useful and with his sense-realism borrowed from Locke. They wanted a boy to learn what would be practically important to him as well as mentally stimulating and formative, and they wanted him to learn it through experience with kindly help and encouragement from a master.[2]

These ideas, in part or as a whole, were shared by most of the radical reformers of the time and later. Adam Smith, himself a Scotsman and therefore familiar with a broader system of education,[3] showed, in a fragmentary comment on Public Schools, that he was infected by Locke's preoccupation with usefulness. He criticized schools because a boy, after going through a Public School, could 'come into the world completely ignorant of everything which is the common subject of conversation among gentlemen and men of the world'.[4] Godwin, a radical though a defender of schools in most respects, shows evidence of innoculation with the other part of the radical theory. He wanted teachers to help and inspire boys to love of work rather than to be tyrants stuffing knowledge into unwilling heads.[5] Cobbett, at odds with the middle-class radicals on so many issues, could agree with them in their hate for the unreality of the 'Learned

---

[1] Maria and Richard Lovell Edgeworth, *Practical Education*, London, 1798, pp. 499 ff.
[2] Day, *Sandford and Merton*, pp. 253 ff.; *Memoirs of Richard Lovell Edgeworth*, 2 vols., London, 1820, Vol. I, p. 108.
[3] For remarks on Scotch education, cf. below, p. 201.
[4] Smith, *Wealth of Nations*, Vol. II, p. 263.
[5] William Godwin, *The Enquirer*, Edinburgh, 1823 (1797), p. 50.

Languages', 'which were once so serviceable to the monks and friars, and which are now kept as much in use as possible by all those who are desirous of making a mystery of what ought to be clearly and universally understood'.[1]

The most important group of nineteenth-century radicals were the Benthamites. It was they who most vigorously and thoroughly applied liberal doctrine to Public Schools.

Bentham himself had worked out a complete system of education along the lines suggested by the Edgeworths. He had intended to put his ideas into practice in a school based on Bell's system of mutual instruction, which was, like Hazelwood, to be a boarding-school for the upper classes.[2] But he alienated his backers by excluding theology, and all that remains is his plan, described in the *Chrestomathia*. Unlike the Hills, Bentham concentrated his attention on intellectual education. His book is a detailed discussion of the subjects to be taught and the methods of teaching them. They are to be such useful disciplines as arithmetic, botany, zoology, mechanics, languages, which will strengthen the mind, end superstition, and provide the groundwork for an occupation. These subjects are to be taught cheaply, in an interesting manner, and without the necessity for flogging. Bentham's aims and methods were thus completely revolutionary, since he desired useful knowledge with classics reduced to a minimum, and a pedagogical method which appealed to a child's love of learning. That Bentham was directly contrasting his system with that of Public Schools is evident from the following passage:

> 'It is a question not unworthy the consideration of mothers, even in the highest rank, whether they will have their sons taught a smattering of Latin and Greek by tasks and flogging at Eton, Winchester, and the Royal School at

[1] G. D. H. Cole, *The Life of William Cobbett*, p. 140. Cobbett's remarks appeared in the *Political Register*, August 15th 1807.
[2] Bentham apparently believed that Russell had been very successful in teaching the classics at Charterhouse with the aid of Bell's system. Bell, in his *Elements of Tuition*, also testified to Russell's success, as did Thomas Campbell in the *New Monthly* (1825, p. 7.) They were all, as we shall see, mistaken. (Cf. Jeremy Bentham, *Chrestomathia*, Vol. VIII of *Works of Jeremy Bentham*, by John Bowring, Edinburgh, 1843, introduction by Southwold Smith; and *Westminster*, January, 1824, pp. 64-65.)

Westminster, or in the way of pastime (without flogging) at the Chrestomathic School, within view of the august royal one.'[1]

The *Westminster*, organ of the philosophic radicals, in a review of Bentham's book in 1824, brought up the whole subject of intellectual education in Public Schools. This review contained the first really thorough attack on Public School subjects and methods. In keeping with Benthamite logic, the *Westminster* felt that the whole problem of what was useful to know and conducive to happiness, together with the methods of teaching, ought to be the subject of scientific study.

To-day, it complained, there is neither a plan in regard to subjects nor methods. We educate only scholars. 'No plan of instruction has been adopted for those who are to be engaged in the active business of life';[2] boys are taught nothing of the age or country in which they live nor of science. As to method, we have only the execrable Eton grammar. 'We are by no means unfriendly to the cultivation of classical literature; ... it is of great value, especially as a means of exercising the intellectual faculties, and as conducive to the formation of a pure and correct taste; to a gentleman it is highly ornamental; to a member of the learned professions, it is indispensable; but we object altogether to the mode in which it is taught; we object still more to the space which it is allowed to occupy in the common course of instruction; and we object to its forming any part of the education of a very important class of the community, to whom, at least as it is at present communicated, experience proves it to be utterly useless.'[3]

In July 1825 the Benthamites further expanded their

---

[1] *Chrestomathia*, p. 16.
[2] *Westminster*, January 1824, p. 45.
[3] *Westminster*, January 1824, p. 46. While the education of the rich was confined to the classics with hardly a dissenting voice, it is important to remember that the education of the poor, partly at least in very different hands and with no hampering traditions, was proceeding along very different lines. The left wing anti-clerical forces especially were providing for them the rudiments of an education that was later to frighten the Public Schools into reform. Brougham, Bell, Owen, Bentham, and others all agreed that education of the poor ought to be useful. Brougham's 'Society for the Diffusion of Useful

Criticism and Defence, 1780–1830   149

ideas. The modern world, they insisted, arose and flourished by despising its ancestors. It has progressed by politics, law, and chemistry, and 'in these ought we to seek for the objects of education'. Languages, words, are not enough. Even modern languages will not 'conduce towards cotton-spinning' or 'abolishing the poor laws'. There must be 'science, on which the wealth and power of Britain depend'.[1] Three years later the *Westminster* devoted an entire article to convincing the 'uppermost and middle classes of society' of the usefulness of science. 'We desire that science should at least take a conspicuous share in all general education,'[2] in proportion 'to its utility'.

The Benthamites have been accused of desiring an education that consisted in the mere stuffing of knowledge into boys' heads for practical materialistic purposes. In part the accusation is just. Desiring a happiness for man that consisted in satisfying his interests, they believed that man

Knowledge' encouraged the studying of politics, mathematics, economics, and the sciences through cheap popular texts. (A study of economics would not only teach boys to improve their lot, but—not at all incidentally—would show them that it was useless to revolt against the laws of nature as stated by Ricardo, which were so favourable to the rich.) Brougham approved the lecture system as instituted by Dr. Birkbeck at Glasgow as early as 1800 and furthered by the Mechanics Institute in London in 1823, as it would save time. (Cf. Brougham, *Practical Observations*, p. 21.) The poor were to be dosed with practical knowledge. They were also to be given moral instruction. Though the liberals were against religious instruction, they were very anxious to discourage crime among the poor. They therefore encouraged the Benthamite doctrine of rewards and punishments as a scientific means of getting boys to associate the moral with the pleasurable. Owen, who praised Bell's and Lancaster's work in this field, carried the principles of the French Rationalists and the English Utilitarians to their logical conclusions. Environment makes crimes. 'Any character . . . may be given to any community . . . by applying certain means; which are to a great extent at the command . . . of those who possess the government of nations.' (Owen, *New View*, p. 9.) You prevent crime by teaching that happiness can be obtained only by attaining conduct conducive to the happiness of the community.

Against the doctrines of the Whigs and Utilitarians the Tories opposed ideas which resembled, in origin at any rate, their views on Public School education. Thus Christopher North pled for the doctrine that, since the mind was not a *tabula rasa*, education ought to be a 'silent and spontaneous growth' not a stuffing of knowledge by the schoolmaster, and that it ought to be emotional and religious as well as intellectual. On the whole, Tory doctrines, really aimed at keeping the poor under the thumb of the Church, made less headway in the struggle over the education of the poor than liberal ones. (Cf. Professor Wilson, *Noctes Ambrosianae*, Edinburgh, 1855, Vol. II, pp. 106, 130, 394; Vol. III, pp. 201, 346.)

[1] *Westminster*, July 1825, pp. 150, 155, 175.
[2] Ibid., April, 1828, pp. 328, 330, 361.

must first know those interests. In order to do this he must grow intellectually. And, since the mind was conceived of as a machine, it grew by being fed with knowledge. This knowledge and the mental vigour derived from it could then be used to practical advantage.[1] Thus, Dr. Southwood Smith defines education as 'the process by which the mind of man, possessed with powers but unfurnished with ideas, is stored with knowledge and enabled to apply this to the business of life'.[2] In this definition lies the faith both in mere useful knowledge as the means to happiness and in success as its end.

The Benthamites were certainly concerned, in good part, with the inculcation of knowledge and its application to competition in the practical world. Yet their conception was broader than this, and included truly liberal ends. Dr. Southwood Smith, in the same article in which appeared the definition of education just quoted, penned another which claimed that to educate was 'to cultivate and enlarge the capacity to its utmost verge'.[3] Useful knowledge alone was not his end; even at its narrowest mental vigour was included in his conception of education. He merely claimed that 'the memory, the attention, and the taste, may be cultivated by useful as well as by useless knowledge'.[4] The *Westminster*, indeed, felt that clear thinking could be learned through the sciences better than through the classics.[5] At the same time it by no means despised literature; if it over-emphasized things as against words, this was in part a reaction against the complete denial of things by its opponents. Finally, the ultimate end of education was not a narrow individual success. The Benthamites were social reformers and wanted to enlighten the world in order to produce justice and humanity. If, later on, the accusation of interest in mere knowledge and in utilitarian ends levelled against many pleaders for new subjects was justified, the Benthamites are hardly to blame. False liberals speaking for a Philistine middle class narrowed and corrupted what was in essence, with all its faults, a noble liberal ideal.

[1] Cf. George L. Nesbitt, *Benthamite Reviewing*, New York, 1934, pp. 66 ff.
[2] *Westminster*, July 1825, p. 150.   [3] *Westminster*, July 1825, p. 154.
[4] Ibid., p. 153.   [5] Ibid., April 1828, p. 361.

2. MORAL EDUCATION

The fiercest controversy in the years before 1830 centred in those features of Public School life which were directly or indirectly responsible for moral and spiritual welfare; the institutions and life of boy society, and master discipline and religious teaching. Of these aspects the first was, as already indicated, the most important part of a Public School. The life that boys lived together was the chief agent in the moulding of character and the chief cause of the happiness or unhappiness of an individual's time at school. Consequently, boy social life received the bulk of the adverse—no less than of the favourable—comment aimed at upper-class institutions.

(a) BOY LIFE

All sections of critical opinion agreed to a certain extent in their attitude towards the miniature world of a Public School. Reactionaries and liberals alike found that it produced immorality. Boy society possessed moral standards, but they were those of boys and barbarians, not of civilized religious Englishmen; it developed character, but character of the wrong kind.[1] Here agreement ended, however. In

---

[1] That critics had solid grounds for their contentions in this respect seems undeniable. Much of what occurred at schools was undoubtedly contrary to any civilized conception of ethical conduct. *The Times* reported on one occasion that Harrow boys attacked a master smith 'with bludgeons and other weapons' (March 2nd 1825, p. 4). Poaching, theft, cruel practical jokes, gambling, heavy drinking, and sexual indulgence were common occurrences reported by friends no less than by enemies. (For detailed accounts cf. Moore, *Life of Byron*, pp. 86 ff.; Rouse, *Rugby*, pp. 170 ff.; Peake, *Memoirs of the Colman Family*, pp. 312 ff.; Tucker, *Eton of Old*, pp. 55 ff.; Moultrie, *Dream of Life*, pp. 62 ff.; Wilkinson, *Reminiscences*, p. 305; *Legacy of an Etonian*, pp. 105 ff.)

Even those who were most passionately attached to their alma maters suggested that school life was generally immoral. What Roundell Palmer wrote of his father was typical of the attitude of many. 'My father's experience of school life and of the world had, of course, made him aware of the moral evils, to the existence of which at Rugby (in a general way) our letters, more or less, bore witness; and, while it was not without full consideration that he determined to incur those risks for the sake of what he thought greater good, he felt them much.' (Roundell Palmer's *Memorials*, p. 79.) Palmer himself, though he loved school, found much bullying as well as a good deal of immorality at Rugby. His father advised him to bear the persecution and to report things 'of a corrupting as well as a tormenting kind'. (Roundell Palmer's *Memorials*, p. 78.) Thackeray, a warm defender of schools by the fifties, wrote in *Pendennis*,

the first place, liberals were at odds with reactionaries over the nature of the moral traits which they desired to inculcate. In the second place, they were concerned over other than strictly ethical matters. They were passionately interested in the happiness and freedom of the individual, and attacked boy society as much for tyranically and cruelly thwarting the weak and the eccentric as for encouraging immoral action.[1] As previously suggested, liberals were libertarians,

'Before he was twelve years old little Pen had heard talk enough to make him quite awfully wise upon certain points. . . . I don't say that the boy is lost . . . but that the shades of the prison house are closing very fast over him, and that we are helping as much as possible to corrupt him.' (Thackeray, *Pendennis*, edited by George Saintsbury, n.d., p. 20.) Just what 'corrupting' and 'corrupt' meant is, it may be added, one of the mysteries seldom explained by the Victorian reminiscers. Whether, for example, there was much of the later prevalent homosexuality, it is almost impossible to discover. Reference to unnamed evils by such as John Allen (Rev. R. M. Grier, *John Allen*, A Memoir by his son-in-law, London, 1889, p. 20) would lead one to suspect that there might have been. It was probably less widespread than later, since in earlier days, the older boys, having more freedom, could find more natural outlets for sexual desires outside of school grounds.

[1] As in the case of immorality there was ample evidence from friends no less than from enemies to substantiate liberal charges. Rowland Williams, on the whole a defender of schools, was a pale, shy boy who was almost killed by being tossed in a blanket; his biographer claims that he was scalped. (E. Williams, *Life of Rowland Williams*, Vol. I, p. 6.) Milnes Gaskell, adorer of Eton, reported bullyings and hardships in his first letters home. (Charles Milnes Gaskell, Editor, *Records of an Eton Schoolboy*, 1883, pp. 2 ff.) The friendly De Quincey stated that Dr. Mapleton took his sons from Winchester because fagging ruined their healths and could not be abolished since it was 'too venerable and sacred to be touched by profane hands'. (De Quincey, *Autobiographic Sketches*, p. 233.) De Quincey himself was threatened with annihilation if he continued to write good verses. (Ibid., p. 174.)

The less happy alumni gave, of course, more prolific, if less reliable evidence. Bentham agreed with Cowper that 'great schools suit best the sturdy and the rough'. Dean Hook is reported as saying of Winchester that 'the racket and bullying out of school are so great that he can get no time to pursue his favourite studies and meditations.' (Stephens, *Life of Dean Hook*, Vol. I, p. 9.) Macready wrote of Rugby that 'the system of bullying seemed to have banished humanity from most of the boys above me, or rather of those between me and the highest forms'. (W. C. Macready, *Reminiscences*, 1875, pp. 8 ff.) The Earl of Albemarle said that when he revolted against the prefect system his fag master used to make him stand at attention and then repeatedly knocked him down. He hated this 'promising pupil' of Dr. Page who made 'what were facetiously called my "hours for recreation"' so bitter. (George Thomas Keppel, Earl of Albemarle, *Fifty Years of My Life*, New York, 1876, p. 26.) The pious John Allen—later a friend of Tennyson and Thackeray and supposedly the prototype of Major Dobbin in *Vanity Fair*—found that his fear of God increased the bullying which was the order of the day, 'and more, perhaps, at Westminster then elsewhere'. The boys forced him to toast bread with his naked hands and broke forks over his back when he tried to resist looking at dirty pictures. (Grier, *Allen*, pp. 20 ff.) Lamb, in his second and unfavourable picture of Christ's Hospital, tells much of the

Criticism and Defence, 1780–1830   153

reactionaries authoritarians in the manner of older school traditions.

The earliest and, until 1810, the only critics of boy life were the Rousseauists and those under Evangelical influence. The latter, particularly the Evangelicals themselves, reserved their most concentrated efforts for attack on master failings, but many of them voiced objection to the conditions which were positively rather than negatively responsible for immorality. Francis Hodgson, who in 1840 became provost of

cruelties of monitors; 'the oppressions of these young brutes are heart-sickening to call to recollection'. They kept one from the fire on cold nights. They licked one for trivialities. One 'Nero' branded a boy. (Lamb, *Essays of Elia*, 'Christ's Hospital Five and Thirty Years Ago', Vol. II of Lucas Edition of Lamb's Works, p. 14.) On the other hand, Lamb could criticize the more aristocratic schools for faults not shared by his school. A Christ's Hospital boy had not the 'disgusting forwardness of a lad brought up at some other of the Public Schools'. (*Gentleman's Magazine*, June, 1813, p. 542.)

Peter Priggins (edited by Theodore Hook, Paris, 1841), written in the early forties, satirized Russell and his predecessor at Charterhouse under fictitious names. Before Russell there were the usual bullying, cowardly, sneaking fagmasters who would flog one for not warming their beds and against whom one could not complain (pp. 186 ff.). Peter learned at Charterhouse 'the sciences of cookery and shoe-blackery' and arts 'which, excepting at Rotherwick and other public schools, are generally profitably pursued by individuals beneath the grade of gentlemen' (p. 197). After Russell came, things were worse. Anthony Trollope, who suffered because of personal defects and his father's poverty as well as for the ordinary reasons that made schools unpleasant, has criticism for all phases of school life. (Trollope, *Autobiography*, p. 11.) As a child even his older brother Thomas Adolphus had whipped him daily—on the basis of prevention. That this is possible 'as a continual part of one's daily life, seems to me to argue a very ill condition of school discipline'. (Trollope, *Autobiography*, p. 8.) (In this connexion Thackeray himself spoke of 'the sacred privilege that an upper boy at a public school always has of beating a junior, especially when they happen to be brothers'.) (Cf. *Men's Wives*, p. 317, 'The Fight at Slaughter House', edited by George Saintsbury, London, n.d.)

Finally, it ought to be added that often the troubles of those who hated schools were admittedly not entirely the fault of the school, though an ideal educational institution might have made them happy. Of Sidney Walker, next to Shelley Eton's unhappiest offspring, Moultrie, his friend, could say that his abstractedness, his eccentricity, his slovenliness, coupled with his sarcasm and stubbornness caused a ridicule which became 'aggravated into a regular and permanent system of unrelenting persecution; disgraceful indeed to its perpetrators and abettors, but not altogether unprovoked on the part of its victim'. Walker was not meant for a Public School. (Cf. J. Moultrie, *The Poetical Remains of William Sidney Walker*, London, 1852, pp. x–xii.) Trollope admits that part of the reason that 'I was never spared', was his dirty, ugly slovenliness. (Cf. *Autobiography*, p. 4.) Even Mrs. Shelley can see that Shelley was a difficult boy for any school. 'On being placed at Eton, Shelley had to undergo aggravated miseries from his systematic and determined resistance to that law of a public school, denominated fagging. . . . Shelley would never obey. And this incapacity on his part was the cause of whatever persecutions might attend him, both at school and in his future life.' (Thomas Jefferson Hogg, *The Life of Percy Bysshe Shelley*, 2 vols., London, 1858, Vol. I, p. 27.)

Eton and helped Hawtrey in his work of reform, attacked the immorality of Harrow's and Eton's miniature world as early as 1801 in a letter to Harry Drury.[1] The future Bishop Thirlwall read Cowper at an early age and remarked that 'the intercourse of a number of boys, apart from their literary studies, I think fraught of necessity with all the evils the poet mentions'.[2] Knox, the Evangelical defender of schools, was only too conscious of the evils that resulted from unsuperintended boy life. Though in his *Liberal Education* he was careful to avoid speaking of them, in his more personal *Winter Evenings* he wrote of the daily torture that he suffered as a fag; his health and growth were affected by the 'wanton tyranny of my schoolfellows'. As an older boy he was a slave to public opinion that considered wickedness spirit and genius.[3] In another place he says that public opinion is a great danger because it makes virtue ridiculous.[4] Hannah More was well enough informed about schools to fight against Macaulay's going to one: 'Throwing boys headlong into those great public schools always puts me in mind of the practice of the Scythian mothers, who threw their new-born infants into the river;—the greater part perished, but the few who possessed great natural strength . . . came out with additional vigour from the experiment.'[5] Finally an anonymous author wrote a novel called *The History of a Schoolboy*, which well summed up the Evangelical position. *The History of a Schoolboy* tells of the trials and tribulations of a good boy at an 'eminent grammar school'. He has to cope not only with tyrannical leaders who, by their strength, make him obey 'what was called the custom of the school', and join them in illicit acts, but also with the negligent master, who does not support his moral monitors and beats boys only when they harm his property. In this novel, it may be added, the moral benefit that may be derived from

[1] James T. Hodgson, *Memoir of the Rev. Francis Hodgson*, 2 vols., London, 1878, Vol. I, p. 33.
[2] Connop Thirlwall, *Letters Literary and Theological*, London, 1881, p. 14.
[3] Vicesimus Knox, *Winter Evenings*, 2 vols., London, 1790, Vol. II, p. 232.
[4] Vicesimus Knox, *Essays, Moral and Literary*, 2 vols., New York, 1793, Vol. II, p. 33.
[5] Timbs, *Schooldays of Eminent Men*, p. 301.

Criticism and Defence, 1780–1830 155

fighting public opinion, emphasized by conservatives and later by Arnold, is made explicit in the hero.[1]

The Rousseauists, though for the most part they were not directly interested in Public Schools, voiced a number of pertinent criticisms of the life of those institutions. Though they desired a more democratic, humanitarian ethics than did the reactionaries, an ethics that glorified work and simplicity rather than obedience, they offered criticisms similar to those of Knox and Hannah More. Day's attitude was the most exaggerated and hostile. The Public School boy in his somewhat naïve book had 'every vice and folly that are usually taught at such places, without the least improvement of either his character or his understanding.'[2] He talked of actresses, mischief, pleasure parties, robbing orchards, insulting travellers, and rebelling against masters. All he cared for was the externals of dress and manner, and he had no heart.[3] Edgeworth, more practical than Day, was not content with mere accusation. If he found that boys learned in school that strength, power, and cunning govern society, he was concerned to find the cause of this state of affairs. He discovered it to lie in the fact that the leaders of the school were so often those who could not be improved at home.[4] Finally, Edgeworth's daughter Maria attacked directly in her novels that vicious public opinion which taught many of the most notorious of school vices. The *Barring Out* is the story of a rebellion in a small school against a good and kind master, led by a Public School boy who had learned ambition and party spirit at his former place of instruction.[5]

As the century entered its second decade the reactionaries and Rousseauists were joined by moderate liberals and radicals led by Sydney Smith. Smith's 1810 *Edinburgh*

[1] *The History of a Schoolboy*, London, 1787, pp. 18, 34–73.
[2] Day, *Sandford and Merton*, p. 263.
[3] Day's reverse snobbery influenced these last criticisms; they were probably less true than Chesterfield's very opposite stricture.
[4] Edgeworth, *Practical Education*, pp. 499 ff.
[5] *The Parent's Assistant*, London, 1897, p. 307. Maria has another story involving Public Schools. Her 'Eton Montem' is not an attack on public education, however; it uses two contrasting types of Eton boys as examples of honesty and independence on the one hand and of extravagance and snobbery on the other. (Cf. Ibid., pp. 172 ff.)

article and the support that it elicited immeasurably widened the arena of discussion. From the fall of Napoleon until the middle of the thirties all aspects of Public School boy life were the subject of continual comment by all shades of British opinion. And as time went on pressure for reform grew more and more powerful until, by the thirties, it proved an irresistible force.

Smith's attack was violent and provocative. It was the more forceful in that, since he had been a success at Winchester in both mischief and learning, he could not be accused of being personally spiteful. He always hated Winchester in spite of his success there. His wife reports that even 'in old age he used to shudder at the recollections of Winchester, and I have heard him speak with horror of the wretchedness of the years he spent there: the whole system was then, my father used to say, one of abuse, neglect, and vice'.[1] In the *Edinburgh* the tyranny of boy control chiefly aroused his ire. The sufferings and the obedience to tyranny of younger boys was out of all proportion, he felt, to what a boy would find in life. Injustice produced hatred, suspicion, and cunning in the young, and insolence and arrogance in the tyrants. The knowledge of the world that was gained was the mere knowledge of vice. There were not enough masters to take care of the average, the result being the survival of the fittest. 'This neglect is called a spirited and manly education.'[2]

Though Smith was viciously attacked at first, by the twenties he found many supporters. Brougham, co-editor of the Whig *Edinburgh* and leader of the fight on endowments, agreed with Smith that 'the only benefit that I ever heard ascribed to a premature emancipation of children is, that it is supposed to give them manly habits'. He did not think, however, that manliness was worth the price of 'such scenes of early manhood as have lately disgraced one of our public seminaries'.[3] Similarly, a *Times*' correspondent could warn the public that bullying and fagging were fatal to the lives of many, the health of more, and 'to the moral character

---

[1] Lady Holland, *Memoir of Sydney Smith*, Vol. I, pp. 17–18.
[2] Sydney Smith, in *Public Education*, pp. 3–10, 16, 17.
[3] Brougham, *Practical Observations*, p. 36, note.

and temper of all the unfortunate victims of them', and that 'the contamination arising from the licentious habits of the boys . . . poison the sources of moral dignity and self-esteem'. He threatened that the public would get a 'general dread of public education' if 'domestic discipline and superintendence' were not included in it.[1] Southey, though by the twenties neither a Whig nor a liberal in most matters, found himself in complete agreement with Smith. Though he saw that schools helped a boy to know himself and to conform to the world, he did not believe that as constituted these advantages made up for the disadvantages. For many students, particularly those with 'a tendency to . . . low vices, such schools are fatal'.[2] Southey's considered opinion was that at a Public School not only does a boy suffer from 'tyranny, which is carried to excess in schools,' but he has an excellent 'opportunity of acquiring or indulging malicious and tyrannical propensities himself'. 'His religious habits' are 'almost impossible to retain at school'.[3] In 1827 the *New Monthly* contained two fierce attacks on the cruelty and immorality of schools. The author of one of these felt that the eulogistic 'commonplaces which are trumpeted forth about public schools, are little less than dull, old, impudent delusions'. He had found fagging to consist of beatings, tyranny, kicks, curses, and reproaches, which made his school life one of 'toil and misery and neglect'. The system was 'the most barbarous and senseless tyranny that ever was exercised by fools of a larger size over poor creatures of a less', and produced cruelty and 'abject, pining submission'.[4]

[1] *The Times*, November 26th 1823, p. 3.
[2] 'Recollections of the Early Life of Robert Southey,' from *The Life and Correspondence of Robert Southey*, edited by his son, the Rev. Charles Cuthbert Southey, New York, 1855, p. 56.   [3] Ibid., p. 38.
[4] *New Monthly*, 1827, pp. 171, 175, 177, 478. That Public Schools were not the only ones attacked for producing tyranny and vice is evident from many of Crabbe's poems, which certainly do not deal with English Public Schools. In one poem he wrote:
      'You saw, . . . in that still-hated school,
      How the meek suffer, how the haughty rule;
      There soft, ingenuous, gentle minds endure
      Ills that ease, time, and friendship fail to cure:
      There the best hearts, and those who shrink from sin,
      Find some seducing imp to draw them in.'
(Cf. *The Life and Poetical Works of George Crabbe*, 'Tales of the Hall', Book III, p. 385, Boys at School, London, 1901.)

In 1828, in what was called the Winchester fagging row, liberals and others were given a chance to air their views about the central bone of contention, the government of boys by boys. The quarrel is particularly interesting as revealing the relative importance to liberals of freedom and kindness in comparison with morality. The fight was precipitated by the expulsion of six boys who had rebelled against prefectorial authority. Dr. Williams, the head master, supported W. G. Ward, the head prefect, and the liberals rose up to denounce cruelty and absolutist discipline on the part of the head master and the head prefect. The interesting thing is that Ward, far from representing the old Tory attitude, was a representative of the new religious revival, just the kind of boy whom Arnold at Rugby was supporting with might and main. Later a leader in the Oxford Movement, and as a boy sensitive, melancholy, and unathletic, it was his religious earnestness and conscientiousness that precipitated the rebellion. 'His ideas of discipline, and of his own duty in enforcing it, were very strict and high.'[1] He felt 'horror at the immorality prevalent at Winchester, startling in its degree to most of those who conversed with him on the subject', and tried to stop it.[2] Sir Alexander Malet, the brother of an expelled boy, claiming that he loved his school and was not against prefects or fagging, protested modestly against the doctrine that prefects should be upheld whether they were right or wrong.[3] Dr. Williams replied, in typical official fashion, that the authority of prefects must be vindicated if discipline was to continue. 'Obedience to the Praefects is required by the usage and laws of the School.'[4] Malet replied a bit testily that he objected to the doctrine of submission to anything a prefect did.[5]

After this the fight became general. The philosophic radicals were, as one would expect, the most passionate adversaries of the system of fagging. The *Westminster*'s

[1] Cf. Wilfred Ward, *William George Ward and the Oxford Movement*, London, 1889, p. 15. [2] Ibid., p. 10.
[3] Sir Alexander Malet, *Some Account of the System of Fagging at Winchester School, etc.*, London (1828 (?)), pp. 3 ff.
[4] Malet, *Account of Fagging*, p. 16. [5] Ibid., p. 21.

contribution to the controversy was a slashing libertarian assault on the whole school system. The worst possible training for the upper classes, it felt, was teaching tyranny by first teaching slavery. Those who rebelled were—grandiloquently—symbols of man's struggle for good government. 'To black shoes under penalty of being beaten for noncompliance, is slavery in man or boy.' Defenders say that if fagging goes, the whole system goes. Splendid. Already the middle and upper classes have founded the University of London. Why not a school in connexion with this? 'The new institution is the legitimate produce of the disgust universally entertained for the absurdities of the old ones.'[1]

The moderate liberals, though less sweeping in their attacks, were no less violent than the radicals. The *Literary Gazette*[2] stated that Malet's pamphlet brought 'the detestable system of *fagging* as practised at our leading schools distinctly before the public'. The system produced tyrants, for fags, 'when raised to authority cannot be expected to resist the malevolent passion for making others suffer in turn as they have suffered'. Boys 'have their lives sacrificed' or at best lose for ever a 'right tone of feeling', 'purity', 'high notions of self-respect', and 'every gentleman-like sense of dignity'. In true liberal fashion, the writer said that the purpose of the system was to make juniors 'the passive, though discontented—the obedient, though growling, menials of a set of premature despots'. 'Woe be to the lad of independent and honest spirit' who revolts. He will be expelled by a master whose 'prejudices are in favour of that system out of which he has come an eminently learned and estimable man' and who will therefore prefer discipline to common sense. The *New Monthly* joined the fray with an attack on the outworn systems of discipline in Public Schools, which 'tend to cow the timid spirit, to repress talent of the higher order, to stifle genius, and to uphold the physically, in preference to the intellectually strong'. Public Schools are 'models of instruction in arbitrary power and abject slavery'.

[1] *Westminster*, January 1829, pp. 244–48.
[2] November 22nd 1828, pp. 745 ff.

Fagging results in the degradation of free spirit. It makes most Public School graduates the 'most overbearing, haughty, irrational men of their order upon the face of the earth'.[1]

Finally, even the *Quarterly Review* joined in the controversy on the liberal side, indicating that some political Tories were ceasing to be thorough educational conservatives. It believed that fagging could not much longer 'be permitted to continue in schools'. How, it asked, could masters 'have suffered boys to establish among themselves the law of the strongest, and reduce tyranny to a system'. 'There is nothing to be said in defence of the system which might not be applied in defence of the slave-trade, or the Turkish despotism.'[2]

(b) THE MASTERS

The chief criticism of the masters was negative rather than positive: they were accused not of causing but failing to prevent tyranny and immorality. Liberals and reactionaries alike levelled their attacks in the main at what they believed to be master neglect of the happiness or moral welfare of their pupils.[3] Knox, for example, wrote, 'It is to be regretted, that . . . very little attention has been paid to moral instruction. . . . the whole time appropriated to instruction is engaged in the pursuit of literature alone'.[4] Southey, in his liberal days, condemned Public Schools

---

[1] *New Monthly*, 1829, pp. 186, 188.   [2] *Quarterly*, January 1829, p. 142.

[3] Writers of reminiscences, many of them friendly to Public Schools, admitted the justice of the charge of neglect. Rowcroft wrote in the thirties that 'at a public school it is not a moral, but a classical education that is aimed at'. Boys 'were exposed to the caprices, or the tyranny, and to the bad examples of one another, almost without check or control'. (Rowcroft, *Confessions of an Etonian*, Vol. I, p. 38.) Lord John Russell found that masters 'confine their attention to the Latin and Greek which they are engaged to teach'. (Spencer Walpole, *The Life of Lord John Russell*, 2 vols., London, 1899, Vol. I, p. 9.) Dean Merivale contended that the neglect of boys was unbelievable; the idea of teaching godliness had perished from the land. (Merivale, op. cit., p. 217.)

A few masters such as Parr and Butler, it will be remembered, did concern themselves about morals. Parr claimed that he taught boys to respect themselves and thus prevented low and unworthy actions. Butler felt that he 'has the charge' of boys' 'morals as well as their learning'. (Cf. Field, *Life of Parr*, Vol. I, p. 51; S. Butler, *Life of S. Butler*, Vol. I, p. [11].)

[4] Vicesimus Knox, *Liberal Education*, 2 vols., London, 1789, Vol. II, pp. 77–78.

Criticism and Defence, 1780–1830   161

chiefly 'for the abominable tyranny which the masters, knowingly, allow to exist'.[1]

In part the blame for master neglect was laid elsewhere than at the master's door. Sydney Smith and others realized that there were too few teachers to handle the hordes of young aristocrats that peopled Eton and Harrow. Knox blamed master failure on a 'defect in . . . [the] constitution' of schools and not on 'the present superintendents'.[2] A great many critics were at pains to point out that it was outworn instruments of education that were responsible for inadequate moral training. But most writers censored the masters at least in part, accusing them of making no use of existing means of ethical instruction. Particularly was this true of a group of Evangelicals who, at the turn of the century, led a direct and concentrated attack on the inadequate religious education given at schools.

The reactionary attack was opened by an important Churchman, Dr. Rennell, who, in a note to a sermon, accused Public School masters of failing to provide adequate religious instruction. Somewhat later the Bishop of Meath stated in a sermon that he had intended to say a few words on the 'sad degeneracy of our Public Schools, in this most important part of education, and their systematic neglect of that religious instruction which in the earlier parts of the Reformation, and even to a much later date, was so carefully provided for the . . . wealthier classes of the British youth', but that Dr. Rennell had anticipated him in calling attention 'to this portentous evil.'[3] This evoked an answer from Dr. Vincent, head master of Westminster School, for Vincent had had Westminster especially exempted from Rennell's charge, and now felt unjustly treated. Vincent's defence drew fire from a number of Evangelicals and thus precipitated a public controversy.[4]

---
[1] *Selections from the Letters of Robert Southey*, by John Wood Warter, 4 vols. London, 1856, Vol. IV, p. 158.
[2] Knox, *Liberal Education*, Vol. II, pp. 177–78.
[3] Quoted from William Vincent, D.D., *A Defence of Public Education*, London, 1802, p. 10.
[4] There were few to defend religious teaching in the schools. Even the staunchest of later defenders admitted deficiencies in this respect. At the ecclesiastical schools religion had, in the hands of fellows, become a dead letter, and at the other schools things were little better. Boys were irreligious. As

Dr. Rennell's original words, both in content and tone well illustrate the reactionary point of view with its concern for out-moded ideals and the preservation of the political *status quo*. It is ironical that Dr. Vincent should have considered Rennell radical enough to be compared with Tom Paine. 'We cannot but lament,' wrote Rennell, 'that in very few of our best-endowed seminaries, the study of Christianity has that portion of time and regard allotted to it, which the welfare of society, the progress of delusive and ruinous errors, and the true interest of sound learning itself, seems at the present time, peculiarly to call for. In some of them, and those not of small celebrity or importance, all consideration of the revealed will of God is passed over with a resolute, systematic, and contemptuous neglect, which is not exceeded by that which the French call their national institute.' The gloomy results of this neglect are that learning, 'deprived of the blessing of Almighty God,' declines, 'indolence and dissipation, even in these retreats, will have their perfect work, and in a short period even the very form and external appearance of discipline and instruction will perish'. 'Young men of rank and talents are dismissed into

T. A. Trollope said: 'We Englishmen were not a devout people in the days when George the Third was king'; boys' religion consisted in abhoring religious feelings as 'very ungentlemanlike propensities'. (T. A. Trollope, *What I Remember*, pp. 136–37.) At Eton, chapel was cheerless, dull, and mechanical; sermons were long, and, since given by old men, tedious and impossible to hear. The whole proceeding bred indifference. Confirmation was a joke. (Tucker, *Eton of Old*, p. 121.) As Gladstone wrote: 'Religion was non-existent then at Eton.' The only religion he received was a plea against Catholic Emancipation. Bishop Pelham had told him 'to maintain the practice of piety, without lukewarmness, and above all, without enthusiasm'. (Cf. Benson, *Fasti Etonenses*, pp. 499–500.) Convention ruled in the formal world of Church religion; if a boy carried a Prayer Book on a weekday, he was denounced as a Methodist; if he did not on a Sunday, he was an atheist. At Winchester, despite surface loyalty to ecclesiastical traditions and to great churchmen like Lowth and Ken, the same conventionality and failure to come to grips with the religious problem prevailed. (Cf. John Henry Overton and Elizabeth Wordsworth, *Christopher Wordsworth*, London, p. 15; Stephens, *Lord Hatherley*, Vol. I, pp. 14–15.) Manning wrote that at Harrow there was no religious guidance, no piety, not even a chapel to go to. (Purcell, *Manning*, Vol. I, p. 18; Charles Wordsworth, *Early Life*, p. 20.) At Charterhouse 'morality and religion were ignored by the seven clergymen who reaped fortunes by neglecting five hundred boys'. (Martin Farquhar Tupper, *My Life as an Author*, London, 1886, p. 21.) Even Butler at Shrewsbury was unable to fight irreligion: the trustees, fearing a Popish or Methodist Head, would not allow him to have a chapel and end the disorders caused by boys going to the town chapel. (Butler, *Life of S. Butler*, Vol. I, p. 82.)

the world, without one single safeguard against those plausible and tremendous theories, which have turned more than one quarter of the world into an Aceldama, or hell of blood.' Without religion these men may work for 'the subversion of order, and the destruction of their native country'.[1]

The supporters of Rennell were legion,[2] but only the two most important need be mentioned here, John Bowdler and William Wilberforce, the leaders of the Evangelical movement. Their points of view were identical with Rennell's. Both were ardent supporters of a traditional religion which they felt was being neglected at Public Schools. Wilberforce, reporting a conversation with Bowdler, noted: 'Much talk about education. He agreed that public school inadmissible, from its probable effects on eternal state.'[3] Bowdler himself wrote: 'In contemplating the characters of both boys and men in the higher classes of society, the most general and radical defects appear to be,—the want of *devotion* and the not making Religion *the rule of life*'.[4]

Evangelical criticism implied change despite its reactionary purposes. An anonymous supporter of Rennell railed in very modern terms against unreasoning loyalty to institutions which needed to have the ravages of centuries remedied. He did not consider himself an innovator; but he felt that changed times demanded changed institutions, a very liberal sentiment. Realizing that the age was increasingly democratic, rational, and materialistic, he saw that only change could fight change.[5]

Though the chief accusation against masters was negative, there was a positive criticism levelled at them as well. Because they flogged boys, they were attacked as creators of no less than as connivers at slavery and unhappiness.

[1] Thomas Rennell, *A Sermon Preached in the Cathedral Church of St. Paul, London, on Thursday, June 6, 1799*, London, 1799, note A, p. 18.
[2] Such Evangelical writings as Jones's *Considerations on the Religious Worship of the Heathens*, Gisborne's *Familiar Survey of the Christian Religion*, and Dr. Randolph's *Sermons Preached during Advent*, all mention the pagan nature of Public School education.
[3] Robert Isaac Wilberforce, *Life of William Wilberforce*, 5 vols., London, 1838, Vol. III, p. 348.
[4] Thomas Bowdler, *Memoir of the late John Bowdler*, London, 1825, p. 191.
[5] *Remarks on the Rev. Dr. Vincent's Defence of Public Education*, London, 1802, pp. 26–28.

The tyranny of the brutal master with the rod had been a favourite theme of unhappy alumni and liberals long before the end of the eighteenth century. But after the French Revolution, attacks on flogging became more frequent, and continued to increase through most of the nineteenth century.[1]

Since the numerous criticisms of masters' severity exhibit a monotonous similarity, it is not necessary to discuss most of them here. Only two, one by Southey, written while he was at school, and one by Thackeray penned long years after his Charterhouse days, merit attention as representing important and rather different points of view.[2]

Southey's attack, which caused his expulsion from Westminster despite an apology to the head master, appeared as the fifth number of a magazine which he edited in the early nineties called the *Flagellant*. This attack is interesting as illustrating the political libertarianism which, under the influence of French philosophy, animated the discontented at the end of the eighteenth century. Southey argued, in terms familiar to Tom Paine, 'I never yet heard of the divine right of schoolmasters.' He has found them 'illiterate,

[1] Even at the end of the eighteenth century there was still a comparative reticence in regard to master cruelty. Men like Landor, Coleridge, Shelley, and Bentham, who suffered most from it, have studiously refrained from writing diatribes on the subject. Landor, whose 'hot and resentful impatience alike of contradiction and of authority' caused him so much trouble, was entirely silent in regard to his schooldays. (Sidney Colvin, *Landor*, New York, 1881, p. 11.) Coleridge, except for an occasional remark about the stern Bowyer, was equally uncommunicative. Bentham mentioned, though he did not protest directly against, the brutal flogging at the Westminster of his day. (Everett, *Bentham*, p. 11.) Shelley hated speaking of his schooldays at all. His wife, however—who, it must be admitted, knew very little about schools—denounced Shelley's masters for him. She painted the tyrant in vivid colours: 'His frowning brow; the rod uplifted in one hand; the book, the fatal, incomprehensible book, in the other; the slave, that cowed, fearful, and stammering, stands before him, his cheek already tingling with the expected blow! This is no caricature of a schoolmaster; such is the picture universally acknowledged as his prototype'. (Hogg, *Life of Shelley*, Vol. I, p. 29.)

[2] Thackeray's attack belongs technically to a later period, but it refers so definitely to the twenties that it seems best to include it here. The same may be said for two bitter reminiscences of master brutality at the great day schools. In one of these Charles Mathews accused his master at Merchant Taylors of a perverted love of flogging. 'I was "too lively" for him, and animal spirits were unpardonable things in his eyes.' (Charles Dickens, editor, *Life of Charles J. Mathews*, New York, 1879, p. 4.) In the other, Ballantine contended that the masters at St. Paul's were in the habit of throwing books at yawning boys. If they produced contusions, they were overjoyed. All that they knew of 'human nature' was that boys were capable of suffering. (Mr. Serjeant Ballantine, *Some Experiences of a Barrister's Life*, London, 1883, p. 4.)

Criticism and Defence, 1780–1830

savage, and unrelenting. They endeavour, by discipline, to inculcate the doctrine of passive obedience, enforce it by stripes, and sour the tempers, and break the spirit of their unfortunate subjects, who in their turn, exercise the same tyranny over their inferiors, till the hall of learning becomes only a seminary for brutality.' 'Corporal punishment appears to me to be a method equally disgraceful and ineffectual.' Southey has heard that sixpence a quarter is paid for birches at 'a certain royal and illustrious seminary', and he feels that the whole business is an invention of the devil and therefore a form of idolatry.[1] Southey's bitterness at tyranny was increased by expulsion, and in 1798 he could write: 'I am no friend of public schools. Where they are beneficial to one they are ruinous to twenty.'[2] Later on, like Coleridge, Southey lost his revolutionary fervour, and even his hate of schools. But memories of flogging continued to infuse bitterness into his comments.

Thackeray's diatribe, unlike Southey's and like Steele's, was more that of the soft-hearted humanitarian than of the libertarian radical. Though political liberalism entered in, Thackeray, along with so many Victorians, cared less to cultivate moral freedom than to produce happiness.

Thackeray's inspiration was the pompous and unsympathetic Russell at Charterhouse, of whom Tupper had said that he 'despotically drilled' a large school 'into passive servility and pedantic scholarship', and who once, when angry, supposedly smashed a child's head between two books.[3] But Thackeray generalized his hate for Russell in his *Punch in the East* into a crucifixion of the schoolmaster in general: 'I always had my doubts about the classics,' he wrote. 'When I saw a brute of a schoolmaster, whose mind was as coarse-grained as any ploughboy's in Christendom; whose manners were those of the most insufferable of Heaven's creatures, the English snob trying to turn gentleman; whose lips, when they were not mouthing Greek or grammar, were yelling out the most brutal abuse of poor little cowering gentlemen standing before him; when I saw this

---
[1] *The Flagellant*, London, 1792, signed Robert Southey, p. 77.
[2] Southey, *Letters*, Vol. I, p. 60.   [3] Tupper, *My Life*, p. 14.

kind of man (and the instructors of our youth are selected very frequently indeed out of this favoured class) and heard him roar out praises of, and pump himself up into enthusiasm for, certain Greek poetry,—I say I had my doubts about the genuineness of the article.' Standing in Athens, Thackeray 'cursed the country which has made thousands of little boys miserable'; he wanted to make 'a sacrifice to the manes of little boys flogged into premature Hades'.[1] All through his life Thackeray kept returning to this question of master tyranny. As late as the sixties he wrote: 'Remember . . . the tingling cheeks, burning ears, bursting heart, and passion of desperate tears, with which you looked up, after having performed some blunder, whilst the doctor held you to public scorn before the class, and cracked his great clumsy jokes upon you—helpless, and a prisoner! Better the block itself, and the lictors, with their fasces of birch-twigs, than the maddening torture of those jokes.'[2]

(c) REMEDIES

To a certain extent reactionaries and liberals were in agreement as to the remedies for immorality and tyranny. They both believed that more master control of boy activity was necessary if the schools were to continue. The reactionaries, theoretic believers in authority, naturally favoured stricter surveillance. But moderate liberals like Thomas Campbell of the *New Monthly*[3] and Sydney Smith[4] no less than radicals like Maria Edgeworth[5] realized that a *laissez-faire* system was bound to have effects which they deplored.

Reactionaries and liberals differed chiefly in their conception of master government and in the extent to which they were interested in disrupting the existing institutions of boy life. As to the first, reactionaries, since they aimed at

[1] *Punch in the East*, edited by George Saintsbury, London, n.d., p. 36.
[2] *Roundabout Papers*, No. 5, 'Thorns in the Cushion', p. 39.
[3] *New Monthly*, Vol. XIX, 1827, p. 478. Campbell, indeed, committed himself to the very reactionary sentiment that boys come to school not to command but to obey.
[4] Sydney Smith, in *Public Education*, pp. 86 ff. Also *The Times*, November 26, 1823, p. 3.
[5] *Parent's Assistant*, p. 307.

returning to old ideals, were satisfied with previously existing conditions. Except for their desire to censor the classics, they offered no suggestions as to changes in the methods used by masters. Flogging and formal religious instruction were to be increased, not changed. There were to be compulsory prayers and frequent Scripture readings.[1] Liberals, on the other hand, were dissatisfied with present methods. The Rousseauists and philosophical radicals in particular hated the reliance on both severity and precept, and advocated kindness, rational punishments, and teaching by example.[2] Human nature, essentially good, was to be allowed to develop naturally. Morality was to be produced by conditioning (to use the modern phrase) not by direct inculcation. As Edgeworth wrote, 'The general principle that we should associate pleasure with whatever we wish that our pupils should pursue, and pain with whatsoever we wish that they should avoid, forms, our readers will perceive, the basis of our plan of education.'[3] This conception was, unfortunately, abhorrent to the religious people who ran schools. For it implied the absence of that absolute morality which, to them, was a *sine qua non* of Christianity.

In regard to boy government and the question of boarding-schools in general, the reactionaries were not prepared to offer suggestions. Occasionally, like the extreme liberals, they lost interest in Public Schools entirely,[4] but in so far as they had any positive remedies for conditions, they seldom advocated drastic changes in school organization. The liberals, on the other hand, moderates and radicals alike, almost all urged considerable modification in the structure of school life. Indeed, had these reformers had their way, Public Schools would have been unrecognizable to one who had known them at the beginning of the nineteenth century.

There were two schools of thought among the liberals. On the one hand were those like Southey, Sydney Smith, Brougham, and almost all of those who contributed on the

[1] Cf. J. Bowdler, *Memoirs*, p. 191; *Remarks on Dr. Vincent's Defence*, pp. 26 ff. Bowdler claimed that the works of pagan authors contained 'the dangerous poison of impure ideas, adorned with all the charms of elegance and harmony'.
[2] *Parent's Assistant*, p. 307; *Westminster*, January 1824, p. 75.
[3] Edgeworth, *Practical Education*, p. 713.
[4] Cf. *History of a Schoolboy* and *Westminster Review*, January 1829, pp. 244 ff.

critical side to the Winchester fagging controversy, who entirely despaired not only of boy self-government but of boarding-schools as well. Southey wrote that he would 'gladly send a son to a good school by day; but rather than board him at the best, I would, at whatever inconvenience, educate him myself'.[1] Brougham and Smith both wanted schools, preferably day schools, of twenty or thirty boys in which the so-called freedom of boys would be checked by parents or masters.[2]

On the other hand, there were many who, innoculated with *laissez-faire* ideas, were, though equally radical, unwilling to destroy entirely the self-government of boys in a large boarding-school. One of these, Thomas Wright Hill, concocted a plan, which, with the subsequent help of his sons, Matthew Davenport and Rowland, he put into practice in an actual school at Hazelwood, that would preserve freedom and yet do away with its worst evils. This plan and its concrete results they outlined in 1822 in a book called *Public Education*.[3]

For a time there was great enthusiasm in England about the Hills' plan. Bentham approved of it, Jeffrey reviewed *Public Education* favourably in the *Edinburgh*, and De Quincey, though he objected to the Hills' Jacobinism, called it the most original experiment since the Edgeworths.[4] Even Dr. Arnold was influenced by it. The school itself was a huge success. Then interest began to flag, and before long the school had disappeared. It has been virtually forgotten to-day.

Why this was so we shall have plenty of opportunity to see later. Its ideas were too new and its break with the past too abrupt to appeal to most upper-class Englishmen so long as a more moderate substitute could be found. Middle-class attachment to the Hills' doctrine was predicated on despair of such a substitute. But at the end of the twenties Arnold

[1] 'Recollections of the Early Life of Robert Southey', in Southey, *Life and Correspondence of Robert Southey*, p. 38.
[2] Sydney Smith in *Public Education*, pp. 21 ff.; Brougham, *Practical Observations*, p. 36, note.
[3] Cf. R. and G. Hill, *The Life of Sir Rowland Hill*, 2 vols., London, 1880, Vol. I, pp. 100 ff. For the more extended title see Note I, p. 170.
[4] Thomas De Quincey, *The Collected Writings*, edited by David Masson, London, 1897, Vol. XIV, p. 9.

provided a solution of the moral problem which did not necessitate destruction of the schools or involve a thoroughgoing liberalism, and thus it was Arnold and not the Hills who has lived as England's great educator.

The Hills started from scratch and produced a revolutionary and scientific system by the aid of reason, in much the same way that the English thought that the French Revolution produced a government. They felt that education was in so bad a state that one had to sweep away all past ideas. The Hills' scheme was thoroughly libertarian in nature; even more than immorality the Hills disliked tyranny and authoritarian morality. The words of their biographer in regard to Arnold indicate their divergence from him in this respect. 'Had he thought a little more of suffering and a little less of sin, he would have been a better master and a greater man.'[1] As to Public Schools in general, Hill wrote, 'These ancient foundations boast, and with justice, of the famous men whom they have reared. They are proud of their traditions; and yet I can never visit one of those old schools without seeing rise before my mind a long line of unhappy children who were too gentle, too delicately wrought for the rough and brutal world into which they were suddenly thrown.'[2]

The object of the Hills was to encourage self-development and a democratic and humanitarian morality. In order to bring about these ends they scientifically applied the principles of the Edgeworths and of Bell and Lancaster to moral training in a school.[3] To begin with, they substituted a kindly and rational control by masters for the brutal laxity of the older schools. They frowned on undue restraint, and they encouraged self-instruction by attempting to arouse the interest of boys in studies of their own choice. As Rowland Hill's biographer said, there was 'a great want of reverence for authority in his school'.[4] The Hills believed, contrary to the opinion of Cowper and others, that there was too much at least of the wrong kind of surveillance in Public Schools.

[1] R. and G. Hill, *Life of Rowland Hill*, Vol. I, p. 100.
[2] Ibid., p. 101.
[3] Cf. De Quincey, *Works*, Vol. XIV, pp. 9-12.
[4] R. and G. Hill, *Life of Rowland Hill*, Vol. I, pp. 102-3.

Their object was to break down the barrier between boy and master, and thus to encourage originality as well as morality.[1] Most important of all, they substituted for the oligarchical prefect system based on tradition, a form of democratic self-government based on a written constitution. Nothing so well indicates the difference between Hazelwood and say Winchester as this particular, for it symbolized the difference in the spirit of the two systems. One was rational and equalitarian, the other prescriptive and aristocratic. At Hazelwood rank was conferred by mental or moral excellence, not by age or strength, a feature which Arnold copied to a large extent. Punishments were given at trials conducted by the boys themselves and were based on complicated written laws. Boys were elected to important offices.[2]

How this system worked out in practice it is hard to say. In theory it seems very close in many ways to modern progressive education, certainly a great deal closer than Public Schools were able to come for many years. It has remained, however, a mere curiosity of early radical educational ideals. The main line of development ran elsewhere.[3]

C. THE DEFENCE OF PUBLIC SCHOOL EDUCATION

The defence of Public School education was no more a consistent whole than was the liberal and reactionary attack on upper-class training. Different conservatives[4] concentrated their praise on diverse aspects of the educational

[1] (Matthew Davenport Hill, *Public Education*) *Plans for the Government and Liberal Instruction of Boys in Large Numbers*, etc., London, 1894 (1822), pp. 165 ff.
[2] (M. D. Hill, *Public Education*) pp. 9 ff., and R. and G. Hill, *Life of Rowland Hill*, Vol. I, pp. 122 ff.
[3] In one way Hazelwood seems to have been similar to Rugby under Arnold. According to one old boy, at any rate, the responsibility that was encouraged was disastrous. Hazelwood became a moral hotbed, a home of prigs. 'The thoughtlessness, the spring, the elation of childhood were taken from us. We were premature men. . . . The school was, in truth, a moral hotbed, which forced us into a precocious imitation of maturity. . . . Some of us had a great deal of the prig about us.' (Quoted in John Corbin, *Schoolboy Life in England*, New York, 1898, p. 157.)
[4] A man who was a conservative in respect to certain aspects, might, of course, not be one as a whole. Such were those who, when we discuss the thirties, we will call liberal-conservatives. Or he might, though approving the ends for which the established system stood, fight for change because those ends were not being fulfilled. This was, as we have seen, the position of the

process, and found a variety of reasons for their objections to reform. Out of the various pleas in favour of the *status quo* there developed, however, a complete if often inconsistent philosophy of conservatism in respect to all aspects of school life.

As suggested previously a great many conservatives defended Public School educational instruments in good part merely because they were old. Knox, for example, contends that 'established practices' must be good since they are 'supported by the uniform decisions of long experience'.[1] Barrow finds that 'that which is most generally adopted, is usually found to be most expedient'. 'In our public schools novel experiments will not be tried.' After all, there are, in education, 'fewer improvements and discoveries' to be made than one would expect.[2] But the antiquity of a practice could hardly be by itself a convincing argument in its favour. Even Knox feels it is necessary to assert that Public School methods were once reasonable. Most conservatives supported the upper-class educational system because they believed that, advertently or inadvertently, it furthered the welfare of those who came under its influence. They stressed the happiness of boys at school, or the intellectual and moral benefits of school training, or both. They believed that the Public School product had been in the past and was to-day a fine man, and they gave the school credit for his creation. As Barrow says, Public Schools ought to be preserved because, 'were the most illustrious examples to be selected from our history of men, who had united virtue with learning, professional skill with integrity of conduct, they would generally be found amongst the pupils of our publick schools'.[3] It was felt that 'these establishments, with all

reactionaries. In those respects in which they were defenders of the *status quo*, these two groups presented the same arguments as did thorough-going conservatives, and have not been distinguished from them in the following pages.

[1] Knox, *Liberal Education*, Vol. I, p. 2.
[2] Barrow, *Essay on Education*, Vol. I, pp. vii, 230, 242–44.
[3] Similarly, many other writers cite the great men, the 'Heroes and Statesmen', the 'Poets and Philosophers', turned out by schools as justification for the maintenance of the *status quo*. (Cf. E. Williams, *Life of Rowland Williams*, p. 10; *Microcosm*, p. 450; Vincent, *Defence of Public Education*, p. 42; *Public Education* (from the *Classical Journal*), pp. 43 ff., Old Etonian, *A Letter to Sir Alexander Malet*, (1829?), p. 20; *Eton System Vindicated*, p. 66.)

their faults, do mainly contribute to make England what it is . . .,'[1] and that, 'the knowledge, learned attainments, and virtue' which boys acquire there 'continue to advance the literary glory of England'.[2] Bowles, defending Winchester, sums up the conservative attitude in this respect when he asks rhetorically, 'If the general system pursued creates, not only for the church, but for all services political and moral, a class of learned and liberal men, PECULIAR TO OUR OWN COUNTRY, and which is one of the moral causes of its preeminence as a nation; a wise Legislator would be most anxious to preserve, not only *inviolate*, but uninjured in the high public estimation, these Establishments.'[3] The statesman Canning echoed these sentiments when he wrote, 'England would not be what she is, without her system of public education', whose discipline prepares boys for the duties of statesmen and churchmen.[4]

In their relationship to their opponents, conservatives divide on any particular question into two groups. The first of these refused to meet the liberals on their own ground. It tacitly admitted or ignored the narrowness of the curriculum, the general ineffectiveness of intellectual training, unhappiness, or immorality, and contended that Public School practice was good because it effected different and far more important ends. Others directly opposed critical objections, claiming, usually without proof, that the classics were taught or that boys were happy or virtuous. It is important to remember, however, that no one attempted to refute directly all critical objections. From the nature of the case no one who was an extreme libertarian or who favoured a broad intellectual training could be a thoroughgoing conservative.

I. INTELLECTUAL EDUCATION

As previously suggested, the intellectual side of school life was relatively less interesting to most Englishmen than was

[1] *Quarterly*, July 1818, p. 568.
[2] Ackermann, *History of Public Schools, Eton*, p. 3.
[3] Bowles, *Vindiciae Wykehamicae*, p. 24.
[4] Lyte, *History of Eton*, p. 349. Quoted from Canning's notes to Byron's *Don Juan*.

the moral. There were a good many conservatives, nevertheless, who raised their voices in defence of Public School mental training. In general these fall into two groups in accordance with the ends that they emphasized and consequently the practice which they defended.

The first of these groups was concerned less over whether all boys learned the classics than whether most were stimulated to self-education and to love of knowledge; they concentrated their applause on the voluntary nature of Public School education rather than on the virtues of the masters or their methods. Thus a youthful writer in the *Etonian* claims that it is its free intellectual atmosphere that explains Eton's leadership in the world. Eton encourages, it does not thwart; therefore her education is effective. 'I should ascribe its [Eton's] influence to that hatred of immoderate restriction which generous talents naturally entertain, and the elevation and expansion which they feel on being principally left to their spontaneous exertions, and experiencing gentle direction rather than positive and harsh control.'[1] Thus the *Quarterly* claims that freedom produces love of learning. 'Education cannot, perhaps, implant, but it may foster and stimulate, to an incalculable degree, this self-improving spirit; and it has certainly been the good fortune, if not the deliberate aim, [*sic*] of the great school to which most of these pamphlets refer, to justify, by its success, in thus kindling the enthusiasm of youth towards the studies of the place' the admiration of its worshippers.[2] Boys are encouraged to a 'generous emulation' of their schoolfellows,[3] and thus learn the classics better than they would under a tutor. Even the 'very ancient and venerable walls of those seats of learning, the recollection of the illustrious dead', are an inspiration to learn, a motive for study.[4]

These arguments, it must be admitted, have a very liberal sound; they have been to a great extent the stock in trade of modern progressivism. Indeed many conservatives believed themselves with some justification to be the champions of a

---
[1] *The Etonian*, Vol. I, p. 55, 'A Visit to Eton.'
[2] *Quarterly*, August 1834, p. 129.   [3] Ibid., p. 130.
[4] Cf. *Public Education* (from *The Pamphleteer*), p. 136.

truly liberal education against the tyranny of examinations and forced learning, and as the century wore on and reform became imminent, they grew more and more belligerent and self-righteous in their claims that the old system was the fountain-head of liberal teaching. Unfortunately, however, a sincere believer in progressive education can hardly take conservative arguments seriously. In the face of the obvious fact that most boys were not mentally stimulated at a Public School, they seem intolerably unreal, a naïve and hollow rationalization of current laxity in teaching.

A few boys undoubtedly were, however, so stimulated. Particularly was this true of two groups of Etonians in the twenties, one led by Praed, Moultrie, and H. N. Coleridge, the other by Gladstone, Hallam, and Milnes Gaskell. These boys used their time at school to educate themselves, and they were grateful to Eton for having provided them with a free and congenial background. They secured for themselves, in the first place, a broad literary education, as is evidenced by the magazines they produced, the *Etonian* and the *Miscellany*, the former under the editorship of Praed, the latter under that of Gladstone. Praed's magazine in particular, had higher literary merit than any subsequent school production, and was rivalled only by Canning's *Microcosm* in the late eighteenth century. These boys also acquired a political education not equalled by that of any subsequent generation. In the Debating Society, 'Pop'—now an athletic society—they discussed topics of the day in imitation of the political world around them, and kept the traditions of statesmanship alive at Eton. Gladstone, for example, was a worshipper of his predecessor Canning, and Eton was divided into Canningites and orthodox Tories with a fervour that one would never find to-day. Gaskell, especially, as Gladstone said, took 'more interest in the leading article of a newspaper than in feathering an oar or handling a bat'. He knew all about Pitt and Fox, nothing about Homer and Virgil. He defended Canningite policies with regard to Ireland and parliamentary reform with quotations from Caesar and with the oratory of Burke. Politics, writes Gaskell, 'is a passport to favour with every one at Eton whose acquaintance is an object of interest, or whose friendship is sought for'.[1]

The second and probably larger group of conservatives interested in mental training took a stand almost diametrically opposed to that of the first group, though that did not prevent many Englishmen from accepting both points of view at once. This group explicitly defended the classics and the authoritarian methods by which masters had for centuries taught them. They fought against elasticity both in the curriculum and in the system of instruction.

A successful defence of this position necessarily involved two steps, a proof that boys did learn the classics at a Public School and that such training was of such value that all else ought to be neglected to procure it. Conservatives seldom attempted such proof.

What they did was, in the first place, to contend arbitrarily that only present methods could be successful in teaching the classics. The classical languages were difficult to learn, and boys do not like to study. Therefore, as Barrow says, only censure, extra work, and compulsion could be used to inculcate them. The final punishment, indeed, must always be the rod; without fear boys will follow the pleasures of the hour, and not a single student will be made.[2]

In the second place they loudly insisted that the present

[1] Cf. F. Doyle, *Reminiscences*, pp. 32 ff.; Praed, *Poems*, Memoir by Derwent Coleridge, p. xxii; Morley, *Gladstone*, Vol. I, p. 34; Gaskell, *Records of an Eton Schoolboy*, pp. 11, 39, 72.)
Many boys who educated themselves at a Public School did so not only without the direct help of the school but actually in the teeth of school opposition. Shelley was persecuted at Eton, and his tutor actually may, as Medwin's story goes, have sent back to its owner a book on chemistry that Shelley had borrowed, 'as it is a forbidden thing at Eton'. (Cf. Peck, *Life of Shelley*, p. 22.) Nevertheless, he conducted his experiments in sensational chemistry. He read wild romances, some, like the revery of Albertus Magnus, in Latin, perused Godwin's *Political Justice* (Ibid., pp. 24 ff.) and read books on metaphysics, from all of which he derived more 'than from all the discipline of Eton'. (Hogg, *Life of Shelley*, Vol. II, pp. 110, 111.) Similarly, Darwin, who could not learn languages, or write verses, learned geometry, Shakespeare's historical plays, Byron and Scott, and dabbled in mineral and insect collecting. Above all, he read chemistry with his brother; 'the fact that we worked at chemistry somehow got known at school, and as it was an unprecedented fact, I was nicknamed "Gas",' and rebuked by Butler. (Cf. Darwin, *Life and Autobiography*, etc., p. 11.) Darwin and Shelley were as much examples to temper praise of Public School 'freedom' as was the average uneducated boy.
[2] Barrow, *Essay on Education*, Vol. II, pp. 131 ff.

masters using the traditional methods were actually successful in teaching the classics. Barrow writes that Public Schools are fine places if one wants to learn the classics.¹ Several defenders of Eton claim that boys do distinguish themselves at the University.² Parr, who, in 1811, expressed his 'unalterable attachment to the cause of public education as conducted in the public schools of this kingdom' and who applauded the fact that no corruption enters into the election of masters, believed that Public Schools taught classics in their purest form.³ Clarke writes that Winchester is known all over 'for the strictness of its discipline, the soundness of its system of instruction, and the inculcation of moral and religious principles'.⁴ The *Quarterly* agrees vehemently with a book which had said that the Public School has 'not *widely* degenerated from its original objects and utility', and adds, 'our public schools are subject to the best regulations which vigilant attention and prospective caution on the part of those who preside, can devise; . . . in them the faculties of the mind are stirred to activity, and that species of emulation excited, which draws forth various talent.'⁵ When Miss Edgeworth, in one of her books, claimed that her hero learned nothing at Harrow, the *Quarterly* writes: 'If there is any school of which less perhaps than of another this charge can be truly made, it is, we believe, Harrow.' Such words are 'flippant injustice' and 'inconsiderate depreciation of an institution, to which we look, with affectionate reverence'.⁶

¹ Barrow, *Essay on Education*, Vol. I, p. 117.
² *Etonensis, a Few Words in Reply, etc.*, p. 7; *Quarterly*, August 1834, p. 131. Neither of the writers of these articles are thoroughgoing conservatives.
³ Field, *Life of Parr*, Vol. II, p. 78.   ⁴ *Letter to Brougham*, p. 6.
⁵ *Quarterly*, May 1811, p. 355.
⁶ Ibid., June 1812, p. 333. Undoubtedly some boys did learn the classics, either with or without master help. Landor, for example, though he constantly resented authority and even went to the extreme of writing an attack on Dr. James in Latin alcaics, nevertheless did learn Latin because he liked it. He wrote and spoke the language and modelled his behaviour on the Romans. As his biographer says, with some exaggeration, 'he is the one known instance in which the traditional classical education of our schools took full effect'. (Colvin, *Landor*, p. 10.) Gladstone says that in his early days, though he learned little, and found that mostly plodding, he did learn what he knew accurately. (Morley, *Gladstone*, Vol. I, p. 30.) Bentham, though masters had little to give and paid no attention to him as long as his work was not noticeably bad, picked up a mastery of Latin composition by working for older boys. (Everett, *Bentham*, p. 9.) A boy like the Puseyite poet, Isaac Williams, to whom 'the great charm of my life at Harrow was composition, especially Latin', was

Criticism and Defence, 1780–1830

Praise of individual masters is as frequent among conservatives—though not confined to them[1]—as is more general eulogy. The *Microcosm* loudly extolled the Eton masters of its day for making boys love the classics.[2] An Old Westminster speaks of 'that loved and venerated Sage to whom I owe my first awakening to the value of letters'.[3] Byron was devoted, as we have seen, to Drury.[4] Many writers had special praise for Keate, and it is worthy of note that he was applauded in early days for, rather than in spite of, his strictness. Defenders contended that Keate was a great and successful trainer of the will no less than of the mind. According to one Etonian he had steadily and ably maintained discipline by 'firm and judicious management'.[5] According to another he had brought the 'morals and discipline of the school, under a regulated and wisely ordered control, which has never been equalled or approached at any similar establishment'.[6] He has so reformed Eton, according to the *Quarterly*, that students are 'ardent in their sentiments and lavish in their expressions of personal attachment and gratitude'.[7] Later on sentimentality entered in, and by the forties Keate could be cheered by hundreds who had once professed to hate him.

---

not prevented from enjoying himself and even obtaining the approval of Butler. (Williams, *Autobiography*, p. 6.) In a similar way Selwyn acquired scholarship at Eton (Tucker, *Selwyn*, p. 8), and the shy and retiring Peel at Harrow. (*Sir Robert Peel*, from his *Private Papers*, edited by Charles Stuart Parker, 3 vols., London, 1891, Vol. I, pp. 12 ff.) Even Thackeray learned some Horace, though, hating schoolmasters, he 'always had . . . doubts about the classics'. (*Punch in the East*, p. 36; Melville, *Life of Thackeray*, Vol. I, p. 27.) In 'The Fight at Slaughter House' in *Men's Wives* (p. 317) Thackeray refers to Charterhouse jokingly as the place where he got 'that immense fund of classical knowledge which in after life has been so exceedingly useful' to him. Melville (loc. cit.), however, says Thackeray was not much of a student and knew little except Horace.

[1] Coleridge, for example, though he hated Bowyer, is full of praise for him
[2] *Microcosm*, pp. 200, 375.   [3] *Letter from one Old Westminster, etc.*, p. 13.
[4] Moore, *Byron*, p. 64. Byron was so attached to Drury that he led a rebellion against his successor, George Butler. (Cf. poem 'On a Change of Masters at a Great Public School', July 1805, *Works*, p. 393.) In 1809 Byron was reconciled to Butler and regretted such actions as tearing the grating from his hall window and such expressions about Butler in his poetry as 'of narrow brain, yet of a narrower soul'. How much Byron learned from Drury is another story. He probably got a better general education than he did a classical one, despite his half-humorous statement in *Don Juan* that it was at a Public School that 'I pick'd up my own knowledge'. (Cf. *Don Juan*, *Works*, p. 606.)
[5] *Etonensis, A Few Words in Reply to Some Remarks*, p. 8.
[6] *Vindication of Eton*, p. 5.   [7] *Quarterly*, August 1834, p. 131.

In the third place conservatives praised the virtues to be derived from the classics, and implied or stated, though without attempt at proof, that other subjects could not be successfully taught in conjunction with them. The supposed intellectual benefits of a classical education which won praise were two in number.[1] In the first place, the classics were defended as the creators of taste and style. They produce such a one as Praed, whose scholarship was 'elegant, refined and tasteful, characterized by an unconscious, and, as it were, living sympathy with the graces and proprieties of diction'.[2] Public Schools teach, in other words, something the very opposite of the lucrative and mechanical arts; they are 'free schools' chiefly in the sense that they teach the genteel, the elegant, the graceful in contrast to the useful.[3] In its best sense this means an 'enlargement, refinement, and embellishment of the mind', which 'is the best and noblest effect of classical discipline'.[4] But the indirect effects of this acquisition of taste are certainly more appealing than the direct effects. Knox shows us the real motive for studying the classics when he says that a classical education makes the gentleman, and that a sense of classic style is necessary for good society.[5] It opens up a 'source of pure pleasure unknown to the vulgar'.[6] As Thackeray, who knew English snobbery as well as any one, says sarcastically, 'I know there is nothing like a knowledge of the classics to give a man good breeding.'[7] In other words, classic taste is a passport to society, and separates the elect from the general. The *Quarterly*, fiercely attacking those who want to enlarge curricula enough to let in boys who need the useful for their professions, shows the direct connexion between the classics and social divisions. It says, with fine venom, that 'such unguarded attacks . . . pamper self-complacency, petulance, and the silly ambition of knowing a little of everything, in a rising generation, already more than enough tinged with such phantasies'. The 'hollow and unworthy cant of

---

[1] There were moral benefits as well, and these will be discussed later. Moreover, there were obvious practical advantages to a classical education. It gave one entrée into the Church or the legal profession.
[2] *Memoir of Praed*, by Derwent Coleridge in Praed, *Poems*, Vol. I, p. xxvi.
[3] Knox, *Liberal Education*, Vol. I, Dedication. [4] Ibid., Vol. I, p. 4.
[5] Ibid., Vol. I, p. 81. [6] Ibid., Vol. I, p. 5. [7] *The Newcomes*, p. 69.

Criticism and Defence, 1780–1830

liberalism' in education parallels the aristocracy's stooping in other respects to flatter the jealousy of social distinctions of the classes underneath.[1] Similarly, Barrow claims that a boy meant for trade ought not to go to a Public School; it will make him look down on his intended profession.[2]

Secondly, classics discipline the mind. This, as we have seen, was the theory that Locke bequeathed the schools. Knowledge of the classics may not be useful, but the process of learning Greek and Latin, just because they are difficult, toughens the mind, builds character, and produces leaders. As John Hookham Frere remarks, 'at school a boy's business is not simply or mainly to gain knowledge, but to learn how to gain it'. He adds that science is not necessary; Canning knew nothing of frogs, and yet he could rule men.[3] From Knox to the vindicators of Eton in the thirties and for that matter to Public School defenders in the twentieth century, the classics have been extolled as mental training.[4]

2. HAPPINESS AND MORAL TRAINING

If Public Schools were often praised for their effect on the minds of boys, much more frequently were they applauded for the happiness or character training which they offered to those who went to them. As Knox wrote, 'goodness of heart is superior to intellectual excellence, and the possession of innocence more to be desired than taste'.[5]

Very few conservatives believed that all boys were happy at school; consequently they seldom used the general pleasurableness of schooldays as a direct argument in favour of the *status quo*. But, as previously suggested, a number of individuals did enjoy their days at Eton or Harrow or Rugby, and wrote glowingly about those days. By implication if not by direct statement many of them contended that, because they were happy at school, no change ought to be made

---
[1] *Quarterly*, January 1831, p. 174.
[2] Barrow, *Essay on Education*, Vol. I, p. 115.
[3] *The Works of the Rt. Hon. John Hookham Frere*, Vol. I, Memoir by the Rt. Hon. Sir Bartle Frere, London, 1874, p. 16.
[4] *Liberal Education*, p. 4; *Eton System Vindicated*, p. 30; *Quarterly*, August 1834, p. 152.
[5] Knox, *Liberal Education*, Vol. I, p. 12.

in the character of Public School life or at least in those aspects which had conduced to enjoyment.

The sources of happiness were, as also mentioned earlier, certain special results of the independent life of boys, and it was this life that therefore seemed important and sacred to conservative alumni. As Moultrie wrote:

> . . . in the lengthening retrospect of years,
> The sports and conflicts of the schoolboy world,—
> Its microcosmic cares, and joys, and griefs,—
> The daily intercourse of boy with boy,—
> Appear the true realities.[1]

Similarly, Praed has words of praise chiefly for the freedom of youth. He longs to give his soul

> Back to thy cherishing control.
> Control? Ah no! thy chain was meant
> Far less for bond than ornament;[2]

The chief results of boy independence which conduced to happiness were such things as scrapes, feasts, and games, and reminiscers from the scoundrel Westmacott to the virtuous Thackeray have written with joy of robbing orchards, acting in plays, indulging in late feasts, and escaping from windows at night.[3] Above all it was friendships formed which produced happiness, and thus endeared their schools to many. As a sentimental Old Westminster wrote to an old schoolfellow, 'our friendship—firm, sincere, and disinterested, as it is—is but one among many thousands of like kind—begun, cemented, and consolidated at a great Public School; and I cannot but think that such bonds, which are not to be knit so closely elsewhere are among the many national benefits produced by these establishments'.[4] Similarly, Gladstone, writing of the long dead Hallam in 1890, speaks of 'the memory of a friendship surpassing every other that has ever been enjoyed by one greatly blessed both in the number and in the excellence of his friends', as a reason for loving Eton.[5] Byron, telling sentimentally of 'ye scenes of my childhood, whose loved recollections . . . Embitters the

[1] *Dream of Life*, p. 67.   [2] Praed, *Poems*, Vol. II, p. 128.
[3] (Charles Malloy Westmacott) Bernard Blackmantle, *The English Spy*, London, 2 vols., 1825, Vol. I, pp. 25 ff.; Thackeray, *The Newcomes*, p. 26.
[4] *Letter from an Old Westminster*, p. 4.   [5] Gladstone, *Hallam*, p. 7.

present', finds Harrow lovely because 'friendships were form'd, too romantic to last'.[1]

Happiness was, however, much less often a sufficient reason for defending the *status quo* than was the belief that Public Schools had beneficent effects on the characters of boys. What most conservatives contended above all else was that Public Schools educated the will, and that, since the social life and the formal training of schools conduced to this result, these features ought to be preserved.

Upholders of the moral effects of schools naturally divide themselves into two groups in accordance both with the ends which they praised schools for bringing about and the means which they defended as effecting these ends. The first of these groups, made up mostly of masters, was concerned chiefly about the traditional moral virtues and the formal discipline and instruction given by the masters. They contended, in effect, that Public School masters and the methods which they used were good because they produced virtuous and patriotic boys, and that that was the most important purpose of education.

In actual practice the arguments of this group rarely took the above form, however. In the first place, the individuals composing it all tended to assume what needed above all to be proved, that schools actually did produce virtuous schoolboys. Occasionally they admitted that immorality sometimes existed at schools, but, as Barrow said, 'I have seldom known a youth deeply involved in depravity at school, who did not bring the seeds of it along with him.'[2] These few wicked boys—and there cannot be many or, according to one defender, boys would not love their schools so much[3]—

---

[1] Obviously many who were not conservatives were happy in the memory of friendships. Southey, so often bitter about Westminster, can say of the friends made there: 'If I were beholden to the old school for nothing more than their friendship, I should have reason enough to bless the day on which I entered it'. (Haller, *Early Life of Southey*, p. 34.) Lamb, whose 'Christ's Hospital Five and Thirty Years Ago' is as unfavourable to his school as his earlier article is favourable, has in it that great tribute to his boyhood friend Coleridge: 'Come back into memory like as thou wert in the day spring of thy fancies, with hope like a fiery column before thee, the dark pillar not yet turned——,' and talk 'while the walls of the old Grey Friars re-echo . . . to the accents of the inspired charity boy.' (*Essays of Elia*, *Works*, Vol. II, p. 21.)

[2] Barrow, *Essay on Education*, Vol. I, p. 94.

[3] *Public Education* (from *The Pamphleteer*), p. 143.

offer the rest an opportunity to test their virtuousness.¹ Moreover, this group made little attempt to show that masters were on the whole faithful and industrious in carrying out Public School moral aims. Dr. Vincent, thinking himself accused of incompetence, wrote a detailed defence of the masters in this respect. He insisted, rather feebly it must be confessed, that they fulfil the statutes with prayers five to nine times a day and enforce these prayers 'with as much external decency as can be exacted, allowing for the natural impatience of boys under restraint, and the levity of youth'.² Aside from Dr. Vincent's words there was little written in praise of the masters as moral educators except for occasional tributes such as the one to Keate cited above.³ Actually what conservatives did for the most part was to defend masters' methods in the abstract as ideally conducive to the production of virtue.⁴

To begin with, the curriculum itself was considered a most potent instrument in the creation of virtue and patriotism. According to Knox the classics promote virtuous affections, soften the disposition, and restrain the passions. Indeed, upon the learning of the writings of antiquity depends 'the religion, the virtue, and I will add the liberties of our countrymen'.⁵ In contrast, the writings of the French— even, according to Barrow, their grammar—house savagery and materialism.⁶ Similarly, Dr. Vincent, answering the charge that pagan authors are responsible for the French Revolution, insists, on the contrary, that they are indispensible instruments in the production of virtue.⁷ Another writer compares the civilized Greeks and Romans, who

---

¹ Knox, *Liberal Education*, Vol. I, pp. 34 ff.; Godwin, *Enquirer*, pp. 50 ff. Some boys were strengthened in well-doing by the opposition of their fellows. Among these may be cited John Allen, Havelock, Isaac Williams, Rowland Williams, Robert Peel, Palmerston, and Gladstone.
² Vincent, *Defence of Public Education*, p. 34. Vincent makes a most amusing comment. Even if Public Schools did not give a good religious education, though this is hardly likely, since they have the best masters in Europe, criticism is evil since it makes the poor believe that they get a better education and thus renders them insubordinate.
³ See p. 177.
⁴ In these arguments they were joined by the reactionaries.
⁵ Knox, *Liberal Education*, Vol. I, pp. 4, 11.
⁶ Barrow, *Essay on Education*, Vol. II, p. 121.
⁷ Vincent, *Defence of Public Education*, p. 21.

Criticism and Defence, 1780–1830 183

teach virtue by example, with the barbarous northern peoples, and claims that a knowledge of the classics will almost inevitably lead to manly action and to a defence of British independence.[1]

The curriculum alone, however, was not enough to induce morality. Since humanity was considered to be corrupt, instruction in religion was also necessary in order to check vice.[2] Moreover, strict discipline as practised in the Public Schools was an indispensable aid to virtue. We need authority to help govern the passions. A master will punish more than he will reward, for the vice of the age is indulgence, leading to selfishness.[3] Knox advises the use of the rod when necessary, for man is naturally imbecile and idle. Ill-judged lenity is cruelty, particularly in moral offences.[4] Finally, compulsion itself was considered valuable morally, or rather its absence was supposed to entail dire consequences. Thus the *Quarterly* in 1812 fought the *Edinburgh*'s scheme for voluntary learning of Latin verses. 'Of all Utopian schemes, it appears to us the most objectionable. It is one which in modern cant may be possibly styled "liberal", inasmuch as it gives children a power of *veto* over their instructors. It opens a door for the grossest infringements of discipline; indeed it discards all idea of that school virtue.'[5]

There are political implications in the whole defence of Public School formal education. This education was supported in good part because it presumably turned out men who possessed an ethical code which was hostile to that of the French, and moral qualities which would be useful in a war against France. These political implications are made explicit by Barrow and Knox. Barrow openly denounced the French Revolution as having taught an indulgence of appetites in education. When you consult the wishes of children you make Jacobins. Only more parental discipline and a right education can prevent revolution.[6] Knox is even more specific. He claims that the old Roman gravity and

---

[1] *Letters from a Nobleman to his Son*, pp. 18–26.
[2] Knox, *Liberal Education*, Vol. II, p. 51; Barrow, *Essay on Education*, Vol. II, p. 181.   [3] Barrow, *Essay on Education*, Vol. II, pp. 218, 225.
[4] Knox, *Liberal Education*, Vol. II, p. 35.
[5] *Quarterly*, December 1812, p. 401.   [6] Barrow, op. cit., Vol. II, p. 320.

dignity of the English character are degenerating, that French levity and 'the levelling principle' have infected England.[1] This is disastious since 'The existence of society comfessedly depends on a regular subordination'.[2] The superior ought to exact deference and express his superiority by dress or external decorum. To fail to do so indicates a lack of real dignity and solid merit. We need a manly education, a tough bite of the classics, to save the national character from French levity.

The second group of defenders of moral education were not primarily interested in virtue but rather in a conception of character which may be designated by the term socialized manliness. Indeed, some, like John Tweddell, were willing to admit without much concern that by 'deduction' schools often initiate a boy early in vice.[3] Moreover, they concerned themselves less about the part played by masters in the educational process than about that played by the boys. What they fought to preserve were the institutions of boy life, and they did so because they believed that these institutions were ideal educational instruments, and as such furthered the moral ends which they considered of first importance.

To some extent all features of a Public School miniature world were praised, from raids on farmers to fights between boys. Writers all the way from Trollope to Thackeray have a good word for 'mills' or fights, though usually as pleasant memories rather than as educational elements. Anthony Trollope's only satisfactory school memory was of 'the way in which I licked a boy who had to be taken home to be cured'.[4] Thackeray talks pleasantly of 'bartering a black eye per bearer, against a bloody nose drawn at sight, with a schoolfellow'.[5] Even masters liked fighting. 'The "science of self-defence" was inculcated upon us boys as one of the essentials of a gentleman's education. It was the point upon which no difference of opinion existed either between masters and pupils or between sons and fathers.'[6] What occasionally happened and what are seldom mentioned were incidents

[1] Knox, op. cit., Vol. II, pp. 311, 321.   [2] Ibid., p. 315.
[3] *Quarterly*, October 1815, p. 229.   [4] *Autobiography*, p. 17.
[5] *The Newcomes*, p. 26.   [6] Earl of Albemarle, *Fifty Years*, p. 65.

like the death of Lord Shaftesbury's son after a fight with Colonel Wood's.[1]

But it was the prefect fagging system which was most often considered the educational instrument on which the formation of English character depended. This system seemed to embody most perfectly the educational principles which appealed to conservatives. As suggested previously, the average upper-class Englishman, in contrast to that special class who were either Churchmen or masters, was a libertarian as well as an authoritarian, and was as proud of his heritage of defence of freedom as were liberals. Consequently, he found particularly to his taste those aspects of English life which he felt combined freedom with authority. The prefect system in the Public Schools appeared to embody just this combination. It seemed to give—and in fact to a great extent it did give—a boy the opportunity for self-discipline, for the management of his own destiny, at the same time that it subjected him to a powerful discipline, which changed from that of direct force at first to that of the indirect pressure of custom and public opinion later on.

Conservatives have never grown weary of praising the prefect system as an ideal solution to the claims of both extreme libertarians and extreme authoritarians. Some of them—particularly Etonians, since at Eton the system was less regularized than at other places—have emphasized freedom. Thus the *Microcosm* called a Public School a republic in which 'honours and offices of State' are 'equally divided', but even more: 'an aristocracy of such gradual progression from despotism to slavery, as to render the distance less oppressive, though not less aweful'.[2] Almost half a century later Moultrie describes Eton government in even more flattering terms. He had come prepared to fight for his rights:

>   . . . but amidst
> Thy peaceful dwellings slender need I found
> Of such heroic daring:—there, enthroned
> On neat gradations of ascending ranks,
> Reign'd Order;—there, by firmest law secured,
> Right triumphed over Might . . .

[1] *The Times*, March 2nd 1825, p. 3. [2] *Microcosm*, p. 278.

> No robber horde were we,
> Anarchical, self-will'd, by force alone
> From mutual wrong and violence restrain'd;
> But a well-governed people, proud to own
> Legitimate control, and to maintain
> Our glorious constitution unimpair'd
> And what if aristocracy, upheld
> By right prescriptive, ruled with feudal sway
> Her unenfranchised vassals,—still her yoke
> Was milder and less grievous to be borne
> Than arbitrary bondage, forced elsewhere
> By strength of fist, on the reluctant necks
> Of trembling urchins, all too weak to win
> The freedom which they sigh'd for.[1]

Others emphasized the authoritative aspect of the system. Indeed, to one Old Etonian who was shocked at the revolt against the prefects at Winchester in 1829, boy government seemed to symbolize the majesty of the established law in the same way that masters did to others. The Old Etonian's political comparison is as amusing as it is significant. Speaking of the revolters he says: 'These indomitable heroes, who, like Daniel O'Connell and his crew, had taken the law into their own hands, to redress their imaginary grievances, found, as all real Englishmen must, what O'Connell and his friends will find to their cost that they were at once resolutely banished from the scene of their illegal and unconstitutional violence.' Only 'mawkish sentimentality' can object to fagging. The rebels could have appealed to the Head, the 'constitutional means' of redress.[2]

The prefect system was praised, in the second place, because it seemed the chief source of the moral qualities and standards which conservatives loved. These standards and qualities resembled those of the institutions which produced them. The Public School graduate was admired for being both independent and socialized, both free and disciplined.

On the libertarian side the most admired virtue and the one for the production of which the Public School and in particular the prefect system was defended, was self-reliance

---
[1] Moultrie, *Dream of Life*, pp. 56–58.
[2] Old Etonian, *A Letter to Sir Alexander Malet*, p. 3.

Criticism and Defence, 1780–1830

or manliness. Conservatives applauded schools in good part because they believed that in them a boy had his ego developed and was given the instruments with which to satisfy his desires. He was taught to stand on his own feet, to overcome, with courage, the obstacles presented by the world, and to lead others.[1] Thus the *Quarterly* in 1834 can speak of the 'emulation', the 'manly strength of mind', and the early habituation to 'self-dependence' through freedom that schools give, as a justification of those institutions.[2] Much earlier the *Quarterly* had quoted with approval the praise of John Tweddell, who had written: Schools 'teach a man that confidence in himself, which is useful in a world where modesty is a poor thriver'.[3] Rowcroft, who was by no means blind to the faults of Eton, says that it fits a boy for competition in the world. It makes him 'rough and rude; but life is rough and rude'. It gives him strength of character and self-reliance.[4] Godwin, a political radical, but in good part an educational conservative defends public education on the basis that its emulation is good for the robust, and produces poise, generosity, and boldness.[5] De Quincey, himself a weakling, whom one would surely not expect to find among defenders, has praise for the 'manliness' and masculine energy of schools.[6]

If conservatives were concerned over independence, they were equally if not—in the face of school rebellions led by 'manly' boys like Byron—more interested in checking freedom. Their libertarianism never was whole-hearted enough

[1] Many impartial or hostile writers of a later time have admitted that schools did produce manliness. Trollope, for example, claims that the prefect system teaches self-reliance. (T. A. Trollope, *What I Remember*, p. 122.) Lord Hatherley wrote that fagging 'was to a young and rather sensitive boy very severe, but it was just that which was wanting to brace one up to face the realities of life'. (Stephens, *Lord Hatherley*, Vol. I, p. 106.)

[2] *Quarterly*, August 1834, pp. 138–29.   [3] *Quarterly*, October, 1815, p. 229.

[4] Rowcroft, *Confessions of an Etonian*, Vol. I, p. 42. These may, he says, become hardness, rivalry, and egotism; nevertheless they are good.

[5] *Enquirer*, pp. 50 ff.

[6] *Autobiographic Sketches*, pp. 72, 172. De Quincey's case is surely curious. He was the kind of boy who thought that life was finished at six because the love and peace and security of an older sister-brother relationship was destroyed. He loved solitary dreaming and was glad he did not have 'horrid, pugilistic brothers'. Always shy, he hated all brutality and violence, and was inclined to be effeminate. His praise of schools—for which he had as many kind words as any one who wrote—seems almost to be psychological compensation. (Cf. op. cit., pp. 27 ff.)

to include a love of the original, the eccentric, or the intellectually independent. They wanted boys socialized in various ways, and they praised schools for disciplining desires and clipping individuality to fit into a social pattern. If they disagreed with reactionaries and moralists generally, it was not over the question of socialization itself but over the particular standards to which a boy ought to conform and the type of character into which he ought to be moulded.

To begin with, the Public Schools were applauded for a negative kind of socialization. As the complement of self-reliance, they were supposed to teach a boy his limitations,[1] what he could not do, and thus adjust him to the world of reality. They were believed to destroy conceit, pride, selfishness, and 'overbearing conduct'.[2] As Frere says, they teach a boy 'his own place in the world, and, in a practical fashion, his duty towards other boys, and to his superiors as well as to his inferiors'.[3] One learns at a Public School to endure and to live with equals.[4] According to Southey—who is always trying to defend schools at the same time that he is attacking—'a juster estimate of one's self is acquired at school than can be formed in the course of domestic instruction, and, what is of much more consequence, a better intuition into the characters of others than there is any chance of learning in after life'. He adds, rather cynically, that the school teaches boys to conform 'to the world's fashion and the world's uses'.[5]

As is evident, one can draw no definite line between a mere negative disciplining and the inculcation of positive virtues. Presumably the eradication of conceit, for example, fosters humility. Thus conservatives often claim that Public

[1] *Public Education*, p. 36, from the *Classical Journal*.
[2] *Public Education*, p. 124, from *The Pamphleteer*; *Quarterly*, August, 1834; Nimrod, in *Fraser's*, September 1842. Even Anthony Trollope could admit, in regard to one of his heroes, that he had 'a conceit which public school education would not have created'. (Cf. *Orley Farm*, London, 1871, p. 16.) Critics like Cowper, on the other hand, hated the schools chiefly, as we have seen, for creating arrogant boys.
[3] Bartle Frere, *Memoir of Frere*, in *Works* of Frere, Vol. I, p. 16.
[4] Godwin, *Enquirer*, pp. 50 ff.
[5] 'Recollections of the Early Life of Robert Southey', in *Life and Correspondence*, pp. 38, 56.

Criticism and Defence, 1780–1830

Schools create at the same time that they destroy. Particularly was this considered to be true with respect to their inculcation of what conservatives called a democratic feeling. On the one hand, Public Schools presumably destroyed the 'false pride' of rank and fortune.[1] As Nimrod says, 'the lord . . . as well as the lord's son, was certain to have his turn in the routine of tyranny'.[2] On the other hand, they led to respect for talent, since, as the *Quarterly* says, at a Public School 'the aristocracy of title and fortune has its first collision with the aristocracy of talent'. 'Unless he is gentlemanly in his manners, courteous and unpresuming in his behaviour, the young patrician will come in for his share of that ruder discipline by which boys are apt to correct presumption and insolence'.[3] In the words of Lord John Russell—before he 'recanted' and got to believe in the Reform Bill—'The democratic character of the nobility of England . . . is very much to be attributed to the gregarious education they receive.'[4] 'A public school does form character. It takes a boy from home, where he is a darling, where his folly is wit, and his obstinacy spirit, to a place where he takes rank according to his real powers and talents.'[5] Similarly, Frere, the friend of Canning and co-editor of the *Microcosm*, wrote, 'No one who has not seen it can estimate the good Eton does in teaching the little boys of great men that they have superiors. . . . Neither rank nor money had any consideration there compared with that which was paid to age, ability, and standing in the school.'[6]

Besides a democratic spirit, it was claimed that Public School life produced many other positive moral virtues, such as generosity, honourableness, and loyalty. This list, it will be noted, did not include either chastity and other Puritan virtues, or the courage to defy group *mores*. Standards of boy society seldom contain such ideals, and, as already mentioned, conservative alumni were as unconcerned over them as were the boys.

[1] Old Etonian, *A Letter to Sir Alexander Malet*, p. 19.
[2] *Fraser's*, September 1842, p. 323.
[3] *Quarterly*, August 1834, p. 137.   [4] Ibid., p. 138.
[5] Spencer Walpole, *Life of Lord John Russell*, Vol. I, p. 10.
[6] Bartle Frere, *Memoir of Frere*, p. 16.

To such as De Quincey and Rowcroft generosity and honourableness seemed the most important. De Quincey speaks eloquently of the 'superior manliness, generosity, and self-control of those generally who had benefited by [the] ... discipline—[of a Public School] so systematically hostile to all meanness, pusillanimity, or indirectness'.[1] 'No discipline will better aid' in developing masculine energy than a classical school, that 'Areopagus for fair play, and abhorrence of all crooked ways', where the selfish are forced to accommodate to a 'public standard of generosity'.[2] Similarly, Rowcroft writes that Eton boys were gentlemen in manner and mind, were liberal and generous and never deserted their comrades. They might do wicked and foolish, but never mean things. Such was the spirit that Eton handed on to each generation.[3]

To others loyalty—in its less conscious form conformity—seemed the most essential virtue created by schools. In a sense it was, because it developed into patriotism and thus proved of extreme political importance. Defenders of Public Schools as instillers of loyalty were quite aware of its broader implications. In the eighteenth century the *Microcosm* could write, 'he, who hereafter may sing the glories of Britain, must first celebrate at Eton the smaller glories of his College'.[4] Twenty years later a pamphleteer echoed the same sentiments: A Public School boy is a member of a body. 'Here he receives the germ of that public spirit which afterwards expands into warm and elevated patriotism. His glowing zeal for the honour of his class, of his party, and of his school, gives the first spring to that noble principle which

---

[1] *Autobiographic Sketches*, p. 62.   [2] Ibid., p. 173.
[3] Rowcroft, *Confessions*, Vol. I, p. 132. Whether schools did actually produce liberality and honour is, of course, another story. Tucker's righteous insistence that Eton men could always be trusted, and always hated the mean, the braggart, and the bully is probably exaggerated. (Tucker, *Eton of Old*, pp. 135–36.) Yet even the critical Trollope could say that the prefect system, even in early days created, through the trust implied by it, a high tone of honour in the school. He spoke of the 'conscious responsibility' created 'in the individual as forming an unit in an organized whole'. He even went so far—probably in order to contrast Winchester favourably with Harrow—as to claim that a public tunding (the Winchester name for a prefectorial whipping) 'was eminently calculated to foster among us a high tone of moral and gentlemanlike feeling'. (T. A. Trollope, *What I Remember*, pp. 113, 122.)
[4] *Microcosm*, p. 10.

Criticism and Defence, 1780–1830   191

it exhibits in beautiful miniature.' Genius expands and at the same time 'new strength is added to the national cause'.[1]

An illustration of the way in which the imperialistic tradition was carried on is provided by Lord Dalhousie. When, in 1823, he was at Harrow, the Marquis of Hastings returned from India, visited the school, and gave sovereigns to the boys: 'so princely a largesse from a grey-haired hero of such fine manners, of a presence so commanding, must have filled many a boyish heart with other sentiments than gratitude alone'. To Dalhousie Hastings became the 'embodiment of a greatness which he, too, might hope some day to rival'.[2] Conservatives knew only too well what purposes the Public Schools really served. As long as they continued to further political ends vital to the class to which they catered they could not be changed in any fundamental way.

To conclude this chapter without mention of the Public Schools as inculcators of good manners—except in passing in relation to the classics—may seem to some, familiar with the importance of the subject to-day, a vital omission. The truth of the matter is that, though schools could hardly be justly attacked in the early nineteenth century, as they were by Chesterfield in the eighteenth, for teaching bad manners, they were not as yet primarily concerned with superficial good form. Neither, it should be noted, were the upper classes. As a result, though Coleridge could speak of the manners and courtesy, the ability to move in the best society that boys learn from one another in a Public School,[3] no one defended schools primarily because they taught manners.

[1] *Public Education* (from *The Pamphleteer*), pp. 115–16.
[2] Trotter, *Life of Dalhousie*, p. 6.
[3] Coleridge, *Table Talk*, Vol. II, p. 114, July 8th 1833.

CHAPTER IV

THE EARLY THIRTIES

A. THE VICTORIAN COMPROMISE

UNTIL the twenties criticism was too scattered to have any noticeable effect either on schools or on defenders of them. The forces of conservatism were in the saddle in educational as well as in political affairs, and reform of any kind seemed out of the question. With the later twenties there came a change. In politics, religion, and education, revolt against existing conditions grew in volume and strength. Liberal and reactionary criticism increased both in power and effectiveness until it reached an unparalleled climax in the thirties. By 1835 it had become clear that if no reforms were to occur the middle classes would desert the schools entirely.

Neither liberals nor reactionaries, however, directly caused reform or dictated its nature. What happened was that in the twenties the radicals and religious reformers made their influence felt among the groups who habitually defended schools. Political, religious, and educational conservatives began to feel the necessity of making some concessions to new ideas. As a result, they initiated, with the aid of moderates among liberals and reactionaries, various movements whose object was, in part at least, to bring about reform. They became what we may call liberal-conservatives, and it was these liberal-conservatives who dominated early Victorian thought. From them came much of the Public School criticism of the early thirties, and it was their ideas which dictated the nature of reform in the thirties and forties. Arnold was successful in reforming Rugby because he embodied and put into practice their ideals and methods. We must therefore examine for a moment the general nature of liberal-conservative philosophy.

Liberal-conservatism was, as its name indicates, essentially a doctrine of compromise or meliorism. Its initiators attempted by certain concessions—different for different people—to domesticate reform movements. They admitted the idea of change in institutions, at the same time that they desired slow changes based on experience, and wanted to preserve these institutions substantially intact. They attempted to further such ideals as democracy, reason, and liberty, and reconcile them with older ideals such as class divisions, experience, emotion, and authoritarian morality, which they preferred and favoured, and which they viewed with a new fervour derived partly from the reactionaries. In philosophy they tried to compromise between religion and science, between emotion and reason, between the moral and the intellectual, with emphasis on the former in each case. In politics they favoured democracy and progress and held fast to stability. The liberal-conservative Canningites best represented this tendency in the twenties, and symbolized the break with rigid Toryism of many members of the party. The Tory Meliorists were, after 1832, joined by many increasingly conservative Whigs. In economics they favoured *laissez-faire* and yet tried to preserve social values, even going so far as to favour state interference. Whig and Tory joined, under the inspiration of the moral and humanitarian revival, in an attack on extreme rationalist *laissez-faire* radicalism; this movement, called by Professor Cazamian, who describes it in *Le Roman Social en Angleterre*, paternalistic interventionism, attempted to moralize and regularize through Government agency the chaos of industrialism. In educational matters meliorism favoured intellectual and moral freedom at the same time that it advocated more vigorous socialization and ultimately an authoritarian morality.

From our point of view the most important aspects of the Victorian Compromise are, on the one hand, its philosophic attitude towards old institutions, and, on the other, its stand on the relative importance of the intellectual and the moral in education, together with its conception of the basis and nature of morality. Conservatism, liberalism, and reaction all found their places in the Victorian attitude on these subjects. With regard to institutions, the liberal-conservatives desired to be preservers through change: schools and

Parliament and Church were to be liberalized in a way to make old-time Tories shudder, at the same time that they were to be given more authority than either liberals or conservatives had ever desired. In regard to the moral question, character was to remain more important than intellect and was to be grounded in religious absolutism. But the intellectual was to find a place and the moral was to be based more on reason and individual conscience than either conservatives or evangelicals desired. In accordance with reactionary wishes, moral fervour was to be revived and strengthened in a manner unknown during the Regency.

The new attitude was for the most part English in origin, being merely a compromise of various earlier positions. But a number of ideas came from the intellectual and emotional revival in Germany, just as radicalism had come from France. The Germans provided, in the first place, a defence of old institutions that was more effective and at the same time allowed for more change than did Burke's. Coleridge brought this defence back from his trip to Germany in 1798 and Carlyle picked it up from a reading (or misreading) of Goethe. Together Coleridge and Carlyle had much influence on early Victorian thought as transmitters of German ideas.[1]

In Germany a powerful philosophic reaction to French revolutionary ideas had grown up at the beginning of the nineteenth century. Just as Germany is to-day reacting against liberalism in the name of racial nationalism, so in the years following the Battle of Jena (1807) she evolved a philosophy opposed to scientific rationalism and democratic individualism. As part of this philosophy she developed a conception of history and of institutions that was both nationalistic and conservative. From Herder to Hegel[2] she was the exponent of an organic conception of history. The Germans saw history not as a series of external forces

[1] It is significant that Carlyle in part and Coleridge as a whole were defenders of Public Schools. Coleridge's remark, made in 1833, 'I am clear for public schools as the general rule' (*Table Talk*, Vol. II, p. 114), is of particular interest in the light of the fact that he was unhappy at school. What the pantisocratic rebel of 1790 hated was the object of love for the Coleridge of 1833.
[2] And for that matter, from Hegel to Spengler.

working on mankind, which could be controlled or modified by reason, but as an organism's gradual unfolding from within. A nation was an organism—which Carlyle symbolizes by the tree Igdrasil—with its own innate direction and possible life history. To both Coleridge and Carlyle, institutions are concrete embodiments of the spiritual ideas in each culture. Coleridge showed his attachment to this idea by writing a book on Church and State according to the 'idea' of each. Carlyle wrote, in *Sartor Resartus*, of institutions as clothes concealing and illuminating the naked idea. Both Coleridge and Carlyle, in their emphasis on the spiritual and the organic, are opposed to the mechanistic interpretations of eighteenth-century science. Both were intellectual leaders in the fight against industrialism, materialism, democracy, and individualism. They differed fundamentally, however, on the question of the worth of old institutions. Carlyle, particularly before he joined the ranks of the reactionaries in the forties with his strong-man theory, was a radical in that he believed that English institutions were old clothes that ought to be discarded because they did not fit the new spiritual ideas of the age. He was thus no guide in this respect for liberal-conservatism. Coleridge, on the other hand, like Burke, believed that Church and State had a spiritual purpose to serve. The Church, for example, is an implement with which to achieve one of the ends of a State: education. Reform should not destroy, but see to it that old institutions serve the purpose for which they were originally intended. Coleridge was an enlightened conservative. He advocated the sloughing off of useless forms and intellectually invalid conceptions. The Church must use reason to distinguish that which is eternal from that which is merely dogmatic. There must be social and institutional change, but it must be in accordance with deep-rooted English sentiments. A revivified and reformed Church and State can then be the leaders of a new age. Coleridge's liberal-conservatism went beyond either conservative or liberal English theory in the power it wished to give to Church and State, and was thus an early progenitor of what to-day we call socialist or more often fascist theory;

Coleridge's control was control by the powers that be, not by the democracy. The idea of a powerful State and Church, whether socialist or fascist, was against English tradition of all kinds, but it gradually grew in favour, and was advocated by such diverse people as the liberal Arnolds, Matthew and Thomas, and the reactionary Disraeli and the later Carlyle.[1] In educational matters, be it noted, neither conservatives nor liberal-conservatives were willing to include upper-class education in any plan of State control.

The Germans again, through Coleridge and Carlyle, stimulated a moral revival in England and at the same time liberalized the dogmatic basis of morality. Kant, Fichte, and Schleiermacher gave philosophic justification to the idea of a morality that was of the heart, and thus individualistic and yet which came from God and was thus absolute in contrast to utilitarian morality. Fichte carried this moral revival into German education. Though Kant as early as 1803 in *On Education* introduced the idea of discipline as a means of subjecting the will in the interests of social regeneration,[2] it was Fichte who, in his *Nature of the Scholar* and more particularly in his *Addresses to the German Nation*, evolved the idea of a moral education as the way to a national cultural revival following Napoleon's disastrous invasions. As indicated above, Fichte borrowed his methods from Pestalozzi; his aim was, however, of the very opposite nature.[3] What Fichte wanted was a nation moulded into

---

[1] From Coleridge's and Carlyle's doctrines grew up a powerful reactionary movement as well as the liberal-conservative one that we have been discussing. Disraeli admits the influence of Coleridge and of Carlyle's *Past and Present* in his attempt to turn back the clock and revive the Church and Royalty as paternalistic preservers of the people against Parliament and manufacturer. The dogmatic and reactionary Oxford Movement also drew sustenance from Coleridge, as Newman willingly admits.

[2] Cf. Monroe, *Education*, pp. 595, 612.

[3] It is difficult, in the light of modern Germany's use of his doctrines, to be fair to Fichte. It must be remembered, however, that he wrote his addresses as patriotic pleas under trying circumstances, not as philosophic discourses. Further, Fichte, a scholar and philosopher, was making a plea for cultural unity to a nation which had no political unity, nor had had for hundreds of years; he hardly envisioned either the blood and iron of Bismarck or the perverted sadism of Hitler. And yet many of Hitler's doctrines can be found in the pages of Fichte: both are the product of a political inferiority complex. The whole doctrine of Germany's cultural superiority to other nations is a proof of this, and it can be found in the *Addresses*. Only the German has depth of soul, real seriousness, real freedom, real devotion. When the Germans

The Early Thirties

a corporate body. Self-development was still praised, but in some curious way one achieved it by subjecting one's individual will to that of the State. The individual was to find his greatest good by subordinating himself to a higher power—the State, conceived of as a living and divine organism.[1]

In many ways the English Public Schools were doing just what Fichte desired—training men to be servants of the State. Yet the English have never approved of German education. Tories and liberals alike, as we have seen, prided themselves on the freedom of their education from the tyranny of the State. They gloried in the freedom from moral pressure and authority which a boy was supposed to have in a Public School. If Rousseau's doctrines spelt anarchy, Fichte's meant tyranny. The English were shocked at the idea of directly moulding a boy to be an instrument of the State; they feared State education, and they objected to the authoritarian methods which Fichte advocated. But indirectly, they welcomed the new moral idealism behind the German movement. Carlyle and Coleridge gave impetus to the moral revival both inside and outside of the Church, Carlyle demanding a complete destruction of dead forms and a return to intuitional religion and morality, Coleridge desiring a purging away of untenable ideas and a re-animation of the Church.

---

borrow from another people it is borrowing; when others do it it is imitation. Only the German language is alive, because it has not fused with other languages. The German is great because he believes in the eternal development of spirituality through freedom. (Freedom is gained through voluntary subjection to the State.) The German Fatherland is an organic spiritual unity; the French State is merely a mechanism. Therefore only the German can really love his State. The German wins wars because he travails under the inspiration of eternity, of a Divine Idea. (Hegel later developed this last idea.) Cf. Johann Gottlieb Fichte, *Addresses to the German Nation*, Chicago, 1922, pp. 54–138.

[1] Cf. *Addresses to the German Nation*, pp. 4, 14, 38, 158. So, in a sense, Rousseau's ideas have come full circle. The appeal to the senses, the slow development of natural capacity through pleasurable action, the idea of natural goodness with which one starts, the appeal to feeling, not reason, remains. But Fichte's education is a discipline of the will and his instrument is the State, and Rousseau would never have countenanced either idea. Rousseau wanted individual self-expression; Fichte wanted an ascetic group morality, voluntary self-sacrifice. He pleaded for State education, for the State is responsible only to God. It should compel men to be free, that is, to sacrifice themselves for the State.

How relatively important German and native influence were, it is hard to say. In any case one of the most noticeable features of the new upper-class attitude was an increased concern with religion and authoritarian morality. The Evangelical insistence on virtue and spiritual revival spread rapidly, until it found advocates among all of the middle and most of the upper class. Carlyle's 'close thy Byron: open thy Goethe' was a battle-cry that became as fatal to fatuous and slumbering formalism as it did to empiricism and rationalism. One has only to read the memoirs of important Victorians to realize their preoccupation with religious and moral problems. Most interesting from our point of view is the emergence, in the schools of the day, of a race of romantic prudes. Of Charles Wordsworth, Manning, and Isaac Williams, who criticized their schools on moral grounds despite their happiness there, we have already spoken.[1] Beside them may be placed other future Churchmen like John Allen, who resisted sin at Westminster by remembering his mother's prayers and the book of Proverbs;[2] or Havelock, the Indian warrior, of whom it is recorded that 'there were early indications of the strivings of the good Spirit of God in his soul' even at Charterhouse, where he and others met to read sermons and were dubbed Methodists;[3] or Rowland Williams who is described as 'a really religious boy, one who dared to kneel down and say his prayers in the "long chamber", to do which, in those days, required no little moral courage'.[4] Even more important were a group of future statesmen. Of Gladstone, for example, his biographer wrote: 'If it be said that his character was moulded by Eton, it must be added that it was not cast in the Eton mould; but got formed somehow outside it.'[5] Palmerston, at Harrow many years earlier, spoke of the 'drinking and swearing, which . . . fashionable at present, I think extremely ungentlemanlike'.[6] Peel, a schoolmate of Byron, kept free from the latter's influence through home

---

[1] Cf. *supra*, p. 98.   [2] Grier, *Allen*, pp. 20 ff.   [3] Brock, *Havelock*, pp. 13 ff.
[4] E. Williams, *Life of Rowland Williams*, Vol. I, p. 8.
[5] James Brinsley-Richards, *Seven Years at Eton*, London, 1883, p. 395.
[6] Sir Henry Lytton Bulwer, *The Life of Henry John Temple, Viscount Palmerston*, Vol. I, Philadelphia, 1871, p. 23.

training. In later years he could write, 'I would not send my boys there [Harrow] unless I believed, what I have reason to believe, that it is better conducted now than it was when I misspent my time there.'[1]

The Established Church itself was the centre of much of the moral revival of the time. The Evangelicals had indirectly succeeded in arousing it from its century or more of stupor into a realization that it must lead or be destroyed. Out of the ferment of the time arose a number of movements which can be vaguely classed as liberal. Since Arnold and others associated with reform were connected with various of these movements, Church liberalism has peculiar importance for schools. Arnold's attitude will be discussed later. Here it is enough to indicate that Angelican liberalism in all its manifestations was the religious expression of the Victorian Compromise. However much they differed in detail, men like Arnold and Whately, Hare and Thirlwall, Maurice and Sterling, Stanley and Kingsley, all had the same general point of view. They wanted to save the Church as an institution and revive it as a religious and moral influence. They appealed to the moral authority of God and were uncompromising in their hate of Benthamism and rationalism in general. On the other hand they realized—unlike Evangelicals or Newmanites—that irrational dogma and ritual as well as the exclusiveness of the Church must go. They preached an undogmatic, personal morality. In political and social questions, they were humanitarians and mild democrats who hated Tories no less than philosophic radicals; many of them, taking their lead from Coleridge, were believers in a paternalism that was at least as far from Disraeli's as it was from Robert Owen's.

B. CRITICISM: 1830–1835

I. CARLYLE

Discussion of the Public Schools between 1830 and 1835[2] differed from that in the previous period in two important

[1] Parker, *Robert Peel*, Vol. I, p. 15. Peel did send his son to a Public School.
[2] Though Arnold was already at Rugby in these years it seems logical to discuss criticism contemporary with his head-mastership at this point rather

respects. In the first place it was more copious: there was nearly as much expression of opinion about upper-class education in these five years as there had been in the preceding thirty. The time just preceding and following the Reform Bill was one of almost unparalleled intellectual ferment, and the Public Schools received, if anything, more than their share of attention. In the second place, the discussion of the thirties, although participated in by the same social groups as joined into it in the preceding period, manifested a new alignment of intellectual groups. Most important, there were virtually no thoroughgoing conservatives; almost all classes of Englishmen saw the need for some change. Moreover, there was no reactionary criticism in the thirties, though later on a new group arose which expressed a philosophy allied in some respects to that of the older reactionaries. The controversy of the thirties was between middle-class liberals of varying degrees of radicalism on the one side and upper-class liberal-conservatives on the other. During the early thirties the upper middle classses tended to join the advanced liberals; later on they swung over to the liberal-conservatives.

Most of the criticism of the time was part of a controversy carried on in the periodicals. Before we consider this controversy and the ideas that emerged from it, it seems advisable to say a word about the educational theories of one critic who stood somewhat apart from the battle. Though Carlyle actually wrote no direct attack on Public Schools, and though much of what he did say about them was written long after the thirties, he deserves special attention here because in educational as in so many other matters Carlyle was the symbol as well as the spokesman of the Victorian Compromise.

In one sense Carlyle was far from typical of the liberal-conservatism we have been discussing: he was a radical in his attitude towards educational as well as towards political

than later. Though several criticisms were directed at Arnold, for the most part opinion was as yet uninfluenced by him. On the other hand, Arnold is best understood when one can contrast and compare his work with the ferment of thought on Public Schools that was stirring in England during the beginnings of his reign at Rugby.

The Early Thirties

and religious institutions; he wanted to sweep them away as outworn. It was in the ends he desired that Carlyle typified and led the new Victorian upper-class mind. He preferred the moral and the emotional to the intellectual, and preached an authoritarian though individualistic morality as the great end of education. The intellectual must give way to the practical; men must learn to do, not to think. Carlyle's masters were Goethe and Pestalozzi,[1] and from them he got such modern ideas as the need for experience as an educational method; but like Fichte he used his masters' ideas in the service of training in obedience and allied virtues.

This is not to say that Carlyle had no concern for things mental. In his early days especially, intellectual education was of vital concern to him; and because of this concern and of his realization, from his own experience, of the nature of an adequate training, he was one of the most radical critics of the curriculum of Public Schools. Both at the Scotch day school at Annan to which he went and at Edinburgh University, then still the centre of a great cultural tradition, he was brought into contact with those modern subjects neglected by Public Schools and English universities. Algebra, geometry, and French were a prelude to an introduction to mathematical physics and modern geology under men like John Playfair and John Leslie, who were in contact with the best minds of the day.[2] As a result Carlyle reacted violently in later years against the dead classical tradition that still existed at Annan despite its comparative modernity. 'Greek and Latin were "mechanically" taught' and other things not at all. 'How,' he asks, 'can an inanimate . . . Gerund Grinder . . . foster the growth of anything?'[3] He was equally severe on the English schools. Speaking in 1823 of Charles Buller whom he tutored, he wrote: he 'had been fed

---

[1] Carlyle wrote that Goethe's ideas could be found 'under a very inferior but more practical form, in the writings of Pestalozzi'. (Cf. David Alec Wilson, *Carlyle*, 5 vols., London, 1923-9, Vol. V, pp. 231 ff.)

[2] Emery Neff, *Carlyle*, New York, 1932, pp. 17, 23-24. Unfortunately, though Edinburgh taught boys to 'act in terms of the mechanical age', teachers were so few and classes so crowded that Carlyle learned less than the programme offered him would suggest.

[3] *Sartor Resartus*, Centenary Edition, London, 1899, Vol. I, p. 84.

at Harrow on Latin and Greek *husks*, unsatisfying to a young fellow of the keenest sense for everything from the sublime to the ridiculous. . . . I tried to guide him into reading, into solid enquiry and reflection; he got some mathematics from me, and might have had more. He got what expansion into wider fields of intellect, and more manful modes of thinking and working my poor possibilities could yield him.'[1] All through his life the proper kind of intellectual education was precious to him, no less at the time of his Inaugural Address at Edinburgh (1867) with its praise of libraries, than in 1839 when he wrote *Chartism* with its passionate plea for learning.[2]

But even in early years learning was seldom for its own sake. Action, practical doing, was the primary end of education. And since action in itself, and particularly the kind that Carlyle desired, necessitated the possession of certain ethical qualities, moral training became an essential feature of education. As Carlyle became the reactionary imperialist and authoritarian of his later years, he grew more and more insistent on doing and less and less patient with mere understanding. Consequently, since learning was not the chief method of reaching moral ends, it became increasingly subordinated in Carlyle's thought to practical experience as the means of education.

As early as the thirties he had written: 'as if it were by universities and libraries and lecture-rooms, that man's Education, what we can call Education, were accomplished. . . . Foolish Pedant, that sittest there compassionately descanting on the learning of Shakespeare. . . . The grand result of schooling is a mind with just vision to discern, with free force to do: the grand schoolmaster is Practice.'[3] In the *Life of Sterling* he indicated that, though Public Schools might give a deficient intellectual education, they offered—unfortunately, for the most part inadvertently—something far more valuable: 'perhaps,—as is the singular case in most

---

[1] Wilson, *Carlyle*, Vol. I, p. 286.
[2] Carlyle was an ardent supporter of the radicals in their efforts to further popular education. (Cf. Neff, *Carlyle*, pp. 170–71.)
[3] *Corn Law Rhymes, Critical and Miscellaneous Essays*, 4 vols., Boston, 1861 Vol. III, p. 222.

The Early Thirties

schools and educational establishments of this unexampled epoch,—it was not the express set of arrangements in this or any extant University that could essentially forward him, [Sterling] but only the implied and silent ones; less in the prescribed "course of study", which seems to tend no whither, than—if you will consider it,—in the generous (not ungenerous) rebellion against said prescribed course . . . does help lie for a brave youth in such places'. Rebellion teaches vigorous mutual fidelity, reticence, steadfastness, mild stoicism; and, in the last analysis, 'What is Greek accidence, compared to Spartan discipline?'[1] In another place he wrote, this time with less of even indirect praise of schools, 'I foresee that our Etons and Oxfords with their nonsense-verses, college-logics, and broken crumbs of mere *speech*,—which is not even English or Teutonic speech, but old Grecian and Italian speech, dead and buried and much lying out of our way these two thousand years last past,— will be found a most astonishing seminary for the training of young English souls to take command in human Industries, and act a valiant part under the sun! The State does not want vocables, but manly wisdom and virtues.' 'Wise command, wise obedience: the capability of these two is the net measure of culture, and human virtue, in every man.'[2]

2. CONTROL

Meliorists no less than radicals among the controversialists of the thirties were agreed that substantial changes were necessary if Public Schools were to survive. As a fairly moderate liberal critic of Eton wrote, reform is in the air:

[1] Carlyle, *Life of Starling* (World's Classics V), London, 1907, p. 35.
[2] *Latter Day Pamphlets*, Vol. 5, Ashburton Edition, London, 1885, No. 4, p. 143. Carlyle continued to repeat these sentiments in varying forms all through his life. In 1854 he wrote that 'education should aim at teaching men to work'. This has been ignored in the educational system from primary school to Oxford. (Wilson, *Carlyle*, Vol. V, p. 86.) By 1866 he was shouting with a fierce despair that, like any army, we need 'bullying and drilling and compelling', for we live in an age of disobedience and anarchy. (Vol. XXIX of Centenary Edition, *Critical and Miscellaneous Essays*, Vol. IV, p. 476.) The following year he wrote hysterically that we must learn to 'work, to behave and do', not to talk. 'Beyond all other schooling' military service is the best. He cites the Prussia of Bismarck as the example to follow. (*Shooting Niagara and After*, Vol. XXX, Centenary Edition, pp. 39–41.)

institutions that show a 'scornful rejection of the demands of a reasoning and enlightened age' and, like Eton, hold 'an unfortunate pre-eminence' in 'undeviating adherence to antiquated errors', fighting 'single-handed the battle of prejudice and wrong', had better watch out or real revolution will overtake them.[1] Moreover, most critics were agreed that the immediate source of the resistance to change was the governing bodies of the Public Schools. In the words of the writer quoted above, 'there is in the constitution of Eton College an inherent principle, directly repulsive of reform', and by this 'principle' he referred to the control of the Head by the Provost.[2]

Moderates differed from thoroughgoing liberals in their unwillingness to make suggestions in regard to a new system of control, without which no radical changes, particularly in the ecclesiastical schools, were likely to occur. They even apologized to the authorities for seeming to be disrespectful, and hoped that school governors would not 'confound a demand for reasonable improvement, with a cry for total and indiscriminate revolution'.[3] The radicals on the other hand, realized that the problem of control was basic.

Unfortunately, those who wanted governmental reform were in no sense agreed on a programme. The largest group favoured a compromise between independent endowments and State control. Though dissatisfied with present conditions, they were not—with typical *laissez-faire* tenacity —willing to admit the idea of complete State control of upper-class education. On the other hand, dispensing entirely with any control would, they felt, produce unsatisfactory results. Most parents, not having the sense to demand a truly liberal education, would secure only inferior professors, and scholarship would be impaired.[4] It is notable that this is the position taken later by John Stuart Mill. Liberals were constantly being caught in this dilemma. Fearing the State, they allowed themselves to be seduced by Coleridge into defending endowments, and thus supporting a form of control which was less democratic, though not

---

[1] A Parent, *Some Remarks on the Present Studies, etc.*, London, 1834, p. 12.
[2] Ibid.   [3] Ibid, p. 6.   [4] Lytton, *England and the English*, p. 147.

more elastic, than management by Parliament would have been.

To the left of the main body of liberals were a few extremists in the tradition of Adam Smith. The *Westminster*, for example, continued, as late as 1835, to favour complete *laissez-faire* on the basis that endowments ruin industry.[1] These doctrinaire liberals were, however, far less important than were a group of liberals who were finally won over, in the thirties, to the idea of parliamentary control.

In January 1834 the *Quarterly Journal of Education*, sponsored by the Society for the Diffusion of Useful Knowledge, made a plea for a system of State education for all classes.[2] Though the *Journal* was willing to let the endowed schools remain, on the basis that no one would go to them if there was a good State system, its proposal was the most radical that had so far been made. Emboldened by its first sally, the *Journal* resumed its militant advocacy of Government schools in subsequent numbers, and by the fall of the year it had ceased to desire the preservation of the independence of the Public School. In October it wrote that endowed schools had conferred less benefit on the country 'than we might reasonably expect from their number and their wealth'.[3] 'We hope soon to see the time when the State will interfere with the management of every endowed school in the kingdom.' The State will direct knowledge, procure masters, and see that others except clergymen are heads of schools.[4] In July 1835, in answer to Arnold's anonymous defence of flogging, the *Journal* again insisted that endowed schools 'required to be remodelled, and to be placed under the superintendence of the State', for real reform could come only from the outside.[5] Though the *Quarterly Journal* remained for long almost alone in its advocacy of these ideas— the *British and Foreign Review* asked tentatively in 1835 if it might not be necessary to call in the State to control schools[6]

[1] *Westminster*, January 1835, pp. 119 ff.
[2] *Quarterly Journal of Education*, January 1834, p. 36.
[3] Ibid., October 1834, p. 237.
[4] Ibid., p. 239. This last statement alone would have been anathema to ninety per cent of school critics, and was the very antithesis of Arnoldianism.
[5] Ibid., July 1835, p. 82.
[6] *British and Foreign Review*, October 1835, p. 312.

—the campaign to bring the Public Schools into the service of the whole nation had finally been launched in earnest.

3. SCHOOLS AS SOCIAL INSTITUTIONS

If liberals attacked the government of the Public Schools, it was chiefly because they felt that the rulers were responsible for the shortcomings of the schools. Even more than in the previous period these shortcomings seemed to critics both serious and of varied nature, involving the nature of schools as social no less than as educational institutions.

Two groups of questions centred around the Public Schools as social institutions: those pertaining to the rights of foundations and those arising out of class stratification among non-foundationers. Few critics concerned themselves directly, any more than they had in the twenties, with the problem of doing away entirely with the caste system. With regard to the question of foundationers it is noteworthy that by 1834 even the *Quarterly* could admit that possibly Eton collegers had not been receiving all the money due to them.[1] Liberal-conservatives did not, however, take the matter very seriously. It was left for more radical writers to compare the fellows at Public Schools to the Rotten Boroughs dispensed with by the Reform Bill and to say grandiloquently, 'these are not the times when abuses can escape public notice, or, when once discovered, be allowed to exist'.[2] It was a left-wing writer who pointed out that 'a poor and indigent boy' of the foundation of Eton, costs his parents at the very lowest calculation, 70 £ a year, and that the statutes are obeyed only when they please the fellows.[3] Above all it was the radicals alone who proposed that the natives of Harrow receive a free modern education even if it were necessary to change the laws administered by the trustees,[4] and who suggested that admission to the foundations of Eton and Winchester ought to be by examination

---
[1] *Quarterly Review*, August 1834, p. 144.
[2] *The Times*, February 25th 1833, p. 3, also May 4th 1833, p. 2.
[3] *Quarterly Journal of Education*, October 1834, p. 279.
[4] Ibid., January 1835, p. 75.

since patronage was part of the old political system of pre-Reform Bill days.¹

To the class nature of the schools there were several objections. In the first place, the snobbery which it fostered was deplored by radicals and moderates alike. The *Quarterly Review* no less than the *Quarterly Journal of Education* contended that social distinctions ought not to exist within a school.² In the second place, upper-class predominance was accused of partial responsibility for the educational failure of schools. The *Quarterly Review* stated that idleness was the result of aristocratic prejudice against work, and would exist as long as many aristocrats went to Public Schools.³ The *Westminster* claimed that schools were run by aristocratic dunces who snubbed the aristocracy of talent, and, by endorsing fagging, taught that the slave-tyrant relationship is the normal one in life.⁴ Bulwer-Lytton insisted that, since aristocratic predominance encouraged snobbish competition among non-aristocrats, it vitiated any attempt to improve Public School education. 'Social prejudices . . . constitute our chief obstacle in obtaining, for the youth of the wealthier orders, a more practical and nobler system of education.' The petty aristocracy of merchants and lawyers want connexions and not an education; ironically enough, they will fail to attain their desire since rank will assert itself at the University and break the friendship between peer and commoner.⁵

4. INTELLECTUAL EDUCATION

By 1830 the industrial revolution and lower-class education had made themselves felt among the upper classes to the extent that the latter, along with the middle classes, began at least to take an interest in the intellectual side of education. In the thirties for the first time the radicals

¹ Ibid., October 1834, p. 293. Entrance by examination did not prove to be a help to the poor. It cost too much to prepare for the examination.
² *Quarterly Journal of Education*, January 1834, p. 39; October 1834, p. 281; *Quarterly Review*, August 1834, p. 138. In the case of the *Quarterly Review* this may have meant a desire to dispense with the poor altogether.
³ Ibid., January 1829, p. 112.   ⁴ *Westminster*, October 1835, p. 314.
⁵ Lytton, *England and the English*, p. 133.

were able to gain the support of moderates in insisting on some changes in the formal education given at schools. Though widespread reform had to wait many years, the end of complete inertia was in sight.

With regard to almost all the questions of the day there was some measure of agreement between liberals and liberal-conservatives. The latter were, however, more loath to admit difficulties and consequently less willing to suggest widespread changes than were the former. To begin with, critics were unanimous in their belief that the intellect deserved more attention than it had received in the past. Thus the *Quarterly Review* and other defenders of Eton praised the 'desire after knowledge' which had been growing in the previous twenty years.[1] One *Quarterly* writer even admitted that a certain amount of idleness existed at Eton.[2] At the same time moderates were still of the opinion that studies were but the skeleton of an education.[3] Moreover, they were inclined to believe that on the whole the Public Schools achieved their intellectual aims.[4] For sweeping charges in regard to the barrenness of the intellectual results achieved by Public Schools one must turn to the advanced liberals who, it must be remembered, now included, at least in regard to certain questions, individuals from the upper middle classes who had formerly been moderates. The *Edinburgh Review*, an Eton pamphleteer, and Bulwer-Lytton claimed that not only did Public Schools not teach anything useful, but they failed even to impart a classical training.[5] The *Edinburgh*, incidentally, suggested, thirty years before the actual formation of such a body, that a Royal Commission was needed to put 'fresh blood into the diseased frame of Eton'.[6] The *British and Foreign Review* accused the Public Schools of providing neither a professional nor a general education, and added, with significant reference to sentimental attachment, that education should make a man

[1] *Quarterly*, August 1834, p. 174; *Reply to Some Remarks*, p. 8. The *Quarterly* felt that, among other things, knowledge checked immorality.
[2] *Quarterly*, January 1829, p. 112.   [3] Ibid., August 1834, pp. 128 ff.
[4] Ibid., p. 141.
[5] *Edinburgh*, March 1831, pp. 68 ff., 77; *Eton Abuses Considered, etc.*, London, 1834, p. 16; Lytton, *England and the English*, pp. 133-4.
[6] *Edinburgh*, April 1830, pp. 67, 80.

The Early Thirties

look forward, not backward to his schooldays.[1] The *New Monthly* asserted that the upper classes thought that fives-courts and race-tracks were places of instruction; it felt that reformers 'in their eagerness for educating the poor . . . have overlooked a main preliminary, the education of the rich'.[2] The *Journal of Education* launched the fiercest attack. It contended that it was only the 'chance of a fellowship of King's which keeps up the number of scholars at Eton College'. Without this chance no parent would send his son into college for the sake of an exceedingly imperfect education, 'at a higher cost than he would incur at the greater number of the best private schools of the country.'[3] The *Journal* added bitterly that no important people have come from the College. Examinations were instituted some years ago, but 'the waters of reform did not rush in through this breach'. Eton has 'preserved an ample stock of venerable abuses'.[4]

Over remedies which did not involve changes in the subjects of study there was general agreement. In the first place, all shades of opinion realized that there ought to be more supervision, and therefore more teachers if boys were actually to learn anything.[5] In the second place, there was a general demand for more incentive to learn by way of examinations, etc., rather than by flogging. There were advocates of competitive examinations within schools no less than for admission to the Public Schools and universities.[6]

If extremists and moderates differed over ways of improving classical teaching, these differences were matters of degree much oftener than of kind. Liberal-conservatives

---

[1] *British and Foreign Review*, October 1835, pp. 298, 306.
[2] *New Monthly*, January 1838, p. 109.
[3] *Quarterly Journal of Education*, October 1834, p. 278.   [4] Ibid., p. 278.
[5] Cf. *British and Foreign Review*, October 1835, p. 313; *Quarterly*, October 1834, p. 284. This supervision, at Eton especially, was needed for the idle average. (*Eton Abuses Considered*, p. 16.) As it was, tutors had no time for any but candidates for the Newcastle. Moreover, what a boy did learn from them was in 'private business', for which he paid extra, and not in the form room. (*Some Remarks*, p. 20.) This is a disgrace to Eton, which is responsible for doing more than offering voluntary education at fancy prices. (*Edinburgh*, March 1831, p. 78.)
[6] *Quarterly*, January 1829, p. 124; August 1834, p. 142; *Reply to Some Remarks*, p. 7; *Edinburgh*, March 1831, p. 73; April 1830, p. 67. Cf. *Some Remarks*, p. 27; *Eton Abuses Considered*, pp. 3 ff.

seldom followed liberals in their advocacy of trained teachers[1] or more friendly relations between boys and masters; these ideas were either occasional or suggested only by extremists. The important split occurred over the question of the extent to which supervision and the installation of examinations ought to be carried. The moderates refused to give up self-help entirely in order to accept a routine that might help the average boy, and fought an excess of examinations on the basis that they would cause 'envious competition' to supersede 'generous emulation'.[2]

In asserting these stock conservative arguments in the face of a growing demand for regularization and forced study, the liberal-conservatives of the thirties were, it may be added, far more conscious than were their conservative predecessors that they were the defenders of true liberal methods in education.

Where liberal-conservatives and liberals disagreed most profoundly was over the question of the curriculum. The former might be willing to substitute prose for verse composition[3] and to allow more time for translation and less for grammar.[4] They might even suggest on occasion that mathematics or possibly French might be added to the curriculum so long as they did not interfere with other work, or, as the *Quarterly* says, destroy love of knowledge.[5] But they were concerned primarily over the classics, which they defended with all the old arguments.

Liberals of all shades, on the other hand, were passionately interested in widening the curriculum to include useful subjects. Indeed, the urgent desire for practical studies became a touchstone of liberalism in the thirties, and continued to be so for sixty years or more. Most liberals at this early date were still willing to retain the classics and, unlike later reformers, to relegate science to the background.

---

[1] Cf. *Edinburgh*, April 1830, p. 67; *Eton Abuses Considered*, p. 14; Lytton, *England and the English*, p. 141. The *Quarterly* opposed this on the basis that only Kingsmen could know the Eton system. (Cf. *Quarterly*, August 1834, p. 143.)

[2] *Quarterly*, August 1834, p. 130.   [3] *Eton System Vindicated*, p. 38.

[4] *Reply to Some Remarks*, p. 7.

[5] *Quarterly*, August 1834, pp. 128, 167; January 1829, p. 140; January 1831 p. 174.

The Early Thirties

Nevertheless their frequent and spirited attacks on the meagreness of Public School studies and their insistent propaganda in favour of history, mathematics, and modern languages seemed radical enough to liberal-conservatives.

The opening gun in the war on the curriculum was fired by the *Edinburgh* early in 1830.[1] In an article full of invective it pointed out that a boy at Eton learns only fragments of Greek and Roman authors from a wretched text-book of selections, a little grammar from a worse book, the way to make absurd Latin verses and a smattering of divinity and geography. 'He has not read a single book of Herodotus, or Thucydides, or Xenophon, or Livy, or Polybius, or Tacitus; he has not read a single Greek tragedy or comedy, he is utterly ignorant of mathematical or physical science, and even of arithmetic; the very names of logical, moral, or political science, are unknown to him. Modern history and modern languages are, of course, out of the question.' Is this creditable to the 'most celebrated public school of England?'[2] The accusations and suggestions of the *Edinburgh* were echoed in book, pamphlet, and article with increasing frequency through the next five years. Over and over again critics attacked the preoccupation with the ' "dead apples" of verbal pedantry' and pleaded for what were considered practical subjects, 'realities ... not phantoms'.[3] As one writer pointed out, Greek and Latin were useful in the sixteenth century; if we would really follow the lead of our ancestors we should teach French, English, mathematics, and history to-day.[4]

Unfortunately, in the struggle for curricular change the real educational ends for which, ideally, liberals stood were often lost sight of. To such an extent was this true that conservatives could claim—as they did in regard to methods —that they stood more for genuine liberal ends than did

[1] The *Edinburgh*'s attack was undoubtedly inspired in part by its perception of the superiority of Scottish education.
[2] *Edinburgh*, April 1830, p. 73.
[3] Cf. *Edinburgh*, March 1831, pp. 73, 77; Lytton, *England and the English*, p. 141; *Eton Abuses Considered*, p. 18; *Quarterly Journal of Education*, October 1834, p. 290; *British and Foreign Review*, pp. 298, 307; *Westminster*, April 1834, p. 303.
[4] *Eton Abuses Considered*, p. 18.

those who professed to be liberals. The great libertarians like Huxley and Mill saw that a broad understanding of life and of method coupled with love of thinking and of knowledge were the ends of education. If they advised a broadening of the curriculum it was in order to secure these ends, and they did not believe that a mere installing of new subjects taught by a sufficiency of masters and tested by examinations was automatically going to secure mental freedom and intellectual interest. Unfortunately, however, many proponents of change thought of useful subjects as a panacea for all educational difficulties. They believed that intellectual freedom would be the automatic result of a new curriculum or—much worse—were not especially interested in intellectual freedom. Their demand for new studies was a product of economic need, and was never far-sighted enough to rise above this need and realize that the new civilization demanded intellectual elasticity and originality. What was wanted was knowledge that was directly useful in a new competitive world. Consequently new subjects and more efficient teaching were all that was cared about. Writers like Bulwer-Lytton spent their time warning the upper classes that if they wished to compete with the new middle classes they had better learn practical subjects.[1] As he said many years after the thirties, 'if one learnt nothing out of school at Eton and Harrow, would what one learns at the school enable one to keep up with the sons of traders?'[2] Magazines like the *British and Foreign Review* fought against the 'antiquated lumber' with which the Etonian mind was filled because it had no direct use in the world of competition.[3] The new capitalism was making its presence felt in the schools: those who were far-sighted enough to see the need to adjust to it by learning contemporary subjects failed to take the further step of fighting for an education that would create individuals able to control this new world as well as compete in it.

To anticipate for a minute, if, from a broadly liberal point of view Public School intellectual reform failed, it

[1] *England and the English*, p. 133.
[2] Earl of Lytton, *Life of Edward Bulwer*, 2 vols., London, 1913, Vol. II, p. 249.
[3] *British and Foreign Review*, October 1835, pp. 298, 307.

was partly the result of liberal narrowness. If the education given at a Public School has never given mental sustenance or taught elasticity of mind or intellectual curiosity, the narrow or false liberals of the thirties and after must bear much of the blame, since, through their lack of vision, they failed to take into consideration the need for real teaching and for a substitute for the freedom and leisure that boys had under the old system. At the same time it is equally true that the reformers of the thirties were probably in any event helpless to control events. Even with vision—and true liberals did have it—they probably could not have improved circumstances. The schools in the nineties with their hodgepodge curriculum weighted with lifeless examinations would have been uncongenial to the narrowest of the reformers. Conditions were, on the intellectual side, the result of the demands of the machine age and the unavoidable compromise between classicist and scientist. Capitalistic civilization inevitably encouraged competition and discouraged self-development. It was responsible in the moral field, I believe, for the corruption of Arnold's ideals. In the intellectual field it created the fetish of examinations and the worship of mere knowledge. Finally, the tenacity of the classic tradition and of English distaste for learning, while they could not forestall the tendencies of the age, succeeded in preventing Public Schools from being effective in any way at all. The late nineteenth-century school tried to teach all subjects including the classics to boys who did not want to learn any subjects; as a result Public School men were neither self-developed individuals nor effective business men.

5. MORAL EDUCATION

As in the preceding period, the chief accusation against Public School life was that it produced unhappiness, slavery, and immorality. On this score all writers of the thirties were agreed. Differences between liberal-conservatives, moderate liberals, and radicals existed partly in the relatively greater concern of the radicals over freedom, but chiefly in the comparative vehemence and bitterness of the leftist groups.

The liberal-conservatives, as represented by the *Quarterly*, contented themselves with admitting that the morals of collegers were not all that they ought to be and that religious instruction was less than inspiring.[1] The more moderate, moreover, claimed to be reformers, not destroyers; they pictured themselves as loving Public Schools even to idolatry.[2] Bulwer-Lytton, indeed, despite a good many hard words about Public Schools, wished that he had gone to one.

Moderate liberal criticism, as exemplified by the *Edinburgh*, was restrained, though thorough. It accused Eton education —Eton being the centre of much of the discussion of the time—of completely failing to create virtuous and honourable characters.[3] 'The number of scholars is so great [there were 612 at Eton in 1829], the tutor's time is necessarily so much occupied, both with the revision of school exercises and other school business, and so much liberty is very properly given to the boys, that a considerable laxity of conduct may exist in the youths of older standing, without being either restrained or detected; and the smaller and weaker boys are exposed, without hope of redress, to the merciless tyranny of their superiors in age and strength.' 'By a tacit agreement between the stronger and weaker parties, has been established at Eton the system of fagging—the only regular institution of slave-labour, enforced by brute violence, which now exists in these islands.' Strength, tempered by a sense of honour, rules. The masters connive without approving, since neither flogging nor the weak efforts at religious education produce either order or virtue. Older boys are freely allowed to break the spirit of the younger or produce in them revenge and deceit. Moreover, legalizing fagging is no remedy. 'The practice of fagging does not diminish tyranny —it authorizes and multiplies it.'[4]

Occasionally, as indicated by the reference to slave labour, the *Edinburgh* could be bitter enough. Similarly, one moderate pamphleteer could, with considerable asperity, compare the 'hardships and privations' of life in college to

[1] *Quarterly*, August 1834, pp. 145, 149.
[2] *Edinburgh*, April 1830, p. 74; *Eton Abuses*, pp. 30–31.
[3] *Edinburgh*, April 1830, p. 74.   [4] Ibid., March 1831, p. 75.

The Early Thirties

those of 'the most miserable slave in the West Indies, or the most wretched inmate of a modern manufactory'.[1] Bulwer-Lytton railed in no measured terms against the creation by schools of cruelty and duplicity. 'It is no disgrace to insult the weak and lie to the strong, to torment the fag and deceive the Master.' Parents think a boy learns to know the world; instead he learns merely its vices, and comes out 'at once arrogant and servile'.[2] But for a bitterness which was not satisfied until it revolutionized the system one must turn to the radicals.

The *Westminster*, for example, showed the most utter contempt for the whole paraphernalia of aristocratic education. The English aristocrat is a slave to the institutions that mould him. 'They render him as much as possible, an instrument of misery, both to himself and to his fellow-beings.' At home and at school he learns to gratify his animal instincts of insubordination, idleness, insolence, lying, gluttony, ignorance, and vice. Fagging, reputed to teach equality, actually makes the young nobleman see life in terms of tyrants and slaves.[3] Similarly, a writer in the *New Monthly*, an Etonian himself, claimed, after revisiting his school, that he had no further use for it. He promised, indeed, never to return there. Attacking the cant of youthful happiness, which prevents any attempt being made to produce real happiness, this alumnus asserted that he spent a youth of 'almost uninterrupted suffering' at Eton and learnt little except the 'knowledge of the worst corners of the human heart'. The school is without doubt a 'world

[1] *Eton Abuses Considered*, p. 26. The comparison with workers indicates that one source of Public School criticism was that humanitarianism which investigated mines and passed Factory Acts in 1833 and 1847.
Besides this comparison, *Eton Abuses Considered* contains another comment of interest. It directly attacked Eton's great master Keate for the cavalier way in which he treated his older boys, who were to be the hereditary legislators and upholders of the rights and liberties of Englishmen and 'the established religion'. Keate, by using the rod on them and always assuming they lie, creates an enmity between boy and masters which makes moral guidance impossible, and produces the very vices he fears. If you regard a boy as a liar, you produce the 'horrible system of falsehood which prevails among the boys in their intercourse with the Masters', which is 'inconsistent with the name and character of a gentleman'. Flogging sensitive boys is repulsive, insensitive ones, inefficacious. (Ibid., p. 10.)
[2] Lytton, *England and the English*, p. 144.
[3] *Westminster*, October 1835, p. 314.

in miniature', but it is a 'world of anarchy and lawless violence' where strength and passion are king and 'malice, falsehood, and hypocrisy', 'cringing to superiors', 'insolence where it was safe' are the commonest phenomena.[1] To-day nothing has changed because no effort is made to break through established usage in the 'headquarters of conservatism'. Eton is in all respects behind working-class education.[2]

The most constant radical depreciation of Public School moral education was voiced by the *Quarterly Journal of Education*. In four long articles it attacked every aspect of school life.[3] 'The great boarding-house system of our public schools,' it felt, 'is one of the most unfavourable that could be devised for forming the character of boys.'[4] Referring specifically to Eton, it asserted that 'There is not the slightest moral superintendence exercised by any one master or tutor of Eton over the conduct of his pupils, except during the hours of business'.[5] As a result, one witnesses 'the moral contamination and the personal wretchedness of the college life of Eton'.[6] Cunning, not virtue is bred; dullness is punished, and wickedness goes free. As for the supposed 'high and honourable tone' of Eton, it can mean no more than the ethics[7] of the aristocratic and corrupt court of Charles II and Louis XV.

Flogging 'as a remedy, is ineffectual, as a punishment inconsiderate, and as an exercise of power, cruel'.[8] It teaches injustice and appeals to fear; vice goes on just the same, and 'boys often not only hate but despise their masters'.[9] The fagging system is inexcusable. Fags 'are the slaves and drudges of the school, performing the most menial offices,

---

[1] *New Monthly*, October 1836, p. 156.
[2] Ibid., pp. 159–62. The author reveals his political bias when he suggests that Canning's betrayal of reform may have been due to his education.
[3] All its articles were not attacks on Public Schools. In January 1833, for example, the *Journal* published an apology for Westminster School in which it contended that fagging had been reduced to 'such trifling services as secure patronage to a little boy, without in any degree subjecting him to hardship or ill-treatment'. Usually, favourable articles were not, however, by the editors, but by schoolmasters like Dr. Arnold. (Ibid., January 1833, p. 47.)
[4] *Quarterly Journal of Education*, January 1834, pp. 36–40.
[5] Ibid., October 1834, p. 285. [6] Ibid., p. 278.
[7] Ibid., p. 282. [8] Ibid., January 1835, p. 84.
[9] Ibid., January 1834, pp. 36–40.

subjected to the most wanton caprice, and often to the most cruel personal ill usage'.[1] Irresponsible power leads to abuse: bullying, confusion, and legal tyranny.[2] Moreover—this is the first overt mention of sex that I have found—the older will teach sexual dirt to the younger and create a 'prurient disposition'. Impurity is bound to and does occur in the dormitories.[3] Finally—and most important in liberal eyes—to fagging is due the 'want of independence, both politically and in private life, which has characterized too many of our countrymen'. 'The humbling of the growing spirit of youth, which is the great ruling principle of our public schools, is every way objectionable.'[4] Fagging destroys the timid whose independence must be protected and applauded.

Over suggested remedies for tyranny and immorality liberal-conservatives and liberals were fundamentally at odds. The former wished to retain most features of Public School life, and to secure improvement chiefly by a revival in formal religious teaching.[5] The latter felt that it was necessary to scrap the essential features of the old Public School, such as flogging, fagging,[6] and above all formal religious teaching, which they felt was a failure and interfered with real discipline.[7] They desired to make a scientific study of the 'principles of human nature' in order to reach a programme of action.[8]

The *Quarterly Journal* was the only liberal publication to present in print the outline of a positive alternative to current methods.[9] Its programme is interesting since it was formulated

---

[1] Ibid., January 1835, p. 86.   [2] Ibid., July 1835, p. 96.
[3] Ibid., p. 99.   [4] Ibid., January 1835, p. 88.
[5] *Quarterly Review*, August 1834, pp. 142, 149, 174. The *Quarterly* had other suggestions also; interestingly enough it was the first to suggest manly sport as a cure for vice.
[6] As the *Quarterly Journal of Education* said, younger and older boys ought to have a very different relationship from that of fagging: the older ought to be good examples to the younger. (July 1835, p. 94.)
[7] *Quarterly Journal of Education*, July 1835, p. 85. Some of the more moderate liberals objected to doing away with religious instruction entirely, but they did want to abolish compulsory chapel. (Cf. *Some Remarks*, pp. 14, 16; *Eton Abuses*, p. 22.) It will be noted that even the *Quarterly Journal* liked Dr. Arnold's sermons. (Cf. January 1834, p. 43.)
[8] Ibid., July 1835, p. 85.
[9] Others made tentative suggestions. The Eton pamphleteers urged the appeal to a boy's honourable feelings by a master who should know each

as a direct answer to Dr. Arnold's defence of flogging and formal religion, which appeared in the columns of the *Quarterly Journal*. One thus sees the scheme which most directly threatened to destroy the Public School system set in relief against the ideas which were to preserve it.

As in the socialist solution for the evils of a *laissez-faire* economic society, the prime necessity according to the *Quarterly Journal* was closer superintendence by masters. There ought to be more masters, and they ought to delegate no power of any kind or tolerate any custom which they did not approve.[1] Boys must be governed out of school hours; athletics—and here the *Journal* agrees with the *Quarterly Review*—may help, but they are not enough.[2] 'There is a great deal of freedom ... in the life of an Eton boy'; though freedom is theoretically good, it must be controlled.[3] In the second place, masters ought to teach by example and encouragement, not by force. They ought to be in *loco parentis* to a boy. Master-boy enmity must be broken down and replaced by love, esteem, and sympathy.[4] Only by the inspiration and example of a man who 'shall be a proper model for imitation' can real freedom be fostered and youth be formed 'for his future social duties as a citizen'.[5]

As more and more people became dissatisfied with the *status quo*, these doctrines, with their fundamental assumption that the old school must disappear, won an ever greater number of converts. But they were never to be actualized as far as upper-class education was concerned. For even

---

boy intimately and take a friendly interest in him. (*Eton Abuses*, pp. 8, 10.) The *New Monthly* urged the checking of fagging and the teaching of morals. (October 1836, p. 159.) The *Edinburgh* wanted flogging reduced, fagging abolished. The editors felt that it was up to masters to stop tyranny and to carry their labours into the moral field. (*Edinburgh*, March 1831, p. 73.)

[1] *Quarterly Journal of Education*, July 1835, pp. 88 ff., 94 ff.
[2] Ibid., p. 93.   [3] Ibid., October 1834, p. 284.
[4] *Quarterly Journal of Education*, January 1834, pp. 36, 40. Cf. also October 1834, p. 285; July 1835, p. 99. In this connexion the *Journal* cites Pestalozzi's teaching. Taken with De Quincey's mention of the subject in a review of the Hills' book and a favourable comment by Bulwer-Lytton, this reference indicates that among advanced liberals at any rate foreign educational theories were becoming known.
[5] Ibid., July 1835, pp. 85, 88, 99.

while they were being most loudly voiced, Arnold was proving at Rugby that he could accomplish what all but a few extremists desired without destroying the old order. To the reforms of Arnold and of several of his immediate predecessors we must, therefore, now turn our attention.

PART III
THREE REFORMERS

CHAPTER I

RUSSELL AND BUTLER

SINCE any reform of Public Schools through State agency was out of the question during the first half of the nineteenth century, change could be effected only by individual masters in individual schools.[1] Furthermore, it could be brought about only by the strongest leader in a particularly favourable situation. In schools where conservative or hostile traditions were especially powerful or where there were conservative ecclesiastical governors, progress was relatively difficult, if not, at times, impossible. Hawtrey, head master of Eton, complained to Samuel Butler in 1834 that he could never have reformed Eton on Shrewsbury lines, partly because of ecclesiastical governors, and partly because of the 'nature of the materials which we have to work upon—sons of people who do not care about Latin and Greek, and who would much rather hear that a boy was captain of the boats than that he had gained the Newcastle Scholarship'.[2]

John Russell of Charterhouse, Samuel Butler of Shrewsbury, and Thomas Arnold of Rugby, were the agents of the most radical changes made in Public Schools in the first third of the nineteenth century. They were all powerful individuals and they all worked under favourable circumstances. In none of the three schools over which they presided were there ecclesiastical bodies to hamper them. Even Arnold admitted that he could not have succeeded in reforming Eton or Winchester.[3] He had, as it was, serious difficulties with the trustees of Rugby. Moreover, all three schools were in a relatively decadent state and were thus ready for reform. Finally, the classes that patronized them,

[1] It is worthy of note in this connexion that the opposition to State interference found powerful allies in great individual reformers like Butler, Arnold, and Thring. (Cf. Butler, *Life of S. Butler*, Vol. II, p. 203; Arthur Penryhn Stanley, *The Life and Correspondence of Thomas Arnold*, New York, 1846, p. 78.)
[2] Butler, *Life of S. Butler*, Vol. II, pp. 92–3.
[3] Cf. Stanley, *Life and Correspondence of Thomas Arnold*, p. 78.

the middle classes rather than the aristocracy, were the ones that most wanted change.

In all other respects, however, the three reformers present a contrast rather than a comparison. They differed profoundly in personality, in ideas, in the success which crowned their efforts, and in their influence on the future. Arnold is by far the most powerful individual and the most thoroughgoing reformer of the three. Moreover, he was, in a way that Butler and surely Russell were not, an instrument in the re-establishment of the Public School system as a popular and living institution.

Arnold, therefore, has the greatest claim on our attention. Primarily, we must study his system and his personality, his success and his influence if we are to understand how Public Schools change. But Russell and Butler have their importance in the story of Public School development. Both had an immediate success at least comparable to Arnold's; Butler had an influence on the future as well. What makes it chiefly desirable, however, to link together with Arnold's the names of these schoolmasters of a previous period[1] is more a contrast than a comparison. Russell's and Butler's careers throw a light on Arnold's achievement. Why did Russell fail completely in the end? Why was Butler's ultimate influence relatively small? The answers to these questions are vital to an understanding of Public School evolution in general and of the success and importance of Arnold's work in particular.

(a) RUSSELL

To compare Russell to either Butler or Arnold is in a sense a travesty. As a man he deserves in no sense to be put beside them. His innovation was as limited in extent as Arnold's was inclusive, and as disastrous as the latter's was successful. Russell changed neither the intellectual nor the moral ends of school life except inadvertently and for the worse. He merely tinkered vainly with methods. But this tinkering,

---

[1] Butler was at Shrewsbury from 1798 to 1836. Russell did his chief work before 1820.

though limited, was more radical in a way than anything Arnold or Butler attempted.

Russell became head master of Charterhouse in 1811, and in 1813 began the experiment for which he is chiefly known. This was simply the use of boy teachers. The brightest boys were to act as assistant masters in order to make it possible to give more instruction than the limited staff of teachers could possibly secure for the students. Russell had only five masters for 431 students in 1821.[1] It is notable that no attempt to change the curriculum was included in the experiment. The idea of mutual instruction was Russell's only positive contribution to Public School education. But his abolition of fagging in order to terminate the master-slave relationship between boys was equally radical, as was, in a way, his changing the names of the forms in the interests of logic.[2]

In the ends Russell meant to serve and in the means he used, one sees the forces that were moulding him. New upper middle-class demands dictated his purposes, and the new middle-class radical intellectualism his methods. The moderately rich who patronized or wished to patronize Charterhouse desired more knowledge at cheaper prices. Russell could answer this demand only by drawing on the Madras system of Bell. This had been evolved as a way of reconciling middle-class humanitarian anxiety to educate the poor with the limitations of middle-class pocket-books.[3] Russell applied it to a Public School because, to give a boarding-school education, always an expensive affair, at even moderate rates, meant that teachers could not be paid very much. By using the Madras system, he offered the middle classes a way of solving their difficulties in regard to their own education just as Bell had in regard to that of the poor. For the first and last time a practice used in schools for the lower classes was applied to a traditional Public School; the ultimate failure of the attempt did not encourage further borrowing.

[1] Davies, *Charterhouse in London*, p. 264.
[2] Russell decided, quite reasonably, that the highest form ought to be the first, not the sixth.
[3] Cf. Note 6, p. 137.

The abolition of fagging was also an answer to middle-class sentiment; it was part of the growing humanitarian objection both to tyranny and to the undemocratic relationship between boys. Russell's was, it may be added, the only attempt except Butler's to do away with fagging in a Public School.

In the way in which Russell went about his task of providing a cheap, intellectual education and a less tyrannical social life, he illustrated the nature of radical practice. Hewlett in *Peter Priggins* calls him, appropriately, Mr. Innovate. For Russell seemed to share the intellectualist belief that reform meant overturn, and that the installation or abolition of a mechanism would, if it were essentially logical, produce automatically the ends designed. The boy-monitor system had proved a fruitful idea elsewhere; he therefore introduced it at Charterhouse without any consideration of the peculiar conditions of a Public School and expected it to function in practice as it was supposed to do in theory. Fagging was evil; he therefore abolished it without taking into account its causes or the purpose it served.

The middle classes readily responded to Russell's innovations. At one time there were 460 students at Charterhouse. For over a decade parents sent boys to Russell, confidently expecting them to learn the classics under ideal social conditions. Then came the reaction; numbers began dropping off, and by 1830 the school was nearly deserted. One wonders only that the catastrophe did not happen sooner. Despite Wellington's statement that in 1820 Charterhouse was the best school in England, and Bentham's uninformed belief that Russell successfully taught languages, the school was apparently noted chiefly, according to Thackeray, Mozley, Tupper, Liddell, and Hewlett, for the paucity of its intellectual training, the severity and ineffectiveness of its discipline, and the brutality and immorality of its life. According to Mozley Charterhouse was unlike other schools —and worse. There was probably less, rather than more learning and humanity at Russell's school than at Keate's or George Butler's.

There were many reasons for Russell's failure, some of more particular interest and application to the problem of Public School reform than others. To begin with, it is doubtful whether any boarding-school, with or without the Bell system, could have given an education to so many boys with the aid of so few masters, or prevented tyranny and vice under conditions as crowded as those existing at Charterhouse. In the second place, Russell was apparently unfitted either to teach or to manage boys. According to Tupper and Thackeray he was a pedant and a despot; even had he not worked under intolerable conditions to install an unworkable system, he could probably not have built up a successful school.

In the third place, Russell failed because his plan was unsuited to a Public School. Had he started from scratch as had the Hills, he might have run an effective if not an influential school. But the attempt to inject piecemeal innovation into a traditional situation was doomed to failure from the start in any but exceptional hands. Russell's legislative fiats produced resentment, and thus accentuated the evils they were meant to cure. At one time the boys burned the head master in effigy for his attempt to do away with old customs and privileges.[1] They refused to obey boy monitors because they were unaccustomed to obeying unathletic scholars. The boy-monitor, indeed, was likely to be found under the desk when there was a disturbance.[2] Fagging was a sympton of a disease, not its cause; boys resented its abolition and continued to act as they always had, if not worse. Wingfield claims that 'The abolition of fagging by Russell brought about a far worse and cruel system of bullying'.[3] Removing a name does not remove a practice. Both Butler and Arnold, in different ways, understood this fact.

The one aspect of a traditional Public School that was absent from Charterhouse was the only one that could, perhaps, have brought order out of the chaos. Because of its heterogeneous patronage, Charterhouse had not the unity

[1] Cf. (Hewlett) *Peter Priggins*, p. 206.
[2] Cf. Davies, *Charterhouse in London*, p. 265.
[3] Cf. W. W. Wingfield, in Mozley, *Reminiscences*, Vol. I, p. vi.

that made for order at Eton: 'we were, in fact, a mob of boys, suddenly gathered, and as quickly dispersed. There was no cohesion or common vitality in the whole affair.'[1]

Clearly no half-way system was possible. One either destroyed the traditional Public School or worked within its limits. If one chose the latter way, one did not expect to work miracles by reforms as superficial as they were thought to be radical. One changed important practices; and one reformed with as little actual overt change as possible.

(b) BUTLER

Samuel Butler's system at Shrewsbury was in no sense a failure. Unlike Russell he embodied his aims successfully in the school that he administered for over thirty years. He turned out probably a larger number of boys educated according to his principles than did any early nineteenth-century schoolmaster except Arnold. Moreover, his work was appreciated at the time as well as later. The West-Midland upper middle and professional classes flocked to Shrewsbury all through his reign. During his head-mastership, Dr. Drury and Dr. Longley of Harrow and Dr. Hawtrey of Eton came to Butler for advice. In after years his system exerted an influence on Public School education which, if not always direct and all decisive, cannot be neglected. As the *Quarterly* wrote in 1842:

'If . . . it be reasonable to suppose that the education of the higher classes, and in particular of the clergy, is at least as important as that of the poor,—and if the silent but most practical reformation which has been at work in our public schools for many years past ever attracts the notice which it deserves,—then the time will come when men will feel an interest in tracing the steps of the improvement; and they will hardly fail to give honour due to that scholar who set the first example in remodelling our public education, and gave a stimulus which is now acting on almost all the public schools in the country.'[2]

---

[1] Cf. Mozley, *Reminiscences*, Vol. I, p. 415.
[2] *Quarterly*, September 1842, p. 315.

Butler managed a successful school and influenced Public School growth because, in the first place, he was a powerful personality. He had what every great schoolmaster from Busby to Sanderson possessed, a combination of wisdom and understanding, and a good deal of severity. He was able to build a system and turn it into a living and functioning institution by the sheer force of his individuality. And this very force, working on and through individual boys and permeating the school, established a living tradition which radiated beyond the school. Butler, no less than Arnold it may be added, was very conscious of this influence of personality on Public School growth, and if he fought State control of Public Schools, it was partly because he feared that Parliament would obstruct the functioning of individuals.

If, however, personality was important and even indispensable, it was, if anything, less important in accounting for his success and influence than the fact that his ideas and methods were in accordance with the desires and needs of his age and the possibilities of reform in a Public School. Original and radical in some ways he may have been, but it was because his ideas were not too different or too far in advance of those of important sections of public opinion within and outside of schools that he was able to accomplish his reforms and serve as a guide to future generations. To a certain extent successful reformers are deliberate originators; much more, however, are they likely to guide and materialize forces already present around them.

Butler came in 1798 to a school with only eighteen boys in it. The town of Shrewsbury, disgusted with the failure of their once flourishing educational institution, had reorganized the management. The mayor and twelve gentlemen now replaced the corporation as a governing body, though the burgesses still retained the right of free education. St. John's College secured the power to appoint the head master. It immediately secured Samuel Butler with the hope that he would make Shrewsbury into a great school.[1] Butler had virtually a free hand in making reforms, being unhampered by traditions among either scholars or parents or

[1] *History of Shrewsbury*, p. 132.

governing body. Innovation of the kind Russell attempted might even have worked at Shrewsbury. But Butler was no theorist or radical. As he grew older he became, indeed, more and more averse to innovation. As he wrote in 1836, regarding the management of a Public School, 'My advice would be to let things alone; let the improvements gradually develop themselves.'[1] Brought up at Rugby under her first rebuilder, James, he was devoted to the Public School system. James had rebuilt Rugby along Etonian lines. Butler, who greatly admired James, built Shrewsbury for the most part on Rugbeian lines. He developed a school that resembled in most respects the Public School described in Part II, with all its faults and virtues. There was no better model at the time, and Butler was no original genius. Furthermore, Butler as a master resembled the traditional Busby type more than he differed from him.

Shrewsbury was a strictly classical school. The classics were to form the taste and the mind and teach noble thoughts. With James, Butler frowned on mathematics or history as being too much for young people.[2] He defended Latin and Greek composition.[3] He taught the classics for their style rather than for their content. Furthermore, Butler's system —exaggerated by Kennedy later—was made for a few scholars only. It aimed towards university honours, and was inclined to neglect the average boy.

As with most masters of the period, the intellectual was more directly and ostensibly important to Butler than the moral. The master's main business was to teach the classics. Moreover, in so far as Butler did concern himself over morals, he was, for the most part, the old-fashioned schoolmaster. He was the stern master with the rod, and was, indeed, known all through his head mastership for undue severity.[4] Consequently, there was continued violence of one kind or another at Shrewsbury. Butler solved the

[1] Butler, *Life of S. Butler*, Vol. II, p. 205.
[2] Ibid., Vol. I, p. 18.   [3] Ibid., p. 25.
[4] In 1806 he had to justify himself for flogging so much by claiming that his punishments were the same as those of other Public Schools. By 1835 he could tell parents that he whipped little boys for idleness, and that if they (the parents) disliked this, they had better remove their sons. (Butler, *Life of S. Butler*, Vol. I, p. 48; Vol. II, p. 107.)

problem of a united and secret public opinion among the boys much less well than did Arnold, who himself had troubles on this score.[1] In 1818 there were town and gown battles in which Butler was even threatened with violence. The boys struck twice over the boiled beef and the harsh life that they had to live, and Butler, who put down revolt with promptness and severity, was forced to expel some of the ringleaders in 1829.[2] On the whole, life at Shrewsbury was none too pleasant. Butler made little effort to overcome the fact that the school was 'almost Spartan in the fewness of its comforts and the hardness of its discipline'.[3] He even discouraged such sports as football and boating, thus permitting little outlet for the boys' energies.[4] Butler shared the general contemporary blindness to the need for new means of securing humanity and morality.

Yet Butler did make important changes. Even in the moral field, about which he cared relatively little, he tried tentatively and less successfully than Arnold to introduce some of the ideas shared by both masters. Compared with Keate or even James, Butler was a great innovator. He believed that he had 'charge of boys' . . . morals as well as their learning,'[5] and took measures to put this belief into practice. Most important, he tried to break down the barrier between boy and master. He trusted his boys, and, as a result, they were often attached to him and transmitted his orders like the barons of old.[6] However, though he depended on the example and influence of his older boys, he avoided—and Shrewsbury continued to avoid—a full-fledged prefect system: Kennedy had refused the headmastership of Harrow because he would 'take no school where fagging is a legalized system'.[7] Though towards the little boys Butler remained the severe master whom boys are bound, he believes, to fear,[8] he deprecated flogging except

---

[1] Butler, *Life of S. Butler*, Vol. I, p. 108. Butler was head master in a more turbulent age, it must be remembered.
[2] Cf. ibid., pp. 156, 353, and *History of Shrewsbury*, pp. 137–39.
[3] *History of Shrewsbury*, p. 139. [4] Ibid., p. 138.
[5] Cf. Butler, *Life of S. Butler*, Vol. I, p. 11.
[6] Charles Clarke, *The Beauclercs, Father and Son*, New York, 1866, p. 9.
[7] Butler, *Life of S. Butler*, Vol. II, p. 134.
[8] Ibid., Vol. I, p. 10.

when necessary,[1] and tried to reason with boys as much as possible.[2] Moreover, he occasionally had a sense of humour, often laughing at—though he reprimanded—misdemeanours that Arnold would have considered sins.[3] He could be kindly even in dismissing boys for unbecoming conduct, idleness, or having too much influence over other boys. He watched over his small boys like a hawk, particularly those who were good only at games and would therefore—he believed—have trouble in a competitive world.[4]

But what Butler did of most importance was in the intellectual field. He increased the educational efficiency of a Public School, and thus, like Russell, answered the demand of the middle class for more learning. He made Shrewsbury a place where the classics not only could be, but were learned. And he did it chiefly neither by the older method of severity not by the modern method of stimulation of interest; 'his crowning merit was the establishment of an emulative system, in which talent and industry always gained their just recognition in good examinations.'[5] It was Butler's examinations that 'changed the face of public education all through the public schools of England, and hence throughout the world'.[6] As we have seen, up to Butler's time there was at most schools, especially at Eton, virtually no competition— the Newcastle was a product of the twenties. There had been and continued to be much talk about emulation, but Butler was the first Public School master who, by marking carefully and having periodic examinations, stimulated the spirit of competition in scholarship. He was the first Public School master to respond tentatively to the spirit of a competitive scientific and democratic age. And incidentally he opened, as far as Public Schools were concerned, the long fight over the value of cramming, examinations, and scholarships which to-day is still raging in American and English academic circles. Butler himself had to defend the system against the liberal as well as the conservative charge of

[1] Butler, *Life of S. Butler*, Vol. I., p. 296. [2] Ibid., p. 217. [3] Ibid., p. 187.
[4] Clarke, *The Beauclercs*, p. 9; Butler, *Life of S. Butler*, Vol. I, p. 11.
[5] Statement by Dr. Kennedy, April 30th 1887, quoted from Butler, *Life of S. Butler*, Vol. I, p. 5.
[6] Butler, *Life of S. Butler*, Vol. I, p. 5.

Russell and Butler

cramming by unfair methods in the same way that our tutoring establishments connected with universities do.[1]

Despite his other achievements Butler's importance and influence were chiefly in the intellectual field: Shrewsbury became famous primarily as a place of learning.[2] Even at Shrewsbury itself the tradition of learning became so strong that other interests were forgotten; the school disturbed and influenced other schools because its boys were doing better at the universities than theirs.[3] When Butler retired in 1836 the speeches praised chiefly educational achievements at Shrewsbury. Kennedy was chosen as Butler's successor because he was the school's best scholar;[4] he accepted the headship because he had 'an earnest confidence in the wisdom and power of' the Shrewsbury system. 'I loved classical literature, and I have always found a high and exciting pleasure in pouring its treasures into minds desirous and prepared to receive them, minds such as I justly expected to find in the Sixth Form of Shrewsbury School.'[5] Shrewsbury men have always been more remarkable as 'scholars and teachers than' as 'public men' because 'the halo that was thrown over learning by such men as Butler and Kennedy inclined them to a career of literature'.[6]

If Butler was an important figure, he did not have the influence in later years on other schools that Arnold had. Even his own school, which was administered by Butler's capable successor, Dr. Kennedy, in strict accordance with Butler's theory, lost in the competition for students. Shrewsbury's decline was due, it must be granted, in good part to its paucity of comforts and its inadequacy in the matter of

---

[1] Ibid., Vol. II, p. 35.   [2] *History of Shrewsbury*, p. 144.
[3] *History of Shrewsbury*, p. 135. When Dr. Drury and Dr. Longley of Harrow, and Dr. Hawtrey of Eton came to Butler for advice, it was with regard to the 'advance of learning' which he had accomplished. (Butler, *Life of S. Butler*, Vol. I, p. 2.) The *Quarterly* in 1842 gives him credit for remodelling education in the intellectual field only. The Reverend S. Tillbrook wrote as early as 1824 that 'your scholastic fame spreads like wildfire here. Nothing is talked of but Shrewsbury school.' (Butler, *Life of S. Butler*, Vol. I, p. 263.)
[4] Butler, *Life of S. Butler*, Vol. II, p. 158.
[5] *History of Shrewsbury*, p. 150.
[6] Ibid., p. 217.

railway communication. But such material considerations do not account for the failure of the school substantially to influence other schools. This failure must be laid at Butler's door. It can be accounted for only by inadequacies in his personality and in the educational ideas for which he stood. Butler lacked some inexplicable personal magnetism which Arnold possessed. Even more important, he did not offer to the Victorian world of the thirties an answer to its needs in the same way that the Rugby master did; unlike Arnold, he failed to symbolize the desires of the thirties and forties. Public opinion by 1835 demanded reforms that were more thorough than Butler's and in a different direction. Butler's concentration on the intellectual side of school life and indeed on a conception of intellectual training that was stale and outmoded vitiated his best efforts.

While Butler's star was fading Arnold's was rising. Even while Butler was still at Shrewsbury Rugby was drawing students away from his school.[1] It was from Rugby that the reinvigoration of the system of upper-class education was to come, not from Shrewsbury. Butler's school was to remain an anomaly among Public Schools until, after Kennedy's day, it merged into the general stream of Public School tradition under Arnold's dominating influence. Dr. Arnold's fame was to become a byword whereas Samuel Butler was to be known to the outside world only by the bitter travesty of him as Mr. Pontifex in *The Way of all Flesh*.[2] Fortunately, this irony was hidden from Butler. The great Shrewsbury master, was indeed, not even aware as late as 1835, of the shadow that was arising to dim his future fame. 'I don't know what you mean by Arnold's reform of Rugby,' he wrote to Kennedy, 'You are probably better informed than I am, and allude to something with which I am unacquainted, but I can only say that I never heard of such an act. I know he increased the numbers very much, and I hear that they are now considerably on the decline again,

[1] Butler, *Life of S. Butler*, Vol. II, p. 120.
[2] The younger Butler, it will be noted, changed his mind about his grandfather between the writing of *The Way of All Flesh* and *The Life and Letters of Samuel Butler*. *The Way of All Flesh*, though not published until after 1900, was finished in the early eighties.

but I do not know anything more.'[1] Had he lived a few years longer he would unquestionably have known a great deal more. For within seven years Arnold's name was on every one's lips, and the great transformation of the Public School system under Rugby influence had begun.

[1] Butler, *Life of S. Butler*, Vol. II, p. 123.

CHAPTER II

ARNOLD

A. SUCCESS AND INFLUENCE

SINCE Arnold is a much more important figure in the evolution of Public Schools than either Russell or Butler, he deserves much more extended treatment. He has not, however, suffered from neglect even among modern scholars and literary men. Stanley's well-known life has now been supplemented and partially corrected by Dr. Whitridge. It would be presumptuous as well as relatively fruitless, therefore, to attempt, by a detailed discussion, to add to the important facts in regard either to Arnold's life or his work. What I propose to do in the following pages is of a different nature. I believe that much can be learned both about Arnold and about his age by a study of the schoolmaster chiefly in his relations to the past and future of Public Schools.

Arnold, like Butler, was, it seems to me, successful during his life and influential after his death primarily because he satisfied general educational demands of the public, and secondarily because he was a powerful personality. As previously suggested, he was more important and influential than Butler because he was both a more complete embodiment of Victorian desires and a greater man.

Though one cannot actually prove this thesis, one can give almost conclusive evidence in its favour if one can show that the successful and influential Arnold gave expression in his educational schemes less to new ideas than to those that we have seen advocated in various criticisms during the twenty years preceding his head-mastership, and that Arnold's contribution was chiefly that of combination, emphasis, and power to make these schemes effective.[1] My chief interest,

[1] It is not, of course, true that because one combines the dominant ideas of an age one is bound to be successful. In the religious and political fields Arnold's attempt had just the opposite effect. Because various parties were irreconcilably opposed, the effort to satisfy all succeeded in pleasing nobody. In the educational field, on the other hand, Arnold managed to combine ideas so that all groups were satisfied.

therefore, will be in viewing Arnold's ideas and methods in their relation to those of the pre-Arnoldian school and to the suggestions of various critics.

But, first, two considerations have to be dealt with, considerations which will be enlarged upon in Part IV. These are the actual facts of Arnold's success in his own school and in his own day, and of his influence abroad after his death. As to the first, whether one defines success as popularity with parents, praise from informed critics, or the accomplishment of the aims which a man sets himself, Arnold has been shown so conclusively by students of his work to have been among the most successful of schoolmasters that the subject needs no extended treatment. On the other hand, he was not an unqualified success, and a few words defining his position in this respect are essential to an understanding of later developments.

When Arnold went to Rugby in 1828 only a few Oxford friends and liberals knew his power and possibilities. Augustus Hare could write to Stanley's mother[1] that Arnold was 'a man calculated beyond all others to engraft modern scholarship and modern improvements on the old-fashioned stem of a public education. Winchester under him would be the best school in Europe; what Rugby may turn out, I cannot say, for I know not the materials he has there to work on.' But to the world at large he was virtually unknown. For long years this lack of recognition persisted. We have seen Samuel Butler's comparative ignorance of Arnold and his work as late as 1835.[2] Charles Wordsworth, second master of Winchester, could say that he had never heard of Arnold until 1838.[3]

In his early days at Rugby he created chiefly opposition except among a few in the school who were growing devoted to him. Liberals attacked him for brutality,[4] conservatives for his theological and political liberalism. In 1834, when

[1] Augustus J. C. Hare, *Biographical Sketches*, London, 1895, p. 19.
[2] Cf. *supra*, p. 234.   [3] Charles Wordsworth, *Early Life*, p. 205.
[4] A *Times*' correspondent, commenting on the expulsion of four boys for illegal angling, wrote: 'I have often thought . . . that there ought to be some controlling power to regulate the expulsions from Public Schools.' (Cf. *The Times*, May 15th 1833, p. 4, and May 16th 1833, p. 7.)

his pamphlet on Church Reform appeared, the smouldering dislike of his school reforms grew strong enough to cause worry to faithful disciples like Clough and Stanley. The *Northampton Herald* as late as 1836 published a scathing denunciation of Arnold for having expelled a boy for resisting a prefectorial whipping. The *Herald* said that Arnold's attitude in refusing to give the boy or his parents a hearing may be an example of the courtesy of schoolmasters, but it hardly agrees with that of other classes of gentlemen.[1]

But by 1838 all this had changed. He had won the loyalty of his sixth form[2] and the freedom from the trustees for which he had been fighting.[3] There was peace and victory as far as his educational ideas were concerned.[4] Parents rushed to send boys to Rugby. When Arnold died in 1842 all England realized that he had been a great educator, and the chorus of praise that emanated from the *Reviews* contained a dissent only in regard to details. Though, as the years progressed, new as well as old criticisms began to make their appearance, Arnold had won an enduring place as England's greatest educator.

If Arnold won unstinted parental and general support during his lifetime for his work at Rugby, it cannot be said that this was because he succeeded in creating a school that was a complete embodiment of his ideals. In general he undoubtedly succeeded in both his moral and intellectual aims. Carlyle could from personal observation speak of Rugby as a 'temple of industrious peace',[5] and of Arnold as 'likely to be the far best Schoolmaster I had ever in my life seen. A brave man.'[6] Most of Arnold's contemporaries, as well as later writers, have echoed these sentiments so copiously that the point needs no further elaboration. On the other hand, Arnold never succeeded entirely even in the

[1] *The Times*, January 2nd 1836, p. 3.
[2] Cf. Stanley, *Life and Correspondence of Thomas Arnold*, p. 208.
[3] As early as 1827 Arnold had claimed that he would not go to Rugby unless he were free from prying trustees. (Cf. Stanley, op. cit., Letter 21, p. 70.)
[4] Cf. Stanley, op. cit., pp. 326, 400.
[5] Cf. Sir Joshua Fitch, *Thomas and Matthew Arnold and Their Influence on English Education*, New York, 1897, p. 107.
[6] *Letters of Thomas Carlyle to John Stuart Mill*, etc., London, 1923, p. 263. Carlyle and Arnold met only in 1842, the year of Arnold's death. (Cf. Wilson, *Carlyle*, Vol. III, p. 153.)

moral field in producing conditions that suited him. Rugby life was, despite Arnold, full of many of the evils of the older schools; for on many boys Arnold had no effect whatever. Clough could write that 'even here at Rugby, the best of all public schools, which are the best kind of schools, even here there is a vast deal of bad'.[1] As late as 1838 many boys drank brandy at the Cock Robin and were expelled.[2] Games of hare and hounds and poaching proceeded despite the strenuous objections of farmers.[3] There was bullying at 'footer'.[4] Not all boys were allowed to say their prayers in peace.[5] There was plenty of insubordination against the prefects,[6] whom Arnold indeed did not always trust. As one writer says, 'the sixth-form system' was 'liable at any time' 'to disruption, even during the height of Arnold's influence'.[7] As late as 1840 Tom Hughes's brother, a prefect, was expelled for not punishing the breakers of an Italian's plaster casts.[8] Arnold, indeed, rode his prefect hobby to death. He forgot, as Corbin says, that boys will be boys and that not even his influence could cause them to tell on one another.[9] This fact, indeed, depressed Arnold so much that to the very end of his days he lamented the evils in Public Schools, and insisted that he could not conscientiously recommend sending a boy to one of them.

If Arnold failed completely with some boys, even with

[1] Arthur Hugh Clough, *Poems and Prose Remains*, edited by his Wife, 2 vols., London, 1869, Vol. I, pp. 56–7.
[2] An Old Rugbaean, *Recollections of Rugby*, London, 1848, p. 28.
[3] Ibid., p. 135.   [4] *The Parents' Review*, November 1895, p. 641.
[5] Ibid., November 1895, p. 834.   [6] Ibid., March 1896, p. 31.
[7] Ibid., April 1896, p. 134.
[8] Thomas Hughes, *Memoir of a Brother*, London, 1873, pp. 32 ff.
[9] Corbin, *Schoolboy Life in England*, p. 169. Martineau, after reading Stanley's *Life of Arnold* could still write in 1845: 'If there is any place in the world where everybody is convinced that he has a right to everything, and with unlimited voracity of claim absorbs whatever is within his reach, until he dashes against the appetences, no less universal and no less entitled, of his neighbours in the scramble; where a state of war is the state of nature, ever and anon resumed to settle the exact sphere of every new-comer, and all determination of rights has to be fought out; where order and law prevail in unstable equilibrium (like the right of search among our French allies) as disagreeable conditions of a treaty of peace, and the only principle truly and heartily respected is, Do, if you dare—certainly that place is an English public school.' No wonder, he adds, Arnold laments the power of public opinion and his inability to get boys to fight it and make the moral overcome the strong. (James Martineau, *Essays, Reviews, and Addresses*, 4 vols., London, 1890, Vol. I, p. 68.)

those on whom he made some impression he had varying degrees of reward for his labours. Only to the very few did he transmit his ideals in entirety. The Cloughs and the Stanleys imbibed the complete spiritual and intellectual fare that Arnold served, but, though they have made a disproportionate amount of stir, they were inevitably few in number. Most of the minds that Arnold touched were unquickened. They may have been moved to work harder than they would have, but they were in no sense permeated with the joy of intellectual adventure that Arnold cherished. Indeed, if Rugby had a greater reputation for industriousness than Harrow it was as much because the middle classes who patronized Rugby favoured work more than the aristocracy, as it was because of Arnold's special influence.[1] 'As far as scholarship and numbers go, the Rugby of Dr. James was not far inferior to the Rugby of Dr. Arnold.'[2] Moreover, the average admirer received Arnold's religious and moral ideals only in a debased form. The Tom Browns were a product of Arnold's moral training, but they were never a direct embodiment of Arnold's most exalted teaching. This fact has vast implications. For, as we shall see, it was the Tom Browns as much as the Stanleys who later on formed a nexus between Arnold and the world.

This brings us to the question of influence. As has just been suggested, Arnold did not pass on his ideals in unmodified form. Even in his own school when he was alive, the power of his personality did not prevent a partial failure of transmission. Even more after this death his purposes suffered modification through misunderstanding and ineptitudes on the part of his disciples and conscious distortions by those less sympathetic. As we shall see, the Public Schools accepted Arnold only on their own terms. But they did accept him: Arnold influenced to some extent every Public School in England.

There have been, however, some writers who have questioned this influence, who have refused to give Arnold any

[1] Cf. Michael Sadler's Introduction to Arnold Whitridge, *Dr. Arnold of Rugby*, New York, 1928, p. xxii.
[2] Whitridge, op. cit., p. 84. Arnold purposely kept down the numbers in the school.

credit at all for the changes in the system of upper-class education that have taken place since his death. Though these writers—people like Samuel Butler the younger, or Leach and W. A. Fearon—are prejudiced witnesses since they are trying to extol Dr. Butler or William of Wykeham at the expense of Arnold, their ideas are worth a moment's pause.[1] In the life of his grandfather, Butler wrote, 'Dr. Arnold unquestionably made a deep impression on those boys who were brought into close communication with himself, but I cannot find that his influence over the school survived longer than that of any subsequent head master, while upon other schools, so far as I have been able to ascertain, he produced—I believe it is not too much to say—no effect whatever.'[2] This contention is quite unfounded, but in so far as Butler did realize the difference just pointed out between Arnold's immediate effect on a few and his remoter general effects, his opinion has value. Butler merely failed to recognize an influence because it was a modified one. Leach and in particular Fearon claim that since Arnold's methods—prefectorial government, *esprit de corps*, religious education—were of Wykehamist origin, Arnold contributed nothing of importance to Public School development.[3] Fearon's facts are half true; his conclusions are wrong. Arnold did preserve old forms. But he changed their spirit and thereby effected fully as much real change as if he had destroyed the forms more and the spirit less, as did Russell. It was indeed, as we shall see, just because he did keep the old moulds that Arnold was able to interest and satisfy his conservative countrymen.

A much better case than Fearon's could be made out for the contention that, since Arnold was, as I have suggested, expressing the demands of his age rather than inventing ideas, it was not he but his ideas that were influential and that these ideas would have permeated schools had Arnold

[1] Wykehamists were not, according to Archer (*Secondary Education in the Nineteenth Century*, p. 75) the only ones to give Winchester credit for the ideas of the modern Public School. 'As time went on, there was a tendency, especially in the case of High Church schools, which could not forget Arnold's theological views, to look to Winchester as the fountain of the system.'
[2] Butler, *Life of S. Butler*, Vol. I, p. 9.
[3] Cf. Old Wykehamists, *Winchester*, p. 21.

never lived. This argument could be buttressed by pointing to the fact that Eton and a few other schools changed without much direct Arnoldian influence, an indication that there could be reform on Rugby lines without Rugby aid. In the last analysis, however, there is really little ground for believing that the Public School system would have been substantially the same without Arnold. For after all, it was Arnold who was directly responsible for reform at Rugby, Harrow, Marlborough, and other schools, and who indirectly influenced Winchester, Westminster, and even Eton. Moreover, one cannot but believe that ideas need to be embodied in a personality who can make them effective if they are to permeate the minds of men. And one hesitates to say that the moment always produces its man. It is conceivable that had Arnold not come along to personify stray ideas they would have found similar expression, but one has no right to assume it. One thing is sure: if reform had come through another than Arnold, it would have been very different, since no two men are alike, and since one of Arnold's important contributions was the peculiar way in which he combined various ideas.

B. CHARACTER, BACKGROUND, AND EARLY STRUGGLES

Arnold's character is a series of paradoxes. He was at once a strong and awesome personality, 'in the succession of the prophets'[1] and a naïve child; he was both tyrannical and gentle, dogmatic and enlightened, conservative and liberal, a man of principle and an opportunist, an idealist and a practical realist. He had in his nature all the apparent contradictions that one associates with the story-book Englishman, and, like Dr. Johnson, he has been admired in part because one cannot fit his character into a logical pattern. Any attempt to see him as a simple one-sided individual has led to caricature. Most of Strachey's picture of the awesome Jehovah is true, but because it is made up of only one half of a series of opposites, it is as a whole grossly misleading.

---

[1] Cf. Michael Sadler in Introduction to Whitridge, *Dr. Arnold of Rugby*, p. xvii.

To say that Arnold was an orthodox liberal who believed in progress, hated most liberal movements, and encouraged 'toleration of those with whom he agreed' is to convert, by unfair juxtaposition, a pair of perfectly real opposites into an implied hypocrisy.[1] G. F. Bradby, on the other hand, errs by implication just as far in the other direction. By seeing Arnold's dogmatisms as the faults of his age, he is able to clear Arnold the man of all implication that he was not a modern liberal. When Bradby writes that 'it was as a stimulator of thought in others, rather than as a propagandist of new ideas that Dr. Arnold most influenced his own generation', that Arnold 'did not impose his own views on them [his boys] unduly', and that, since he was 'a passionate seeker after truth, . . . the boys who grew up under his influence grew up with independent minds and judgements', he is, like Strachey, enunciating a number of half truths.[2]

In point of fact there were at least two Arnolds, and one could find grounds for the statement that there were many more. The best known and probably the most important is the Arnold who was a passionate moral preacher, a dogmatist, and an authoritarian.

Even in his early years the outlines of this figure were beginning to emerge. Being, like the members of the school over which he later ruled, a member of the upper middle classes,[3] he had, even at school, a good deal of piety and seriousness. The scant picture that we get of him at Winchester, where he went from 1807 to 1811 under Dr. Goddard and then under Dr. Gabell, is in part a replica of those pictures of model youths of which the unregenerate Public School was full. Like Peel or Isaac Williams or Havelock, Arnold brought from home a moral training which flourished in spite of rather than because of Public Schools. There was indeed much of the pious, industrious prig about him. He loved Greek and Latin, took an exceptionally keen interest in politics and history for a boy, and had a rather overdeveloped moral sense and solemnity.[4] He lived too much

[1] Lytton Strachey, *Eminent Victorians*, London, 1918, p. 197.
[2] G. F. Bradby, *The Brontës and other Essays*, London, 1932, pp. 51, 54.
[3] He was the son of a Collector of Customs.
[4] Cf. Whitridge, op. cit., pp. 6, 7.

with elders, and thus acquired a stiff formality and a precocity which changed him too quickly from boy to man.[1] Further, his association with officers gave direction to his innate liking for discipline.[2]

But in his school and even in his college days at Oxford, the lines of his character were not tightly drawn. Only after he had spent some ten years in the comparative peace of Laleham, where he engaged in private tutoring, in preparation for his life's work,[3] did the authoritarian side of his personality take final shape. The man who went to Rugby in 1828, however, was already the dynamic and Jehovah-like prophet with whose portrait the world has become familiar.

This well-known Arnold was essentially a man in whom 'intellect and affection waited upon the conscience and the will; and became great and rich and tender in the divine hardships of duty and the strenuous service of God'.[4] He was a strong personality who could move others to action by his influence more easily than he could convince their judgments.[5] Believing deeply in the philosophy he had worked out for himself in his early years, he made it his business to penetrate the heart and will rather than to argue. He was himself the Carlylean strong man that he so much admired, practical, healthy, and at the same time spiritual. And he was just the man to inspire others with a doctrine of Carlylean work and duty rather than abstract thought. Essentially a practical man himself, severe, often ruthless with a 'remarkable capacity for government', he was as great in action as he was merely 'respectable in scholarship, insensible to art'.[6] In a sense his very narrowness combined with moral earnestness and insight and untiring devotion to an ideal made him a power of the first order.[7]

But this, if the most important, is not the only side of Arnold's character. All through his life an over-seriousness

---

[1] J. J. Findlay, *Arnold of Rugby*, Cambridge, 1897, pp. 1, 2.
[2] Michael Sadler in Whitridge, op. cit., p. xxi.
[3] Stanley, op. cit., p. 41.   [4] Martineau, *Essays and Addresses*, p. 62.
[5] Cf. Sadler in Whitridge, *Dr. Arnold of Rugby*, p. xvii.
[6] Cf. Martineau, op. cit., Vol. I, p. 62, and Stanley, op. cit., p. 78.
[7] Cf. Findlay, *Arnold of Rugby*, p. vii.

and moral urgency were combined with both intellectual tolerance and boyish good spirits. Arnold will always be chiefly the Puritan prophet, unable to sympathize with 'moral thoughtlessness' or to unbend entirely even with his best boys,[1] but as Whitridge has pointed out, there were other sides that Stanley failed to emphasize sufficiently.[2] At Winchester he was very much a boy believing in boys' conventions. One is pleased to find him caught playing lou, which was strictly forbidden, and justifying himself for caning the sentinel who allowed him to be caught on the grounds of 'custom immemorial'. His idea of prefectorial dignity was much like that of East in *Tom Brown's Schooldays*. Masters and boys were enemies and all was fair except lying.[3]

Later on, we find that Arnold could be an ideal companion to his wife and children.[4] Moreover, if he was Jehovah to the younger boys at Rugby, towards the chosen few he could sometimes, despite his own shyness be friend and companion, one whose tenderness was as manifest as his strictness.[5] Despite his dogmatism he could be tolerant and, within certain moral limits, encourage freedom of thought.[6]

The paradoxes in Arnold's character coupled with the exigencies of the age in which he grew up accounted for the intellectual difficulties that early assailed him and the ultimate direction and characteristics of the political, religious, and educational philosophy at which he finally arrived.

Born in 1795, the same year as Carlyle, who was so similar to him in many ways, Arnold lived his first thirty-five years in that age of transition and turmoil which followed the outburst of the French Revolution. He was forced, like so many of his contemporaries, to adjust old values to a new and changing world. Arnold floundered about for years in

---

[1] Stanley, op. cit., p. 117.   [2] Whitridge, op. cit., p. 10.
[3] Sadler in Whitridge, op. cit., p. xxix. When Arnold was caught in his offence he told the truth, though how much this was from fear that Gabell would tell his family, we do not know. At any rate the code that forbade lying to a master Arnold transported to Rugby.
[4] Cf. Whitridge, op. cit., p. 4, also Stanley, op. cit., p. 140. In return his wife exercised a restraining and sympathetic influence on the over-passionate and over-serious Arnold.   [5] Cf. Stanley, op. cit., p. 78.
[6] Bishop of Hereford in Findlay, *Arnold of Rugby*, p. xvi.

the twilight world of half beliefs and shifting points of view until, in the years at Laleham before he went to Rugby, his beliefs solidified.

Even at Winchester Arnold's moral and intellectual emancipation precluded an acceptance of the old dogmas of religion and politics. It is reported that in his schooldays he was strongly influenced by Jacobinism.[1] But it was at Oxford where he became in 1814 a fellow of Oriel that what have been called to-day the 'acids of modernity' presented the greatest challenge both to Arnold's political conservatism and to his religious orthodoxy. Though at first the influence of Coleridge and Keble and the poetry of Wordsworth made Arnold a Tory and inclined him to orthodox religious views,[2] he could not long escape the insistence of new Whig and Church-liberal rationalism. In particular the Oriel liberalism of Whateley and others, with its persistent intellectual inquiry into the Scripture, shook his religious faith. Arnold had such trouble about the Thirty-nine Articles that he nearly gave up the Rugby position rather than sign them.[3] Eventually, along with Copleston, Hawkins, Hampden, and Whateley himself, Arnold solved his difficulties, but he went through struggles which it is hard for us to-day to appreciate. Strachey, ever ready to see the rent in a strong man's armour, infers from Stanley's rather too careless slurring over of Arnold's doubts, that there were difficulties not admitted and accuses Arnold of an evasion which implies hypocrisy.[4] This is an unjust accusation. At the same time, though Arnold refused to subscribe to Keble's insistence that doubt itself was vice, he can hardly be said to have overcome his difficulties in a manner satisfactory to modern eyes. As James Martineau, who did not find his sister Harriet's religious troubles exactly to his liking, says, 'We cannot satisfy ourselves that Arnold got rid of his doubts about the Trinity by fair means: and in the advice given to him on the subject, we see so much of the mischievous sophistry and

---

[1] Stanley, op. cit., pp. 28 ff.; Whitridge, op. cit., p. xxx.
[2] Stanley, op. cit., pp. 28 ff.   [3] Whitridge, op. cit., p. 52.
[4] Strachey, *Eminent Victorians*, p. 186. Strachey does this chiefly by inserting at the end of a paragraph a casual remark about the slightly puzzled expression on the face of Dr. Arnold.

dishonest morality current on these matters among divines that we feel bound to enter our protest as we pass.'[1]

The truth of the matter seems to be that Arnold, like Carlyle, was greater as an actor than as a thinker. Moreover, he was gifted with a will to believe and was innately religious; thus he was bound to win through to belief. His was a search for truth prejudiced by the fact that his nature demanded belief; whatever compromises he had to make he would find a God to reverence because it was in his nature to worship.

By the time he went to Rugby Arnold had resolved his doubts and developed for himself a philosophy which, if not entirely self-consistent, was for him a satisfactory basis for action. He had discovered a number of sources from which he could elicit an answer to the problems of existence satisfactory to the needs of his nature in the world in which it found itself. First and foremost he came in contact with the political and religious philosophy of Burke and Coleridge. Secondly, in 1825, he read the writings of the German historian, Niebuhr, whose Roman history, according to Stanley, freed Arnold from both Jacobinism and Toryism.[2] Finally, he made, with the help of the Germans, what amounted to a rediscovery of the classics. Lessing, Winckelmann, Goethe and others revived, at the end of the eighteenth century, an interest in the 'true classics'. The Germans emphasized the Greek and Roman writers as expressors of great ideas which should serve as lessons to the present, not as mere masters of language to be studied for stylistic reasons. And they discovered in these writers, as will any one who studies them with that intent, just those ideas which were most appealing to nineteenth-century Germans. They found that the ideal of Greek and Roman civilization was a combination of liberty and law. Classic civilization was free; at the same time it was moral and disciplined, very unlike the negativistic and chaotic condition of contemporary France.[3] These ideas found a ready response in England,

[1] Martineau, *Essays and Addresses*, Vol. I, p. 50.
[2] Cf. Stanley, op. cit., p. 49. Arnold had little use for German theology.
[3] For a discussion of the classic revival in Germany and its relation to English education, cf. Archer, *Secondary Education in the Nineteenth Century*, pp. 25 ff.

particularly at Oxford when Arnold and his friends were students and tutors there. To Arnold they were the solution of the central political problem which had been disturbing him.[1]

The philosophy at which Arnold arrived was one form of that Victorian Compromise whose principles we have already discussed. It was an attempt to unite and thus to reconcile those political, economic, and educational ideals which were struggling for mastery in the fluid society of the thirties. Arnold was at one and the same time a defender of freedom and of authority, of reason and emotion, of change and stability, of democracy and of aristocracy, of tolerance and of dogmatism.[2] He was, indeed, to a certain extent, a vindicator and reconciler of every theory and attitude which had found expression in the preceding fifty years. Particularly was this so in educational matters. Arnold's purposes and methods at Rugby included and attempted to fuse all the ideas which we have seen battling for supremacy in the tens, twenties and early thirties.

C. ARNOLD'S EDUCATIONAL PURPOSES

As we have seen, there were, from the point of view of educational purposes, two extremes of opinion in the tens and twenties. On the one hand, there were those individuals whose only care was that boys should be more virtuous and religious, who wanted socialization and discipline of thought and action to conform with the doctrines of old-time Christianity. On the other hand, there were those who believed in individual freedom, in a broader intellectual training, and in a morality which laid less stress on discipline —conformity to authority and repression—and more on free co-operation, kindness, and democratic feeling. Between these two extremes were the alumni defenders of schools,

[1] Stanley, op. cit., p. 129.
[2] It is important to note that the two sides of Arnold's character do not, in most cases, directly parallel the above pairs of opposites. Thus Arnold's moral earnestness accounts for his love of freedom as much as it does for his love of authority. On the other hand, his tolerant side worked as often to make him conservative or undemocratic as it did to foster radicalism or equalitarianism. It was constantly enlisted to modify the one-sided intensity and austerity with which he held all his views, even many of his compromise positions.

who wanted moral independence if not real freedom and cared more for the manly virtues than for an undue preoccupation with the avoidance of unchristian sin.

In general we may divide Arnold's educational purposes into those which were eminently suited to answer the needs of the first of these groups, the Public School masters and the Evangelical religious reformers, and those which were acceptable to the second group, the liberals, and to a certain extent to the third, the alumni defenders of the miniature world idea of a Public School. Obviously the various groups within each of the halves of this dichotomy often disagreed among themselves. But the division is nevertheless a useful one, since in the main it separates the authoritarians from the libertarians and semi-libertarians, and Arnold's philosophy naturally divides itself into his authoritarian and his libertarian ideas. It will be noted that this division cuts across any division between the conservative Arnold and the Arnold who desired change, a division to be enlarged upon when we deal with Arnold's methods.

The most obvious and in a sense the most important side of Arnold's teaching is the reactionary one. Above all, Arnold was a moral reformer along Christian lines.[1] Arnold himself listed his aims as 'first, religious and moral principle; second, gentlemanly conduct, thirdly, intellectual ability'.[2] He wanted to form Christian characters and to inculcate Christian principles. The English gentleman being assumed, the aim of education was to teach Christian self-regulation.[3] His first thought on going to Rugby was that he would be able to 'try whether my notions of Christian education are really impracticable' in a Public School,[4] to find out whether he could make Christian men out of the very imperfect boys who came to the schools.[5]

Now up to a point not even extreme liberals would have disagreed with these aims of Arnold's. Almost every one thought that there should be some moral reform, and only

---

[1] His liberalism was never proof against irreverence: he resigned from active interest in London University because it excluded theology. (Cf. Stanley, op. cit., p. 264.) His *Roman History* was written partly at least to refute Gibbon.
[2] Quoted in Strachey, *Eminent Victorians*, p. 188.
[3] Findlay, op. cit., p. xx.   [4] Stanley, op. cit., p. 70, Letter 22.
[5] Ibid., pp. 71, 72, Letters 25, 26.

the most radical were entirely anti-Christian. Moreover, as we shall see, there were certain aspects of Arnold's moral ideas that were, if anything, more appealing to liberals than to orthodox conservatives and to reactionaries. Nevertheless, many of the essential doctrines of Arnold the religious teacher and the implications of those doctrines were totally inconsistent with the ideals of most liberals as well as, in part, with those of the defenders of the miniature world idea of a Public School. Moreover, the passion that he brought to the task of religious reform and the manner in which religion and morality seemed to absorb all other interests were contrary to the ideals of conservatives of all kinds as well as of liberals. Arnold was indeed nearer in these last respects to the Evangelical religious reformers than to any other group.

Christian teaching claimed a disproportionate amount of Arnold's attention in comparison with such things as intellectual training or the larger attempt to make boys freely functioning individuals. Everywhere, even in the intellectual field, the moral seemed to rule. One was to learn the classics because mental cultivation was a religious and moral duty.[1] The chief end of learning was neither knowledge nor, essentially, mental training, but the spirit of work. As with Carlyle, the moral trait of industriousness was the most important thing a boy could acquire through study.[2] To Arnold the effort, not the result, was what counted; he would have admired Browning's *Andrea del Sarto* had he lived to read it. Ignorance or dullness Arnold could forgive, but never 'wilful irregularity'.[3] In so far as knowledge itself was important, it was so, in good part, for ethical reasons. As we shall see, Arnold taught the classics for their moral lessons. He believed that the intelligent were always the moral because they were in sympathy with great minds and not with animals.[4] In all fields of life what Arnold cared about was the glory of righteousness, the reality of evil, and the thrill of high endeavour.[5]

---

[1] Cf. Fitch, *Thomas and Matthew Arnold*, p. 90; Whitridge, op. cit., p. 111
[2] Whitridge, op. cit., p. 107. [3] Stanley, op. cit., p. 46.
[4] Cf. Findlay, *Arnold of Rugby*, p. 74.
[5] *The Letters of Matthew Arnold to Arthur Hugh Clough*, edited with an Introductory Study by Howard Forster Lowry, London, 1932, p. 3.

The intensity of Arnold's concern for moral behaviour was no less remarkable than the extent of that concern. Arnold was passionately in earnest to a degree that was probably as startling in his own day as it seems excessive in ours. One cannot read more than a few pages of his letters or sermons without being impressed by the way in which the contrast between sin and virtue haunted him. He appears as the Hebrew prophet, humble before his God, stern and commanding before man, solemnly exhorting boys to become virtuous and be saved. Sin was ever at his shoulder ready to fasten upon those who for a moment relaxed from duty.[1] He was so profoundly inspired by righteousness that, as Stanley says, even boys were bound to be impressed.[2]

As a result of his deep concern for virtue, Arnold was profoundly depressed by the conduct of the pupils of the Public Schools. He saw the seeds of vice sprouting everywhere,[3] and was, indeed, as severe a critic as the Evangelical Bowdler, to whom he refers.[4] Schools are nurseries of vice, places where modesty, respect for truth, and affection are stifled and unrestraint and coarseness run rampant. 'Now it is certain that education, like everything else, was not brought to perfection when our great schools were first founded . . . I am afraid that Christian principles were not enough brought forward, that lower motives were encouraged, and a lower standard altogether suffered to prevail. The system also was too much one of fear and outward obedience; the obedience of the heart and the understanding were little thought of.'[5] Arnold was obsessed by the idea that it ought to be otherwise: that evil must be eradicated, and that even the youngest boy, despite the fact that he has no sense of sin, can commit a moral crime.[6] Though the sins of the young are different from those of adults, they are sins, and no less inexcusable. Elisha cursed the children for calling him bald. God does not consider boys' sins trifling. If you displease

---

[1] *Westminster Review*, February 1843, p. 29.   [2] Stanley, op. cit., p. 48.
[3] Ibid., p. 79.
[4] Thomas Arnold, *Sermons Preached in the Chapel of Rugby School*, New York, 1846, No. 12, p. 102.
[5] Arnold, *Rugby Sermons*, No. 12; pp. 106–70.   [6] Ibid., No. 10, p. 84.

God, the evil of your conduct is infinite, and its consequences are infinite.[1]

As already pointed out, this ultra-religious spirit was in evidence long before Arnold. It had indeed reached Rugby before his arrival in the person of a boy named Spencer Thornton, who was an older member of the school when Arnold became head master. Arnold, be it noted, highly approved of this embodiment of Evangelical fanaticism. 'From the day of his confirmation Thornton regarded himself as one publicly and solemnly given to the service of God,' and spent his time visiting 'the poor in the town and neighbourhood of Rugby, distributing tracts, and labouring earnestly for the conversion of his schoolfellows.'[2] When he 'received a cuff' for remonstrating with a boy for swearing, he gave in return 'a tract on swearing', which, 'although it may not have had the desired effect upon the offender, was at least not without permanent benefit to others, who were touched by this unusual example of courage and devotedness in so young a boy.'[3] That Thornton was tolerated at all by his fellows is an evidence of a new spirit abroad; one rather doubts, however, that he could have had as much influence as Collins claims.[4] Arnold, at any rate, appreciated his services, and spoke of Thornton's zeal in a sermon, though he did not mention him by name. To Thornton's father he wrote, 'My obligations to your son are great'.[5] The most interesting thing about Arnold's relations to Spencer Thornton is the former's failure to see how bad for a boy such exaggerated piety was. Arnold made the same mistake with some of his best pupils, for he was blinded by his deep religiosity to the dangers inherent in developing a boy's moral sense too early and too strongly.

When we turn to examine the implications of Arnold's Christianity, we find even more grounds for liberal objection than in the mere fact of his over-emphasis of religion. After all qualifications have been made, Arnold's religious conception still remained fundamentally the traditional

[1] Arnold, *Rugby Sermons*, No. 7, p. 57.
[2] Cf. W. R. Fremantle, *Memoir of the Rev. Spencer Thornton*, London, 1850, p. 3.
[3] Fremantle, *Memoir of Spencer Thornton*, p. 14.
[4] Cf. Collins, *Public Schools*, pp. 383 ff.   [5] Fremantle, op. cit., p. 36.

Christian one. Arnold held moral views that did not differ essentially from those of churchmen and Public School masters of the past, no matter how much he might himself differ from them in the passion with which he carried out these views or the relative emphasis he gave to them. Above all he was, in the first place, a dogmatic believer in an absolute universal moral law outside of the individual, and in the second place a subscriber to the notion of the essential evil of human nature, two ideas which set him definitely apart, despite compromises which he made, from the empiricists, relativists, and libertarians of his own and later times.[1] From these philosophic notions proceeded certain important educational ideas of an equally anti-liberal nature. Since the individual was not the measure of all things, and since he was fundamentally base, he must find his highest good in disciplining his natural instincts into obedience to authority. Consequently, the first purpose of education must be to socialize a boy. Like the best of the Public School masters, like Locke, and indeed, like boy society itself, Arnold wanted to mould and discipline the individual rather than to encourage self-expression.

With Arnold the socialization of the individual was of various kinds. First and foremost there was the fact that all boys were to be fundamentally the same kinds of men and to believe certain essential truths. Arnold wanted his boys to subscribe emotionally and unthinkingly to the truth rather than to evolve their own scale of values, and to be boys of the right moral type rather than of diverse types. As Stanley records naïvely, Arnold would not dictate, but he wanted his boys to be right, and he used his tremendous emotional power to influence them.[2]

But Arnold went further in socializing the individual than merely encouraging conformity. Conformity to truth implies nothing about the truths themselves. A boy might, in the old Public School, be subjected to pressure to adopt himself to anti-social standards. Arnold, on the other hand, wanted to socialize the individual in the sense that he desired him to have standards that were beneficial to society. Most

---

[1] As it did Kant and Carlyle.   [2] Stanley, op. cit., pp. 98 ff.

of a boy's moral qualities were to be anti-individualistic, anti-egoistic, anti-instinctive in nature. A boy was, essentially, to be loyal, reverent, and dutiful. He was to be humble and obedient. He was to be pure and honourable. All these characteristics imply either a repression of the normal instincts or at least the glorification of those aspects of human life that are at the opposite pole from self-expression.

Arnold wanted essentially to create a world of boys who were altruistic rather than egoistic, and who had chastened their instincts in accordance with Christian principle. He wanted to teach a boy to do his duty to his fellow-men, and to sacrifice his own interests to the good of others.[1] As Sadler says, he contributed to English education the idea of corporate duty. And since, it may be added, Arnold effected his purposes in his school, and was thus able to turn out boys who would carry his ideas beyond the educational world, he also contributed this idea of corporate duty to the new Civil Service and local government.[2] The importance of this achievement cannot be exaggerated.

The most important of Arnold's moral ideals were loyalty, self-sacrifice, and obedience. They were the essence of his Christian code; moreover, they had a double interest for Arnold: they were means to an end as well as ends in themselves. Arnold taught loyalty and obedience to God, to school, and to himself[3] because he believed that the best means of furthering ideals was to secure allegiance to objects which embodied those ideals.

Between loyalty and self-sacrifice on the one hand and obedience on the other there is an important and significant difference.[4] Loyalty and self-sacrifice were willing and conscious subjections of the ego. In so far as Arnold taught these characteristics he was only partially an authoritarian in the tradition of the older masters; he was nearer to boy

[1] Cf. Whitridge, op. cit., p. 206.   [2] Ibid., p. xlii.
[3] Strachey accused Arnold of identifying himself with God when in chapel he 'propounded the general principles of his own conduct and that of the Almighty', but there is no reason to believe that he did. It was some of Arnold's pupils who made the identification.
[4] Between loyalty and self-sacrifice viewed as means to an end there is also an important difference. Self-sacrifice is a step farther along in the process than loyalty. One sacrifices one's own desires in order to make others live up to an ideal to which one is loyal.

ideals. Indeed, he went farther in the direction of libertarianism than did boy ideals, because in practice boy loyalty was virtually a forced loyalty, whereas Arnold's was based on a more conscious individual choice. But Arnold taught voluntary suppression of instinct chiefly to his older boys. With his younger boys he emphasized obedience more than any other virtue, and obedience was a strictly authoritarian ideal.

Arnold's theories about the training of little boys show him in his most antipathetic and ludicrous light, and place him more definitely than do any other of his ideas among the conservative and reactionary authoritarians. In contrast to Rousseau and to most modern educators, Arnold believed that, since man was fallen and thus evil,[1] little boys were sinful creatures. He never really felt at home with the young, no matter how hard he tried to be kindly, for he was constantly seeing the corruption of man in the grimy youngsters in the lower forms at Rugby. Over and over again he wrote such things as: 'It is quite surprising to see the wickedness of young boys; or would be surprising, if I had not my own school experience and a good deal since to enlighten me,'[2] or 'a school shows as undisguisedly as any place the corruption of human nature.'[3] Arnold's sermons echo these sentiments. 'It shows you plainly, how strong must be our evil dispositions, when you see them, in so short a time, getting the better of those that have had ten or twelve years to ripen.' 'Every boy brings some good with him, at least, from home, as well as some evil; and yet you see how very much more catching the evil is than the good, or else you would make one another better by mixing together.'[4] Childhood indeed was an inferior state, in which selfishness and ignorance ruled. Childishness was the worst of vices.[5]

Since youth is an inferior state, it has no right to entertain barbarous unchristian ideas of independence. A sense of personal dignity in those who have no sense of sin but are

---

[1] Thomas Arnold, *Sermons Preached mostly in the Chapel of Rugby School* called *Christian Life, its Course, its Hindrances, and its Helps*, London, 1841, No. 1, p. 1.
[2] Stanley, op. cit., p. 168, Letter 15.
[3] Ibid., p. 227, Letter 77.
[4] Arnold, *Rugby Sermons*, No. 5, pp. 48, 49; Arnold, *Christian Life Sermons* No. 2, p. 14.
[5] Arnold, *Christian Life Sermons*, No. 4, p. 35.

none the less sinful is improper. A child must be restrained and curbed, and taught, above all, humility and obedience. Arnold found no difficulty in squaring such ideas with liberal ones, since he felt that the latter, unlike popular principles, were opposed only to unjust restraint. Freedom was but a means to moral happiness.[1] A boy should learn to obey the authority of the Church which taught the eternal verities and the virtues dear to Arnold. He would then and then only be a genuinely free man.

Fortunately, Arnold believed that man was fallen, not hopelessly evil. He might be improved by judicious disciplining. The object of education was to turn the boy into the man as fast as possible, since only thereby could his soul be saved.[2] And the business of the schoolmaster was to save the souls of sinful boys. A boy's nature was not to be developed but moulded and disciplined until no trace of youthfulness was left, until he was a man endowed with the moral qualities of which Arnold approved.[3]

From the most authoritarian and anti-individualistic side of Arnold let us turn to the individualistic and liberal-humanitarian aspects of his doctrines, those aspects which in one way or another were calculated to please conservative alumni or liberals. To begin with, many of Arnold's ideals were democratic or humanitarian. If boys were to sacrifice their natural instincts, it was to serve liberal ends. In Church matters Arnold was an equalitarian, who fought against exclusiveness in the interests of a universal church, which was to include all except Jews and possibly Unitarians. In political affairs he was liberal enough to earn the praise of the radical *Westminster Review*.[4] He fought for an extension of the voting franchise and for middle-class education, and was in general a friend of the poor.[5] His sermons are full of references to a brotherly love which was to be much more inclusive than a narrow class ethics would have

---

[1] *The Miscellaneous Works of Thomas Arnold, D.D.*, New York, 1845, pp. 355 ff. As Carlyle said, freedom meant the ability to find the right track on which to run.
[2] Arnold, *Christian Life Sermons*, No. 3, p. 22.   [3] Stanley, op. cit., p. 83.
[4] *Westminster Review*, February 1843, pp. 1 ff.; December 1844, pp. 363 ff.
[5] Cf. Stanley, op. cit., pp. 129, 258; Arnold, *Miscellaneous Works*, p. 372.

advocated. Moreover, loving one's neighbour meant actually denying oneself to help the poor. It meant getting to know the less well off, mixing with them, and cultivating democratic feeling, not contempt.[1] According to an old boy, Arnold considered fighting with the town boys, with those 'of lower social position' contemptible; instead one should help them by acting towards them as 'Christians and gentlemen'. The author of this piece of information adds that had Arnold's ideas been followed, there would have been no Indian Mutiny.[2]

That there is something patronizing and a trifle fatuous in Arnold's attitude towards the poor there is no denying.[3] Nevertheless, such ideas were an advance in a democratic direction. Duty had for Arnold a broader base than it had for Wellington or than it has, for that matter, for all but a few modern Public School masters. Arnold would have been profoundly shocked had he known that for many Public School men duty has become confined to the willingness to sacrifice one's life to save one's class. Moreover, Arnold's attitude towards the poor is important as one indication that his morality was not merely the stern Calvinist conception that dominated so much of his thought. Love and kindness, humanitarianism in a word, were as essential a part of what he tried to teach as was repression. Just as in his own life the prophetic Jehovah warred with the kindly, boyish, and sympathetic man, so in the ethics which he tried to inculcate in his boys there was as much of an expansive forward-looking Christianity as of an authoritarian conservative Hebraism.

Turning from his world view to the school, one sees Arnold's humanitarian and liberal ideals exemplified in his attitude towards his little boys. For, though he had a hard time being kindly to them in practice and wanted to discipline them, he desired at the same time that they should

[1] Cf. Arnold, *Rugby Sermons*, No. 16, p. 140; No. 24, p. 214.
[2] *Parents' Review*, December 1895, p. 759.
[3] Strachey makes much of the fact that Arnold limited his interests to the respectable poor. While this does indicate that Arnold was narrow, it does not mean that he was a faint-hearted liberal. He did not necessarily like only the poor who obeyed their masters. What it does mean is that Arnold's interest in morality was so great that it blinded him to purely economic considerations.

lead a happier life than they had led in the older Public School. Stanley, indeed, claims that he felt a sympathy for the young which, because of his shyness, exceeded his manifestation of it; with the very young, in whom the evil inevitably associated with boyhood had not yet appeared, he could apparently even be playful.[1] Bullying or cruelty he would not stand for. One of the prime objects of the system of government which Arnold set up in the school was the elimination of tyranny.[2] Life in Arnold's school was to be at least tolerably free and happy for the weak and the eccentric. Indeed, the very altruism and repression of instinct which Arnold cultivated in his older boys had as its object the liberation of the small boy. As mentioned so often, the freedom of the young and of the old must be distinguished, for they were so often mutually exclusive, since the freedom of the stronger often meant autocracy and tyranny towards the less strong.

As a matter of fact Arnold involved himself in this dilemma. For along with his desire to protect the young and to socialize the older boys went an almost equally strong urge to inculcate in the latter the kind of independence that Public Schools had always produced.

This desire was part of a general belief in individualism which was as essential a part of Arnold's doctrine as was his authoritarianism or his humanitarianism. Despite his belief in absolute moral law and in authority Arnold was a romantic individualist who shared his age's respect for the sanctity of the personal and the subjective as against external law. His philosophy was in good part an attempt to reconcile this idea of individual liberty with that conception of transcendent authority which we have previously discussed. In order to do this he posited, as did Kant and Carlyle, the idea of an innate moral sense.[3] In other words, he contended that absolute moral law was in the heart of each individual. When the individual's actions did not seem to square with morality, that meant that they were dictated by the lower senses, by the sinful side of man. Fortunately, the individual

---

[1] Cf. Stanley, op. cit., pp. 117-21.
[2] Arnold, *Miscellaneous Works*, pp. 360 ff.
[3] Martineau, *Essays and Addresses*, I, p. 73.

had within himself the will and the instinct to do right if it could only be disentangled from and given more power over those basely selfish instincts which man possessed as a result of his fall from grace in the Garden of Eden.

Armed with this doctrine, Arnold contended, in the first place, as did Carlyle, that the great individual represented the most important gift of God to civilization.[1] Therefore, he insisted that the individual schoolmaster ought to be an autocrat. In the second place, he fought for a personal religion as against a dogmatic one. Though, unlike Carlyle, he did not attack the existence of the Church—there was a point beyond which individual reason and intuition dared not go—he was radical enough in his insistence that all formalism and sacerdotalism within the Church must disappear, that religion ought to be an affair of individual feelings, and that each man had the right to exercise his private judgment in the interpretation of the Scriptures.[2] For these doctrines he was condemned as a latitudinarian by the Newmanites even more vociferously than, for his authoritarianism, he was attacked by the Benthamites as a bigot.[3] Finally, in educational matters he insisted that moral independence in the right boy was a virtue, and attempted to inculcate it at Rugby.

The adjective 'right' indicates that Arnold did not believe unqualifiedly in independence. His doctrine indeed was a compromise between his belief in the necessity of virtue and his desire for self-reliance. Younger boys or those without the proper character and principles had no right to independence. But once a boy had learned willingly to suppress his egoistic traits, and to conform in thought to Arnold's doctrines, in other words, once he was properly socialized, he was encouraged to stand on his own feet. In fact he was asked to be more than merely self-reliant. He was to be a moral reformer himself, a courageous fighter in the war on moral evil. Arnold wanted his best boys, those who in their innermost hearts were servants of righteousness, to be the leaders of a new crusade.

[1] Stanley, op. cit., Letter 98, p. 244.
[2] Ibid., p. 140.   [3] Ibid., p. 306.

So far we have seen that Arnold was a libertarian in that he was a humanitarian and an individualist. But he was also one in the sense that he believed in the cultivation of free intellectual inquiry. Though Arnold's intellectual aims, not heretofore dealt with, were of secondary importance, they are by no means to be neglected, particularly as it was on the intellectual side that a good deal of Arnold's liberalism found expression.

As already suggested, the aim of much intellectual training was purely moral in the double sense that effort itself would cultivate industriousness and that classic learning would provide moral lessons. Moreover, a good deal of Arnold's purpose was the time-honoured one of disciplining the mind, of making it a perfect instrument;[1] not knowledge, but the means of gaining it, is the end of education.[2] At the same time some of his principles were nearer to what to-day we mean by a liberal education than were the principles of the most advanced liberals of the day. Arnold was a humanist, and with Sir Richard Jebb he liked the classics in good part because they represented 'forces hostile to obscurantism, pedantry, and superstition, forces making for intellectual light, for the advance of knowledge in every field'.[3] Since the classics were our mind 'developed to an extraordinary degree of perfection', by studying the literature of the classics we obtain the 'general liberality of its tastes and the comparative comprehensiveness of its views and notions'.[4] In other words, Arnold wanted to broaden the intellectual outlook of boys. Further, he wanted to 'create an appetite for knowledge' through study.[5] He wished to stimulate the mind to free intellectual inquiry, to make boys think for themselves.[6]

Arnold's educational purposes were not only exceedingly diverse, but were often potentially or actually self-contradictory. But the genius of Arnold was able to preserve a balance between his various ideals, and to effect his diverse purposes without involving his boys in any irreconcilable difficulties. It is worth noting, however, that after Arnold

[1] Cf. Arnold's *Miscellaneous Works*, p. 296. [2] Stanley, op. cit., p. 98.
[3] Cf. Whitridge, op. cit., p. 72. [4] Arnold, *Miscellaneous Works*, p. 340.
[5] Ibid., p. 352. [6] Stanley, op. cit., p. 98.

was dead, and thus no longer able to lend support to his pupils, many of them found themselves involved in what appeared to be very real contradictions.

The central difficulty was Arnold's attempt to reconcile dogma and individualism, faith, and thought. Whether he was philosophically right or wrong, Arnold's insistence on the omnipotence of individual conscience and the right of private judgment was ultimately fatal to the religious principles which he taught. So long as Arnold was alive the magnetism of his personality made his disciples take these principles for granted, in spite of the innoculation of individualism and intellectualism which he administered. In a sense, too, Arnold, the man, took the place, for his followers, of infallible dogma. Once he was dead, however, it was discovered that he had succeeded chiefly in 'stimulating earnestness of what we might fairly call a destructive kind, a kind that dissipates faith even while it scores deep the lines of ethical zeal'.[1] The acids of modernity bit deeper and deeper into the metal of doctrinal Christianity in the forties and fifties, and some of Arnold's best pupils, like his son Matthew and Arthur Hugh Clough, found themselves floating, unhappy and alone, on the vast and unstable sea of scepticism.

D. ARNOLD'S EDUCATIONAL METHODS

In order to carry his heterogeneous combination of purposes into practice, Arnold used a variety of methods. But very seldom did he import these methods from the outside world: the distinctive feature of Arnold's system of education is its almost exclusive use of the means already at its disposal in a Public School. Arnold maintained the traditional customs, ways of doing things, and organization that he found at Rugby. Even where he modified most radically, he left the established forms as they were before his day.

That Arnold was able to reform and yet preserve is of primary significance. Just as a resolution of various conflicting educational aims was a necessary premise to his

[1] *Spectator*, June 18th 1892, p. 840.

success, so was the ability to accomplish these aims without destroying the traditions of the system. For English opinion before Arnold was fairly well divided between those who believed that an educational revolution was necessary and those who did not. The conflict between conservative and modificationist was solved by Arnold as was that between individualist and dogmatist by giving to each what he desired. The advocate of change secured many of those educational ends for the accomplishment of which he had been willing to overturn the system. The conservative retained many of his beloved customs and traditions. Arnold thus preserved the popularity of the Public School system among all those classes who had the money to go to them. Had he, instead of using old customs, tried, like Rowland Hill, to create an entirely new school with a paper constitution, he would probably not have had any permanent influence in England.

If we ask why Arnold retained most of the important characteristics of the old school system, we are confronted with one aspect of his educational philosophy not so far enlarged upon. In dealing with educational purposes, we have assumed that all Arnold's aims were the result of educational and philosophical principles, and were not influenced by the former aims of the institution in which he worked. Probably this was not entirely true. It was certainly not true of Arnold's methods. In other words, it hardly seems logical to conclude that the retention of so many old traditions was based entirely on Arnold's abstract belief that these traditions represented the most efficacious methods for training youth or embodied the highest moral ideals. That undoubtedly was his motive in many instances, and it is certainly true that he seldom retained a tradition which he felt to be definitely bad. However, two other factors assuredly entered in. In the first place, Arnold probably adopted some customs because, given the inertia of schools and the force of public opinion, he found it easier to do so. That tolerance which we have discovered in his nature helped him to be an opportunist where it was most necessary that he should be. Far more important and more easily demonstrable, he retained many old ways of doing things because he had a fondness for the established and the old, for the traditional and authoritative. If a custom or a purpose or a whole institution had existed for a long time, if it bore the authority of ages, that entitled it, all other things being equal, to be viewed with favour. In other words, Arnold, like so many Englishmen, loved the old and believed in the authority of that which is established.

As Sadler says, Arnold was always 'sensitive in a marked degree to the influences of any spiritual tradition which appealed to him by its beauty, tenderness or justice.'[1] In his early days at Winchester he was permeated by a feeling for the 'peculiar constitution of a public school', and had strengthened in him an innate 'feeling of reverence for what is ancient and noble'.[2] 'In after years he always cherished a strong Wykehamist feeling',[3] and defended Public Schools against radicals because of their 'historical associations and beauty'[4] and the 'great and venerable traditions', the 'long historic record' which they represented.[5] It always meant much to Arnold that he could 'breathe the atmosphere of a renowned public school',[6] and he regretted exceedingly that Rugby was not older. He wanted, indeed, to have a medal of rank for his school so that it would have historical associations like Eton.[7] He particularly lamented the fact that there were so few old associations in the chapel as reminders of nobleness, and early consecrated this scene of his greatest labours to the graves of those future Rugby dead who would give the place traditions.[8]

If Arnold's love of established institutions was primarily based on prejudice of a personal or class nature, it must be remembered that he, no less than other conservatives, found justification for his emotions. In the first place, he contended that age embodied wisdom, and propounded the thesis, derived from Burke and Coleridge, that old institutions were moral beings and that history was a moral

[1] Whitridge, op. cit., p. xxxii.
[2] Stanley, op. cit., p. 3; Fitch, *Thomas and Matthew Arnold*, p. 9.
[3] Stanley, op. cit., p. 3. Dr. Arnold sent his son Matthew to Winchester.
[4] Michael Sadler in Whitridge, op. cit., p. xlix.
[5] Fitch, op. cit., p. 93. [6] Ibid., p. 9.
[7] Stanley, op. cit., p. 84. [8] Ibid., p. 109.

evolution.¹ In the second place, he argued, as suggested previously, that wisdom embodied in custom was the best means of education. He felt that education could best be conducted by establishing traditions and inducing boys to be loyal to them. If this belief did not in any sense preclude the destruction of bad traditions, it acted as an incentive to preserve the *status quo* and an argument justifying that preservation. Even more important, it provided a reason for the belief in tradition, that is, traditionalism, and immensely strengthened its hold on the Public Schools.² Because Arnold had an instinctive reverence and loyalty for the old and the established and because he found a rational justification for these feelings, he was doubly eager to impart them to others, and thus, without really intending to, he furthered the unreasoning adoration which English boys had for long displayed towards their schools without magisterial encouragement.

Whatever the causes, Arnold retained most of the internal structure of schools. He preserved almost intact the general nature and organization of a Public School, the apparatus of study and discipline and moral instruction, the customs and traditions of boy life.

To begin with, Arnold accepted in general the existing form of government of schools. He believed that the Public Schools ought to be independent endowments retaining their individuality. Though he worked for co-operation between schools, he was a bitter opponent of Government regulation.³ In the second place, he tacitly assumed the class nature of Public Schools; he was governing an upper-class institution and it never occurred to him that the membership of Rugby ought to be more democratic.

Apropos of Arnold's feeling in regard to the government of Public Schools, there was what seems to be an inconsistency in his philosophy. Though he fought against State control over upper-class schools, he strongly advocated such control with regard to middle-class education. Thus, like his

---

[1] Thomas Arnold, *Introductory Lectures on Modern History*, New York, 1845, p. 78.
[2] Archer, *Secondary Education in the Nineteenth Century*, p. 64.
[3] Stanley, op. cit., p. 240, Letter to Longley.

son Matthew, he anticipated later development of the democratic state, which the orthodox liberals opposed. Thomas felt that only the State could force the teaching of other than commercial subjects and bring about the inculcation of habits of work rather than mere knowledge.[1] Furthermore, in the economic field he was a supporter of Government interference with private industry, again in opposition to the orthodox liberals. Realizing that the condition of industrial society was one of anarchy, not civilization, he joined with Disraeli and Dickens and Carlyle in advocating as a remedy paternalistic intervention by the State. In both these matters Arnold appeared to be drifting towards socialism.

In so far as these ideas are actually inconsistent with his ideas about Public Schools, the explanation must rest on his sense of personal and class superiority. Arnold could favour a kind of control for the middle classes which he could not countenance for the upper classes or for himself. But his doctrines were not as self-contradictory as they seem. In the first place, he conceived of the State not in socialistic terms but as a union of Parliament and the Church, a curious idea, which, it may be added, pleased no one, neither political conservatives, High Churchmen, nor liberals. In the second place, membership in the State was not to be on a democratic basis, but on one of 'race', which meant to Arnold the proper religious and moral feeling.[2] Though this conception is highly equivocal, it would probably have meant in practice a control chiefly by the superior classes, those who already managed the Public Schools.

Returning to Arnold's methods at Rugby, we find that he retained the old system of formal education very nearly intact, even to some of its worst features. He refused, indeed, to be the leader in intellectual reform to a greater degree than in other fields. The classics and even Greek and Latin verse composition were retained as the basis of education, and were defended with most of the familiar arguments, the most essential of which were that the classics trained the

[1] Arnold, *Miscellaneous Works*, p. 372, Education of the Middle Classes.
[2] Arnold, *Introductory Lectures on Modern History*, Appendix.

mind, developed the taste, and familiarized the boy with the culture of a great nation.[1] Fundamentally, he believed in the disciplinary theory of education, which he reinforced by his theory of work as a sacred duty.[2] Interest and pleasure would not have appealed to Arnold as general motives for learning. He fought bitterly against the liberal insistence on useful knowledge,[3] and was opposed to Butler's method of stimulation by marks, to Arnold a utilitarian business-world idea.[4]

As a disciplinarian and moral teacher he followed in good part the old methods. Above all he found it necessary to retain flogging in order to maintain discipline. Only the lower form boys, and these for moral offences—lying, drinking, idleness—could be whipped. Yet flogging and fear of it were none the less an essential obverse to the freedom allowed to a large and unruly school. Arnold justified himself on the old-time theory that only the appeal to fear will move children.[5] As mentioned above, Arnold believed that there was a real inferiority in a boy which justified the use of fear; fear in its turn impresses on a boy his imperfection.[6] To Strachey this meant that you must beat boys or they will think that they are men.[7] Moreover, Arnold went further than merely using the rod himself: like a general pacifying a province, he delegated powers of corporal punishment to his prefects.[8] Finally, since Arnold had to have discipline, if he could not secure it by the rod of either prefect or master, he would expel ruthlessly.[9]

Needless to say, Arnold retained the religious part of Public School education. Against such liberals as the *Quarterly Journal of Education* and the Eton pamphleteers he was a staunch supporter of clerical head masters,[10] compulsory chapel, and lessons in Scripture. It is hard to believe that

---

[1] Cf. Whitridge, op. cit., p. 128; Arnold, *Miscellaneous Works*, pp. 346, 352.
[2] Arnold believed that all work was a consecration to God, and offered up prayers before first lesson.
[3] Arnold, op. cit., p. 352.   [4] Whitridge, op. cit., p. 126.
[5] Arnold, *Christian Life Sermons*, No. 10, p. 105.
[6] Arnold, *Miscellaneous Works*, pp. 355 ff.
[7] Strachey, *Eminent Victorians*, p. 191.   [8] Whitridge, op. cit., p. 143.
[9] Cf. Stanley, op. cit., pp. 87 ff. Arnold called this removal, and his reason for it was usually that the boy in question, being too childish for responsibilities, was harmed by a Public School.   [10] Stanley, op. cit., p. 337.

he could have succeeded in finding a following among the middle classes had he felt otherwise. But, since religious teaching was the core of his system, this seems a gratuitous speculation. As it was, he lent the weight of his influence towards the maintenance of the tenets of the Church of England in the Public Schools, though clerical head masters have not been a permanent part of the system.

Finally, Arnold's conception of a Public School as an independent society of boys had to be fundamental if he were not to destroy the whole idea of a Public School. And indeed it was. Even from the point of view of morality Arnold argued in favour of a life free from espionage. A school was a testing-place of virtue, and untried goodness was worthless.[1] Arnold admitted that schools did encourage roughness, pride, and profanity, but added that 'the victory of fallen man is to be sought for, not in innocence, but in tried virtue'.[2] Further, Arnold saw, as did most defenders of schools, that it was more advantageous to legalize the system of boy self-government, of fagging and monitors than to allow privileges to be merely usurped. In the legalized system Arnold found all the virtues that schools were accustomed to find. It gave a regular government and avoided the anarchy that resulted from the 'lawless tyranny of physical strength'. An aristocracy of the oldest, strongest, and cleverest would put down the bullying of the overgrown dunces. Boys would complain if their legal superiors ill-treated them; public opinion would prevent their telling on a bully. As to fagging—and here he shows his authoritarian conservatism—Arnold supported it because he believed that it was good for a boy to obey a real superiority. Fagging taught that quickness, punctuality, helpfulness, and endurance which the boys in the Peninsular War found so helpful, and had nothing to do with real servility.[3]

[1] Ibid., p. 83.   [2] Arnold, *Christian Life Sermons*, p. 7.
[3] Arnold, *Miscellaneous Works*, p. 360. Arnold has convinced even modern liberals of the virtues of the prefect system. Whitridge sees no alternative to self-government of Arnold's kind except Keate's form of espionage (op. cit., p. 135). Though Archer attacks the 'class of croakers who believed that a Spartan discipline' imposed by boys on one another 'was an actual benefit to character', he does not object to the prefect system. (*Education in the Nineteenth Century*, p. 62.)

If Arnold was a conservative, he was also a believer in change. In politics he was a mild liberal who wanted to improve in order to preserve. Though no revolutionary—he was scandalized at Jacobin excesses, and would not even read Byron's *Don Juan*—he hated the diehard Tories for their failure to move with the times. He approved of the French Revolution of 1830 because it was the suppression of an aristocratic revolution against society.[1] In religion, as we have seen, he attacked both Church doctrine and Church exclusiveness. In general he shared Carlyle's belief that the individual should attack worn-out dogmas and dead formalisms; change and progress were necessary; age was no guarantee of sanctity. As he wrote to Stanley, 'My love for any place or person, or institution, is exactly the measure of my desire to reform them.'[2]

Arnold's changes at Rugby were of two kinds. There were technical changes, actual innovations. But these were of minor importance compared with other less tangible reforms. What made Arnold a great reformer was not modification of form, but shifts in emphasis, the imbuing of old forms with a new spirit, the redirecting of old traditions to serve new purposes.

In the non-educational aspects of schools, Arnold made the fewest changes either in form or spirit. He made no actual innovations. If he fought for supreme control as against the trustees, he was merely following the precedent of every strong master before him from Busby to Samuel Butler.[3] Despite his democracy he never tried to have the poor taught at Rugby. He did, however, as we have seen, try to make his boys more democratic. Further, Whitridge reports that Arnold did not want a school filled with nothing but country gentlemen, though the alternative of professional men was not a new departure.[4]

In the intellectual sphere his actual changes were extremely tentative. He introduced modern history, modern languages, and mathematics, but, as Stanley admits, he did

---

[1] Stanley, op. cit., pp. 59, 129, 170, 178.   [2] Ibid., p. 244.
[3] For Arnold's attitude in these matters, cf. Stanley, op. cit., p. 70, Letter 21, and p. 78.
[4] Cf. Whitridge, op. cit., p. 107.

not give enough time or importance to the last two.¹ Science he did not teach at all, on the basis that one had to give all or nothing to science, and, as Strachey adds sarcastically, science surely ought not to be all for a Christian and an Englishman.² Arnold, who cared more about Duty and mind training than about facts, felt that religion and the humanities were more important than science.³ He was, however, becoming less averse to the idea of the natural sciences.⁴ As we have seen, many liberals from Bentham down were far ahead of Arnold in curricular changes. Nevertheless, it does remain true that Arnold was ahead of all Public Schools; all these subjects were unknown at Eton except as extras; at Harrow there was one lecture a week on modern history and literature. Only at such schools as the Quaker School at Bootham and at Hazelwood were science, algebra, or drawing taught.⁵

The most important reforms in intellectual training that Arnold made were in the spirit in which he taught the classics. Though he clung to composition and mind-training through grammar, he concentrated, as had not been done for hundreds of years, on the content of the classics. Derived, as we have seen, from Germany, this new interest in the ideas in the classics proved tremendously fruitful with Arnold. He taught them for the moral ideas in them applicable to modern times. This meant that he encouraged comparisons with the present, and cared much more for idiomatic translations than he did for the dissection of construing.⁶ Arnold felt that the classical mind was useful only if its relation to modern literature and politics was shown. In like manner he approved of translations because they helped one to know English by the comparative study of language that emerged.⁷ The classics thus served Arnold as instruments for moral teaching and mental stimulation, the two purposes that he had most in his heart.

Finally, the greatest change that Arnold made was in his

[1] Cf. Stanley, op. cit., p. 98.   [2] Strachey, *Eminent Victorians*, p. 194.
[3] Cf. Arnold, *Miscellaneous Works*, p. 296.
[4] Cf. Whitridge, op. cit., pp. 112 ff. [5] Ibid., pp. 119 ff. [6] Ibid., p. 128.
[7] Cf. Arnold, *Miscellaneous Works*, pp. 346 ff. Arnold carried his ideas of comparative study so far that he wanted Homer translated with Saxon and early French words, and the tragedians into Elizabethan.

method of teaching. With the sixth form—he taught the lower forms relatively seldom—he was no longer the forbidding schoolmaster, but the familiar guide and mentor. Though he never allowed impertinence, he established an informality in the classroom which, though not entirely new, was certainly very far from the ordinary practice of the day. Moreover, he made learning a personal relationship between teacher and boy; each of Arnold's best students knew that the master had a thorough familiarity with and concern for his intellectual development. As a result the boy was aroused, as he could have been in no other way, to an interest in the new mental worlds to which Arnold introduced him.[1]

In formal discipline and moral instruction, Arnold made important modifications. He flogged much less than former masters. He was, whenever possible, kind to his younger boys, trying to improve them by example and encouragement, and to prevent undue severity by the older boys. Even more important was his attitude towards the older boys. Unlike Keate or Gabell he trusted all his boys to some extent. It was the prefects, however, who received the direct benefit of Arnold's belief that boys had a better nature that was not proof against reason and love.[2] To a greater degree than any previous master, he made his best pupils his friends and companions, often inviting them to go for walks with him or to dine at his house.

Unfortunately, it was impossible for Arnold to have personal contact with most of his students. Only the sixth formers ever saw him informally, and even these complained that he did not guide them enough.[3] The younger boys were bound, after all, to know him chiefly as a superior being dispensing punishment. Arnold's problem was to find some way of making his moral influence felt over the entire school. He needed avenues along which his means for bringing about moral reform—persuasion, encouragement, and severity—might travel. He found these means in the two apparently out-moded forms of school life which the

[1] Stanley, op. cit., pp. 98 ff.
[2] Cf. Stanley, op. cit., p. 83; Whitridge, op. cit., pp. 95 ff.
[3] Stanley, op. cit., pp. 117 ff.

Arnold

radicals had wanted to discard—the chapel service and the prefect system.

In Arnold's hands the formal religious part of school life, once mere mechanism, became a living thing; he personalized it. He made his warm and powerful personality the instrument for the diffusion of religious ideas. Or to put it in another way, he used the chapel pulpit as a means for disseminating his moral ideas. The older Public Schools limited themselves to teaching formal dogmatic religion through dry-as-dust sermons and long, uninspired services. Arnold created the modern school sermon, short, simple, and intimate. He himself became chaplain and personally took care of the religious education of boys, a function that older schoolmasters had not considered part of their duty. Communion especially was sacred to him.

In all his sermons his method was to talk intimately about ordinary, practical subjects. He spoke of the evils of schools, the 'common things of your daily life;—common faults which you every day commit, common feelings which every day pass through your hearts and minds', and compared them with the laws of Christianity.[1] In modern eyes, his insistence on sin was repellent and austere, but in comparison with the practice of his day, intimate and gentle.[2] Moreover, as time went on, he grew gentler and more full of love and less of hate. Sternness was always mixed with affectionate entreaty.[3] On the positive side, though there was some dogma —he was constantly trying to point out how such things as the Resurrection and the Church were visible symbols of the unseen life[4]—for the most part he appealed straight to the personality of Christ in order to reach a boy's heart. He made his pupils feel that Christianity had some personal relation to them, that believing in Christ helped to overcome temptation, and that religion, while taking away none of the gaiety of youth, could bring manliness and save souls.[5] As he said in one sermon, typical of many, 'Only may God grant, that what I have hitherto said, may lead some of you, at least, to acquire a greater familiarity with the words and

---
[1] Stanley, op. cit., pp. 109 ff.; Whitridge, op. cit., p. 91.
[2] Cf. Strachey, op. cit., pp. 195, 196.   [3] Stanley, op. cit., pp. 109 ff.
[4] Arnold, *Christian Life Sermons*, No. 28, pp. 307, 309.   [5] Ibid., No. 3, p. 22.

deeds of Christ; that your own experience might tell you whether I have over-valued the advantages of knowing them and loving them.'[1]

Arnold's use of the prefect system was central to his whole method and illustrates better than anything else the way in which he made an old form serve a new purpose. In the old days the prefect system had been in a sense a symbol of the division between master and boy. Arnold was always especially aware of and hostile to this disunity in the school, so fatal to morality. As he said dejectedly in one of his sermons, 'boys have learnt to regard themselves and their masters as opposite to one another, as having two distinct interests;—it being the master's object to lay on restrictions, and abridge their liberty, while it was their business [by] . . . combinations amongst themselves, concealment, trick, open falsehood, or open disobedience . . . to baffle his watchfulness, and escape his severity'. Boy custom or public opinion dictated hostility, and, unfortunately, 'at no place, or time of life, are people so much the slaves of custom, as boys at school'.[2] As we have seen, Arnold broke down this barrier to a great extent by kindness and persuasion out of school, in school, and in chapel. But above all, he broke it down by striking at its root, the independent prefect system. He turned a prefectorial government which had been a nearly autonomous system acquiesced in or supported by the master into a link between master and boy. He made prefects instruments for carrying his moral ideas to the school. He transformed an organization of boys with their own laws and *esprit de corps* into an agency for humanizing and reforming the life of a Public School. The leading boys, which to Arnold meant the entire sixth form, were to assume the master's function of persuading and disciplining the younger boys into conformity to Arnold's wishes. For Arnold believed that, since the example of schoolfellows is more important than the discipline of a master, the sixth form would better be able to raise the moral tone of the school than could a master unaided.[3]

[1] Arnold, *Rugby Sermons*, No. 2, p. 25.
[2] Arnold, *Rugby Sermons*, No. 12, pp. 103, 106; No. 9, p. 71.
[3] Old Rugbaean, *Recollections of Rugby*, p. 99.

There were two halves to Arnold's transformation of the prefect system. He gave his sixth form both more and less independence than they had had before. On the one hand, he trusted his prefects implicitly and gave them a power and importance that they had seldom had before. Prefects became young gods. At the same time he made them realize what few had understood before his day, that a prefect must be loyal to ideals and that power implied willingness to spread these ideals abroad. He gave authority in order to demand service, and delegated it only to those who took their moral lead from him and showed that they felt responsive to him. The spirit that Arnold wished to cultivate in his boys was echoed by Hughes's grandfather when Thomas's brother George was expelled from Rugby: it is the duty of prefects to have school spirit and to uphold Arnold if they really esteem him.[1] Sadler has stated the whole matter in modern terms. 'He turned the Sixth Form into a corps of young commissioned officers for a campaign against offences in school. Hodson, afterwards the leader of Hodson's Horse in the Indian Mutiny, was the boy he chose to put down disorder in a boarding-house.'[2]

Obviously the crux of Arnold's system was his ability to instil loyalty to his ideals and the willingness to further them. In part loyalty and the crusading spirit were implicit in his system, for giving trust and responsibility inspires affectionate loyalty towards him who gives it. As Whitridge suggests rather cynically, Arnold's delegating of power gave more people a stake in the system as it was, and thus made them loyal to it.[3] But beyond that, Arnold had consciously to persuade his prefects into being loyal and helpful. He had constantly to preach the doctrine that all were members of one institution whose honour all should guard,[4] and that the few thoughtful must help the others.[5] In other words, Arnold's method was one of personal influence, not merely of a delegation of power to the sixth form.[6] No more than

[1] T. Hughes, *Memoir of a Brother*, pp. 32 ff. At the same time the sturdy Old Westminster was not quite won over to Arnold's extreme position: he objected to tale-bearing and to slavery to Arnold's ideals.
[2] In Whitridge, op. cit., p. xxi.   [3] Cf. Whitridge, op. cit., p. 143.
[4] Stanley, op. cit., p. 83.   [5] Arnold, *Christian Life Sermons*, No. 5, p. 49.
[6] Corbin, *Schoolboy Life in England*, p. 169.

an account of his teaching of the classics, nor of his system of religious training, is a discussion of the prefect system complete without reference to Arnold's personality.

This brings us to two final and in a sense all-important points in regard to Arnold's methods. In the first place, no analysis of the separate aspects of Rugby education is tantamount to a complete picture of that education. Arnold's Rugby was not a collection of discrete and lifeless mechanisms, but an organic unity created by the genius of one man. In order, therefore, really and fully to comprehend its nature and quality, one must re-create a picture of the school as a whole and as a living and functioning institution. In so far as this can be done it must be the work of the artist, not of the analyst. But even the artist is severely handicapped by the barrier of years; for the essence of a living thing is unique and individual, and can be completely understood, intimately, only by those who have experienced it.

In the second place, and closely related to the first point, an account of Arnold's methods is not identical with an explanation of the effectiveness of those methods. If Arnold was a successful schoolmaster partly because of the adroit synthesis he made of various popular means of education, that is by no means the whole story. In the last analysis Arnold's effectiveness was due to the force of his personality; Arnold accomplished his aims at Rugby and thus influenced the world because he was a man of unique power.

A mere statement of this fact is not, it must be confessed, very illuminating. A convincing explanation of Arnold's success would involve an attempt to grasp the nature and causes of the personal power which he possessed. Unfortunately, one is as handicapped in such an undertaking as one is in an effort fully to understand Arnold's system, and for much the same reasons. One can describe in detail Arnold's character and his actions. But the man himself escapes one, and, as Stanley says, 'it was the man himself' as a unique whole whose magnetism moved boys and inspired them to carry on his system.[1] His power was over and above any combination of qualities that he possessed or any

[1] Stanley, op. cit., p. 82.

actions that he performed. As Bradley says, the source of his inspiration was secret and mystic, was Life itself.[1]

The most fruitful thing that one can do is to study the glowing words of Arnold's disciples in regard to their master, and thus indirectly acquire some sense of the nature of the force that inspired these words. Almost all of Arnold's best pupils were left with a 'peculiarity of character' which 'was derived not from the genius of the place, but from the genius of the man';[2] and almost all have regarded their mentor with affectionate awe and loyalty, even with adoration.[3] Especially was this true of Stanley, Clough, and Dr. Arnold's son Matthew. And it was the last of these who has given the world the most moving eulogy of the Rugby master, and who has thus come nearer than any one else to making us feel his power. 'Rugby Chapel' expresses both Matthew's love and the quality of the man who inspired it.

> . . . thou would'st not *alone*
> Be saved, my father! *alone*
> Conquer and come to thy goal
> Leaving the rest in the wild . . .
>
> . . . . .
>
> Still thou turnedst, and still
> Beckonedst the trembler, and still
> Gavest the weary thy hand.
>
> . . . . .
>
> Therefore to thee it was given
> Many to save with thyself;
> And, at the end of thy day,
> O faithful shepherd! to come,
> Bringing thy sheep in thy hand.

E. THE FRUITS OF ARNOLD'S DOCTRINES

Throughout the foregoing pages I have maintained the thesis that Arnold's educational aims and the system which he evolved to effect those aims point to the fact that the Rugby schoolmaster was at once a liberal, a conservative, and a reactionary. Since Arnold's day there have been

---
[1] *Nineteenth Century*, March 1884, G. G. Bradley, 'Rugby and Arnold'.
[2] Stanley, op. cit., p. 82. [3] Ibid., p. 117.

many writers who have denied this thesis, especially that part of it which claims that Arnold was a liberal. Of these the most important has been a group of modern progressives led by Lytton Strachey and Bertrand Russell. For this group, besides accusing Arnold of being a black reactionary, has held him responsible for most of the anti-liberal conditions which they feel exist in our day both within the Public School and in the outside world.

Strachey has insisted that Arnold's emphasis on morality and religion and his deification of the prefect have meant slavery for the young and the creation of a type of older boy who follows orders blindly and is at the same time ruthless in enforcing on others a rigorous and repressive code. He has blamed Arnold for modern anti-intellectualism, athleticism, and the worship of good form.[1] Russell has emphasized chiefly the effect of Arnold's system on the outside world. Arnold, he contended, was responsible for the creation of the modern empire builder, a man who, because he was 'energetic, stoical, physically fit, possessed of certain unalterable beliefs', imbued with 'high standards of rectitude, and convinced that [he] . . . had an important mission in the world', was adapted to exert authority at home and in the empire.[2] His mission was to reform the benighted heathen. 'Not unnaturally,' adds Russell, 'the pupils of his [Arnold's] disciples . . . believe in flogging natives of India when they are deficient in "humbleness of mind".' 'It is tragic when we think of the generations of cruelty that he put into the world by creating an atmosphere of abhorrence of "moral evil".'[3] According to Russell, 'Dr. Arnold sacrificed intelligence to "virtue". The battle of Waterloo may have been won on the playing-fields of Eton, but the British Empire is being lost there. The modern world needs a different type, with more imaginative sympathy, more intellectual suppleness, less belief in bulldog courage and more belief in technical knowledge.'[4]

Even if we are convinced of the liberal nature of some of Arnold's intentions and of the liberal effect of his teachings

[1] Strachey, *Eminent Victorians*, pp. 190 ff., 212.
[2] Bertrand Russell, *Education and the Good Life*, New York, 1926, pp. 47, 53.
[3] Russell, op. cit., pp. 38-40.   [4] Ibid., p. 54.

Arnold

at Rugby, Strachey's and Russell's accusations cannot be lightly dismissed, for they raise questions that go beyond such considerations. Was the ultimate outcome of Arnold's teachings in accordance with his liberal aims? If it was not, how much of the responsibility for the failure of his designs must Arnold bear?

Of the answer to the first question there can be little doubt. Arnold's system has not, on the whole, borne liberal fruit in the years since his death. Public Schools have seldom been places of kindness or freedom, places where intellectual originality, individual happiness, and democratic co-operation have been cultivated. Arnold's educational instruments have been retained, but they have been used to further ends very different from any that Arnold desired.

Particularly has this been true of the central feature of his system, prefectorial government. Certain achievements of Arnold with respect to boy self-government have been of momentous and lasting importance. In the first place, Arnold established prefectorial government as the most unassailable part of the idea of a Public School. In the second place, he fixed as its permanent working principle the ideas of loyalty, *esprit de corps,* and self-sacrifice. If the system has functioned successfully, it is because prefects have always worked as a loyal and united body. In the third place, Arnold made enduring the idea that it was the duty of prefects to instil loyalty and self-sacrifice in others. Finally, and most important, he made of the prefect system an instrument of government not only recognized but deliberately used by the masters. Indeed, that it was so recognized is what gave it its increased power. Arnold actually did, with qualifications, break down the barrier between boy and master. Prefects were from Arnold's day on to be as universally recognized instruments of master government as flogging and religious instruction. This meant, on the one hand, that prefects were nominally, at any rate, loyal to and defenders of master ideals. Never again, except in certain respects, have boys and masters run separate governments with separate laws. On the other hand, this has meant that the masters have become part of a

Public School. Loyalty and romantic attachment have, ever since Arnold, had as their object an institution belonging to boy and master alike.

But Arnold's prefect system has not always been used to further Arnold's ends; it has seldom protected the weak, encouraged real moral idealism, or instilled liberal principles. In the first place, prefects, enormously strengthened in their positions and considering themselves morally superior to others, have felt entitled vigorously to stamp out individuality and to enforce conformity. When they have left school, it may be added, they have been only too ready to assume their share of the 'white man's burden' in distant lands. In the second place, they have demanded standardization in the name of relatively vulgar ideals. Were such standardization enforced for the sake of promoting Arnold's purposes, one might possibly forgive the suppression of individuality. This has, however, usually not been the case. Prefects have become, once again, the administrators of boy ideals. They have asked boys to conform merely because conformity was considered a virtue, and have held up boy ideals like strength and competitive power as standards for imitation. Thus Arnold's prefect system has indirectly resulted in the worship of mere 'good form', and the deification and imitation of the athlete. As far as the outside world was concerned, it has meant the creation of a large group willing to die to preserve the upper classes in power at home and abroad.

In connexion with this question of Arnold's prefect system and the fruits which it bore, an interesting parallel between educational and politico-economic developments presents itself. That it is more than a parallel I do not venture to say. In a previous chapter I suggested that the condition of boy society before Arnold was analogous to the *laissez-faire* system that prevailed in the outside world. On top were decayed, powerless institutions that, because they embodied legitimate power, thwarted economic advance without checking its evils. Underneath was a seething, chaotic, and yet living society. In Arnold's day Whigs and Tories united to rehabilitate old institutions and make them the instruments for checking the greed and tyranny of the new manufacturing classes through Factory Acts and the like. Of this movement, called by M. Cazamian paternalistic interventionism, Arnold was himself a part. It left *laissez-faire* as the dominant characteristic of society but attempted to control it in the interests of the weak. Though it made some notable advances, it did not really check the advance of a ruthless and powerful monopolistic capitalism. It seems to me that Arnold's work at Rugby may well be called paternalistic interventionism. He left the old system of self-government of the boys intact, but tried to control it from above in the interests of humanity and morality. The ultimate outcome was, despite an improvement in moral tone, chiefly a strengthening of the power of the older boys and a greater crushing of the individuality of the small boy.

For what happened to Arnold's system after his death he cannot be held entirely without responsibility. In the first place, he did create the elements out of which subsequent difficulties developed. He over-emphasized worship of absolute ideals in comparison with independent thought, and obedience, loyalty, and self-sacrifice in comparison with freedom and originality. He was primarily concerned with producing boys who cared for *esprit de corps* rather than individuality. Moreover, he glorified the self-reliant prefect and made him a virtually independent educational instrument. He is responsible for future events in the sense that had he not emphasized these purposes and methods there might have been no deadening conformity, no cruelty, no imperialist leaders. Or, to put it more exactly, had Arnold had other ideas he might have stemmed the tide in those directions.

In the second place, he seems to have been curiously blind to the potentialities for evil that existed in his ideas. He seems not to have realized just how dangerous the delegating of power to boys was, how few were capable of using this power for their own benefit or for that of their fellows. On the one hand, he was oblivious to the harm that he was doing to those who, like Clough and Stanley, absorbed his purposes. On the other hand, he was equally unconscious of how few could be expected to comprehend those purposes in the way that Clough did, or administer them without the constant supervision of an Arnold. He failed, in short, to realize that he was strengthening a system which could yield libertarian and democratic fruit only in exceptional hands. The same thing may be said with regard to Arnold's political views. Arnold believed that it was the duty of the morally superior English state to be helpful to weaker or less civilized peoples.[1] The sincerity of the purely ethical motives which inspired such a belief is beyond question. Yet one cannot help feeling that Arnold was unforgivably blind: one is even justified in feeling that, because of his blindness, he was not an inappropriate leader for the future Public School boy who was to conquer the world in the name of humanity and British capital.

The worst that one can say of Arnold, however, is that he was blind to the implications of his ideas. He was not only not directly responsible for most of what occurred after his death, but would have disliked it as heartily as do Strachey and Russell. Athleticism, the worship of good form, rigid uniformity, and imperialism would have shocked him profoundly. If Arnold preached conformity it was only in essentials, it was never blind, and it was in part obedience to liberal standards. Obedience to 'what is done' was the very opposite of what he wanted. Loyalty to my school, my country, right or wrong, was never even implicit in Arnold's ideals; he preached loyalty and self-sacrifice only for a worthy end. And that end was a moral, not a class end. Whether Arnold could have approved the sacrifice of millions of lives on the altar of capitalist profits would have depended on whether or not he would have been fooled into thinking he was saving the world for democracy. Loyalty to a nation, because it is your nation, or a class because it is your class, was foreign to Arnold's teaching. Even more important, the morality for which he was crusading was at least partly a democratic and humane one. His attitude towards natives, the poor, and small boys in the school may have been one of moral superiority, but it was never one of

---

[1] Arnold, *Miscellaneous Works*, p. 327, 'The Social Progress of States'.

cruelty. Humanitarianism has been proved to be too weak to stop cruelty in the economic world, but to say this is not to accuse Arnold of fomenting cruelty. He fought for protection and sympathy for the small boy in school as well as for the poor outside. The very essence of Arnold's conception was the control of his prefects in the interests of the happiness of the weak. Finally, Arnold taught individuality and free thought within limits to all who were capable of profiting by his teaching. Arnold did not want unthinking servants of even the finest moral principles.

The ultimate responsibility for the failure of Arnold's system to develop in a liberal direction must rest elsewhere than on Arnold's shoulders. In the first place, a good deal of illiberalism, of conformity, and of prefect tyranny existed before 1830, and was merely not permanently destroyed by Arnold. When less powerful masters than he attempted to use his system, evils which had always been inherent in the Public School system gained the upper hand once more. As suggested above, the moral success of Rugby was in good part the result of Arnold's forceful personality. When weaker rulers attempted to use his system, they failed to achieve his ends. They were forced, in order to preserve the friendship with boys which Arnold had won, to accede to boy demands, to allow prefects to administer schools in the name of boy ideals.[1] In the second place, much that occurred was the result of new ideals in society which Arnold could neither have foreseen nor forestalled. Arnold's death in 1842 took place at the dawn of a new era. In the forties and fifties new forces working through other men than Arnold used Arnold's methods for their own ends.

[1] Cf. Oscar Browning, *Aspects of Education*, p. 175.

PART IV
FROM ARNOLD TO THE PUBLIC
SCHOOL COMMISSION

CHAPTER I

ARNOLDIANISM

A. INTRODUCTION

EVEN before Arnold's death most of the neglect and criticism that had pursued his earlier years had disappeared. Through his own writings and speeches and through the influence of his best students at the universities and elsewhere, his name and achievements were coming more and more into prominence.[1] As early as 1838 Moberly, head master of Winchester, credited the Rugby head master with having made a revolution the effects of which were felt even at Winchester.[2] After his death in 1842 and particularly after Stanley's biography two years later, Arnold's public recognition grew to huge proportions. He became the outstanding schoolmaster of his generation and the dominating force in all educational matters.

Since Arnold is the hub around which revolve the history and criticism of the early Victorian Public School, this section must begin with Arnold and work outward. Chapter I will deal with the posthumous career of Arnold's doctrines and will be confined to a record of their impact on the minds of men, excluding their actual effect on the schools themselves. This involves a consideration of Arnold's influence on many diverse personalities, and conversely, of the influence of these personalities on Arnold's doctrines. Chapter II will discuss actual changes in the Public Schools

[1] In 1836 the omnipresent Crabb Robinson wrote that he, as well as Bunsen and the Wordsworths, grew fonder of Arnold all the time. He added: 'The Doctor certainly talks more freely than I ever heard a D.D. talk; and from the head master of so great an establishment as Rugby School (where, I believe, there are 300 pupils) this is a significant sign of the times.' (Henry Crabb Robinson, *Diary, Reminiscences, and Correspondence*, 3 vols., London, 1869, Vol. III, p. 83.)

[2] Though the spirit of the age was in part responsible for his success, it was, according to Moberly, due chiefly to Arnold that boys went to Oxford with a new consciousness of duty. (Stanley, *Life and Correspondence of Thomas Arnold*, p. 125.) Charles Wordsworth believed that Moberly deserved more credit than he gave himself. The poet Wordsworth was inclined to give Charles himself much praise. (Charles Wordsworth, *Early Life*, p. 270.)

285

prior to 1860. It will record the way in which Arnold's ideas were materialized in various educational institutions. But, since the schools and not Arnold will now be the centre of attention, it will not deal only with Arnold, but will tell of other influences that played a part in Public School change. Chapter III will resume the story of Public School defence and criticism. It will concern itself with Arnold only secondarily, in so far as his doctrines are imbedded in conditions defended or criticized. In this résumé of the reaction to the early and mid-Victorian School, we shall be looking, not backward at Arnold, but forward to the liberal outburst of the sixties and the work of the Public School Commission.

Though for clarity and convenience it is well to separate the record of the absorption of Arnold's doctrines by individuals from the concrete changes in the schools, and from the general criticism of the post-Arnoldian school, actually all these phenomena were occurring simultaneously during a period of about thirty years. Their nature and characteristics were governed by certain general forces which dominated the mid-Victorian world.

At the outset it is well to remember that much of what occurred was the result of individual differences, and was therefore neither a general nor a period phenomenon. If Stanley and Hughes generated contrasting ideals, it was partly because they were cast in different individual moulds. If the education of Clough and Stanley had diverse effects on their lives, it was because Clough suffered from a more deep-seated introversion than did Stanley. If Vaughan was more successful in adopting Arnold's ideas than was Christopher Wordsworth or Moberly or Kennedy, the explanation lies in part in Vaughan's greater personal magnetism and temperamental similarity to his master.

But these individual diversities operated within a framework of more general influences. To begin with, throughout the thirties and much of the forties the forces that had produced liberalism and the religious revival were still in the ascendancy. Most of the upper classes continued to subscribe to that union of libertarianism, religious feeling, and conservatism which we have called the Victorian Compromise. As a result, Arnold's doctrines, the embodiment of this compromise, were both enthusiastically praised and eagerly accepted by the schools. Indeed, for some extremists, both liberal and reactionary, even Arnold did not go far enough. The reactionary High Church party wanted more authoritative control in the interest of religion and morality. Though the influence of this party in the forties and fifties was fairly well limited to Winchester, ritualism, a later form of High Church reaction, began to make an impression at Eton and Harrow in the late fifties. Similarly, the intellectual liberals were far from satisfied with Arnold's work. Throughout the forties and fifties they carried on a battle for curricular reform until in the sixties they won at least a Pyrrhic victory. The humanitarian liberals have proved ineffective but persistent foes of the prefect system all through the later nineteenth and into the twentieth century.

But, though in the ascendancy, the reformers were not uncontested. Older Public School traditions were solidly rooted in the hearts of many upper-class Englishmen and in the schools themselves. The forces of conservatism were, however, almost entirely on the defensive until nearly mid-century, and did little but retard and temper reform. Their resistance, it may be added, was stronger at the ecclesiastical schools than at the freer of the old schools or at the new schools. Moreover, it was more powerful, other things being equal, at an aristocratic than at a middle-class school and at a popular than at an unpopular one. As might be expected, Eton was the backbone of conservatism.

But in the forties and especially in the fifties, important anti-liberal as well as anti-religious[1] forces were gaining enough strength partially to reverse the direction of early Victorian thought. Conservative as contrasted to liberal or reactionary educational principles were now commonly held not only by those who had always been conservatives, but by the new middle classes, many of whom had been the

[1] This word is, though convenient, not entirely accurate. Most of the forces to be discussed were merely relatively anti-religious, working more against excessive religious enthusiasm than against religion itself.

pillars of liberalism or had supported the religious revival. In general this meant negatively that there was a renewed distaste for freedom of thought on the one hand and for excessive moral idealism and quixotic self-sacrifice on the other; positively, it denoted a renewed emphasis on solid unthinking conformity, and on the ability to stand on one's feet and compete in the world of reality.

But the reaction against the reform movements of the preceding age was only in part a return to older ideas. History seldom repeats itself in any case, and it must be remembered that much of this reaction was born of forces peculiar to a new age and participated in by groups other than the old upper classes. The middle classes, though they objected to the reformers, were not entirely content with their new team-mates. They supported many of Arnold's moral reforms. They continued to be mildly interested in intellectual training, though they espoused that false intellectual liberalism which saw the curriculum as an instrument for training boys to compete rather than as the doorway to freedom. Above all, they did not, like the conservatives, really approve of the way in which the old Public Schools had permitted boys to remain relatively unsupervised. On the contrary, they wanted the new generation rigorously disciplined; they desired a more efficient, more closely organized Public School than had previously existed.

Some of the social forces that produced the middle- and upper-class reaction were purely negative. In various ways the reform wave had spent itself by the middle forties. In political matters the middle classes had accomplished their ends, and therefore no longer wished to overturn institutions or preach freedom and reason and democracy. Whiggery became innocuous in the hands of a Russell or a Palmerston. Genuine liberalism, except for a last burst of reforming zeal under Gladstone in the sixties, was extinguished until the eighties or nineties. In economic matters the humanitarian movement lost its edge with the return of prosperity and the partial taming of the capitalist beast in the fifties. During a span of thirty or more years following the Factory Act of 1847 men like Carlyle, Ruskin, and Matthew Arnold were lone voices in the wilderness of capitalist Philistinism. Religious enthusiasm reached its height in the controversies of the thirties and early forties and infused a new spirit in the land, but by the fifties passionate attachment to Low, Broad, or High Church tenets had cooled, to be momentarily revived in reaction against the liberalism of the sixties. Similarly, in educational matters insistence on a broader and freer intellectual life and on idealistic adherence to duty and virtue no longer commanded the interest of the upper classes. Important reforms had been accomplished everywhere by about 1845, and the tendency was to deprecate rather than encourage further change. In education as in political and religious matters there was to be only one last burst of liberal enthusiasm in the sixties to light up the midVictorian night that extended from the late forties until the nineties.

Of positive forces conditioning the reaction against liberalism and religion, the growth of science and the scientific outlook deserve first mention. In earlier days, and to some extent later on, these phenomena had a precisely opposite effect, being in good part responsible both for liberalism and successive religious revivals. Particularly was this so in the sixties and in the nineties when waves of scientific discovery reawakened the science versus religion controversy. But for the average middle- or upper-class citizen the growth of science has typically had a very different meaning, especially in the years between 1840 and 1860 when the new science had served his economic purposes. In the first place, the amazing disruptive force of new ideas frightened him into reaction, into a mistrust of free thought of all kinds. More and more he became fearful of genuine liberalism and confined his desire for knowledge to the narrowly useful. This suspicion of free thought reached a climax in the sixties with the publication of the notorious *Essays and Reviews*. Temple, head master of Rugby, who followed in Arnold's liberal footsteps and contributed to this book, roused an opposition as great as any that Arnold had to face in his earlier years at Rugby. Matthew Arnold wrote to his mother that he did not wonder at Temple's troubles, because 'the last quarter in which people in general', particularly those with 'the ecclesiastical attachments of the upper classes', 'wish to admit religious uncertainty is in the education of the young'.[1] In the second place, the middle-class religious faith was tried in the fires of scientific thought and found wanting. The romantic religious resurgence relapsed into a sterile materialistic respectability.

Closely connected in its effects with the growth of science was the stabilization and expansion of capitalist industrialism. In the early years of Victoria's reign modern big business began to come into being with its attendant intensification of the struggle for survival and its atmosphere of materialism. More than anything else the creation of a *bourgeois* industrialism accounts for the absence of spiritual ideals and the suspicion of all intellectual breadth which was characteristic of English Philistinism. Even more important, it accounts for the increased premium which Englishmen began to put on success. They were far more concerned that the schools produce successful competitors than that they turn out educated and adult individuals.

Finally, growing out of industrialism, came imperialism. With the expansion of business enterprise, England's colonies took on a new importance as markets for English goods and as sources for raw materials. The empire founded in the eighteenth century ceased to be a burden in the minds of even traditional small Englanders. Far more use, indeed, was found for the colonies than as a home for surplus population, though Carlyle's suggestion of this use furthered interest in overseas possessions. With the fifties and sixties, and especially the seventies, the consciousness of England as a vast world system whose parts were integrally related began, through the dramatic showmanship of Disraeli, to dawn on the minds of Englishmen. With this new attitude came a reaching out to the far corners of the earth for new colonies. By 1900 the British Empire, both in its size and in its importance to Englishmen, had grown far beyond the Empire of 1800 as the latter had beyond Elizabeth's island kingdom.

[1] Matthew Arnold, *Letters*, Collected and Arranged by George W. E. Russell, 2 vols., New York, 1895, Vol. I, p. 152; March 14th 1861.

It is difficult for the modern liberal or socialist to see in the British Empire more than a cold-blooded exploitation of subject peoples for the enrichment of a few capitalists. Kipling's white man's burden seems hollow pretence, its very hypocrisy demanding an execration that a franker brutality might escape. The curious manner in which oil wells have sprouted almost literally from the bones of dead missionaries has had the appearance of grotesque comedy. In a sense one cannot but subscribe whole-heartedly to this position. The evidence garnered in the last twenty years as to the real nature of capitalist imperialism is too overwhelming to be discarded. What is unfair in the realist's attitude is the assumption that Kipling or the average upper-class Englishman was a conscious hypocrite in his glorification of Empire. Fooled he might be, but it seems to me that one misses the point entirely if one takes for granted that Eton captains whose bones are bleaching under African suns were knowingly fighting to save the world for the owners of oil wells. If one credits the servants of empire—soldiers, poets, civil service employees—with economic motives hypocritically concealed, one fails to understand the nature or power of an attitude of crucial importance for later Public School history. Based on class motives and grounded in economic need it might have been, but essentially love of the Empire was both idealistic and passionately sincere. It was indeed the last of England's romantic faiths. English romanticism, as a parting gesture before it was undermined by the forces of realism, succeeded in transforming the shoddy actuality of colonial exploitation into a dream of a great paternalistic empire on which the sun should never set. To faith in this dream the upper-class Englishman brought all the sentiment and idealism that were gradually being starved by a materialistic age.

For the schools the new imperialism was all important. Business itself was, until late in the nineteenth century, almost exclusively a middle-class occupation, so that the insistence that the Public Schools produce men mentally and morally equipped for careers in industry was not supported by many of those who went to them; industrialism affected the schools indirectly for the most part. But the imperialistic enterprise was led by the whole of the English upper middle class and aristocracy, and its impact on the schools was therefore decisive. The English Public School of the late nineteenth century became directly a training ground for the leaders and servants of the Empire. In a sense this is what the schools had always been, but from the fifties on they were more exclusively, intensely, and effectively so. Whatever criticisms there may be of the middle and late Victorian school, failure to fulfil its tacit or expressed purposes cannot be one of them. What the Empire needed was manly, well-adjusted, honourable boys moulded into unthinking conformity and imbued with a passionate idealistic loyalty towards authority, whether school or nation. Such boys the Public Schools have turned out by the thousands.

B. THE CRITICAL REACTION TO ARNOLD

In the years between 1842 and 1845 there was hardly a dissenting note in the chorus of voices raised in praise of Arnold. Even his unpopular political and theological opinions were tolerated because of the power and greatness that the world began to perceive in the man. If, in the days immediately following his death, there were signs of a rift among Arnold's supporters, they were manifested only in the fact that different people chose different aspects of his work to single out for special praise.

Moderate liberals and liberal-conservatives were the most voluble in eulogy. James Martineau wrote in 1845: 'It is admitted on all hands, that he turned to the best account all the elements of good in the English system of public schools, and struggled manfully and with unexampled success against its peculiar evils.'[1] 'From what a good man *does* there is no higher lesson to be learned than what he is . . . that Arnold has lived, and shown how much nobleness and strength may maintain itself in an age of falsehood, negligence, and pretence,—with this let us rest and be thankful.'[2] Forster,

---
[1] Martineau, *Essays and Addresses*, Vol. I, p. 63.   [2] Ibid., Vol. I, p. 44.

author of the Education Act of 1870 and later the husband of Dr. Arnold's daughter, read Stanley in 1844 and was deeply stirred. He thought that Bentham, Goethe, and Arnold were the three most important men of the century, and that Arnold had the advantage of being a Christian.[1] Dickens, on hearing of Stanley's book, said, 'I respect and reverence his memory . . . beyond all expression. I must have that book. Every sentence that you quote from it is the text-book of my faith.'[2] The liberal Tory, Lord Ashley, was enthusiastic about Arnold, and significantly enough it was chiefly Arnold's moral side that appealed to the great paternalist. He noted in his diary in 1844 that he found Rugby a more satisfactory place than Eton because the new generation 'must have nobler, deeper, and sterner stuff; less of refinement and more of truth; more of the inward, not so much of the outward, gentleman; a rigid sense of duty, not a "delicate sense of honour"; a just estimate of rank and property, not as matters of personal enjoyment and display, but as gifts from God, bringing with them serious responsibilities.'[3]

The three great reviews outdid each other in praise of Arnold, though each emphasized only those aspects of his ideas most congenial to its particular political and social philosophy. The radical *Westminster*, assuming that Arnold's reputation as an educator and historian was well known, concentrated its attention on his love of the working classes and his liberal anti-superstitious theology.[4] In the conservative *Quarterly*, Lake, a disciple of Arnold's but a Tory and a Newmanite, praised his master chiefly for the religious improvement that he had brought about at Public Schools: 'Arrogance, irreligion, an hatred to submission' aggravated by the very 'scope for energy, for freedom, for manliness, which we justly value for its after-effects on the character' are the evils which Lake and the *Quarterly* most extol Arnold for overcoming. Arnold is further admired for working in

[1] T. Wemyss Reid, *Life of the Rt. Hon. William Edward Forster*, 2 vols., London, 1888, Vol. I, pp. 162, 163.
[2] John Forster, *Life of Charles Dickens*, 2 vols., London, 1904, Vol. I, p. 389.
[3] Edwin Hodder, *Life and Work of the 7th Earl of Shaftesbury*, 3 vols., London, 1888, Vol. II, p. 77.
[4] *Westminster*, February 1843, pp. 1, 24.

accordance with tradition and taking cognizance of an aristocracy of birth. Lake would indeed have preferred a trifle more love of the past than Arnold exhibited.[1]

The *Edinburgh*, representing a compromise position itself, and thus being closest to Arnold's ideas, went the furthest in eulogy. It found Arnold 'one of the noblest minds and highest characters of these days', one to inspire boys with a 'higher tincture of reverence' than any other master had ever done. Typically enough it found him admirable for just that reconciliation of opposites which made it possible for Arnold to appeal to liberals and conservatives, libertarians and authoritarians alike. According to the *Edinburgh*, Arnold taught the virtue of both truth and humility, independence and authority. He indicated the truth and allowed boys to judge for themselves. He attacked prejudices, unreasoning patriotism, and pride of birth; yet he was dogmatic and hated scepticism.[2]

Two years after the article that contained these sentiments, the *Edinburgh* published another review of Arnold which voiced some rather different sentiments. Though it gave the Rugby reformer more than a generous allowance of praise, it pointed out some of the directions in which he seemed to be at fault. Above all the *Edinburgh* resented Arnold's religious fanaticism; it was both absurd and dangerous to attempt to infuse even daily acts with a religious spirit.[3]

Though the *Edinburgh* article was followed by no outburst of adverse comment on Arnold, it does mark a turning-point in the critical treatment of the great reformer. From the late forties on, the perfection of Arnold's ideas was no longer taken for granted. Moreover, the *Edinburgh*'s doubts suggest the general direction of the objection that was to ensue.

For the most part it was the point of view of the average conservative Englishman that found expression in criticism. Those sides of Arnold's doctrine which diverged most from older traditions in either a liberal or reactionary direction were those least appreciated. Critics objected on the one

[1] *Quarterly*, October 1844, pp. 475, 494 ff. [2] *Edinburgh*, January 1843, pp. 357 ff.
[3] *Edinburgh*, January 1845, p. 223.

hand to the excessive moral pressure to which Arnold subjected a boy, and on the other to the excessive responsibility that he gave to those who had, in his eyes, profited by the pressure. Arnold turned boys into premature men who were too self-important and self-righteous, too intellectual and too filled with their master's liberal ideals. If they broke away from Arnold's tutelage they were likely to be free-thinkers. Moreover, Arnold's favourites had been trained to be moral crusaders, not realists fit to live in the actual world. Idealists in nineteenth-century England were only too likely to wreck their lives; often when this happened they committed the unforgivable sin of finding shelter in the arms of the Roman Church.

Among the first to criticize Arnold adversely were, significantly enough, some of his closest disciples: Arthur Hugh Clough, Dean Lake, and G. G. Bradley. According to Lake, Clough realized late in life that he had been subjected to an overstrain at Rugby which had crippled his mental and moral growth.[1] In 1852 Clough himself wrote resentfully, 'Certainly, as a boy, I had less of boyish enjoyment of any kind whatever, either at home or at school, than nine-tenths of boys, at any rate of boys who go to school, college, and the like.'[2] In the same year, in a 'Passage Upon Oxford Studies', he said, with probable reference to his Rugby days, that Public Schools push pupils too fast in the classics by means of prizes.[3] Finally, in the epilogue to *Dipsychus*, an imaginary dialogue between Clough and his uncle, he wrote what, despite its lightness and gaiety, proved to be as severe an attack on Rugby education as the fifties produced. Clough seems to defend Arnold, but obviously sympathizes with his uncle's point of view. The latter, having heard Clough say that *Dipsychus* tells about a 'tender conscience' versus the world, says: 'But as for that, I quite agree that consciences are much too tender in your generation— schoolboys' consciences, too! As my old friend the Canon says of the Westminster students, "They're all so pious". It's all Arnold's doing; he spoilt the public schools . . .

[1] Katherine Lake, *Memorials of William Charles Lake*, London, 1901, p. 12; *Good Words*, October 1895, p. 666.
[2] Clough, *Poems and Prose Remains*, Vol. I, p. 174.   [3] Ibid., p. 407.

whatever else they [the old Public Schools] were or did, they certainly were in harmony with the world, and they certainly did not disqualify the country's youth for after-life and the country's service.' The uncle finds that boys are no longer boys: 'they seem to me a sort of hobbadi-hoy cherub, too big to be innocent, and too simple for anything else. They're full of the notion of the world being so wicked, and of their taking a higher line, as they call it. I only fear they'll never take any line at all.' True education should teach the primary law of life, that one has to fight for his own way. After Clough has defended Arnold on the basis that he is not to blame, the other replies, 'Why, my dear boy, how often have I not heard from you, how he used to attack offences, not as offences—the right view—against discipline, but as sin, heinous guilt, I don't know what beside! Why didn't he flog them and hold his tongue? Flog them he did, but why preach?'[1]

Like Clough, Dean Lake and G. G. Bradley attacked chiefly the excess of pressure which Arnold exerted on his students in order to make boys of thirteen into men, thus subjecting them to unhealthy moral and mental strain. Lake wrote that this 'mental strain was, I have little doubt, both intellectually and physically, the one weak point (I cannot think of any other) in Arnold as a schoolmaster.'[2] Bradley added, interestingly enough, that attachment to Arnold proved not only over-stimulating but also limiting since boys saw only Arnold and followed him blindly.[3] This was a legitimate libertarian objection, but it was also used by many Tories, not because they loved free thought, but because they objected to the particular brand of liberal doctrine inculcated by Arnold.[4]

The criticisms voiced by those less close to Arnold personally or politically were naturally less apologetic than those

[1] Clough, *Remains*, Vol. II, p. 170. [2] *Good Words*, October 1895, p. 666.
[3] Cf. *Nineteenth Century*, March 1884, pp. 455 ff. Despite his criticisms, Bradley could write 'I do not hesitate to call those three years in some ways the most fruitful, the most valuable, the most formative, intellectually, morally, and spiritually, of my whole life.' (*Nineteenth Century*, March 1884, p. 464.)
[4] Just as to-day the conservative New York dailies cry for freedom of the Press.

of sympathizers.[1] Charles Pearson, who went to Rugby a year after Arnold's death, is most severe and thorough in his criticism of the reformer of the school. 'Arnold's influence was still paramount among masters and boys. To one who looks back dispassionately, it sometimes seems as if the doctor had been extravagantly overpraised.'[2] According to Pearson, Arnold did not improve the intellectual side of education at all. His moral influence, on the other hand, was great; unfortunately it was for the most part evil. By trying to impel pupils into Holy orders, Arnold produced either positivism or formalism. Pearson added, 'it is, I think, undoubted that Arnold's pupils lived in an atmosphere of priggishness. They were taught to be always feeling their moral muscles, always careful about their schoolfellows' morality. . . . The precepts were more weighty than boys could assimilate without incessant pretentiousness, and before long Rugby was known at Oxford as the "disagreeable school". Its reputation in the Army was, I believe, even worse.'[3] 'The simple fact, however, is that Rugby men were no better than the best set from any good public school—Eton, Harrow, or Winchester. The difference was that the Rugbeians were self-consciously moral. . . . The fault lay in education that had been pretentious and over-strained.'[4] These comments are particularly interesting when one realizes that Pearson approved on the whole of the old Public Schools. He believed that the playground was more important than the teacher, for it encouraged 'manliness and subordination, loyalty and veracity';[5] 'the real advantage of the English public-school system . . . is perhaps to be found in the fact that it discourages overwork. So long as a boy acquires the habit of application, the less he is set to learn before he is fifteen the better.'[6] The English make the best adventurers, explorers, and organizers, and

---

[1] There were, it may be added, sympathetic critics other than direct disciples. Such was the German, Wiese, who found that too early manliness took away the joyousness of youth. (L. Wiese, *German Letters on English Education*, translated by W. D. Arnold, London, 1854, p. 46.)
[2] Charles Henry Pearson, *Memorials*, by Himself, his Wife, and his Friends, New York, 1900, p. 14.
[3] Ibid., p. 17. [4] Ibid., p. 18.
[5] Ibid., p. 24. [6] Ibid., p. 27.

though their education is faulty, it is, he agrees with Talleyrand, the best in the world.[1]

Francis Doyle, a critic along somewhat similar lines, is quite frank about his political position. 'As I am neither a Rugby man nor a Whig, but a high Tory and an Etonian, I may perhaps venture to point out one qualification for a head master which Keate possessed but Arnold did not—I mean the knowledge of God Almighty's intention that there should exist for a certain time, between childhood and manhood, the natural production known as a boy.'[2] He did not give boys a priggish self-importance, and yet Eton men succeeded in the world as well as Rugby men. Pearson, it is worth noting, also uses success in the world as one criterion of a good education. He has, however, enough loyalty to Rugby to point out that if Etonians are more often successful in life than Rugbeians, the reason lies not in Arnold's deficiencies, but in the fact that aristocrats start out with certain practical advantages.[3]

In the fifties, particularly after the publication of *Tom Brown's Schooldays*, which revived public interest in Arnold, the reviews began again to publish articles about him. These were, however, of a much less enthusiastic character than those in the forties. The *North British Review*, though it expressed liking for Arnold as a person, disapproved of his doctrines and of his theological followers. It resented the fact that the myth of Arnold's greatness seemed to be independent of the validity of his teachings, and bitterly derided his inability to sympathize with those with whom he disagreed.[4] The motive for this last criticism was, no more than with most conservatives, a hatred of intolerance; the *North British* objected to the liberal religious doctrines with which Arnold sympathized and his consequent intolerance of conservative and authoritarian ideas. Arnold was considered narrow because he encouraged really dangerous boys like Stanley and distrusted and often expelled those masculine boys who were the pride of England.[5]

[1] Pearson, op. cit., p. 28.   [2] Francis Doyle, *Reminiscences*, p. 48.
[3] Cf. Pearson, op. cit., p. 18.
[4] The *North British* article is full of false statements such as that Arnold lacked the art of teaching.   [5] *North British Review*, February 1858, pp. 123 ff.

The *Quarterly*, praising *Tom Brown's Schooldays*, attacked by implication Arnold's use of moral pressure. On its positive side the *Quarterly*, like Pearson, applauded that aspect of school life which was soon to be so exaggerated: athletics.¹ 'The Isthmian games of our public schools,' it contended, do 'much to make England what it is'; they prevent overwork, which is more dangerous than underwork.² The fear of games was dormant except among extreme radicals until the next decade.

The most interesting attack on Arnold came from the *Edinburgh* in a review of *Tom Brown's Schooldays* by Leslie Stephen's brother James Fitzjames. Stephen was neither an avowed enemy of Arnold's nor a thoroughgoing conservative. He objected to the anti-intellectualism of Hughes's muscular Christianity as much as he did to Arnold's priggishness. He had himself been very unhappy at Eton, where he had learned to hate tyranny and to consider games foolish.³ Moreover, he approved, on the whole, of Arnold's pedagogy and character. Speaking of Hughes's book, Fitzjames wrote: 'Whatever exception may be taken to some of its features, and to some of the characteristics of the school which it eulogizes, it is impossible not to feel that there must be very great merits in a system which could inspire such an affection.'⁴ Arnold's faults, Stephen believed, needed to be pointed out just because his greatness was admitted.

Nevertheless, his attack on Arnold was not only severe, but was the clearest and most complete statement of the conservative attitude that had so far appeared in print. Negatively, Stephen approved of just those characteristics of a Public School that Arnold had tried hardest to eradicate. Despite his dislike of Eton, Stephen applauded the absence of teaching, discipline, and Arnoldian moral enthusiasm that characterized the school.⁵ He liked the pre-Arnoldian

---
¹ It is worth remembering here that it was the *Quarterly* that had, as early as 1834, pointed out the moral advantages of organized sport.
² Cf. *Quarterly*, October 1857, p. 334.
³ Cf. Leslie Stephen, *The Life of James Fitzjames Stephen*, London, 1895, pp. 77 ff.
⁴ *Edinburgh*, January 1858, p. 176.
⁵ Possibly Stephen's unhappy meeting with Arnold in 1841, in which Arnold embarrassed the little boy by seeming to look right through him, prejudiced him against the Rugby master. (L. Stephen, op. cit., p. 82.)

Public School partly because its methods had been tested by time; things that have lasted long are by that very fact good; only the impractical person laughs at religion and marriage.[1] Partly, he defended older ways of doing things because they produced boys eminently suited to the needs of a practical and conservative world. By letting boys discipline themselves, the pre-Arnoldian school produced courage and knowledge of the world; it curbed the 'diseased sensibility' whose dreams from Byron and Shelley down are responsible for most of the world's troubles. Englishmen 'willingly plead guilty' to seeing no visions, and they attribute this to the 'moral influence of our public-school education. We do not believe that any system was ever invented so real, so healthy, and so bracing both to the mind and body.'[2] The exceptional boy may suffer in a school's miniature world, but if he is robust, it will do him good, will teach him to adjust himself to a hard and coarse world, to know his limitations.

Positively, Stephen found Arnold's ideal a bad one. The power of the head master who, with his 'impatient fervour', substituted 'earnest' for 'serious', produced priggishness.[3] 'The total want of humour which characterized him prevented him from seeing that much of what he considered "awful wickedness", was mere fun, and that it was far less desirable than possible to turn boys into men before their time'.[4] A sensitive sixteen-year-old boy is only too willing to believe that he is a priest and a prophet. He needs a curb, not some one to tell him that the world waits on his actions. If a custom is bad, abolish it as Hawtrey, Stephen's Etonian mentor did, do not moralize over it. If you refer every trivial thing to a general principle, it generates a 'diseased consciousness'.

C. ARNOLD'S DISCIPLES—THE TRUE FAITH

The critical reaction to Arnold's ideas suggests some of the lines of spiritual relationship between Arnold and his contemporaries and successors. But the mere record of

[1] *Edinburgh*, January 1858, pp. 180–81. [2] Ibid., p. 177.
[3] Ibid., p. 183. [4] Ibid., p. 185.

praise and dispraise gives only a superficial conception of this relationship. A real understanding of Arnold's impact on his generation involves a detailed analysis of the interaction between the Rugby master and those boys who came in contact with him when they were at school.

This interaction has two aspects, each of which has a special importance. In the first place, Arnold's pupils were the most direct recipients of his doctrines. As such they demonstrated the manner in which Arnold's ideas percolated into other minds. In the second place, they were the chief disseminators of his ideas. By embodying Arnold's ideals, by writing in praise, interpretation, or criticism of those ideals, or finally by attempting to put them into practice in other schools, they acted as the liaison agents between Arnold and the world. Their lives and activities therefore illustrate the process by which Arnold's purposes were carried beyond Rugby.

In a sense there were as many reactions to Arnold's teaching as there were individuals who felt its impact. Moreover, the reactions of individual boys could be highly contradictory. As Hughes, writing of his brother, remarks, 'though Arnold's life influenced him quite as powerfully as it did me, it was in quite a different direction, strengthening specially in him the reverence for national life, and for the laws, traditions, and customs with which it is interwoven, and of which it is the expression. Somehow, his natural dislike to change, and preference for the old ways, seemed to gain as much strength and nourishment from the teaching and example of our old master, as the desire and hope for radical reforms did in me.'[1]

In general, however, there were two main types of boy and two kinds of relationship to Arnold. On the one hand were what may be called the 'intellectuals', those who were temperamentally close to Arnold and who fully comprehended and sympathized with his major aims. Such were Stanley, Clough, Matthew Arnold and to a lesser degree Vaughan and Lake. On the other were the 'ordinary', boys who had less personal contact with the master and for whom

[1] T. Hughes, *Memoir of a Brother*, p. 90.

Arnold's loftiest intellectual and moral ideals were a closed book. Of these one may cite, among hundreds of forgotten boys, the anonymous author of *Recollections of Rugby*, Sir Alexander Arbuthnot, and above all Thomas Hughes.[1]

Arthur Penryhn Stanley was not only the most important but also the first of Arnold's 'true' disciples. But even in 1830 Stanley was not Arnold's sole lieutenant. Before he reached the sixth form, Stanley had passed on to two friends, Charles James Vaughan and William Charles Lake, much of the devotion that he himself felt. He had transformed their awe and admiration for Arnold into a love and a willingness to serve that were equal to his own.[2] Consequently, it was a sixth-form triumvirate made up of Vaughan, Lake, and Stanley that ruled Rugby in the early thirties, disseminated Arnold's doctrines throughout the school, and served as a model for future sixth forms. These three loved Arnold at a time when the rest of the school was relatively indifferent to him.[3] Imbued with Arnold's 'lofty ideal of public school life', they made themselves the responsible trustees of that tone 'at once moral, religious, and highly intellectual', the creation of which was so fundamentally a part of Arnold's pedagogy.[4]

Vaughan is of particular interest to the student of Arnold because he, probably more than any other disciple, wholeheartedly accepted his master's doctrines, embodied them in his own life, and transmitted them directly and successfully beyond Rugby. Even more important, he was the only pupil of Arnold to become head master of one of the seven old Public Schools other than Rugby. In 1844 Vaughan became head master of Harrow and proceeded to reform the school on Arnoldian lines. Though he was never a mere imitator, and though circumstances caused

---

[1] To pigeon-hole in this manner each individual who has told about his Rugby days or about Arnold is obviously impossible. Some such as Walrond, who wrote of Arnold in the *Dictionary of National Biography*, or Cotton and Bradley, whose work at Marlborough we will notice later on, or Tait who succeeded Arnold at Rugby, belong in a sense in both classes, though they are more 'intellectuals' than ordinary boys.
[2] Lake's testimony in *Good Words*, October 1895, p. 666.
[3] Lake, *Memorials of Lake*, p. 16.   [4] Ibid., p. vi.

Arnoldianism

modification of Arnold's doctrines at Harrow, Vaughan came nearer to producing a replica of his master's system in another Public School than did any other disciple. For these reasons his life and activities deserve careful study, but, since they are inextricably interwoven with the history of Harrow, it seems better to reserve discussion of them until the next chapter.

Lake is far less significant as a person and contributed much less to the spread of Arnold's ideas than did Vaughan.[1] He is, however, important as an example of a close admirer of Arnold who 'ceased after leaving Rugby to be as absolute a follower' as was Stanley,[2] and who therefore criticized the school from the inside. The secret of Lake's behaviour seems to have been that he was not naturally the type that could be turned into an Arnoldian hero, but an ordinary boy of the Hughes type who loved games and idleness. Consequently, the interesting thing is not that he was unfaithful to his early allegiance, but that he ever became a true disciple in the first place. Such, however, Arnold and Stanley together seem to have made him, and there is no more conclusive evidence than this of their combined power.

It was Stanley who first taught Lake to love Arnold, to cease to be an idle boy, and to become a serious student with the weight of the world on his shoulders. Lake wrote that he gave up games 'almost as a matter of course, when I became an intimate friend of Stanley'.[3] Once in Arnold's good graces, Lake became the master's most devoted follower; he claims, indeed, that he 'knew Arnold far more intimately than Dean Stanley did.'[4] In any case Arnold exerted a powerful influence over the boy. When Lake had passed his examination to enter the sixth form, Arnold said: 'Now, Lake, I know you can do well if you chose, and I shall expect you to do so.' 'Those few words altered my whole character, intellectually, at all events. Whatever I was, I was never an idle boy again, and my one

---

[1] In 1849 Lake was a candidate for the head-mastership of Rugby. Had he won the position the story of Lake's relation to Arnold would have been a more important and interesting one.
[2] Cf. Lake, *Memorials of Lake*, p. 3.
[3] *Good Words*, October 1895, p. 666.   [4] Lake, op. cit., p. 3.

wish was to be well thought of by Arnold.'[1] Arnold made Lake love his favourite authors such as Thucydides, and hate Caesar. Finally, he inspired his pupil to write the soaring praise of his master in the *Quarterly* article of 1844, to which reference has already been made.

As Arnold's first and chief lieutenant while at Rugby and his mouthpiece to the world in later years, no one is of more importance in connexion with Arnold than Stanley. It was Stanley more than any one else who helped make the real Arnold known: as a student at Rugby when Arnold was but an unknown and mistrusted experimenter, he preached his master's ideas; as a man he wrote an understanding and loyal biography of his teacher. But his importance is not limited to mere discipleship. He wrote not only a faithful but a great biography of Arnold, one which has lived in its own right and thus added to Arnold's name the lustre of having been the inspiration for a work of art. Further, Stanley made more of a success of his own life than did any of Arnold's pupils; as the revered liberal Dean of Westminster he remained for forty years after Arnold's death a living embodiment of the virtues of Arnold's training.

The son of a country rector connected with the aristocracy, Stanley was, as a child, shy, sensitive, and retiring. A typical introvert, moody, loving books, he was anything but the kind of a boy whom, typically, one would have sent to a Public School.[2] Nevertheless, because of Augustus Hare's influence, Stanley was entered at Rugby on January 31st 1829.[3] At his early school 'and even at Rugby, he was never entirely at home in the whole range of schoolboy life'; nevertheless, 'he soon overcame his first feeling of strangeness and isolation, and entered upon his new career with much cheerfulness and spirit'.[4] His account of his first day of school, February 4th 1829, reads much like that of a modern schoolboy in its placid recital of events entirely free from the melodrama of the usual fictional entrance. The boys were kindly and, according to H. C. Allen, an associate of his

---

[1] Lake, op. cit., p. 8.
[2] Cf. Rowland E. Prothero, *The Life and Correspondence of Arthur Penrhyn Stanley*, 2 vols., London, 1894, Vol. I, pp. 8 ff.
[3] Ibid., p. 33.   [4] Cf. Prothero, op. cit., Vol. I, p. 11.

at Anstey's, favourably impressed rather than the reverse by the pre-report of his brilliance. In six months he was free from a fagging which never seemed to bother him much at any time. 'Strange to say, I have only been fagged once, being always excused by praeposters whom I never knew before—and sometimes by the most severe. I am very lucky to be favoured by them.'[1] His feminine, vivacious manners, coupled with a charm whose power, like Arnold's very different power, is indefinable, apparently won over even those most likely to bully him for his fumbling dislike of games. Moreover, what was admittedly 'unparalleled in those rough days of the history of Rugby',[2] Stanley's schoolfellows, including 'those who were least likely to appreciate his intellectual gifts' were greatly impressed by his brilliance.[3] Allen writes that there was 'such respect entertained for intellectual powers in our school society, that none of us held Stanley in less esteem because he was not a cricketer or football-player.'[4] When he won an English essay award or wrote a prize poem, the boys, no less than Arnold, congratulated him.[5] As he advanced in the school the respect grew. Even before he entered the sixth form he could write that boys fagged for him without being asked.[6] His individuality was scrupulously respected; his study was called poet's corner.[7] When he became head of the house he ruled 'without friction or difficulty', and with Lake and Vaughan put down a rebellion, a testimony, it may be added, as much to Arnold's influence over the school as to Stanley's charm.[8] During the four years that he was in the sixth form he became almost a myth. John N. Simpkinson says that the beauty and goodness of his character caused boys to feel that he should not be judged by their standards.[9]

If Stanley was respected, it cannot be said that he was very much loved. Nor, until he came under Arnold's influence, was he very happy. At first, though his foreboding that at Rugby he would have to bid 'a long farewell to all

[1] Ibid., Vol. I, p. 44.
[2] Ibid., Vol. I, p. 67.
[3] Ibid., Vol. I, p. 55.
[4] Ibid. Vol. I p. 62.
[5] Prothero, op. cit., Vol. I, pp. 55, 67.
[6] Ibid., Vol. I, p. 48.
[7] A. J. C. Hare, *Biographical Sketches*, p. 25.
[8] Prothero, op. cit., Vol. I, p. 67.
[9] Ibid., Vol. I, p. 68.

goodness and happiness' was not fulfilled, he certainly was very lonely and was always glad to get home for the holidays.[1] The best that Hare could report was that, considering that he made no friends at first, he was as happy as could be expected.[2] When he got into the sixth form he went with his few literary friends, but at no time was he genuinely popular.[3]

The truth of the matter was that, as Lake says rather bitterly, Stanley was never a boy, a fact that Arnold failed to appreciate.[4] The pressure that Arnold exerted on boys to make them men was successful with Stanley because becoming prematurely adult was a part of his natural development.[5] Surely it would have been better had Arnold checked rather than encouraged this, but few schoolmasters, even to-day, can resist the temptation to exploit a brilliant pupil.

In the early days Stanley tried to enjoy athletics and lamented his introversion.[6] But he never succeeded in liking football or cricket, and records that while playing the former 'I sometimes catch myself looking at the sunset instead of the ball'.[7] In the meantime his intellectual powers were being rewarded by the Balliol scholarship and all six prizes that Rugby had to offer. When he reached the sixth form he no longer tried to play games, but gave himself up to his studies and the worship of Arnold.[8] He hated leaving Rugby for Balliol as much as he had disliked coming,[9] but his love was based on his relationship to Arnold, and not on an absorption of the ordinary spirit of a Public School. When *Tom Brown's Schooldays* appeared, Stanley wrote, significantly: "'Tis an absolute revelation to me: opens up a world of which, though so near me, I was utterly ignorant.'[10]

This then was the boy who was to be Arnold's chief disciple. Stanley's love for Arnold grew slowly, but by the time he left Rugby it amounted to an adoration which, when forty years later Stanley, then Dean of Westminster,

---

[1] Prothero, op. cit., Vol. I, pp. 45, 51.   [2] Hare, op. cit., p. 25.
[3] Prothero, op. cit., Vol. I, p. 67.   [4] *Good Words*, October 1895, p. 666.
[5] Lake, *Memorials of Lake*, p. 11.
[6] Prothero, op. cit., Vol. I, p. 61.   [7] Ibid., Vol. I, p. 48.
[8] Ibid., Vol. I, p. 67.   [9] Ibid., Vol. I, p. 75.   [10] Ibid., Vol. I, p. 68.

spoke in Rugby chapel of Arnold's idea of 'the relation of
the soul to God' and its dependence on moral and spiritual
character, had in no wise diminished.¹ Mrs. Stanley found
her son's letters full of Arnold; 'Arthur's veneration for him
is beautiful,' she wrote, 'what good it must do to grow up
under such a tree.'² Stanley was early quite conscious that
his feeling was almost one of 'idolatrous veneration'.³ At
first, and even as late as 1832, he was still too much in awe
of Arnold to feel quite at home with him,⁴ but later he was
visited by the great master and went himself to stay at Fox
How. He was wary of staying too long with the Arnolds for
fear of idolizing the master too much.⁵

Stanley's love for Arnold was an almost complete immersion. As late as his Oxford days, Stanley, like Clough,
felt lost without Arnold at the same time that he believed
that, because of Arnold, he had a responsiblity to Rugby to
win Oxford distinctions.⁶ In his Rugby days both the man
and his ideas were godlike and untouchable. In one letter
he is even 'rather alarmed at seeing how few of my thoughts
are original, and how many of them come directly or indirectly from Dr. Arnold's sermons.'⁷ Arnold's political
and theological opinions influenced him more and more.
He hated Balliol in advance for its disliking Arnold, and
became a passionate defender of the Rugby master against
both Rugby's and Oxford's opposition, particularly that of
the Newmanites.⁸

Arnold's hold over Stanley was not to end with the latter's
college days, but was to continue all through his life. As
Prothero says, 'In Arnold he encountered, at the most impressionable period of his life, the man who was exactly
fitted to exercise over him a powerful and permanent influence. In him he found strong and deep religious feelings,
which were united with free, trustful views on Scriptural

¹ Prothero, op. cit., Vol. II, p. 454.
² Hare, op. cit., p. 30. Stanley recorded the fact that Arnold and other
masters sometimes went out leaping; to his mother this seemed 'as much a
sign of the times as the Chancellor appearing without a wig'.
³ Prothero, op. cit., Vol. I, p. 78.
⁴ Ibid., Vol. I, p. 94.   ⁵ Ibid., Vol. I, pp. 99–100.
⁶ Ibid., Vol. I, pp. 164, 174. Arnold felt that this last was going too far, and
wrote to Stanley that he need not feel so much responsibility.
⁷ Ibid., Vol. I, p. 64.   ⁸ Ibid., Vol. I., pp. 94, 96, 141.

criticism and interpretation, and which, projecting themselves into the world, sought to christianize, not only society, but the individual.' Despite other influences 'the first impressions preserved their hold, and Stanley in 1846 was still what he had been at the time of his ordination—a follower of Arnold'.[1]

At Balliol, however, Stanley, unlike Clough, found himself as a person. When Arnold's strength was no longer behind him, he did not collapse; nor did the over-serious moral and intellectual seeking cultivated by Arnold lead him into Newmanism or into tortured despair as it did Clough. He became an integrated and forceful individual in whom Arnold's opinions and influence found their appropriate place. The conflicts of the times were to him an incentive to the creation of a new and personally satisfying form of liberalism. If, like Arnold himself, he evaded some issues, he discovered an adjustment which made of him a powerful and useful figure in Victorian England.

Stanley saw some of Arnold's shortcomings with an objectivity denied to those who, like Matthew Arnold and Clough, were emotionally involved in those faults. He felt, for example, that Arnold's excessive radicalism of statement was foolish since it gave the false impression that Arnold was a radical.[2] Arnold was not a latitudinarian, but a stopgap between Low Church and Newman. Stanley, who saw how easily his opinions, gleaned from Arnold, could lead him into Newmanism, believed even after his momentary High Church flirtation had subsided that Arnold was too intolerant towards Newman.[3]

Stanley's biography of his master is a great book because it combines the reverent idealization of a disciple with the powerful realism and objectivity of a mature individual. On the one hand, Stanley's closeness to his master made it possible for him to understand Arnold in a way that few others could have. Stanley was so saturated with the spirit of his master that the *Life and Correspondence* is very nearly,

[1] Prothero, op. cit., Vol. I, p. 381.
[2] Ibid., p. 141.
[3] Ibid., p. 194. Stanley lost a Balliol fellowship because he was an Arnoldian; his tolerance of Newman was therefore no superficial feeling.

from Arnold's point of view, autobiographical. There emerges from its pages that picture of the deeply religious, highly intellectual teacher and friend that has served as inspiration for several generations of Englishmen and Americans. Further, Stanley's love of Arnold suffused the pages of the book with a glow and a warmth that make it in places very nearly poetry. On the other hand, the disciple's independence prevented any omission of the unpleasant—though it is often lightly treated—and dictated a cool impartiality far indeed from saccharine adulation. Stanley allowed Arnold to speak for himself and seldom hesitated to be critical where he felt it warranted. The result is a living portrait, not a flat and unreal daguerrotype.

If Stanley's is a great biography, it is not, however, a complete account of either Arnold or of Rugby under Arnold. Stanley was, as an individual, limited in many ways, and as a result his book suffers from important omissions. He brought to life chiefly Arnold's intellectual and religious liberalism, his passionate devotion to moral earnestness, his relations to boys like Stanley. He has given us, in other words, those sides of Arnold's nature and those aspects of his Rugby life which most concerned Arnold himself. At the same time he has neglected much that seems to us, if not to Arnold and Stanley, of equal importance. In the first place, Stanley omitted or under-estimated the lighter, more human and, in a sense, more animal side of his master. In the second place, and much more important, he failed to record Arnold's relationship to the ordinary boy. For Arnold did not care a great deal about these average boys and the shy recluse, Stanley, did not know anything about them. The impression that Arnold made on this ordinary person and the conception of the schoolmaster entertained by the latter did not find expression until Hughes published *Tom Brown's Schooldays* in 1857.

Except Stanley, no one was a more passionate admirer of Arnold than Arthur Hugh Clough nor more important in the history of the spread of Arnold's ideas. But his significance is chiefly of a very different kind from Stanley's.

Directly, Clough contributed little after leaving school to the development or dissemination of Arnold's doctrines. At Rugby he was a leading disciple and lieutenant in Arnold's war against idleness and immorality, but in later years, except for the few criticisms already noted, he neither wrote nor did anything that pertained to his teacher. Clough is important chiefly negatively, as a tragic example of the evil effects—or what Englishmen took to be the effects—of strict adherence to Arnold's ideas. If Stanley's later life was convincing testimony to the virtues of Arnold's system, Clough's proved to be a solemn warning of its dangers.

Clough, though younger than they, was an intimate friend of the 'clerical' group, Lake, Stanley, and Vaughan. Later Dr. Arnold's sons were his associates. He was, indeed, a boy after Dr. Arnold's as well as Mrs. Stanley's heart.[1] His early boyhood, in his wife's sentimental memoir, reads very much like that of Stanley and other precocious introverts. Considered a genius at the age of seven, he was, according to his sister, a beautiful boy with silky hair who was 'too fastidious to take off his shoes and stockings and paddle about as we did'. He was 'constantly with' his mother, who 'poured out the fulness of her heart' to him.[2] In 1828, when he was nine, Clough came to England from Charleston where he had been living. Surrounded by cousins, 'Arthur could not enter into the boys' rough games and amusements, and missed the constant companionship of his father'. When his father died, Arthur became more than ever the pet and companion of his mother.[3]

Both nature and circumstances made it inevitable that Clough should fall powerfully under Arnold's influence. He was only ten when, in 1829, he went to Rugby. For six years he was quite alone there, since his family were in America. Dr. Arnold and Mrs. Arnold became his second parents, taking him into their home at Rugby and at Fox How.[4] There his relationship to Arnold was bound to be closer even than Stanley's. He was, indeed, more exposed than Arnold's sons to the schoolmaster's powerful personality.

[1] James Insley Osborne, *Arthur Hugh Clough*, London, 1919, p. 19.
[2] Clough, *Poems and Prose Remains*, Vol. I, pp. 4–6.
[3] Ibid., pp. 8–9. [4] Arnold, *Letters to Clough*, p. 1.

Arnoldianism

Clough's adoration of Arnold was comparable only to Stanley's. Just being near him filled the boy with joy,[1] for, as he said himself, Arnold offered him so much to look up to.[2] He dedicated the Rugby magazine to Arnold, 'whom with our very hearts we love and honour', and for whose sake he will try to make the magazine full of 'Christian and moral feeling'.[3] After Arnold died, Clough felt the loss as did no one else. As Stanley said, from that day 'a circle of Rugby men were "on a little island of memory, and all who share in that memory must hold together as long as life lasts." '[4]

Clough's love of Arnold, unlike Stanley's, was most active and important for Public Schools while he was at Rugby. Arnold made of Clough a hero-prefect after his own heart; Clough became the chief instrument in the carrying out of Arnold's aims. 'His school was for Clough his life', and he gave to it the best that was in him.[5] He responded wholeheartedly to Arnold's desire that his prefects should be passionately attached to the school and assistants in his plan to make Rugby a Christian community. In 1836 he wrote to Simpkinson, 'I verily believe my whole being is soaked through with the wishing and hoping and striving to do the school good, or rather to keep it up and hinder it from falling in this, I do think, very critical time, so that all my cares and affections and conversation, thought, words, and deeds, look to that involuntarily.'[6] With an ardour as terrifying as it was pathetic, he threw himself into the task of spreading his master's moral principles among the boys.[7] As he wrote to his sister, 'I am trying, if possible, to show them [his schoolmates] that good is not necessarily disagreeable, and that a Christian may be, and is likely to be, a gentleman; and that he is surely much more than a gentleman.'[8] Clough himself

---

[1] Cf. Letter to his Mother in December 1835, Clough, *Remains*, Vol. I, p. 66.
[2] Ibid., p. 62.
[3] *The Rugby Magazine*, 2 vols., London, 1837, Vol. I, p. vi.
[4] Arnold, *Letters to Clough*, p. 6.   [5] Ibid., p. 1.
[6] Clough, op. cit., Vol. I, p. 68.
[7] Clough's wife makes much of the fact that Clough's having to be idle for a year—he was only fifteen when he was head of the fifth form—before he could enter the sixth gave him an opportunity which he might never otherwise have had to busy himself with moral work among the boys. (Cf. Clough, *Remains*, Vol. I, p. 11.)
[8] Clough, op. cit., Vol. I, p. 60.

was constantly obsessed by the idea that God was near him, issuing orders, judging him, loving him,[1] and he tried to communicate to his fellows both the sense of God's presence, and the purposes that He had in mind. He worried over his own soul and that of others to an extent that is dismaying to a modern reader. He had no time for thinking or beauty or humour or lightness; conduct was his constant preoccupation.[2]

Clough conveyed his ideas to others in two ways. In the first place, he made personal contacts with the boys. Less shy and retiring than Stanley, he was able to gain friends and acquaintances and to play games. But his was no ordinary mingling: To Clough most boys were idle and evil,[3] and he made their acquaintance chiefly as a duty, not as a participation in 'care-free, joyous youth'.[4] He was bent on 'associating with fellows for their good';[5] he mingled with them because it is easier 'to do good to those who like us'.[6] The curious thing is that apparently he did not arouse the resentment of his barbarian companions: Clough seems, on the whole, to have been both popular and a leader, despite his officiousness. How much moral effect he had on his acquaintances is, of course, another story.

Clough's second method of making his influence felt was through the *Rugby Magazine*. This was a periodical started by Clough 'to pay our debt to the mother that has fostered, and is fostering our young intellects; nor we trust, our intellects alone'.[7] 'The political philosopher may find food for his mind in boy-societies; and to spread the knowledge of these societies and their nature, is a rational object of a Boy-Magazine.'[8] Probably never has such a periodical been written either before or since. Next to it the *Microcosm* is

[1] Clough, op. cit., Vol. I, pp. 57, 59, 62.
[2] Osborne, *A. H. Clough*, pp. 24 ff.
[3] Clough, op. cit., Vol. I, p. 62, October 24th 1835, to J. P. Gell. As Clough wrote: 'There is such an excess of acquaintance and such a lack of friends here.' (Clough, op. cit., Vol. I, p. 62, November 9th 1835.)
[4] Osborne, op. cit., p. 20.
[5] Clough, *Remains*, Vol. I, p. 62, Letter to J. P. Gell, November 9th 1835.
[6] Clough, op. cit., Vol. I, p. 60. He wrote to his brother George not to mind the boys' knowing that 'you are trying to serve God'.
[7] *The Rugby Magazine*, July 1835, Vol. I, p. 13. Clough prayed that it might be written for the glory of the school and in the spirit of God. (Arnold, *Letters to Clough*, p. 12.) [8] *The Rugby Magazine*, Vol. I, p. 10.

Arnoldianism

frolicsome farce. Over it hangs the deadening weight of Arnold's principles, reproduced with no saving grace of humour or inspiration. Well might Clough apologize in his preface to the second volume for his magazine's being too serious.[1] It contained little but sermons on such things as the importance of miniature societies in the instruction of youth,[2] the virtues of emulation,[3] the necessity for contact with vice if virtue is to be gained,[4] the saving grace that resides in being 'more sensible of the pleasure and wisdom of living for others,'[5] the greatness of the classics in preparing one 'for the station of a gentlemen,'[6] and the importance of original composition as an instrument in training the mind.[7] In one way or another the whole magazine was a repetition of the plea, expressed in an early article, that, since our school was 'entitled to our gratitude from its many benefits conferred upon us' we ought to express that gratitude by doing our duty to our fellow students, seeing that vice is crushed and that possible future statesmen or Shelleys are not made unhappy.[8]

The small Rugby world of the thirties was very proud of Clough and expected even greater things of him than of Stanley. In 1837 he went up to Oxford with a Balliol scholarship, Dr. Arnold's blessing, and Matthew Arnold's belief that Rugby was sending forth a boy peculiarly her own.[9] But he had not been at Oxford long before the drive towards distinction ceased. His studies fell off, to the disappointment of his friends, and he failed to get a first class. After leaving Oxford he tried his hand at many activities, but never, except at rare moments, succeeded in finding any that were entirely satisfactory. On occasion he wrote poems such as the *Dipsychus* and the *Latest Decalogue* which exhibit an insight and a satirical gift of a high order. Clough, indeed, acquired in general a sense of proportion which made him in later years a pleasanter person than he had been at Rugby. But despite these evidences of a coming to terms

---

[1] Ibid., Vol. II, Preface.
[2] Ibid., Vol. I, p. 95.
[3] Ibid., Vol. II, p. 122.
[4] Ibid., Vol. II, p. 327.
[5] Ibid., Vol. I, p. 120.
[6] Ibid., Vol. I, p. 359.
[7] Ibid., Vol. I, p. 67.
[8] Ibid., Vol. I, p. 104.
[9] Arnold, *Letters to Clough*, pp. 1, 13.

with the world, one cannot but view his life as, in the last analysis, a tragic failure. Compared with the promise of his youth, his subsequent career bore meagre fruit; in place of the hope and energy that animated him at Rugby, his adult life seems burdened with divided purposes and a permanent sense of futility.

What happened to Clough? Granting that he did to a certain extent succeed in expressing himself and in developing into an integrated personality, why was this true to so limited an extent? What part, finally, did Dr. Arnold play in the tragedy of Clough's career? Though there is danger in being too dogmatic in regard to delicate psychological matters, I believe that Clough failed in life because when he went to Oxford he was neither physically, intellectually, nor morally fitted to adjust himself to the world of reality, and that Dr. Arnold was in good part responsible for this unfitness.[1] Arnold was obviously not wholly to blame. Clough had, as part of his essential make-up, those characteristics of withdrawal and over-sensitivity which we term introversion; his adjustment to his environment would have been difficult in any case. Furthermore, his mother, whose influence was early and therefore decisive, probably did more to harm Clough than Arnold could possibly have done: consciously or unconsciously, she did all that she could 'to make a conscientious and idealistic boy quite *too* conscientious and idealistic.'[2] At the same time Arnold deserves censure both negatively and positively. Had he merely failed to try to change his pupil, he would have earned the displeasure of most moderns. But Arnold did much more than that: partly inadvertently and partly consciously, he exploited those sides of Clough's nature that needed curbing, and encouraged the kind and degree of activity and thought and allegiance that were harmful to him. Clough was tremendously and permanently influenced by Arnold, and for the most part in a harmful direction. Dr. Arnold, unfortunately, was

---

[1] Even if Arnold had been responsible for Clough's failure, one can agree with Whitridge that that would be insufficient reason for condemning Arnold's whole system, as Strachey does. (Cf. Whitridge, *Arnold of Rugby*, p. 133; Strachey, *Eminent Victorians*, p. 207.)

[2] Osborne, *A. H. Clough*, p. 12.

proud of his work, though he did not live to see the final result. As Osborne says, Arnold 'really believed such a morally over-trained product as Clough was when he left for Oxford was the proper end of public-school training'.[1]

The most obvious deficiency in the Clough that graduated from Rugby was a physical one, and it can be directly traced to Clough's schooldays. Clough was actually tired out. As early as 1835 Arthur himself wrote, 'I have been in one continued state of excitement for at least the last three years, and now comes the time of exhaustion.'[2] Clough's wife goes so far as to claim that the moral and intellectual strain of Rugby days weakened Clough irreparably and thus caused him to fail to come to grips with life.[3] Though this physical strain was important, it does not seem to me that it was the crux of Clough's difficulty.

Certain intellectual traits, furthered by Arnold, are much nearer the heart of the problem, though they alone are not the whole explanation either. As we have seen, Dr. Arnold had solved to his own satisfaction the problem of faith and scepticism. He could pursue the truth relentlessly because he had hewn for himself an unshakeable foundation of belief. Unfortunately for some, as we suggested earlier, he also taught to his boys the necessity for both faith and intellectual independence. Clough, particularly, imbibed from Arnold the need for belief and the equally strong need for honesty of mind. As long as Clough was at Rugby the truths that Arnold taught remained protected from the acids of scepticism. But at Oxford, Clough, like Stanley, Matthew Arnold, his brother Thomas, and others, felt the impact both of the new science and of the religious upheaval from which Arnold had protected them. The others all eventually found a solution for the problem either in a new liberalism or in Newmanism, but Clough never did. Inhibited from action by Oxford's preoccupation with theological controversy and deeply upset by doubt, Clough threw himself into endless speculation.[4] Unfortunately, the harm that this did to his studies was not counter-balanced by any enlightenment in

[1] Osborne, op. cit., p. 22.
[2] Clough, op. cit., Vol. I, p. 58.
[3] Ibid., p. 46.
[4] Cf. Arnold, *Letters to Clough*, pp. 13 ff.

regard to the problems of existence. Under the inspiration of the dialectical Ward, Clough flirted for a while with Newmanism. Later Carlyle seemed to offer the answer to his problems. But, as Clough's biographer says, Carlyle led Clough into the wilderness and left him there. Arnold's death left him free to find his way out of the Church and to become an unhappy specialist in tiresomely over-earnest intellectual honesty.[1] Clough continued to look for the kind of truth that the modern world simply does not have for those who are honest. Though one admires a refusal to compromise, one recognizes that a scepticism which inhibits action or creation constitutes a failure to come to grips with reality.

But Clough's chief trouble was a moral one, in the broadest sense of the word. Stanley and Matthew Arnold with similar intellectual problems found both a relatively satisfactory solution to the intellectual problem and an adequate adjustment to the Victorian world. Clough found neither. He seems to have lacked from the beginning those traits of character and that practical vision which make successful living possible. And Arnold added immeasurably to Clough's difficulties. In the first place, he over-stimulated the boy's ethical sensibilities to such an extent that the world became to the young idealist a vast moral battlefield on which young Tennysonian Galahads fought and eventually conquered the black knights of unrighteousness. Rugby, in Arnold's eyes, was just such a continual tournament, and he thus implanted in Clough an unreal black-and-white picture of the world, in which he, Clough, was the knight in shining armour whose sacred duty it was to extirpate evil. Though Clough himself was inclined to blame Rugby's hot-house atmosphere on the 'over-excitation of the religious sense' caused by Wesleyanism and Puseyism and not on Arnold, the chief onus nevertheless rests on the latter.[2] In the second place, Arnold acted as moral no less than as mental nurse to Clough. His strength, his backing, imparted to the young idealist an artificial power and courage in much the same way that a dictator or a gang leader provides moral muscle for his followers. He taught Clough idealistic action along lines

[1] Osborne, *Clough*, pp. 64, 177.   [2] Clough, op. cit., Vol. II, p. 172.

Arnoldianism 317

prescribed by a leader and protected him in the exercise of his duties. Despite the seeming conflicts of life at Rugby, Clough's existence was free from the necessity of facing the circumstances of actual existence. It never occurred to Arnold that Clough's independence and sense of responsibility were as illusory as his picture of the world and the part he was to play in it were false. Clough had learned at a Public School neither to stand on his own feet nor to see life as it was: in other words, he failed to acquire the things he most needed and which, incidentally, were just what those who were not crushed by the older Public Schools did learn there.

When Clough arrived at Oxford he was confronted by a world far removed from that of Rugby. He found an environment no longer conveniently and recognizably divided into the saved and the damned. Clough himself, faced by Oxford's intellectual chaos, was not even so sure which was which. And Arnold was not there to offer shelter and inspiration and intellectual certainty. Furthermore, nobody wanted to be reformed through Arnold's teachings by a seventeen-year-old boy. Clough found himself without employment and intellectually and morally at sea; moreover, he had no tools with which to fashion a satisfactory life out of the new materials at hand. The disintegration and loss of energy in the face of new circumstances were permanent.

In one sense Matthew Arnold did not belong to the group composed of Clough, Stanley, Vaughan, and Lake. For Rugby School, to which he went in 1837 for only a short time after having spent a year at Winchester, seems to have been not only not the deciding influence in his life, but not important to him at all.[1] Yet actually and spiritually he was of this coterie. Stanley and even more Clough were his friends. He felt a group solidarity with these and other

[1] M. Arnold, *Letters*, Vol. I, p. 1. Information in regard to Arnold's schooldays is scant. One of the few suggestive touches that has been preserved records that at Winchester he was pelted with balls made of rolls by his schoolmates for telling Moberly that the work was too easy. It is easy to picture Dr. Arnold in the same predicament thirty years previously. (Cf. Thomas Arnold (Matthew's brother), *Passages in a Wandering Life*, London, 1900, pp. 9 ff.)

Rugby leaders which manifested itself in reunions at Rugby and in pleasure at their advancement. When Lake won his deanery Arnold wrote, 'He is one of the old Rugby set, and I like their coming to the front.'[1] Arnold always loved Rugby; after visiting Marlborough School he could say, 'The place is very striking, and interests me the more as a decided offspring of Rugby.'[2] Further, Arnold was spiritually akin to Clough and Stanley: he was an 'intellectual'. Finally, Arnold, more even in some ways than the others, felt the impact of Dr. Arnold's teaching and personality.

Matthew's importance in the history of Dr. Arnold's relationship to the world was twofold. In the first place, he was a direct transmitter of the true Arnold legend. *Rugby Chapel*, written as an answer to Fitzjames Stephen's attack on Dr. Arnold in his review of *Tom Brown's Schooldays*,[3] is the essence of Stanley's book compressed into Matthew's great verse and lifted into a region to which Stanley can scarcely soar. The poet has given immortality to the great spiritual leader and moral prophet whose divine inspiration and fatherly guidance were to lead the chosen religious souls 'on to the City of God'. But *Rugby Chapel* was too short a poem to contain much that was of practical importance for the spread of Arnold's influence in the schools. Matthew contributed nothing else of importance to the portrait or eulogy of Dr. Arnold. Nor did he take part in the conscious dissemination of his father's ideas. And even had he done so, it is doubtful whether he would have preached these to the Public Schools. Always a lover of the Public Schools[4]—he sent his two sons to Harrow—Matthew felt that, even with the leaven of Dr. Arnold's influence, the system was doomed to extinction. He praised and criticized the Public Schools, but he was not an active reformer of them along either Arnoldian or other lines at any time in his career.[5]

---

[1] M. Arnold, *Letters*, Vol. II, pp. 22, 28.
[2] Ibid., p. 78. [3] Arnold, *Letters to Clough*, p. 164.
[4] For a short time in 1845, while waiting for an Oriel fellowship, Matthew was an assistant in the fifth form at Rugby. The experience does not seem to have been very important either for Matthew or for Rugby. (Cf. Arnold, *Letters to Clough*, p. 55.)
[5] Arnold's defence and criticism of the Public School system is a phenomenon of the sixties.

Matthew Arnold's importance in connexion with his father is chiefly, on the one hand, as an example of the effect of the great schoolmaster's personality and ideas on a son who happened to be one of the most brilliant writers of his generation. More even than Clough or Stanley Arnold was to the Victorian age a living illustration of Dr. Arnold's teaching. On the other hand, Matthew was, because of the influence of his father on him, an often unconscious transmitter of Dr. Arnold's ideas. For middle-class education, in which Matthew was interested, this dissemination was direct; but the Public Schools felt indirectly the impact of Matthew's ideas and thus of his father's.

Dr. Arnold's relations to his son are the record of the collision of two distinct and powerful, yet similar individualities, one belonging to the world of the twenties and thirties, the other to that of the forties, fifties, and sixties. Matthew was tremendously influenced by his father, particularly in his ideas. At the same time, through the power of his personality and the influence of an age unborn when Dr. Arnold died, Matthew forged for himself a career and a philosophy very different from those of the older man.

According to his son Thomas, Dr. Arnold was, despite his severity, intimate with his children and averse to interfering directly in their lives.[1] Nevertheless, neither Thomas nor Matthew were ever free from their father's dynamic influence. In the former's case the result was such a destruction of individuality that, as he says himself, had he not borne an honoured name he might not have got along.[2] The freedom that Dr. Arnold gave him led, after many religious troubles, to that sanctuary of lost souls, the Catholic Church, with its acceptance of the comforting oneness of Christian revelation.[3]

But Matthew refused to be consumed by the doctor's fire. He determined, even as a young man, not to be his father's son. As a youth he displayed this determination in the most superficial kind of revolt, aping the extravagance and affectations of a Byron, the pet abhorrence of the earnest

---
[1] T. Arnold, *Passages in a Wandering Life*, p. 9.
[2] T. Arnold, op. cit., Preface, pp. v, vi.   [3] Ibid., p. 155.

Dr. Arnold. He gave himself airs, dressed outrageously, was bumptious and wilfully astonishing. Probably only the influence of Clough kept him from failing completely at Oxford.[1] His letters to Clough from Rugby in 1845 draw the picture of a frivolous Satan, not pompous enough for his conventional colleagues. He wrote Clough such things as the following, the tone of which would have shocked his father profoundly: 'But my dear Clough, have you a great Force of Character? That is the true Question. For me, I am a reed, a very whoreson Bullrush: yet such as I am, I give satisfaction.'[2]

This phase was not of very long duration, but it was succeeded by a mature Arnold who seems in many ways anything but the son of the Rugby schoolmaster. The suave and sophisticated preacher of sweetness and light no less than the bitter lyricist who found the world a place where ignorant armies clash by night seems almost the antithesis of the stern, unbending liberal. Matthew always remained more distinctly an individual than any of Dr. Arnold's close followers. It is therefore doubly interesting to trace the similarities to the elder man which the son exhibited.

After his early revolt, and especially after Dr. Arnold's death, the younger Arnold grew both to love his father and to take pride in being his moral and mental offspring. In 1868 he wrote that he believed Dr. Arnold would have approved and found his son's work indispensable.[3] He was overjoyed, shortly afterwards, to find corroboration for this belief. 'Arthur Stanley moved his chair round to me after dinner, and told me of his delight with my Preface, [to *Culture and Anarchy*] and how entirely the ideas of it . . . were exactly what papa would have approved.'[4] Matthew is always proud to be mentioned along with his father by such critics as Sainte-Beuve and the *North American Review*.[5] He constantly expressed admiration for the schoolmaster, particularly for 'bringing such a torrent of freshness into English religion by placing history and politics in connexion with

[1] Cf. Arnold, *Letters to Clough*, p. 28.   [2] Ibid., p. 56.
[3] M. Arnold, *Letters*, Vol. I, p. 454.
[4] Ibid., Vol. II, p. 4.   [5] Ibid., Vol. I, pp. 213, 252.

it'.[1] On his father's birthday in 1868 he marvelled at what Dr. Arnold did in a span of life the end of which Matthew himself had already reached.[2] He was always planning to write about his father's influence and importance,[3] which, particularly in America, never ceased to astonish him.[4]

The most fundamental likeness to his father that Matthew exhibited, derived probably from both inheritance and training, was his preoccupation with the moral. For Matthew, despite his Hellenism, saw the world essentially in ethical terms. Even in the 1849 poems of the foppish young secretary of Lord Lansdowne, his family were surprised to find a well-developed 'moral consciousness', awakened probably by Clough.[5] Later on, the moral, for which Matthew was always searching in nature, became three-quarters of life. Poetry was to be judged by its ability to teach one how to live. Religion was, in good part, moral law. Education, as with Dr. Arnold, was to a great extent religious and moral training; a boy was to be judged less by what he knew than by what noble qualities he possessed.[6]

The other side of Matthew Arnold, his preoccupation with the mental and the sensuous, seems far from Dr. Arnold. Matthew, under the influence of the anti-emotionalist forces of the fifties and sixties, evolved a philosophy that in many ways would have shocked his Puritan father. Yet the younger Arnold's intellectualism had important connexions with his father's training. For Matthew the classics were the source of his belief in the mental, and he derived his love of the ancients from Dr. Arnold. As he wrote himself, 'I inherit from him a deep sense of what, in the Greek and Roman world, was sound and rational.'[7] Moreover, it must not be forgotten that the classics were for Dr. Arnold as well as for Matthew a source of mental no less than of moral stimulation.

Where Matthew and Dr. Arnold seem closest to-day is in

[1] Ibid., Vol. I, p. 362.
[2] Ibid., Vol. I, p. 454.
[3] Ibid., Vol. II, p. 14.
[4] Ibid., Vol. II, p. 271.
[5] Arnold, *Letters to Clough*, pp. 28 ff.
[6] Cf. Fitch, *Thomas and Matthew Arnold*, p. 270.
[7] M. Arnold, *Letters*, Vol. I, p. 263. Matthew was very conscious, however, of the fact that he lived fifty years later than his father, and thus found new meanings in classic literature. (Cf. M. Arnold, *Letters*, Vol. I, pp. 454, 455.)

the similarity of their compromise between freedom and authority, the old and the new, aristocracy and democracy. In political matters Matthew was very conscious of his unique relation to his father: 'In my notions about the State I am quite papa's son, and his continuator. I often think of this—the more so because in this direction he has had so few who felt with him.'[1] It was probably, though not necessarily, in reference to politics that Gladstone—who was too Tory in the thirties to suit the elder Arnold and too Philistine in the seventies to suit the younger—spoke of the 'Arnoldism of the Arnolds'.[2] Matthew was a lover of England's stable aristocratic heritage, and he loved it all the more because he saw, what Dr. Arnold did not live to see, that the day of privileged classes was over. Referring to the Public School system, he wrote that, 'splendid fruits as it has undoubtedly borne, [it] must go. I say it does not rejoice me to think this, because what a middle class and people we have in England.'[3] Matthew Arnold disliked America because of its vulgarity,[4] and believed that 'few stocks could be trusted to grow up properly without having a priesthood and an aristocracy to act as their schoolmasters at some time or other of their national existence.'[5]

Feeling as he did, Matthew spent his life trying to educate the middle classes, to find a saving remnant to check the onrush of democracy. Like Dr. Arnold, the younger man, in 'Democracy' and other essays, preached the need for a powerful superbody to act as ballast to the ship of *laissez-faire* democracy; this superbody was to be a union of State and Church. Though Matthew found no more hearing in the Whig Philistine world of the sixties than his father had among the philosophical radicals and diehard Tories of the thirties, he was an important link in the chain which led, in its mild forms to State education and State protection of the worker, and in its more radical extension to modern Socialism and Fascism.

In religious matters, finally, Matthew Arnold combined

[1] M. Arnold, *Letters*, Vol. I, p. 263.
[2] *Fortnightly Review*, April 1911, p. 680.
[3] M. Arnold, *Letters*, Vol. I, p. 57 (to Mrs. Forster, February 17th 1856).
[4] Ibid., Vol. I, p. 326.   [5] Ibid., Vol. I, p. 133.

Dr. Arnold's desire for an absolute with his liberal hatred of dogma. But the impact of the new science led Matthew much farther along the road of liberalism than it had Dr. Arnold, and involved him in difficulties nearer to those of Clough than to those of Thomas Arnold at Oxford. Because, like Clough, Matthew possessed a mind trained to demand both truth and faith, contact with the new belief-destroying ideas meant for him a long period of bitter indecision and despair. The deepest emotion in *Rugby Chapel* emanates from Matthew's worship of a Dr. Arnold who was above the doubts and disillusionments of the Victorian world. To his contemporaries, Matthew Arnold provided, as much as Clough, a warning of the dangers of free thought.

Yet Matthew found his way to a solution that made life possible, first by transforming his doubts into poetry, and then by turning to the humanist standards to be found in the classics. Finally, he arrived at a religious solution which, though it stripped the Godhead of all anthropomorphism and religion of all dogma, kept Matthew not only a believer in the Christian religion but a member of the Church of England. Though Matthew had advanced far along the road, first pointed out by Arnold and other liberal theologians, that leads to atheism, he came finally to a compromise position which Dr. Arnold, even if he could not entirely have approved of it, would at least have understood.

D. ARNOLD'S DISCIPLES—THE PRACTICAL FAITH

However relatively important in the history of Arnoldianism the intellectuals may have been, they were certainly a very small proportion of the followers of Arnold. Most of the boys at Rugby were what I have called 'ordinary' boys, stolid, extroverted English youths without the sensitivity or the mental gifts of the Cloughs and the Stanleys. These boys were the privates in Arnold's army, and though he influenced many of them exceedingly, he had in general a very different effect on them than he had on the intellectuals. They either did not get to know or were impervious to the Arnold who made prigs and metaphysicians, and thus became neither prigs nor metaphysicians themselves. These soldiers received an 'inspiration toward devotion to duty' at the same time that they escaped the evils of premature seriousness.[1] It was because they escaped these effects that Lake, in his reaction against Arnold, felt that the Tom Browns profited more from their schooldays than did the scholars.[2]

Unfortunately very few of Arnold's private soldiers have recorded their impressions of Arnold or of their schooldays. Common soldiers are rarely literary men. But two boys have left scattered reminiscences and a third has written probably the most important book about Public Schools that has ever appeared. The two reminiscers are interesting chiefly because they give some impression of the restricted nature of Arnold's contact with the ordinary boy. The 'Old Rugbaean', whose sentimental reminiscences appeared as early as 1848, apparently felt Arnold's influence only indirectly and infrequently, for he talks a good deal more about escapades and old customs than about Arnold, and seems to derive what information he has about the head master from Stanley and not from direct experience.[3] Similarly, Arbuthnot, the author of *Memories of Rugby and India*, was a healthy extrovert whose wretchedly written recollections are more important for what they do not say than for what they do. Though he went to Rugby in 1832 he tells little about Arnold and nothing about school leaders such as Lake and Vaughan. As he says himself, 'I could not regard myself as one of Arnold's favourite pupils.' At the same time 'I do not believe there was one whose future career was so greatly influenced as mine was by my association with Arnold'.[4] Characteristically, what he took away with him was what he brought, mental and physical robustness.[5]

Thomas Hughes, though he defended Arnold all through his life, is a figure of decisive importance because he wrote one great book, *Tom Brown's Schooldays*. If Stanley's *Life and Correspondence of Thomas Arnold* spread the knowledge of

[1] Osborne, *A. H. Clough*, p. 17.
[2] Lake, *Memorials of Lake*, p. 12; *Good Words*, October 18th 1895, p. 667.
[3] Old Rugbaean, *Recollections of Rugby*.
[4] Sir Alexander J. Arbuthnot, *Memories of Rugby and India*, London, 1910, p. 36. [5] Ibid., p. 318.

Arnoldianism 325

Arnold among the leaders of Victorian thought, *Tom Brown's Schooldays* introduced the great head master to thousands in both England and America who had known little or nothing about him. Hughes more than any one else is responsible for the popular deification of Arnold and of the post-Arnoldian school which has been a characteristic feature of Public School literature ever since.

The reasons for the success of Hughes's book are not far to seek. In the first place, though Hughes was not a great writer and though he was overfond of a rather odious kind of preaching, *Tom Brown's Schooldays* remains even to-day one of the most vivid and realistic pictures of boy life that has ever been written. Hughes had lived with passionate enthusiasm many of the scenes that he describes. As a result, though Rugby existence in his pages is more black and white, more melodramatic than actual life usually is, Hughes has been able to invest most of his narrative with the illusion of reality. Some of the most incredible portions of the story have an artistic truth that is more convincing than actuality itself. Moreover, the book is given a vital unity and a living pattern which raises it above most books about schooldays by the loyal attachment to Arnold which pervades its pages. *Tom Brown's Schooldays* is the undying record of healthy English boyhood raised above itself by passionate love of a great leader.

In the second place, Hughes has given an interpretation of Rugby ideals which, however much at odds with reality it may have been, was true to the experience and desires of the vast majority of Englishmen. To begin with, *Tom Brown's Schooldays* dramatized and justified many of the ideas and sentiments about the traditional Public School which conservatives had long entertained. In the second place, it embodied a conception of Arnold which, because it omitted or distorted certain aspects of his character and work emphasized by Stanley, was palatable to the average man. Finally, it adumbrated a relatively new Public School ideal and a new feature of school life which were coming into popular favour in the fifties and sixties.

Hughes's interpretation of Rugby life under Arnold and of

Arnold himself was conditioned by his own personality, by his contacts with the head master and by the philosophy of Maurice and Kingsley. As a person Hughes differed from Stanley or Clough or Matthew Arnold about as much as people can differ from one another. He was John Bull incarnate, a country gentleman, a sportsman, a barrister, and a public man—a healthy extrovert who cared more for action than for thinking and for practical English ways of doing things than for theories or dreams. What he was like as a boy is apparent from the idealized portrait of himself that he has given in *Tom Brown's Schooldays*.[1] Tom was the ordinary boy incarnate, kindly, sturdy, competitive. He was humble before his mother, gracious to the poor, and tenacious of his rights with his peers. Though he loved danger and lawlessness, he had that essential rightness of heart which modern commentators such as another Hughes, author of the *Innocent Voyage*, fail to find in the young. At school, of course, Tom got along magnificently with other boys, particularly when they found out that he could play games and that 'he's got nothing odd about him, and answers straightforward, and holds his head up'.[2] He was, indeed, that ideal boy that the older Public School claimed to produce but seldom did unless such a product were in good part vouchsafed them to begin with.

Hughes was not the kind of boy who could ever have been, as Stanley was, a colonel in Arnold's army. He was, moreover, denied a chance of intimate acquaintance with the head master just because he was not the sort that Arnold readily took to his heart. Fitch says that Hughes probably did not go with the best set at Rugby;[3] whether this was true or not he certainly did not share the friendship with Arnold that this set possessed. Not until the middle of his Rugby career did Tom Brown have close enough contact with the head master even to discover that the latter could be kindly as well as stern; not until his last days in the school did a personal relationship grow up between master and pupil. Even then, Arnold had an effect on Tom's character chiefly

[1] Hughes's denial, in *Tom Brown at Oxford*, that he had written of himself can be discounted.
[2] (Thomas Hughes) An Old Boy, *Tom Brown's School-days*, London, 1928, p. 79.
[3] Fitch, *Thomas and Matthew Arnold*, p. 105.

through the indirect agency of the weak Arthur. Though one has only the evidence of *Tom Brown's Schooldays* to go on, it would seem that Arnold's influence was limited to filling Hughes with a sense of duty and loyalty and stirring in his squire's soul the germs of a few liberal ideals. Hughes never became a boy after Arnold's own image, nor did he ever fully comprehend Arnold's character or his aims.

After Hughes left Rugby he met Frederick Dennison Maurice and Charles Kingsley, and with their help arrived at a political and moral philosophy which profoundly affected his picture of Rugby ideals in *Tom Brown's Schooldays*. Kingsley's Christian Socialism and Maurice's liberal Christianity, in many respects derived from the same sources that produced Arnold's philosophy, were the last early Victorian attempt to forge a compromise between liberalism and Toryism in politics and between individualism and dogma in religion. Christian Socialism as revealed in Kingsley's *Yeast* and *Alton Locke* is an even more curious hodge-podge of democracy, socialism, Christianity, and fascism than was Arnold's philosophy. Though it was radical enough to cause the *Quarterly*, reviewing *Tom Brown's Schooldays*, to attack Farmer Brown's 'specious' idea of the Equality of Man,[1] it was actually much closer to Tory paternalism than to democratic socialism. Similarly, the conception of Christianity voiced by Maurice was, though more personal and broader than Coleridge's liberalism, not radical enough to make necessary a split with an authoritarian Church.

If Kingsley's conception was similar to older compromises, there were significant differences, for Christian Socialism was tainted by the new forces of imperialism and industrialism that were gaining headway in the fifties. Both Kingsley and Hughes were, in politics, extreme nationalists in a way that Arnold certainly was not. The naïve jingoism of *Westward Ho*, written in the sixties, represents in extreme form basic ideas that Kingsley always possessed. In their religious ideas both Kingsley and Hughes tried not only to compromise with liberalism but with materialism as well. Muscular Christianity, out of which the Y.M.C.A. movement has

[1] *Quarterly*, October 1857, p. 344.

grown, was an attempt to bring Christianity down to the level of the average man by showing him that it was really a robust, manly affair. The result was often, like Bruce Barton's effort to prove that Christ was a super-salesman, a vulgarization of Christianity. In Kingsley, Christian practice seems not seldom to mean little more than being clean and physically well developed.

Much of the early part of *Tom Brown's Schooldays* is a rehash of Kingsley's philosophy. Its theme is a glorification of those old English families that had ploughed England's fields and fought her wars, and of English folk-stories and customs from the past. Hughes particularly loved traditional ceremonies like the Veast, and ancient games like cricket and hunting, which he claims were initiated by the Church. In Hughes's mind, interest in these practices is contrasted with love of science, to the detriment of the latter. In loving the past Hughes was actuated in part by a conservative feeling for class and a strong nationalism. This last appears only too clearly in his attack on excessive interest in foreign languages and on the preference for 'bad foreign music' over 'good English cheeses' which he found prevalent among farmers' daughters.[1] At the same time Hughes was also motivated by concern for democracy and for morality. According to Hughes, old customs and country games drew all classes together on an equal basis; the death of these social and universal activities caused the further separation of classes which commercialism had started.[2] Reformers must replace these games with something to try men's muscles and endurance and hearts if the breach between the classes caused by riches and over-civilization is to be repaired. Old Squire Brown, Tory as he was, knew, because he was familiar with ancient traditions, that a man should be valued for himself and not for the externals of rank and fortune.[3]

The conception of Rugby education which emerges in *Tom Brown's Schooldays* is in good part that of the old Public School. Most of Hughes's book is, like *The Recollections of Rugby*, a picture of school life that closely resembles that

[1] Hughes, op. cit., p. 35.   [2] Ibid., p. 25.   [3] Ibid., p. 46.

Arnoldianism

portrayed in the reminiscences of Etonians or Harrovians of the same period. There are the usual games and bullyings and feasts and friendships, the ordinary events of a boy life lived beyond the pale of master activity. Further, the spirit that animates Hughes's pages is that of a former day. In the 'miniature world' of a Public School Tom learns to compete, to know his place, to obey authority, to be 'proud of being a Rugby boy'.[1] With old Brooke he cheers 'the old Schoolhouse—the best house of the best school in England', and he does so in good part because it is his school-house and not because it stands for ideals.[2]

The part that Arnold played in Hughes's world was that of socializer. He intensified *esprit de corps* and gave it an ethical object. The average middle-class gentleman had felt that what was lacking in the old Public School, and what he hoped his son would acquire at Rugby was moral virtue. Farmer Brown sent Tom to school to learn to 'tell the truth, keep a brave and kind heart, and never listen to or say anything you wouldn't have your mother and sister hear';[3] 'if he'll only turn out a brave, helpful, truth-telling Englishman, and a gentleman, and a Christian, that's all I want.'[4] This, in essence, is what Tom did learn. The personal influence of Arnold working through Arthur made him gradually relinquish many of his boyish ideas: he learned to be a responsible man, to stop cribbing, to do his duty by his weaker fellows, and even to pray. Moreover, he acquired a passionate devotion, not merely now to the school, but to Arnold and to the moral ideals for which Arnold stood.[5]

The picture of Arnold the man that Hughes drew was scarcely more than an embodiment of those moral forces whose effect Hughes felt so powerfully. Yet it is a human and moving impression of the great teacher that emerges from the mists of Hughes's adoration. Sitting in chapel every day, the boy was deeply stirred by the 'oak pulpit standing out by itself above the School seats. The tall, gallant form, the kindling eye, the voice, now soft as the low notes of a flute, now clear and stirring as the call of the light infantry bugle,

[1] Ibid., p. 75. [2] Ibid., pp. 106–09. [3] Ibid., p. 62.
[4] Ibid., p. 64. [5] Ibid., p. 110.

of him who stood there Sunday after Sunday, witnessing and pleading for his Lord, the King of righteousness and love and glory, with whose spirit he was filled, and in whose power he spoke.' According to Hughes, Arnold moved even those who had been impervious to religion because they felt that they were listening to a man who was striving 'with all his heart and soul and strength, . . . against whatever was mean and unmanly and unrighteous in our little world'. Arnold spoke not from 'serene heights' but as one fighting 'by our sides, and calling on us to help him and ourselves and one another'. He had 'no misgivings, and gave no uncertain word of command'.[1]

Hughes undoubtedly recaptured, as Stanley could not have, the relationship that existed between Arnold and his ordinary boys and the influence that he had over them. But in part for this very reason, his picture of Arnold and of Arnold's purposes is faulty. To begin with, he omitted an account of Arnold's intellectual interests and spurned those interests himself. Tom's Philistine father did not send his son to Rugby to learn 'Greek particles',[2] and Tom did not learn them. Though he got into the sixth form despite his idleness, he seems to have been so untouched by the Arnold who was a passionate seeker after truth and who spurred on his best boys to disinterested intellectual endeavour that he gave no account of him at all. Indeed, his whole book is permeated by contempt for the intellect. The efforts of masters always seemed to him futile and unimportant; the time between classes was the essence of school life.[3] Old Brooke, voicing the sentiments of all, says, 'I know I'd sooner win two School-house matches running than get the Balliol scholarship any day.'[4] In view of the influence of Hughes's book his anti-intellectuality was unfortunate. It gave sanction to a tradition which Arnold had tried, with some success, to break down. It meant that the tendency of many masters to minimize the intellectual side of school life in order to retain the friendship with boys was encouraged. Further, it helped block reform of the curriculum and prevent

[1] Hughes, op. cit., pp. 121–22. [2] Ibid., p. 64.
[3] Ibid., p. 54. [4] Ibid., p. 107.

respect for industriousness from permeating the schools even when, at the end of the century, such an attitude was vitally needed.

Much more subtle than his omission of the intellectual side of school life was Hughes's partial vulgarization of Arnold's personality and moral ideals. Though the Arnold that inspired Tom Brown from the pulpit seems on the surface very similar to Stanley's Arnold, actually there is a world of difference between these two figures. One of Hughes's self-appointed tasks was to defend Arnold, not only against the liberals who accused him of furthering a cruel monitorial system, but against those who, like Stephen, believed that Arnold made of Rugby a 'semi-sacerdotal fraternity' of premature men. Hughes claimed that Arnold produced earnest and yet genial boys, not prigs.[1] To prove this he emphasized in his portrait of the master those sides of his personality which were human or downright, not prophetic or subtle. He taught that Arnold was boyishly exuberant and kind, not awesome. At the same time, he pictured him as much more the old type of schoolmaster, familiar to Englishmen, than as a fanatical reformer. He flogged when necessary, was patient with bad customs such as fighting, and did not usually encourage boys to tell on one another. The Arnold of Hughes's conception is a 'strong, fearless, and just' captain who leads his lieutenants forth to war against petty selfishness and cruelty.[2] The grandeur of his character, that carried boys to new regions of thought and feeling and sometimes destroyed them, has disappeared. Hughes's Arnold has neither the fanatic idealism, the other worldliness, nor the over-developed sense of sin that the real Arnold possessed. He has become a glorified boy scoutmaster whose strenuous spirituality has been made palatable to Englishmen by presenting it under the guise of the honest manliness of a Kingsley hero.[3]

If Hughes's modification of Rugby ideals was chiefly in the

---

[1] Ibid., Preface to Sixth Edition.
[2] *Great Public Schools*, London, n.d., pp. 154 ff.
[3] Cf. Thomas Hughes, *The Manliness of Christ*, New York, 1880, p. 582. Stephen in the *Edinburgh* (January 1858, p. 189) was the first to point out the relationship between Hughes's Arnold and muscular Christianity.

direction of older school conceptions, it was by no means entirely so. In the method that Hughes advocated for creating moral schoolboys, he added something to the idea of a Public School which had existed neither in the Arnoldian nor in the pre-Arnoldian school. In *Tom Brown's Schooldays* organized games are very nearly the only means of achieving the ethical purposes dear to Hughes and, as Hughes conceived of him, to Arnold. This idea, though not original with Hughes and already in practice at other Public Schools by 1857, grew quite logically out of Hughes's own ideas. Since Hughes loved games, and since he interpreted Arnold's moral ideal as a spiritual kind of courage, it was only natural that he should have believed that sport could achieve the ends that Arnold had in mind. He therefore filled his book with a glorification of organized athletics. Long before the figure of Arnold appears at all, the tone and lesson of *Tom Brown's Schooldays* have been given through a detailed description of a football match with its diverse characters, its true and false courage, and its spirit of team-work. Of this game Hughes can say with a passion evinced only by the picture of Arnold in chapel, 'This is worth living for; the whole sum of schoolboy existence gathered up into one straining, struggling half-hour, a half-hour worth a year of common life.'[1] Now whatever one may think of games, they are not as important relative to other activities as Hughes makes them out to be. Further, they certainly are not, even at their best, perfect instruments for the achievement of moral ends as broadly conceived as were Arnold's. In no other aspect of his book do we feel so strongly the cheapening of Arnold's conception of a Public School as in Hughes's insistence on the almost exclusive value of athletics. Here more concretely than anywhere else is manifest the materialistic spirit of an age of which Kingsley's philosophy was in part an expression.

Though it is apparent from the above discussion that Hughes did much to encourage practices of an anti-liberal nature in the schools, it would be unfair to give the impression that he was directly responsible for or even sympathetic

---

[1] Hughes, *Tom Brown's Schooldays*, p. 96.

Arnoldianism 333

to the manifestations of the new industrialism in the schools of the sixties and seventies. In particular the phenomenon known as athleticism, whose general characteristics we will discuss in the next chapter, cannot be laid at Hughes's door. Hughes was both a sincere liberal and a profoundly religious man, and hated an undemocratic and exploiting capitalist class with its narrow materialistic ideals no less than did Arnold. In an address at Clifton College in 1879 he pleaded for idealism, humility, simplicity, and self-denial and bitterly assailed the luxury, the worship of good form and the cut-throat competitiveness which characterized society. The following year he attacked the over-emphasis of athletics in schools; games, he wrote, might teach self-sacrifice, but they might equally well mean a mere glorification of strength and proficiency.[1] Like Arnold, Hughes has suffered the ironic fate of having prepared the ground for practices which he abhorred.

[1] Hughes, *Manliness of Christ*, p. 583.

CHAPTER II

THE PUBLIC SCHOOLS
1840–1860

SEEN in broad outline, Public School history in the forties and fifties is the story of the conflict between the two main streams of influence suggested in Chapter I, liberalism and the religious revival on the one hand, conservatism and the forces of advanced industrialism on the other. Until the middle fifties the response to the religious reformers, the humanitarians, and the intellectual liberals was the more positive and important. It was as a result of yielding to these forces that the schools not only retained the allegiance of the old upper classes but won the support of thousands who would otherwise probably not have gone to Public Schools at all. New schools grew up in imitation of the most progressive of the older schools until the latter formed but the nucleus of a vast network of educational institutions.

The chief embodiment of the new tendencies was Arnold. Though his influence was slow in making itself felt,[1] and though other head masters like Moberly continued for long to reflect reformist tendencies partly independent of Arnold, the Rugby head master was the spearhead of change. By the fifties his disciples and imitators were busy and continued to be busy for twenty years reforming old schools or founding new ones on Arnoldian lines. Rossall, Cheltenham, Marlborough, Clifton, Haileybury, Harrow, and even day schools like King Edward's at Manchester, St. Paul's, and Bedford felt the direct impact of Arnold's work.[2] All schools felt his influence to some extent, and those like Charterhouse, Westminster, and Shrewsbury which felt it least were the least popular.[3] His sermons found worthy imitations in the

[1] Despite Moberly's mention of Arnold in the thirties and Vaughan's coming to Harrow in 1844, the *Edinburgh* could say as late as 1845 that Arnold's practical effect was virtually nil: he left the problem of education 'pretty much where it was before'. (January 1845, p. 233.)
[2] Cf. Archer, *Secondary Education*, pp. 69 ff.
[3] Parents like Henry Sidgwicks' mother, who had had a rooted dislike of Public Schools for their 'low moral tone', sent boys there in the fifties because

334

sermons of Cotton, Montagu Butler, and Vaughan, as well as ludicrous parodies in those of Sewell of Radley and others.[1] Leopold Wiese, head of the Royal Foundation School in Berlin, surveying the Public Schools from a foreigner's point of view in 1852, could credit Arnold with most of their progressive features. *Punch*, retracting a slur on Public Schools in 1854, wrote that 'there is not a better security for the youth of a public school than the sort of feeling which seems to exist at Rugby'.[2] Finally, the Public School Commission, writing in 1864, could mention Arnold as a chief cause of the improvement which they felt had occurred in the Public School system since his day.[3]

As suggested previously, the liberal and religious forces which Arnold represented held by no means uncontested possession of the field. In the first place, conservative forces were powerful all through the forties, fifties, and sixties, and they had a tendency to inhibit, modify, or redirect Public School purposes as Arnold conceived of them. Leopold Wiese, who visited the Public Schools when Arnold's ideas had been as completely absorbed as they were going to be and when new ideas did not yet loom large on the educational horizon, found in existence a system basically similar to that which we have seen in practice in 1820. It was a system grounded in traditional customs, practices, and institutions,[4] and maintaining as its ideal a combination of heroic manliness and 'due subordination of individuals into one whole'.[5] If Arnold had changed old ways of doing things in that he had suppressed self-seeking, increased *esprit de corps*, brought some humanity into school life, and they heard, as Mrs. Sidgwick did from E. W. Benson, that Arnold had reformed the Public Schools. (A. S. and E. M. S., *Henry Sidgwick, A Memoir*, London, 1906, pp. 6 ff.)

[1] Cf. *Quarterly*, September 1855, pp. 335 ff.
[2] *Punch*, January to June 1854, p. 123.
[3] 'We are satisfied, on the whole, both that it has been eminently successful, and that it has been greatly improved during the last 30 or 40 years, partly by causes of a general kind, partly by the personal influence and exertions of Dr. Arnold and other great schoolmasters.' (*Report of Her Majesty's Commissioners Appointed to Inquire into the Revenues and Management of Certain Colleges and Schools and the Studies Pursued and Instruction Given Therein*, London, 1864, *General Results*, p. 44.)
[4] Wiese found the English naturally conservative, respecting old institutions and clinging to prejudices. (*German Letters on English Education*, pp. 25, 31, 116.)
[5] Wiese, op. cit., p. 21.

broken down somewhat the enmity between master and boy,[1] he had as signally failed in other respects to introduce his purposes into the traditional Public School. Of his attempt to stimulate the mind and create intellectual independence or to inculcate passionate moral idealism there is little evidence in the schools of the fifties.

In the second place, the positive counter-Arnoldian influences exerted by an imperialist and materialist industrialism were already beginning to be felt in Wiese's day. Though these forces manifested themselves in a number of ways, their most concrete expression in the schools was the rise of organized athletics and its development into athleticism. The history of this movement, which was still in its infancy in 1860, provides a beautiful illustration of the nature of the complex forces that were moulding the schools and of the characteristic outcome of the mingling of those forces. To begin with, the interest in games was, as we have seen, of long standing among boys, and had been growing perceptibly during the first forty years of the century. At the same time sport was becoming more and more organized. The impetus, however, which produced the close organization and prestige of athletics came not out of the older schools but from the Arnoldians. To disciples of Arnold like Hughes and Cotton, athletics seemed a useful instrument in effecting Arnold's moral purposes. They were supposed to and surely often did teach loyalty, honourableness, graciousness in defeat, self-sacrifice, co-operation. Since these were highly desired ends, the Arnoldians brought master support to a movement which, without aid from authority, might never have grown to the proportions which it later assumed.

Undoubtedly the disciples of the master believed that, in advocating an increased use of games, they were merely following in Arnold's footsteps. Actually, even when they subordinated games to other activities and to the moral purposes that Arnold had in mind, they were bending ideals to fit the needs of a new age. Arnold would never have

[1] Wiese claims (op. cit., p. 37) that masters trust boys, never suppress free development and have a huge personal influence in forming character.

The Public Schools: 1840–1860

approved of the glorification of the body that games implied. Further, he would surely have felt that the moral ideals that games at their best could teach were a vulgarization and materialization of his high religious purposes. But even granting these limitations inherent in sport as a builder of character, athleticism was innocuous enough as long as it meant merely the playing of games as one method of furthering moral ends. It was not long, however, before the boy love of sport, unchecked by the disapproval of masters and parents, gave a very different meaning to the term, a meaning that would have been as utterly hateful to Arnold as it has been to liberals and moralists ever since. Games became a religion. They grew to be the essence of school life and were engaged in with an earnestness only equalled by the fervour which Arnold inspired in regard to religious activity.

Athletics as an exclusive cult had far-reaching implications. To begin with it meant that other activities, in particular the intellectual side of school life, secured even less interest from boys and, what is more important, from masters than it had earlier in the century. In the second place, it sounded the death-knell to any possible growth of individualism. In the old Public School boys had sought to regiment the individual, but had had no support from masters. In the Arnoldian school, masters had preached conformity, but had advocated standards which could not possibly win the general allegiance of boys. Now, however, masters and boys made common cause in urging individual subordination to a boy god. In the third place, athleticism meant a narrowing of the possible moral aims of Public Schools. Since games could teach none of the democratic humanitarianism, the religious idealism, or even the moral purity that Arnold had advocated, an exclusive preoccupation with them implied the drying up of any broad conception of human worth which might otherwise have flowered in the schools.

Finally, and most important, the turning of athletics into a religion brought about the gradual obliteration in boys' minds of the moral purposes for the sake of which masters had originally encouraged games, and caused the glorification of what had been at first a mere means, the successful playing of the game itself. Consequently, the qualities that made for success became the values most prized at Eton and Rugby. This meant a complete perversion of Arnold's purposes, For, though Public School sport was kept on a relatively high plane, achievement could hardly result chiefly from a subordination of selfish interest to general good. An athlete quickly learned that only by strength and self-assertion could he win a place on his own team or help conquer rival teams. Consequently, worship of the athlete by younger boys came to mean love of physical prowess and of competitiveness. In its final form, the religion of athletics seems the perfect expression of a Philistine age.

Though a bird's-eye view of the Public School system in the first twenty-five years of Victoria's reign presents the general pattern suggested above, intimate contact with various schools reveals wide and important differences in the manner in which individual institutions absorbed the influences of the age. Each school was steeped in its own traditions, which varied in pertinacity in almost direct proportion to the age, wealth and rigidity of governmental structure of the school. Head masters or assistants were all individuals with personalities of varying power and with minds variously adapted to receiving new ideas. As a result, each school accepted dominant ideas at a different time and with different degrees of thoroughness, and imparted an individual quality to the educational pattern that finally emerged.

A. RUGBY

Rugby did not actually degenerate after Arnold's death. It merely remained as it had been under its great master, and, since imitation is likely to be relatively sterile, Rugby lost the leadership it had won. At the same time it continued to be one of the best schools even during the days of Tait and Goulburn, and then took a new lease on life in the sixties under another strong man, Temple.

Tait, who followed Arnold, was neither a scholar nor a favourite of Arnold's. The job of succeeding the great leader was at best a thankless one, and probably no strong man was

The Public Schools: 1840–1860

very anxious to have it. Tait tried to do the only thing that he could do, carry on in Arnold's spirit. Stanley himself had urged Tait's election, and had suggested to him that he read Arnold's sermons, even at the risk of orthodoxy (Tait had High Church leanings, and defended Ward's *Ideals of a Christian Church* in the face of Low Church opposition), in order to acquire spiritual sympathy with his predecessor.[1] Tait himself, the day before his election, wrote that, 'If it were in my power to keep up that system which Dr. Arnold has begun, I should certainly think my life well spent.'[2]

In carrying on Arnold's ideals Tait fell heir to the typical troubles of a weak man imitating a strong one. To begin with, he had difficulty with masters who had worked under Arnold and who therefore felt that they knew what Arnold wanted better than did Tait. Further, not being a scholar—Lake, Pearson, and Shairp all agree in saying this—he was handicapped in his efforts to be, like Arnold, an inspiring teacher. His major difficulty, however, was that he blindly tried to exaggerate the side of Arnold's ideas of which the world disapproved. Bradley, who worked under him, as well as Pearson, said that he overdid the inculcation of moral responsibility.[3] Since he was not, however, as intense a person as Arnold, he seems in practice actually to have made the relations between the sixth form and the rest of the school less rather than more strained. Further, since his influence over individuals was more limited than was Arnold's, he turned out, in spite of himself, far fewer unnaturally mature boys than had his predecessor. Ironically enough, by the end of his reign (1850) Rugby resembled the average Public School much more than it did under Arnold.

Testimony as to the state of Rugby, particularly in the forties, is conflicting. Pearson, writing years later, can say that 'English public schools are, I believe, bad enough now, but they have been immensely improved from Rugby in its palmy days. In reality, we learned nothing but Latin and

---

[1] Cf. Randall Thomas Davidson and William Benham, *Life of Archibald Campbell Tait*, 2 vols., London, 1891, Vol. I, p. 110.
[2] Ibid., p. 112.
[3] Cf. Davidson and Benham, op. cit., Vol. I, p. 116, and Pearson, *Memorials*, pp. 14 ff.

Greek, and those very imperfectly.'[1] But even if one grants the truth of Pearson's evidence and admits that there was some relapse from the spirit of study and the good relations between masters and boys that had existed under Arnold, it remains incontestable that Rugby had a deservedly higher reputation[2] both intellectually and morally than did most schools.[3] The spirit of Arnold survived in the teaching of such men as the dogmatically liberal Bonamy Price,[4] the eccentric Principal Shairp, and others like G. G. Bradley, Cotton, and Walrond.

Though the Rugby of the fifties was very similar to that of the thirties, the new spirit of athleticism and conformity were creeping in. Pearson mentioned it as existing in the forties, but not to any great extent.[5] Ten years later, however, Henry Sidgwick could complain that he was unhappy at Rugby, as any clever unathletic boy of fourteen in a high form and an athletic house would have been.[6] Shairp, who saw Rugby develop through the decade from 1846 to 1857, felt that the Public School system 'had a tendency to dwarf originality'.[7] It was probably true, however, as Rouse says,

---

[1] 'Translation was rather better taught than composition. Other subjects could hardly be said to be taught at all.' There was one French and German lesson a week and one learned little. 'Perhaps, however, the best proof how superficial our studies were is the fact that they had not the slightest influence in lessening the contempt which as British boys we felt for the masters who taught us.' (Pearson, *Memorials*, pp. 13–15.)

[2] Lord Ashley noted in his diary, November 21st 1844: 'Went yesterday to Rugby to examine the physical and moral aspect of the place and see whether it would be a good school for Anthony. Hope—nay, think it will do; universal testimony, so far as I hear, in its favour from all who have sons there.' (Hodder, *Life of Shaftesbury*, Vol. II, p. 77.)

[3] Teachers like Shairp, no less than the Public School Commissioners in the sixties, found Rugby an industrious school. (William Knight, *Principal Shairp and his Friends*, London, 1888, p. 85; Rouse, *History of Rugby*, p. 281.) Shairp stated that he found at Rugby 'the manliness of character, the spirit of honour, and the frankness of manner conspicuous in the better type of public school men'. (Knight, op. cit., p. 100.) Even Pearson admits the honourable spirit of the playground, the relative infrequency of bullying, and the moral tone of the classrooms, where 'it was thought disreputable to lie'. (Pearson, *Memorials*, pp. 24, 26.)

[4] Shairp says that Price was king at Rugby; Pearson called him a tyrant, but admitted that he was a great teacher. (Knight, op. cit., p. 101; Pearson, op. cit., p. 22.)

[5] Pearson, op. cit., p. 24.

[6] A. S. and E. M. S., *Henry Sidgwick, A Memoir*, p. 9.

[7] Cf. Knight, op. cit., p. 100. It was harmful to geniuses and prepared boys for the world by taking conceit and eccentricity out of them.

The Public Schools: 1840–1860 341

that, despite its invention of Rugby football, Rugby did not idolize the athlete as much as did other schools.[1] It probably does not to-day.

B. HARROW

The development of Harrow from 1830 to 1860 is probably of more interest than that of any other school. For it is the story of early failure in incompetent hands, followed by success when Harrow was entrusted to one of the greatest of Arnold's disciples. Harrow's history thus illustrates the factors making for Public School degeneration and revival in early Victorian days. Further, since Harrow was the only old school reformed by an Arnoldian, it provides the best opportunity of studying the relationship of old traditions, reformers, and the new age.

From 1825 to 1844 Harrow degenerated because in the face of public criticism it gave evidence of all of the bad features of the unreformed school.[2] For thirty years what Minchin chooses to call the Byronic influences of drunkenness, dissipation, bullying, and idleness ruled; there was gambling, night hare and hounds, and skylarking of various kinds; one boy died from having his constitution ruined; a bully was nailed into his room.[3] So bad were conditions that Vaughan was told not to throw himself away on Harrow.

If such conditions prevailed, it was not because there was no effort to amend them. The spirit of a reform age affected Dr. Longley (1829–36) and Dr. Christopher Wordsworth (1836–44) almost as much as it did Arnold. But they were not Arnolds, and their efforts were unavailing. Their

[1] Cf. Rouse, *History of Rugby*, p. 312.
[2] Its members fell from 250 in 1825 to 70 in 1844. (Thornton, *Harrow School*, pp. 248–83.)
[3] J. G. Cotton Minchin, *Old Harrow Days*, London, 1898, pp. 87 ff. Except for Kennedy—later head of Shrewsbury—there was no one in Longley's day who could teach. Latin and Greek were dull and formal, history dry husks. Harrow was not an educational institution, but a small world ruled by the bold. (Sir William Gregory, *An Autobiography*, London, 1894, p. 36.) Goldwin Smith calls the government of Harrow in Wordsworth's time 'government in the form of a moderate anarchy'. (Howson, *Harrow*, p. 99.) Charles S. Roundell tells of stone throwing, attacking the head of the house, locking out masters, advertising as matrimonial agents and pelting a suitor from London with rotten eggs.

failure and the reasons for it illuminate by contrast the nature and causes of Arnold's and Vaughan's success.

Longley's failure is interesting evidence of the necessity for Arnold's disciplinary power. Strachey may carp over floggings and Jehovah-like sternness, but it is hard to see how any one but a genius could have entirely dispensed with either in the Harrow of 1830. From all accounts Longley was much too kind and weak to rule boys; he thus failed in his efforts both at discipline and at religious reform.[1] The only positive thing about his unsuccessful reign was the gradual creeping in from Winchester through Eton of legalized fagging and the Rugby monitorial system.

Wordsworth, a stronger and more interesting man than Longley, set out with the intention of reforming Harrow as Arnold had Rugby. He built a chapel and brought Harrow into touch with the religious revival. Through having services in accordance with boys' needs, he tried to encourage religion and to create Christian gentlemen on the Arnoldian pattern.[2] Further, he attempted to organize the budding monitorial system into a paternal despotism based on moral responsibility: the monitors were to deal with bullying and breach of customs, and to report immorality to the masters.[3] Finally, even in intellectual matters, he introduced such innovations as mathematics.[4]

Despite his best efforts Wordsworth was unpopular and unsuccessful. The truth was that his sympathies were not in his job.[5] He was tactless, intolerant and impatient in making badly needed reforms, and thus affronted boys' natural conservatism without being able to overcome it.[6] Further, he alienated the outside world; he 'did his murders openly', that is, he ruthlessly dismissed troublesome boys and thus aggrieved influential people. His best acts turned against him because he was not practical enough to deal with their results.[7] But probably what hurt him most were his high church leanings, a disability from which Arnold was free,

---

[1] Cf. Howson, *Harrow*, p. 82; Thornton, *Harrow School*, p. 267.
[2] Cf. Overton, *Christopher Wordsworth*, pp. 63 ff.; Howson, op. cit., p. 99.
[3] Cf. Howson, op. cit., p. 102. [4] Ibid., p. 98.
[5] Ibid., p. 105. [6] Overton, op. cit., pp. 65 ff.
[7] Cf. Howson, op. cit., p. 89.

and which at another school might have been less of a handicap. His was the theological spirit of Nicaea; his ideal for Harrow boys was the 'catechetical school of Alexandria'.[1] He thought of the grammar schools as nurseries of the Church and wanted to carry on 'school discipline on Church principles.'[2] As a result many Evangelicals deserted the school; even Peel sent his younger sons to Eton.[3]

When Vaughan went to Harrow in 1844, there were some misgivings at turning over the school to so young a man. Vaughan justified his appointment by the speed with which he rebuilt Harrow. In 1845 there were eighty boys in the school, in 1846 one hundred and thirty-eight, in January 1847, two hundred and sixty-four, and in September three hundred and fifteen. In 1859, when he retired, there were four hundred and thirty-eight.[4]

Vaughan rehabilitated the institution over which he ruled partly because he followed Arnold, whose principles were at the height of their popularity in 1844, and partly because he was endowed with the attributes that made for the latter's success.[5] The fact that he believed fully in Arnold's ideals and methods—the especial importance of morals and religion, the insistence on the intellect and on literary originality, the use of the chapel, and the system of monitorial trust[6]—was in itself of great importance. Stanley's book had appeared in 1844 and was eagerly devoured by the sixth form at Harrow and by alumni. As a result, the older boys helped Vaughan,[7] and the authorities gave him *carte blanche* to reform the school by moral suasion.[8] As a *Times* correspondent suggested in 1845, Harrovians were pleased with

[1] Ibid., p. 105. [2] Overton, op. cit., p. 68.
[3] Cf. Thornton, op. cit., p. 280.
[4] Graham, *Harrow Life of H. M. Butler*, pp. xviii ff., 29. [5] Ibid., p. 29.
[6] In 1854 in a letter to Lord Palmerston during a public controversy over the subject, Vaughan defended monitorial discipline as opposed to espionage. He believed that 'faults of turbulence, rudeness, offensive language, annoyance of others, petty oppression, and tyranny', which reflected on the 'gentlemanlike tone of the Houses and of the School' could best be dealt with by boys. Further, he contended that fagging was a necessary part of the system, since it both served as 'a memento of monitorial authority' and was important positively in creating a system of organized rank best calculated to produce the 'character of an English Christian gentleman'. (Quoted from Thornton, *Harrow School*, p. 448.)
[7] Howson, op. cit., p. 107. [8] Thornton, op. cit., p. 286.

Vaughan because of 'the knowledge that Harrow is now under the direction of one who is able and willing to carry out the Arnold system of education'.[1] But at least equally important was Vaughan's possession of qualities which enabled him to teach, to inspire, to discipline, and to sympathize with the boys, and to beget confidence in governors and alumni, without which his principles would have mocked rather than re-created Arnold's. Though it is conceivable, it is hardly likely that Vaughan's ability to teach or to discipline were the mere result of imitation of Arnold rather than of psychological similarity. A mere imitator could hardly have put life or effectiveness into his creation. It is hard to believe that even a Stanley, whose character and ideas were nearer to what Arnold approved than to what Arnold was, could have managed Harrow on Arnoldian lines. A school modelled exactly on Rugby required for its successful governance character traits similar to Arnold's. Moreover, since inspiration is not transferable, those traits had to be inherent, not acquired.

Vaughan had, though this was the least important aspect of his nature, intellectual capabilities of a high order.[2] Far more important, he had the power to move boys' hearts.[3] The deep religious feeling that shone through his sermons seems to have been so contagious that it almost made Harrow into a religious community.[4] Again, Vaughan had just the combination of sternness and sympathetic understanding necessary to make possible a successful monitorial system along the lines that he advocated. He expelled the dullard and the unjust prefect;[5] at the same time he showered responsibility on the worthy. By charm, by understanding of boys and by the freedom that he allowed them, he made his

[1] *The Times*, March 3rd 1845, p. 6.
[2] According to Montagu Butler, he was a penetrating if not a broad scholar. G. O. Trevelyan gives him much credit for the production of the verse writer Calverley. (Graham, *Montagu Butler*, p. 30; Thornton, *Harrow School*, p. 286.)
[3] By the very liking he had for faults, he made people ashamed of them. (Graham, op. cit., p. xx.)
[4] Cf. Thornton, op. cit., p. 297; F. D. How, *Six Great Schoolmasters*, London, 1904, pp. 145 ff. Trevelyan claims that Vaughan's sermons were so treasured that boys were dismayed when he did not speak. (Graham, op. cit., p. xx.)
[5] Cf. Thornton, op. cit., p. 295.

prefects his staunch allies.[1] Finally, Vaughan, even more than Arnold, was tactful. He successfully reformed the conservative Harrow because he did not offend alumni by doing too much, by breaking too decisively with the past. Even though the Arnoldian monitorial system had Arnold's precedent and the support of Stanley's book, Vaughan 'proceeded cautiously and gradually in his reforms. He respected the *genius loci* of the place [sic] and the school traditions.'[2] Old connexions came back as much for his 'sympathizing spirit as regards Harrow custom, combined with a reverence for her great past' as for his reforms.

Vaughan's net effect on Harrow was probably, from all that one can gather, far less profound or far-reaching than was Arnold's at Rugby. That which made Vaughan go so slowly—the relatively greater power of a Harrow tradition that was longer than was Rugby's—acted to prevent as great a change at Harrow as at Rugby. The aristocratic character of the school balked any attempts to create either much general industry or much religious idealism. Moreover, the liberal religious revival was less fresh in 1848 than it was in 1828. No one accused Vaughan of creating prigs. Harrovians at best were, for the most part, merely more moral and less inhumane barbarians than they had been in the old days.[3]

[1] Cf. How, op. cit., p. 145. Like Arnold he had his worshipful disciples. H. M. Butler, Vaughan's successor, 'fell, immediately and literally, into love and hero-worship for his Head-Master'. (Graham, op. cit., p. 28.)

[2] How, op. cit., p. 145.

[3] A Montagu Butler might be a fine student, a liberal, and an overconscientious prefect who fought his fellows in the interests of the master, as well as a good athlete. (Graham, op. cit., pp. 32, 36.) A very few might be moved by the Reverend John Smith, who specialized in saintly example and teaching. (Graham, op. cit., p. 137.) Later Farrar, Bowen, and Bosworth Smith were each to influence a few. But most boys remained, much more even than at Rugby, little animals who spent their time in games and pranks on incompetent masters. As Minchin writes: 'what sense of gentlemanly conduct or even of honour has the average boy when face to face with a master who had not the faculty of keeping order?' (Minchin, *Old Harrow Days*, p. 8.) It was always, for example, against boy rules to learn the mathematics of the unjust Middlemist. Cribbing continued unabated. Hare's description of Harrow in the late forties is anything but encouraging. He speaks of bullying and ceaseless fagging, beatings for bad service to fag-masters, and blankettossings. (Augustus J. C. Hare, *The Story of My Life*, 2 vols., New York, 1896, Vol. I, pp. 169 ff.) Cricket fagging was especially bad. Rows, raids, mischief, and floggings by Oxenham made up much of the life of the time. For amusement big boys made little ones fight until the blood came, and fag at cricket.

If Harrow was less friendly to Arnoldian ideals than Rugby, it proved a more congenial home for the new athleticism than did the midland school. As early as 1836, Kennedy, then an assistant there, wrote that love of games was too strong among the boys for a teacher to get work from them.[1] With the better organization of the prefect system games became a regular means to effect the more manly moral ideals. Though Vaughan did not further athleticism as did Cotton, his system readily served it and his ideals were an excuse for it.[2] Harrow became one of the leaders of the new tendencies that were to reach fulfilment in the Public Schools in the sixties, seventies, and eighties.

C. THE NEW SCHOOLS—MARLBOROUGH

The most interesting early Victorian educational phenomenon was the founding of numbers of new Public Schools. Not for well over two hundred years before the creation of Cheltenham in 1841 had any school been established which either at its foundation or later became a Public School. Only Rugby and Shrewsbury had been added to the list of actual Public Schools in the previous hundred years. But after 1841 the creation of new schools and the transformation of old grammar schools into Public Schools became a familiar occurrence. Cheltenham was followed by Marlborough (1843), Rossall (1844), Wellington (1853), Clifton (1862), and Haileybury (1862) among new schools, and by Repton, Sherborne, and Uppingham among grammar schools converted into Public Schools.

These new schools were essentially the product of the

'Servility was . . . inculcated at Harrow in those days.' Little of mathematics, physical science, or modern languages was learned. Inane Latin verses, wretchedly taught, formed the staple; there was a 'total defect of discipline in tough studies'. (Hare, op. cit., Vol. I, p. 192; Horatio F. Brown, *John Addington Symonds*, 2 vols., London, 1895, Vol. I, p. 218.)

[1] Butler, *Life of S. Butler*, Vol. II, p. 134; Howson, op. cit., pp. 89 ff.
[2] Games probably did lessen chaos and casual bullying, but they exacted their usual toll: uniformity. Frederic Harrison, despite his approval of the 'discipline of some kind, rude as that discipline is' of a Public School, found that that discipline was won at the price not only of freedom but of a really high morality. Schools put pressure on boys to force them into a pattern; the original became rebels. (Frederick Harrison, *Autobiographic Memoirs*, 2 vols., London, 1911, Vol. I, pp. 44, 60–65.)

The Public Schools: 1840-1860 347

demand of the new upper middle classes for an education. What was wanted was a cheaper education than Harrow or Eton or even Rugby supplied. Often, too, some special group was catered to or some modern need which older schools had been too conservative to supply was served. Marlborough, for example, was founded for 'sons chiefly of clergymen of the Church of England' who could not pay the prices of the aristocratic schools.[1] Cheltenham was the result of the efforts of a group of Evangelicals and was thus also, a significant sign of the times, of religious origin. Cheltenham combined day boys and boarders, had a classical and a modern side (or course) of equal rank—a bold innovation—and specialized in training for the Army.[2] Clifton, the last actually new school to be launched until Stowe was opened after the World War, specialized in systematic scientific teaching and the cultivation of individual tastes.[3]

If the demands of the middle classes were responsible for the founding of schools and for some of their features, only the good repute that Arnold gave to the idea of a Public School can account for the fact that these schools became large boarding-schools. As a matter of fact the founders of Cheltenham had no idea that they were going to establish a large Public School.[4] Moreover, it was Arnold who dictated the principles that the new schools followed; oftener than not his disciples became their head masters. At Marlborough, Cotton in 1851 and then Bradley in 1858, both pupils of Arnold and teachers at Rugby, revived a school that had virtually collapsed. Dr. Percival at Clifton was a fervent disciple of Arnold's and made his school a colony of Rugby. In 1879 he claimed that the school had been successful because he had taught 'old school patriotism and public spirit' as had Arnold.[5] Cheltenham conformed to the Rugby system of government and imported football straight from Rugby in 1851.[6] Haileybury, when it was

---

[1] Cf. *Great Public Schools*, p. 259, article by A. G. Bradley.
[2] *Great Public Schools*, pp. 121 ff., article b E. Scot Skirving.
[3] Ibid., p. 203. Founded in 1862, Clifton was a product of the liberal revival of the sixties.
[4] Ibid., p. 121.   [5] Ibid., p. 203.
[6] Ibid., p. 138. The use of the Rugby game is a touchstone of direct Rugby influence.

refounded in 1862—it had closed when Indian civil servants no longer had to be trained together—procured Butler from Rugby as head master.[1]

It is not necessary to discuss all the new schools, since they conform fairly well to one pattern. For several reasons Marlborough seems most worthy of detailed consideration. Starting out as it did on other than Arnoldian lines, it demonstrates most convincingly the way in which Arnold's principles in a strong man's hands can turn a number of boys into a traditional Public School, animated by Rugby ideals. Further, since its great head master, Cotton, was more affected by the spirit of the fifties than most of Arnold's disciples, Marlborough's history also illustrates more directly even than does that of Harrow the effect of new forces.

Marlborough started as a collection of pupils chosen by nomination, of which two-thirds, who had to pay less than others, were clergymen's sons. To make possible the relatively small fees demanded, all the boys were lodged in one ugly dormitory run by the school.[2] The cheapness—and in this as in other respects the early Marlborough resembles Charterhouse under Russell—attracted five hundred boys to the school in five years. Even so the fee was too low and the school almost collapsed financially in 1854 just after Cotton had made it, educationally, as good as any institution in the country.[3] It is noteworthy that it probably would have collapsed had Cotton not been able to recruit idealistic Rugby masters with missionary zeal at low prices.[4]

From 1843 to 1851 social conditions in the school grew worse and worse. To crowd five hundred boys into a small space was bad enough. But Marlborough (like Charterhouse) also lacked a past to give that cohesion and semblance of order which even the worst of the old schools exhibited.[5]

[1] *Great Public Schools*, p. 287, by Rev. L. S. Milford.
[2] Cf. A. G. Bradley, and others, *History of Marlborough*, London, 1893, pp. 56 ff. In the seventies the fees were equalized except for scholarships to seventy clergymen's sons, and a boarding-house system was started, thus bringing the school into conformity with others. (Cf. ibid., p. 192.)
[3] A. G. Bradley, op. cit., p. 112. [4] Ibid., p. 146.
[5] As Bradley says, 'the roughness which distinguished the School throughout its earlier years was due to the absence of traditions'. 'Nor was there yet any corporate reputation to maintain and to feel jealous of, or any intellectual or athletic heroes to emulate and be proud of.' (Bradley, op. cit., pp. 68, 112.)

The boys were a mere crowd without communal solidarity and *esprit de corps* or traditions of decency and morality. There was no prefect system and there were no games, since boys had no precedents in organizing them. Consequently chaos and force dominated Marlborough life.[1] Wilkinson, the head master, did little to improve conditions. With insufficient help and less knowledge of boys, he tried to manage the whole school himself on the old Keatian principle of unmitigated severity.[2] The ultimate effect of his system of spies and tyranny was an open rebellion in 1851, the last recorded in Public School annals.[3] Even in the quieter, more humane mid-Victorian days, a repetition of 1818 was possible wherever conditions were similar.

Soon after the rebellion Cotton was imported from Rugby to effect disciplinary and moral reform of the school. Though in a sense, since he did not have enough masters to try anything else, he had little choice but to use a self-governing system as his means of effecting these ends, it was not inevitable from the nature of the situation that he should have employed Arnold's oligarchical prefect system. But Cotton was an Arnoldian and used Arnold's methods because he believed in them.

Once having determined on the Rugby form of government, he faced a problem very different from Arnold's or Vaughan's. Like them he had to create loyalty to good customs among his older boys. But with Arnold the problem was one of transference of conservative feeling and loyalty from evil traditions to the ideals in which he believed. Cotton had to arouse the sentiments themselves, to create traditionalism, since in early Marlborough there had been no objects, good or bad, to inspire love and reverence. Cotton went about his task, in a sense an easier one than Arnold's, in much the same manner as had the Rugby master. By giving boys responsibility and by mingling sternness, sympathy, and exhortation in just the right proportions in his treatment of them, he secured loyalty to himself both

---

[1] Youthful exuberance made itself felt among the neighbours in poaching and roving games of one kind or another. Gangs formed and re-formed as ever new leaders arose. (Bradley, op. cit., p. 77.)
[2] Ibid., p. 67.   [3] Ibid., p. 126.

as the embodiment of ideals and as the substitute for old customs.[1] Once having secured this loyalty, he transferred it to the ideals for which he stood, of which the school and the customs that he established became the embodiment.

After Cotton's day an interesting and significant transformation took place with regard to the reverence and loyalty which he had created. The school and its customs had become the objects of these sentiments, and it was easy to forget that they were to be worshipped only as embodiments of ideals. Conservatism and snobbery made themselves felt, and, before long, patriotic feeling began to find customs good because they were established and Marlborough a fine place because it was aristocratic and old.

The only difficulty was that Marlborough was neither of ancient nor of upper-class origin. This did not, however, greatly impede those Marlburians who were ashamed of the 'quasi-charitable nature' and the comparative recentness of the school's inception. When fees were raised, upper-class snobbery conveniently forgot the purposes of the school's foundation. As Bradley naïvely remarks, Marlborough outgrew 'any prejudices worth noticing that might have clung to it' because of its original cheapness.[2] Moreover, conservative attachment soon invented a substitute for a long history. Bradley devotes fifty pages of his history—pages which in a history of Eton would discuss the school in the fifteenth century—to the antiquity of the town. He then begins his discussion of the school by saying that the fact that the central building, Seymour Mansion, was an old inn gave Marlburians extra associations and affections to make up for deficiencies of age, and helped to 'stimulate the patriotism for which Marlburians are so unquestionably conspicuous'.[3]

Seen in retrospect, the story of Arnold's influence at Marlborough has thus its ironic aspects. He was—indirectly of course—responsible for creating the very evils that he

[1] Cf. Bradley, op. cit., p. 139.
[2] Ibid., p. 54. To-day, he says, the country gentlemen and clergymen who send their sons there would rather pay more than they can afford than send boys to a charity school.
[3] Bradley, op. cit., p. 61. As a matter of fact sentimentalists did not require great age as an object of feeling. At Cheltenham a thirty-five-year-old chapel was antiquated enough to cause conservative boys to lament its destruction.

fought against in other schools, because his system, growing out of an older one, contained within it the seeds of those evils. Viewed from the point of view of traditionalists, Cotton, by basing the *esprit de corps* which he created on school ideals, served the purpose of providing an object for loyalty as a temporary substitute for old customs and old walls, necessarily lacking at first. Given the desire to worship the past, natural to the upper classes and encouraged by Arnold, it did not take long before Marlborough was able to dispense with ideals as the object of worship and take its place as part of the traditional Public School system.

If Cotton was a loyal Arnoldian, he did not make Marlborough a replica of Rugby. Both Cotton and his successor Bradley were men closer to the spirit of the fifties than were Arnold and Vaughan. They were sterner and blunter men, less passionately religious and intellectual.[1] Moreover, they came to Marlborough when the religious revival was even more on the wane than when Vaughan arrived at Harrow. Further, Cotton, especially, came to a school whose greatest need was discipline. Probably for all these reasons Cotton stressed athletics more than any previous master had done. If Tom Hughes was the first in literature to glorify athletics as moral discipline, Cotton was the first to do so in practice, and it is worth commenting on that Hughes mentions Cotton, then assistant at Rugby, with high praise in *Tom Brown's Schooldays*. Cotton very consciously used organized games, imported from Rugby, as a weapon in the war on immorality, as an antidote to lack of discipline,[2] and as a means of breaking down master-boy hostility. The playing-fields became the centre of school activity.[3] Over a third of the history of Marlborough is a history of athletic records.

If Cotton was an influence tending to debase Arnold's coinage, it is worth nothing that there was one man at Marlborough in its early days who worked in the direction of both Arnold's highest liberal and moral ideas. This man, later so important in connexion with both the Public School Commission and the literature about schools, was Frederick

---

[1] Pearson accused Cotton of undue severity when he was at Rugby. (Pearson, op. cit., p. 28.)
[2] Cf. Bradley, op. cit., p. 137.   [3] Ibid., p. 147.

W. Farrar. He was a fighting liberal in intellectual matters. In regard to social and moral questions he was virtually the last early Victorian who preached the high idealism that was characteristic of Arnold.[1] No Arnoldian prefect was ever as much of a prig as the heroes of *Eric* and *St. Winifred's*. It is significant that Farrar was in politics and religious matters part of the liberal-conservative reform movement which, in different ways, included Arnold, Coleridge, Maurice, Kingsley, and Hughes. At college he was a member of the respectably liberal 'Apostles' whose most famous member was Tennyson.[2] As assistant at Marlborough he won hearts by kindness, stimulated to intellectual achievement, and inspired many to noble and chivalrous idealism.[3] He hated athletics, though using them to cement friendship with boys, and was a bitter opponent of athleticism.[4] Unfortunately Farrar lacked what Arnold, Vaughan, and Cotton had, toughness and sternness. Though a successful master at Harrow for fifteen years, he failed as head master of Marlborough when he returned there in 1870.

D. SHREWSBURY

Of the old schools relatively free from Arnold's direct influence Shrewsbury was the only one that possessed a living tradition both different from Arnold's and from that of the old Public School. Until well into the second half of the century this tradition, with its emphasis on the intellectual and on emulation, dominated Shrewsbury life in the person of Butler's successor, Kennedy. Kennedy had been Butler's favourite pupil and had been enthusiastically recommended by his predecessor.[5] At school he had been a fine scholar, winning an undergraduate ode prize when merely a schoolboy, and was head boy at Shrewsbury when not yet sixteen. He was probably a very poor athlete, and, as we have seen,

---

[1] Marlborough, in its earliest days under Cotton, inspired him with devoted idealism. As he says, 'how we all loved it! How boys and masters alike worked for it! What a pride they felt, even in its humility.' Life, indeed, is made worth while by worship, by surrender to God of self. (Farrar, *Life of Farrar*, p. 66.)
[2] Ibid., p. 39.   [3] Ibid., pp. 53 ff.   [4] Ibid., p. 33.
[5] Butler, *Life of S. Butler*, Vol. II, p. 132.

The Public Schools: 1840-1860

disapproved of the enthusiasm for games at Harrow, where he went as master from 1830 to 1835. Thus equipped by nature and by training, Kennedy was an ideal pilot to steer Shrewsbury along the course already marked out for her. For thirty years he ruled the school in humble imitation of his great predecessor.[1]

But Kennedy was not Butler, and even when most faithful to the latter's ideas he perverted them. He was, in a sense, too enamoured of the Shrewsbury system, and thus changed it by carrying it to an extreme never contemplated by his master. In his passion for classical scholarships he concentrated all his attention on his clever boys and pushed them so fast that they might spend four out of five years in the sixth form.[2] Kennedy thus evinced in the intellectual field the same tendency to exert pressure on his boys that Arnold exhibited in the moral. Samuel Butler the Younger in *The Way of All Flesh* has indeed painted a caricature of his master (Dr. Skinner) which resembles in many ways Strachey's picture of Arnold.[3] He refers to the ' "simpleminded and childlike earnestness of his character", an earnestness which might be perceived by the solemnity with which he spoke even about trifles', and to the power which Kennedy possessed of moulding his pupils' minds after the model of his own, and thus stamping 'an impression upon them which was indelible in after-life'.[4] The reaction to Kennedy which Butler's opinions express was, it may be added, about as successful as the similar conservative reaction

---

[1] Ibid., p. 163.   [2] *History of Shrewsbury*, p. 216.

[3] Butler drew a different picture of Kennedy in the life of his grandfather from the one he painted in the novel. In the *Life and Letters*, the later book, Kennedy appears as one who treated the younger Samuel with forbearance, and administered a school 'free from either priggishness or blackguardism'. But in contrast to the two portraits of Dr. Butler, the early sketch of Kennedy was the considered opinion of his pupil. Speaking of the *Life and Letters*, Butler wrote, 'I do not believe any one would gather from my book what my real opinion of Kennedy is.' That real opinion can be deduced from his remark that he used to call 'that old fool Professor Kennedy a genius'. (Cf. Henry Festing Jones, *Samuel Butler, A Memoir*, 2 vols., 1919, Vol. I, p. 154; Vol. II, p. 267; Butler, *Life of S. Butler*, Vol. II, pp. 163–64.)

[4] Butler hated Kennedy because the head master cared too much about false quantities and believed that work was a duty and pleasure a sin. He revolted consciously against priggishness at school as much as Hughes had revolted unconsciously against it. Butler chose the less desirable boys as his friends, avoiding Kennedy's favourites. (Cf. Samuel Butler, *The Way of All Flesh*, Modern Library, New York, n.d., pp. 110–11.)

to Arnold. Passionate intellectuality as well as passionate moral idealism could be and was checked. But the regularization and complication of school life which implied pressure and the destruction of freedom could not be stopped since they were the result of the dominant forces of the age.

If Kennedy found himself unconsciously receptive to the ideas of the time in his use of pressure, he did not so readily respond to most new tendencies. Towards some, such as organized games, he was definitely hostile, and, though they made their appearance, he held them in check.[1] Towards others he made half-hearted and unsuccessful gestures. Thus, though Shrewsbury introduced French and mathematics, they were not successfully taught until Kennedy resigned in 1866. Again, though, because of humanitarian agitation, Kennedy reduced the number of boys in each house and improved the ventilating system, health conditions were still none too good in 1860.

Finally, and most important, though to the influence of Arnold Kennedy was certainly not hostile, he was only partially successful in translating Arnold's ideas into practice. He introduced a sixth-form system of responsibility and trust,[2] and methods of teaching religion suited to boys. Through these and other means Kennedy seems to have created a reasonably disciplined and moral school: even Samuel Butler admits that the 'awful accounts of Dr. Skinner's temper, and of the bullying' about which he had heard before entering the school were much exaggerated.[3] But Kennedy did not produce, as did Arnold, boys notable for consciousness of duty or high moral idealism. He simply was not fitted to do so. If he produced a few good scholars, it was because he was probably, as How says, the 'greatest teacher of his century', a man able to arouse by his own living interest and encouragement a love of the classics and of work.[4] But he had not Arnold's power in moral matters. He was too tyrannical and stern, and lacked the latter's ability to attach his boys to him or to move them to chivalric

---

[1] How, op. cit., p. 106.
[2] Ibid., pp. 107–08. He fought, however, against legalized fagging, just as Butler had done, and prevented its installation.
[3] Butler, *The Way of All Flesh*, pp. 115, 126.   [4] How, op. cit., p. 116.

deeds. Primarily an intellectualist, with narrow classical gifts, Kennedy committed Shrewsbury to an ideal and a way of life that nearly brought about its destruction. The age demanded a relatively greater concern for the moral than Kennedy evinced. Consequently, despite the latter's abilities, Shrewsbury lost over half of its two hundred and ninety-six students between 1832 and 1841.[1] Kennedy indeed had to fight hard to prevent the townspeople from turning Shrewsbury back into a free non-classical local grammar school.[2] The fight was not over until 1866 when Kennedy's contention that Shrewsbury had always been a royally chartered school preparing for the universities and made up mostly of 'alieni' was finally upheld.[3] In that year the new governing body formed by the Public School Commission reduced the number of burgesses who were to be educated free to forty and provided that these forty were soon to be abolished.[4] By this time Shrewsbury had fairly well conformed to the ordinary Public School pattern; it had discovered that the power of dominant ideas could be denied only at the risk of extinction.

E. WINCHESTER

Winchester historians have always proudly claimed that theirs was the oldest and most conservative and at the same time the most progressive of schools. Wykeham has 'still his seventy faithful boys in these presumptuous' days of Queen Victoria. And still

> Shall his white-robed children, as age on age rolls by,
> At Oxford and at Winchester, give thanks to God most High.

They 'learn the old truths, speak the old words, tread in the ancient ways'.[5] Yet Winchester, the heart and symbol of the Public School system, has grown 'gradually, steadily, and beneficially'.[6]

[1] *History of Shrewsbury*, p. 151.
[2] Though the Harrow tradesmen had carried on a similar struggle, they never came as close to victory as did those of Shrewsbury.
[3] How, *Six Great Schoolmasters*, p. 111.   [4] *History of Shrewsbury*, p. 158.
[5] Charles Wordsworth, *Early Life*, pp. 399, 400.
[6] George Moberly, *Five Short Letters to Sir William Heathcote, etc.*, London, 1861, p. 8.

If these statements mean merely that Winchester has both remained the same and changed with the times they find perfect exemplification in the school's history from 1832 to 1860. The school responded sooner and more readily than any Public School except Rugby to the moral and religious agitation of the twenties and thirties. At the same time the reforms that occurred were not, despite the influence recorded by Moberly, dictated by Arnold, but grew out of the past of the school as interpreted by Winchester's own masters, and assumed a form indigenous to Winchester. If, on the other hand, the contention of historians implies that there was any mystic perfection in the combination of old and new that was the Winchester of 1840 or 1850 there are grounds for serious disagreement. The school was in anything but a progressive condition throughout most of that period and had lost a good deal of its patronage by the sixties when Ridding brought about its rejuvenation.

To the two men who guided Winchester's destinies, George Moberly, head master from 1835 to 1866, and Charles Wordsworth, master in college, moral and religious reform was the great need of the day. If their names are important in Wykehamist history, it is because they tried to bring about, through a revivified religious teaching and a reform of the prefect system, a changed moral tone comparable to that which Arnold had created at Rugby. Undeniably they were partially successful; Wordsworth claims that by 1844 over half the boys were in the habit of being confirmed.[1] At the same time Winchester was never Rugby. There were never many deeply religious boys there; there was always a good deal of bullying and rather odious fagging.[2] Most boys came out of Winchester having imbibed at best little more than the traditional 'judgment, decision, and self-reliance' that made for worldly survival.[3]

The comparative failure of Moberly and Wordsworth can be traced as much to the traditional system and principles which they used as to their personal shortcomings. In the

[1] Wordsworth, *Early Life*, pp. 200 ff.
[2] Cf. How, op. cit., pp. 54 ff.; (R. B. Mansfield) *School Life at Winchester College*, London, 1866, pp. 18 ff.
[3] (Mansfield) op. cit., p. 20.

The Public Schools: 1840–1860

first place, they were handicapped by the religion which they inherited and of which they approved. Winchester had from its foundation been Tory and High Church, and both Moberly and Wordsworth were Newmanites in their sympathies. Moberly was most insistent that there must 'be a system of practical religion, and that practical religion the religion of the Church'.[1] Wordsworth was proud of the fact that the 'general awakening' in religious matters 'with us at Winchester *partook decidedly of a Church character*, such as Arnold's teaching and example, however excellent in their way, had little or no tendency to create'.[2] It was, indeed, to Wykeham himself and to Bishop Thomas Ken in the reign of Charles II that Wordsworth looked for guidance in the religious reforms that he instituted.[3] In practice this meant a religion narrowly formal and forbiddingly authoritative, one that could appeal neither to the personal interests nor the hearts of boys.[4]

Moberly never seems to have understood this fact. Though he took a personal interest in confirmation, he confined his sermons to other than school subjects, and taught his boys a cold if impressive theology in chapel and at divinity lessons. He was an ecclesiastic, a priest in charge of souls, rather than a head master of boys.[5] Wordsworth, on the other hand, saw the unsuitableness of mere formalism, and therefore modified his teachings to suit his hearers. His *Christian Boyhood* sermons, dedicated in book form to the 'cause of Christian Education, especially in our Public Schools', dealt with the practical duties of Christianity in terms that boys could understand.[6] Obedience to God became, in school terms, staying in bounds, responding audibly in chapel, not allowing others to crib, studying hard, and doing one's duty as a prefect.[7] Wordsworth's general theme was, as with Arnold, the irreconcilability of school public opinion and the privileges of a communicant. But even Wordsworth could not escape the authoritarianism

---

[1] How, op. cit., p. 68.   [2] Wordsworth, *Early Life*, p. 278.
[3] Ibid., p. 206.   [4] Leach, *History of Winchester*, pp. 430 ff.
[5] Cf. How, op. cit., pp. 71 ff.
[6] Charles Wordsworth, *Christian Boyhood at a Public School*, 2 vols., London, 1846, Vol. I, p. v.
[7] Ibid., Vol. I, pp. 17, 59, 381, 479.

and conservatism inherent in High Church teachings. He went so far as to insist that all laws from a legitimate authority represent the will of God, a position that hardly leaves much room for the dictates of conscience.[1] Public School boys might by subtle pressures be made to conform to such tenets; they would not find them very inspiring.

If the religion that Moberly and Wordsworth adopted stultified their efforts, the social system from the past, which they attempted to use, thwarted them no less effectively, though in a different way. Winchester had, as we have seen, the most fully developed prefect system of any of the Public Schools. Moberly, like Arnold, borrowed this system and tried to turn it to his own purposes. He felt, on the one hand, that legalized prefectorial government was good in itself, since it meant that boys have a 'place in a series, and, with that place, duties, offices, rights, and privileges'.[2] He believed that a Public School is a desirable institution chiefly because it is a place 'where certain of the most trustworthy boys are empowered to exercise some real authority among their schoolfellows, for the purposes of order, morality, and protection'.[3] At the same time he realized that the master's problem is 'how to cultivate interest and secure their [boys'] habits and character up to eighteen years old.'[4] Moberly and Wordsworth tried to solve this problem by mixing directly with their prefects[5]—Wordsworth was a good athlete and joined the boys in their games[6]—and by treating their lieutenants with manly and respectful confidence.[7]

Yet Moberly did not succeed in creating a prefect system after Arnold's heart. For a man who did not believe in flogging except as a last resort, he had to do a good deal of it.[8] Even so he never secured moral control over the system, and

---

[1] Wordsworth, op. cit., Vol. I, p. 400. [2] How, op. cit., p. 67.
[3] Moberly, *Letters to Heathcote*, p. 13. According to Moberly, the results of the system are that 'there grows for the most part upon young men bred at public schools a facility of using their powers, an easy skill in taking and keeping their position in life, an absence of absurd pretension, a general practical modesty, a self-reliance and moral presence of mind, a good sense, an early maturity of practical judgment, which are of unspeakable value in all the conduct of their lives'. (How, op. cit., p. 66.)
[4] How, op. cit., pp. 66–67. [5] Ibid., p. 54.
[6] Charles Wordsworth, *Early Life*, pp. 229 ff.
[7] Moberly, op. cit., p. 13. [8] Ibid., p. 87.

The Public Schools: 1840–1860

at one time there was almost a rebellion: the morality that boys imbibed—a 'keen sense of honour' and 'patriotic feeling'—continued to be the result of rigid custom among the boys, not of master influence.[1] The system that Moberly inherited from the past, with its traditional independence from master control, proved too strong for Moberly. It is possible that Arnold might have broken through the barrier of boy law, but he would, admittedly, have had a harder time than at Rugby, where tradition was less crusty.

Neither the external conditions already mentioned, nor others such as overcrowding and lack of masters,[2] were of course solely responsible for the failure of Winchester to undergo a moral reform similar to that at Rugby. Had Moberly or Wordsworth been Arnold he might have done a great deal more than he did. But neither Wordsworth nor Moberly was cut after the pattern of the Rugby head master. Particularly was this true of Moberly, who is described as small, elegant, and cautious, and subject to fits of disgust that made him at times incapable of ruling at all.[3] Though often impressive, he had neither his great contemporary's driving energy, his power of creating love, nor his prophetic inspiration as moralist or teacher.[4] It is as doubtful whether he could have reformed Rugby as it is whether Arnold could have remade Winchester.

If Winchester reformed herself at least partially in moral matters, she remained stubbornly behind the times in other ways. For some of Winchester's backwardness Moberly was not responsible. If New Commoners, which Moberly built in 1844, was ugly and small, and so unwholesome that epidemics were frequent, driving away the health-conscious upper classes, the blame lies mostly with the warden and fellows, who continued to steal the surplus funds of the school.[5] On the shoulders of the ecclesiastical governors belongs also the onus of perpetuating the system of drawing

---
[1] (Mansfield) *School Life at Winchester*, pp. 24, 42, 54.
[2] Cf. Leach, op. cit., p. 434; How, op. cit., p. 78.
[3] How, op. cit., pp. 48, 50, 82. [4] Ibid., p. 54.
[5] Cf. Leach, *History of Winchester*, p. 435. Fortunately the University Commission provided competitive scholarships in 1857.

Winchester masters almost exclusively from New College,[1] a system which 'proved fatal to nearly every reform that was not forced on the College from outside'.[2] Yet Moberly was responsible for Winchester's backwardness in several ways, since in other than moral matters he was a conservative. He took masters from outside of New College only as a last resort. Moreover, he impeded reform of the curriculum as long as he was head master. Education was to be literary, that is classical, not modern 'heterogeneous pieces of knowledge'.[3] The only concessions to modernity that he would make, even as late as the sixties, were examinations of a slightly more difficult nature[4] and English explanations in Latin grammar books.[5] The blast of the Public School Commission alone could shake Winchester loose from her customary moorings.

F. THE CITY SCHOOLS—WESTMINSTER, CHARTERHOUSE

The location of Westminster and Charterhouse in London proved the chief conditioning factor in their mid-nineteenth century histories. The Victorian upper classes with their increasing demands for health and for games refused to go to schools crowded into the confines of London's ill-smelling streets. Ancient traditions went for naught when faced by the practical demands of a realistic century. Both schools declined alarmingly in numbers. In 1835 Charterhouse had only ninety-nine boys, and, though in 1853 it had one hundred and seventy-eight, it was hopelessly handicapped in its race for patronage with such schools as Cheltenham

---
[1] Wordsworth was the first non-Wykehamist for three hundred years to be a master.
[2] Leach, op. cit., p. 439.   [3] Cf. How, op. cit., p. 54.   [4] Ibid., p. 51.
[5] Moberly, op. cit., pp. 16 ff. In this connexion Wordsworth's experience with a new Greek grammar that he wrote illuminates humorously the intellectual conservatism and the absurd patriotism of the older schools. Wordsworth's grammar, written, in accordance with tradition, in Latin, was meant to replace the incomplete, incorrect, and confused Eton grammar. Wordsworth, so as not to antagonize Eton, wrote the book only after Hawtrey had declined to do so. Even then Eton refused at first to use it, though Rugby, Harrow and most other schools accepted it immediately. Some time after publishing his book, Wordsworth discovered that the old Eton grammar had been written, not by an Etonian, but by an Old Westminster. The article in which he published his findings was suppressed. (Cf. Wordsworth, *Early Life*, pp. 177 ff.)

and Marlborough.[1] Westminster's enrolment dropped as low as sixty-seven in 1841, and, despite reforms in the fifties, seldom exceeded one hundred.[2]

Progressive Old Westminsters and Old Carthusians became seriously perturbed over the plight of their alma maters. But when, responding to a suggestion in *The Times* in 1858, they advocated the school's removal to the country,[3] the opposition from conservative lovers of the *genius loci* proved unexpectedly strong. The struggle that ensued, which brought into glaring relief the abyss that yawned between conservatism and the forces of a progressive and materialistic age, belongs to the period of the Public School Commission, and cannot, therefore, be discussed in detail here. Suffice it to say that Charterhouse was eventually removed to the country in 1882, whereas Westminster remained in London and became a mixture of day- and boarding-school. Even if one's sympathies are with the progressives, it may be added, it is difficult to walk through quiet little Dean's Yard under the shadow of Westminster Abbey and not feel the force of conservative arguments.

Failing numbers seem to have thrown a pall over the life of both schools and to have reduced their early Victorian histories to the record of intellectual and moral stagnation. Particularly was this true of Charterhouse, where the flat picture of mediocre teaching, a Spartan life, severe fagging and petty, exacting customs is unbroken by any hillock of reform.[4] In many ways Westminster was in a worse condition than Charterhouse. But its history has interest in that there was an attempt, although a relatively unsuccessful one, to reform the school along Arnoldian lines. That such an attempt was made at all is an excellent illustration of the force of Arnold's ideas; that the results were so negligible is convincing evidence of the power of tradition and of conservative governors.

The Reverend Henry George Liddell, Westminster's reformer, came to the head-mastership in 1846. Goodenough's disastrous reign of twenty-five years had convinced Old

[1] Davies, *Charterhouse in London*, pp. 273 ff. [2] Forshall, *Westminster*, p. 107.
[3] *The Times*, August 12th 1858, p. 8.
[4] Davies, *Charterhouse in London*, pp. 282, 287, 289.

Westminsters and even the Dean and Chapter of Westminster Abbey that the school needed a strong man, even an outsider, to revive its fortune. Dean Buckland, indeed, seems to have been so anxious both to improve conditions of health and to end the 'tyranny and cruelty among the boys' that he asked Dean Stanley for 'a detailed account of great parts of the system at Rugby'.[1] With Buckland's support, Liddell was able not only to secure new buildings and masters, but to introduce Arnold's system of trust and simple personal chapel sermons.[2] By such means he seems to have succeeded in making college less rough and independent, and in raising the tone of the school somewhat.[3]

Unfortunately Dean Buckland's support was only limited, and Liddell lost his fight to gain control of the school and to accomplish his reforms in spite of a Dean who admitted that he would never have appointed Arnold head master of Westminster.[4] Moreover, the conservative opposition of boys governed by a rigorous traditional life was as successful against Liddell as it was against Moberly. Reform never cut very deeply into the life of the school. Markham's account of Westminster in the fifties, which almost exactly parallels Froude's in the thirties, pictures the traditional boy life independent of masters and governed by exacting and often cruel customs.[5]

G. ETON

Of all the Public Schools, Eton held out the longest against both liberal religious reform and the forces of industrialism. Oblivious to the severe attacks make on her in the early thirties, she continued to manifest until well into the forties, most of the characteristic vices of the pre-Arnoldian school. Oppidan life, though better than life in college, often led, because of its freedoms, to waste, ruin, and wretchedness.[6]

[1] Henry L. Thompson, *Henry George Liddell, D.D.*, London, 1899, p. 119.
[2] Ibid., pp. 101 ff.   [3] Ibid., p. 93.   [4] Ibid., p. 119.
[5] Cf. Zeta (James Anthony Froude), *Shadows of the Clouds*, London, 1847; Captain F. Markham, *Recollections of a Town Boy at Westminster*, London, 1903.
[6] As Thring, who in later years at Uppingham profited by his experiences at Eton, wrote: 'It was not training, for training does not mean some boys turning out well in spite of disadvantages.' Very few masters tried really to

College was a plague spot. It continued to be Eton's poor relation, and was scorned as such by the rest of the school. No aristocrat would have gone there, for 'such associates, cheek by jowl with the sons of Windsor tradesmen, would no more have amalgamated than the Rhine with the Rhône'.[1] The life led in college was, as in earlier days, crowded and unhealthy, and exhibited in miniature all the evils of the pre-Arnoldian school.[2] Of its effects A. D. Coleridge wrote, 'There is no exaggeration in saying that some of the best men I have ever known ran a considerable risk of becoming the worst, from the ordeal of Long Chamber. . . . Our forefathers, of yore, possibly fared rather worse than their descendants, but ours was a sufficiently stern baptism in the expiring days of Long Chamber.'[3]

Even the worst evils of college were difficult to change. Not only did the 'higher authorities' not want a 'public exposure of the system', but the boys, with their natural conservatism, resented reform and, when it came, shed tears over the 'order and cleanliness' and the hot-water pipes that made

train boys or to teach them. As a result there was idleness, vice, and suffering. If traditions and the absence of legal prefects curbed much tyranny, there was a good deal of casual bullying and usurped authority. (Cf. George R. Parkin, *Edward Thring*, London, 1900, pp. 22–23.)

[1] A. D. Coleridge, *Eton in the Forties*, pp. 82–83. All collegers, but especially the day boys, were treated as inferiors. According to Leslie Stephen, even the masters felt that these latter must be tradesmen or sons of royal footmen spying on old Eton customs. (Leslie Stephen, *Life of J. F. Stephen*; Frederic William Maitland, *The Life and Letters of Leslie Stephen*, New York, 1906, p. 77.) As a compensation for feeling inferior to oppidans, collegers could in turn look down on some in their own ranks. 'The sons of Eton masters were received on equal terms, but the same privileges were not conceded to the sons of Eton or Windsor doctors or solicitors, royal servants, or successful tradesmen. . . . For some mysterious reason, the farther away from Eton a boy lived, the more he was respected.' Among the 'accepted' in college there was a fierce solidarity, which extended to love of 'hereditary dirt', a savoury legacy from the past. (Cf. Coleridge, op. cit., pp. 4, 23.)

[2] Though there was 'frolic' and fun in that 'land of misrule . . . with its strange code of traditional boy-law' (Parkin, *Thring*, p. 22), more often 'six-form tyranny, though disapproved of, remained unchecked' and encouraged brutality in others. Boys often 'underwent privations that might have broken down a cabin-boy, and would be thought inhuman if inflicted on a galley slave'. Boys loved to birch others, rehearsing the formalities of an execution on unoffending victims. Even a man who later was the kindest of men made his fag eat a sandwich of tallow so that his own cold mutton would not taste so bad. Mr. Okes reported that 'my master was a beast and a bully, and the reign of terrorism upon certain occasions was a horror I shall never forget'. (Coleridge, op. cit., pp. 2–4.)

[3] Coleridge, op. cit., p. 1.

life tolerable.¹ Yet change was to come, in Long Chamber and elsewhere. Eton felt the spirit of the age both in practical innovations and in a changed tone and atmosphere. Powerful traditions, deadening ecclesiastical machinery, the prestige which kept Eton's enrolment high even at the worst periods of misrule, might work against change, but Eton could no more remain isolated from her social environment than could Rugby. Her ideals and her organization were as much at the mercy of parents' desires as were those of the meanest grammar school. When her aristocratic supporters ceased to be satisfied with the social prestige that she offered and demanded moral and intellectual reform and efficiency in producing colonial leaders, she had to respond or cease to be England's leading school.

Eton reform differed from reform in other schools less in kind than in the agents that brought it about. Modification was not, as at most schools, the work of one or even of two men. Further, none of Arnold's disciples had a hand in the remoulding of Eton, and most of those who did the work of reform were but very indirectly influenced by the Rugby master. Gladstone went so far as to say that Eton was not 'sensibly affected by any influence extraneous to the place itself'.²

The chief agent of new forces was John Hawtrey, who succeeded Keate as head master in 1834 and ruled Eton until 1852.³ That the idea of reform as well as its difficulties was in his mind when he took over the head mastership is evidenced by a letter he wrote to Samuel Butler of Shrewsbury.

'I am here in great embarrassment. A large body of malcontents who have no responsibility abuse our whole system, and advise all sort of absurd changes. On the other hand I am checked by an attachment to the old course of things

¹ Coleridge, op. cit., pp. 41, 42. Coleridge wrote, 'I saw the last days of Long Chamber, and the first of the new buildings, and, in common with others of my unreasoning comrades, I cordially resented the change.' (Coleridge, op. cit., p. 6.) ² Tucker, *Life of Selwyn*, p. 54.
³ Hawtrey spent most of his sixty-two years of life as student, teacher, head master, and provost at the school to which, as he wrote, 'I owe everything'. (Francis St. John Thackeray, *Memoir of Edward Craven Hawtrey*, London, 1896, p. 2.)

in the ruling power of Eton, which it is very difficult indeed to make any impression upon. I am desirous therefore to get all the authority I can for improvements which seem to me absolutely necessary to meet the demands of the Universities upon us.'[1]

If for years Hawtrey was hindered by the authorities from making reforms, his patience was rewarded when the liberal and friendly Francis Hodgson became provost in 1840. With his aid Hawtrey upset much in the old Eton system.[2] Above all, living conditions in college were improved; Long Chamber was abolished, new buildings erected, and more servants and better meals provided. Probably the boldest, if not the most important of Hawtrey's reforms, was the destruction of Montem, Eton's most cherished ceremony. In the intellectual field mathematics were introduced, though not on an equality with classics. Modern languages were encouraged, though not as part of the regular system. Examinations for all forms and for entrance to Eton and King's were instituted, chiefly at Samuel Butler's instigation. The number of masters was increased, the forms reduced in size, books improved, and the private tutor system abolished. In the moral field Hawtrey began the destruction of houses controlled by dames, who were beyond the reach of school discipline, encouraged better chapel sermons, and helped to organize games, making them compulsory in college.[3]

Probably even more important than any specific reforms was the change in the spirit of teaching and discipline that Hawtrey instituted. He had been trained under Goodall and had thus acquired an understanding of the classics and an enthusiasm for self-culture. His object was to inspire boys to love of learning, not to beat them into passive

---

[1] Butler, *Life of S. Butler*, Vol. II, p. 91.
[2] Hodgson's biographer, as well as others like Tucker, believe that Hodgson was more responsible for reform than was Hawtrey. (Hodgson, *Memoir of the Reverend Francis Hodgson*, 2 vols., London, 1878, Vol. II, p. 254; Tucker, *Eton of Old*, p. 214.)
[3] For full discussion of these reforms, cf. Lyte, *History of Eton*, pp. 438 ff.; Tucker, op. cit., pp. 214 ff.; How, op. cit., p. 16; Thackeray, *Life of Hawtrey*, p. 85; Major Gambier-Parry, *Annals of an Eton House*, London, 1907, pp. 10 ff.

acquiescence, and as assistant under Keate no less than as head master, he produced love of learning in many of his pupils such as Hallam and Praed.[1] The spirit of kindness and encouragement, unknown to Keate, animated the whole of Hawtrey's approach. He trusted his boys and quietly rebuked them when they were not gentlemanly in much the same way that Arnold did.[2] Coleridge records that he preached a stirring sermon in college in protest against bullies; 'never was a message more faithfully delivered on behalf of the timid, the eccentric, and the unsociable'.[3] As a result Hawtrey destroyed much of the hostility between master and boy, and began the spread of a more orderly, moral, and humanitarian spirit throughout Eton.

Unfortunately, Hawtrey not only did not try to make a number of needed reforms, but more important, he often failed to achieve ends in the intellectual and moral fields towards which he was striving. He did not develop a modern liberal system of education, nor did he substantially raise the standard of learning and morality among the many. Though for some of his failures he was not responsible,[4] for most of them he was. If he did not give the school a modern curriculum, it was because, brought up at Eton under a classical system, he was devoted to that system.[5] Again, if he did not make Eton resemble Rugby morally, it was partly from conservative disapproval of pressure and prefect systems, and partly from temperamental incapacity. He was not an Arnold, but a 'refined scholar, a courteous gentleman', the 'innate ceremoniousness' of whose nature often became mere foppishness.[6] He had neither Arnold's force, gusto, and organizing power, nor his prophetic magnetism.

Fortunately, there were many men at Eton who, if they could not entirely make up for Hawtrey's disabilities or overcome forces opposed to change, supplemented the head

[1] Thackeray, op. cit., p. 15.   [2] How, op. cit., p. 25.
[3] Coleridge, *Eton in the Forties*, p. 42.
[4] The redundant tutorial system and lack of masters were situations difficult to cope with at best. And there was opposition on all sides, even the liberal Hodgson fighting Hawtrey on the question of importing other than Kingsmen as masters.
[5] How, op. cit., p. 33. As head master and provost, he fought off the waves of liberal reform with all his strength.
[6] Thackeray, *Life of Hawtrey*, p. 97.

master's work in various ways. Hawtrey had the good sense to give a relative amount of freedom to his assistants,[1] and many of them used their opportunities to advantage. Particularly was this true in the intellectual field, in which, even before Arnold's death, a number of masters contributed to Eton's progress. If Eton education did not collapse in the thirties and forties, it was because the school boasted tutors like the Reverend Edward Coleridge and others who were kind, helpful, and worthy of respect, and who inspired such men as Thring and Northcote and A. D. Coleridge to love of learning.[2]

The most important of Eton's masters from an intellectual point of view was William Johnson Cory. In some respects he was a conservative, ignoring the discipline, manliness, and patriotism initiated by the new materialism and fighting against many important intellectual changes advocated by liberals in the sixties. Yet he called himself a liberal,[3] and in the sense that he believed in mental freedom and breadth and encouraged scientific interests in his students, he deserves the appellation better than many advocates of radical change. Cory's great contribution to Eton education was the literary stimulus that he imparted to those who came under the influence of his eccentric personality. In the increasingly materialistic Eton of the fifties Cory taught boys to read widely in modern authors such as Arnold, Meredith, and Ruskin.[4] With his best pupils he talked on Ptolemy, Copernicus, Newton, and Laplace as well as on Virgil and Cicero, and lectured on botany and political economy.[5] His was the incalculable personal touch for which the old Public School at its best allowed scope.

In the moral field, in which Hawtrey was particularly ineffective, there were numbers of men who helped to bring to Eton the new spirit abroad in the land. Most interesting

[1] Cf. Lyte, *History of Eton*, p. 408.
[2] Cf. Andrew Lang, *Life, Letters, and Diaries of Sir Stafford Northcote*, Edinburgh, 1891, pp. xv, 7; Parkin, op. cit., p. 18; A. D. Coleridge, op. cit., pp. 365 ff.
[3] *Extracts from the Letters and Journals of William Johnson Cory*, selected and arranged by Francis Warre Cornish, Oxford, 1897, pp. 57, 58.
[4] Oscar Browning, *Memories of Sixty Years at Eton, Cambridge and Elsewhere*, London, 1910, pp. 20, 23.
[5] Cf. Cory, *Letters*, pp. 53, 116, 255.

of these was Evans, who acquired one of Eton's large boarding-houses in 1838, and who brought into this world within a world more directly than did any other master the methods and ideals of Arnold.[1] Evans made the government of his house an oligarchy run by the captain and prefects, whom he trusted implicitly, and consequently improved the tone of the house to such an extent that he found admirers among figures in the outside world like Thackeray and Dickens.[2] Among other masters who helped in the work of moral reform Edward Coleridge, who brought religious influences to bear on Lord Northcote and helped to inspire the future Bishop Patteson to missionary zeal, and George Selwyn, whom Gladstone credits with producing most of Eton's religious earnestness in the thirties, and who was Patteson's chief teacher, deserve mention.[3] Later on there were many like Kegan Paul who created at Eton that 'atmosphere of a cultivated home in which impurity was unthinkable'.[4]

More interesting and probably more important than any of these influences was that of Bishop Patteson. In Patteson, who was at Eton in 1838 when Selwyn was at Windsor, about to go to New Zealand, the connexion between missionary fervour and imperialism begins to be explicit. A religious leader like Patteson or Selwyn arouses in boys ideal yearnings and directs them towards reformation of the poor unenlightened heathen in far-off New Zealand. These boys soon become, either consciously or unconsciously, agents in the exploitation of foreign markets. Patteson's biographer has put the matter charmingly: 'Indeed it was from the first understood that Eton, with the wealth that her children enjoyed in such large measure, should furnish "nerves and sinews" to the war which her son was about to wage with the darkness of heathenism, thus turning the minds of the boys to something beyond either their studies or their sports.'[5]

[1] Evans's was technically a dame's house because Evans was a drawing, not a classical master.
[2] Cf. Gambier-Parry, op. cit., pp. 26 ff., 83–84. He started the Arnoldian custom of praying, though with what success it is hard to say.
[3] Cf. Lang, op. cit., p. 10; Tucker, *Selwyn*, p. 24; How, op. cit., p. 29; Charlotte Mary Yonge, *Life of John Coleridge Patteson*, 2 vols., London, 1874, Vol. I, p. 29.
[4] Oscar Browning, op. cit., p. 26.   [5] Yonge, op. cit., Vol. I, p. 28.

The Public Schools: 1840–1860

By the time he was confirmed in 1842 Patteson, who was a cricketer and no puritan, had become a powerful moral force. It was 'very noticeable to Eton men' 'that the most popular oppidan of his day should have utterly ignored the supposed inferiority of the less wealthy section of the school'. When he threatened to leave the cricket team unless bad language was stopped, it apparently gave pause to a good many.[1] When later this popular alumnus became a missionary, his positive influence was as powerful as it was incalculable.

Finally, there was one change at Eton which was coming about in the fifties which required no specific agent. This was the ubiquitous spirit of athleticism. Games, for long Eton's most important activity, were becoming more and more organized and were beginning to exert an increasingly repressive influence on other activities and on individual initiative. By 1860 there were house cups and house colours. Romantic picturesque days on the river were giving place to fierce contests for places in the eight.[2] Public opinion, though without as yet the aid of masters, was beginning to coerce the reluctant into making sport their chief occupation.[3] And along with athleticism came a secularizing and military spirit. By 1860 many masters were laymen, and the rifle corps had been founded.[4] The religious revival had degenerated into Philistine efficiency.

In general, Eton in the late forties and fifties was in a state of transition between the old system of freedom, idleness, vice, and cruelty and the new system of relative humanitarianism, morality, educational efficiency, and conformity.[5] One could, indeed, make out a good case for the fact that Eton in the fifties was in an ideal state. Though athletics, house organization, more studies, closer relationship of master and

[1] Ibid., p. 39.
[2] Arthur Campbell Ainger, *Memories of Eton Sixty Years Ago*, London, 1917, p. 125.
[3] Cf. Gambier-Parry, op. cit., p. 131.   [4] Ainger, op. cit., pp. 241, 275.
[5] Creasy, writing a history of Eton in 1848, can say that though 'there is no place of education which is more frequently ignorantly assailed on the score of supposed defects' than Eton, 'there is no body of men who have made greater exertions to improve that which is committed to their charges than the present authorities of Eton'. They have 'completely remedied' many defects. (E. S. Creasy, *Some Account of the Foundation of Eton College, etc.*, London, 1848, p. iv.)

boy were gradually destroying freedom, individuality, and idealism, they had not completely won the battle. In its forms as well as in actuality the old unhampered freedom from interference existed more than at other schools; Eton, indeed, became the last refuge for Public School ideals that were being destroyed in other schools by Arnoldianism no less than by capitalism. At the same time many evils of the old system were disappearing.[1]

Most illustrative of the transition spirit was the fact that a boy like Swinburne, who, to the Philistine Lord St. Aldwyn was a 'horrid little boy, with a big red head and a pasty complexion, who looked as though a course of physical exercise would have done him good', was at least tolerated at Eton in 1849.[2] Weak and frail and as unable to fit into Eton life as Shelley, he was neither persecuted in the older Eton spirit nor made to conform to the new.[3] He was excused from athletics and spent his time reading, walking, and dreaming in a fairy world. 'None dreamt of interfering with him—as for bullying there was none of it.'[4] If Swinburne's fate was in part attributable to his courage, it must be remembered that courage did not save Shelley in 1800.

Unfortunately one can reverse the picture of Eton with equal truth. The new evils of standardization, vulgarization,

[1] Ainger, op. cit., pp. 17 ff.; Alfred Lubbock, *Memories of Eton and Etonians*, London, 1899, p. 206; Creasy, op. cit., p. 64. Fagging was less severe and was to some extent at any rate controlled by masters, who saw to it that the sixth form in college ruled with some mercy. Millings were much less frequent, a fact regretted by 'old boys', who mumbled threateningly about the next Battle of Waterloo. (Lubbock, op. cit., pp. 208 ff.). More friendly relations between masters and boys were at least beginning to exist.
[2] Edmund Gosse, *The Life of Algernon Charles Swinburne*, London, 1917, p. 14.
[3] Cf. Oscar Browning, op. cit., p. 108.
[4] Gosse, op. cit., p. 322. Henry Salt, whose testimony as a radical is worth having, claims that if Swinburne was not bullied he was teased to such an extent that he hated to face his schoolmates. (Cf. Henry S. Salt, *Memories of Bygone Eton*, London, 1928, p. 125.) Certain it is that if Swinburne was not cruelly treated, he was never really happy at Eton, Francis Warre Cornish's opinion to the contrary. He grew rebellious in 1853, and left the school. (Cf. Gosse, op. cit., p. 18.) Though the traditions of Eton 'touched his poet's soul the memories of the flogging block were his most vivid recollections, and served to alienate him from such of his former schoolmates as Oscar Browning who, Swinburne thought, had the power of flogging.' (Cf. Gosse, op. cit., p. 323; Oscar Browning, op. cit., p. 108.) George Lafourcade claims that Eton cultivated Swinburne's masochistic tendencies expressed in 'A Year's Letter', 'The Flogging Block', 'Lesbia Brandon', 'Eton: Another Ode', and the 'Whippingham Papers'. (Cf. George Lafourcade, *Swinburne, A Literary Biography*, London, 1932, p. 46.)

The Public Schools: 1840–1860

and futile educational efficiency were creeping in, and existed side by side with many of the vices of the old order. Master severity,[1] hostility between master and boy,[2] idleness, bullying, cruel fagging[3] and snobbery towards collegers[4] were still in good part the order of the day. Many of these evils were to remain until the twentieth century. Others were gradually destroyed in the sixties and seventies, but, since the days of Arnold's high idealism and broad intellectual principles were long past, old faults in the system were overcome only at the expense of allowing new enemies into the citadel.

[1] Keate's system of discipline lasted well into the fifties, and the studious Swinburne no less than the idle Lubbock was flogged plentifully. (Ainger, op. cit., p. 83; Lubbock, op. cit., pp. 12, 40; Lafourcade, op. cit., p. 46.) Where masters were too few it was felt necessary to 'cultivate in boys' minds the feeling that authority was always just round the corner'. (Ainger, op. cit., p. '89.) As Oscar Browning said, masters seldom know 'the magic force of sympathy or have wisely exercised it'. (Oscar Browning, op. cit., p. 26.)

[2] The master-boy relationship was one of armed neutrality. A boy seldom went to a tutor for help or advice; the boy world remained distinct, and was managed by the sixth form in college and the captain of the house among the oppidans. (Ainger, op. cit., pp. 36, 57; Lubbock, op. cit., pp. 245–247.)

[3] Cf. Ainger, op. cit., pp. 21, 57; Lubbock, op. cit., pp. 207, 208. As Oscar Browning wrote (op. cit., p. 18), 'If love be the foundation of morality, morality was entirely absent from our society.'

[4] The Eton product considered himself as possessing 'equality with all, and superiority to most'. (*Prospective Review*, July 1848, p. 350.) Oppidans snubbed collegers, and in the lower school there was open war, which included shin-kicking by big, stupid oppidans in the same form with bright collegers. (Ainger, op. cit., pp. 31, 74.)

CHAPTER III

DEFENCE AND CRITICISM

1840–1860

ASIDE from the criticism and glorification of Arnold already dealt with, there was far less comment either favourable or unfavourable with regard to Public Schools between 1840 and 1860 than there had been between 1815 and 1835. Most of what did exist was casual, fragmentary, and miscellaneous, and, unlike earlier discussion, it did not typically cut very deeply into the heart of the problem of Public School education. About only one question was there much open controversy, the curriculum, and, despite Wiese's remark that in 1852 all England was attacking the school system, even this question secured less attention than it had earlier or was to have later.

The comparative dearth of opinion about schools is readily explained. Criticism was hushed because most Englishmen liked their schools as they were in the fifties. Arnold's reforms, especially in the modified form in which they reached the schools, satisfied the increasingly conservative spirit of the age in all fields except the intellectual. As Wiese wrote, if schools are occasionally 'abused' it is only 'because they are loved'.[1] Dickens expressed the common attitude when he said that the Public Schools are fundamentally all right even though 'we may differ about the curriculum and other matters'.[2] There was little praise of schools because there was no need to answer non-existent attacks. When any one dared suggest a fault, as *The Times* did in regard to the prefect system in 1854, innumerable retorts were instantly forthcoming. Moreover, in the forties and fifties every Tom, Dick, and Harry who had been at a Public School did not feel called upon to give the world a gratuitous account of how much he loved his youth and his alma mater as he did in the seventies and after. Thackeray, who indulged his pleasure

[1] Wiese, *German Letters*, p. 14. [2] Forster, *Life of Dickens*, Vol. II, p. 280.

Defence and Criticism: 1840–1860   373

in recalling the past more often than almost any one else, expressed the opinion in *The Newcomes* that usually only the writer of memoirs was interested in his own youth.[1] It was not until Hughes set the example in *Tom Brown's Schooldays* that the flood of novels and recollections about schools began. Yet there were more writers of reminiscences in the second than in the first quarter of the century when the fashion actually began. Long before Hughes's novel there were, besides Thackeray's numerous publications, such books as the anonymous *Reminiscences of Eton* (1831), Nimrod's articles on Rugby (1835, 1842), Rowcroft's *Confessions of an Etonian* (1847), Zeta's (Froude's) *Shadows of the Clouds* (1847), and Old Rugbeian's *Recollections of Rugby* (1848).[2] These evidences of a growing interest in youth and Public Schools as subjects for writing are not numerous enough, however, to compensate for the dearth of controversial literature as compared with the previous period.

A. CONTROL

The problem of Public School government lay behind all questions of ends. Whether one wanted moral or intellectual reform or a change in the class nature of schools, the closed system of endowments stood in the way. Few Englishmen, however, were willing to face this fact in the forties and fifties. Occasionally an old boy would complain about the cost to his schools of fellows and provost and 'not very hardly worked masters', to whom Public Schools were mere 'pecuniary speculations',[3] but only liberal or religious extremists

---

[1] Thackeray, *The Newcomes*, p. 43.
[2] The first three of these books as well as much of Thackeray are of interest to a student of the Arnoldian and post-Arnoldian period chiefly as evidences of literary trends with reference to schools, for they deal with a previous period. On the other hand, there were innumerable books written in the sixties and later that dealt with the forties and fifties. I have—except in factual chapters such as the previous one—used them even more sparingly than I have similar material in Part II. Only when they discuss important new attitudes that were developing in the schools in the fifties which did not find expression in print till much later have I referred to them at all. Common sentimental attitudes and traditional defences of fagging, etc., need no further illustration than that provided by works written within the period.
[3] Cf. *The Times*, February 14th 1845, p. 6; ibid., August 29th 1854, p. 10. The complaint of the Etonian who wrote the earlier of these articles was called

continued the struggle begun by Brougham's Commission in 1818 to change the nature of school administration.

The possible solutions of the problem ranged, as in the previous period, from complete *laissez-faire* to complete State or Church control. But not even the *Westminster Review* advocated in the fifties entire abolition of endowments after the fashion of Adam Smith, though it occasionally showed its *laissez-faire* tendencies by attacking details such as the tyranny of academic degrees, on the basis that the public should be allowed to use quacks if it so desired. At the same time no one pleaded for complete State control of upper-class education. The reactionary High Church party wanted Church control of education, but, since to them the Church was to be independent of the State, this did not mean what it did even to Coleridge, from whom Newman and Ward derived their ideas.[1]

The position advocated by the greatest liberal of the day, John Stuart Mill, and later supported by other liberals and radicals, was a compromise between independent endowments and State control. In earlier days Mill had agreed with Turgot in 'condemning endowments in themselves, and proposing that they should be taken to pay off the national debt.'[2] By 1833 he no longer believed that people knew what they wanted, and was not willing to trust to the market as the best means of providing education.[3] 'On the contrary, I urged strenuously the importance of having a provision for education, not dependent on the mere demand of the market, that is, on the knowledge and discernment of average parents, but calculated to establish and keep up a higher standard of instruction than is likely to be spontaneously demanded by the buyers of the article.'[4] On the other hand,

forth by the attempt of the masters to saddle the public with the cost of Eton improvements. These improvements, he felt, 'ought reasonably and cheerfully to be defrayed by themselves'. To ask the public to pay was 'an impudent and most impolitic act on the part of the Eton masters'.
[1] Cf. Rev. W. G. Ward, *The Ideal of a Christian Church*, London, 1844, p. 34; John Henry, Cardinal Newman, *The Idea of a University*, London, 1919 (1852), pp. 212 ff.
[2] *Autobiography of John Stuart Mill*, with a preface by John Jacob Coss, New York, 1924, p. 128.
[3] John Stuart Mill, *Dissertations and Discussions*, Vol. I, Boston, 1865, p. 51.
[4] Mill, *Autobiography*, p. 128.

—and in this Mill shows, as he does in other respects, the failure of mid-nineteenth century liberalism to come to grips with the problems of a highly organized industrial age —Mill never came round to State control of education. He supported (as did Arnold and Coleridge, the latter of whom he grew to admire so much in the late thirties)[1] the old endowments which had in the past raised man's spiritual culture. His position was advanced, however, for he maintained 'that all endowments are national property, which the Government may and ought to control'.[2] His article in the *Jurist* had the design 'first, of showing that there is no moral hindrance or bar to the interference of the Legislature with endowments, though it should even extend to a total change in their purposes'.[3] The cry of founders' claims and spoliation Mill felt to be merely the frightened clamour of vested interests, which had winked at perversion of trusts by trustees. In reality fellows have no vested rights. As to founders' wishes and Church rights, they are not sacred. In true liberal fashion Mill contended that, unless we are to make the dead our masters, a founder's wishes should be respected only so far as he could have been expected to see into the future. The rule was to employ funds as consistently with founders' wishes as modern usefulness dictated.[4]

Probably the most interesting support of Mill's contentions appeared in 1854 in a book called the *Life and Adventures of George Wilson* by a man named Griffith. Though Griffith's purposes were more radical than Mill's, he agreed with the latter's ideas about Public School government. He believed that the public ought to interfere with endowments, and that the election of trustees should be changed. English fear of Government regulation, he contended, prevented decent education.[5] In the sixties Mill's ideas found a good deal of support from moderates as well as extremists. In part they were carried into practice by the Public School Commission, though they failed, for a number of reasons, to effect the radical reforms expected of them.

[1] Cf. Mill, *Dissertations*, Vol. I, p. 64.
[3] Cf. Mill, *Dissertations*, Vol. I, p. 28.
[5] Cf. op. cit., Preface and p. 126.
[2] Mill, *Autobiography*, p. 128.
[4] Ibid., Vol. I, p. 62.

B. MEMBERSHIP

To propose destruction of the class nature of Public Schools in the forties and fifties required a temerity and a fundamental radicalism of outlook which few upper-class Englishmen possessed. If there were many who felt that the few poor who were still admitted into these august institutions were being shamefully treated, they were more likely to favour the withdrawal of the disturbing elements than the reform of the schools to make life possible for them. Even such an enemy of Public Schools as the *Prospective Review*, despairing of changing the system, sought instead to minimize its importance. 'We cannot admit,' it wrote in 1852, 'that these institutions are a characteristic national institution: we have, on the contrary, always been accustomed to regard them as a national anomaly.' Since, it insisted, the aristocracy is dying out, the schools are losing their distinctive character and will propagate nothing similar.[1]

The only direct plea for the return of the Public Schools to the poor was contained in that curious book of Griffith's just mentioned, the *Life and Adventures of George Wilson*. This long, rambling, badly written novel makes amusing reading if only because of its hopelessly inaccurate and unrealistic picture of Public School life. As a virtually lone example of passionate radicalism it is both interesting and important. Griffith wrote his book as a protest against the perversion of endowments from their original purpose of educating the poor, and dedicated it to the dispossessed middle and working classes.[2] In order to effect his purpose he traced in melodramatic fashion the sorry lot of a foundation boy at a Public School. This boy, for whom Public Schools were, presumably, founded, is the victim of a system of snobbery, favouritism, and contempt which it would be hard to discover at even the worst of Public Schools.[3] And even, if, despite

[1] *Prospective Review*, April 1852, p. 189. The *Prospective* is, at the same time, loath to admit that the Public Schools are responsible for the character traits of the classes that they do educate.
[2] George Griffith, *The Life and Adventures of George Wilson, A Foundation Scholar*, London, 1854, Preface. As he says, the noble and opulent are those chiefly taught by masters paid from large endowments.
[3] The foundationers fag for the boarders in the place of menials, as

handicaps, he does well in the classics, he will not, according to Griffith, get the fat livings which are supposedly the reward of scholarship. 'A rich man's son trained in the poor man's foundation school is sent to college instead of the poor man's son, and when his studies are completed there, his rich connexions place him in some official position, and then we hear a great deal of praise bestowed on our benevolent and pious forefathers.'[1] The solution offered by Griffith is in the best democratic anti-clerical tradition: an educational system based on the Continental model, with a broad curriculum, a mixture of social classes on a basis of equality, and State regulation.[2]

C. SOCIAL LIFE AND MORAL TRAINING

Until well into the fifties the thin stream of protest against the social life and moral training of Public Schools proceeded either from introverts and individuals whom a Public School could never please or from those diehard liberals and moralists who had produced the reforms of Arnold and now felt cheated by the compromises with their cherished aims that passed, in most schools, as reform.

The only unified group of critics were the reactionary High Church party, many of whose members were gradually drifting into Catholicism. Later on in the sixties and seventies they continued the fight against the Public Schools in the pages of the *Dublin Review*. But neither later nor in the forties and fifties were Newman, W. G. Ward and their followers heeded, for they represented an extreme point of view from which the English recoiled as much as they did from the opposite libertarian extreme. The Newmanites cared above all else for religious idealism and moral humility,

compensation for their 'conceit' in coming 'to a gentleman's boarding-school'. In Griffith's bitter eyes the masters are more cruel and snobbish even than the boys. The head master warns the hero not to mix with the boarders or he will be flogged. When George says that it hurts his feelings to be a servant, the Head is outraged. 'Feelings indeed! did ever anybody hear of foundation boys having feelings. How can men learn the humility taught them in the Scriptures if they are not trained to do humble tasks in their youth.' Society is preserved by keeping the lower classes in submission. (Griffith, op. cit., p. 67.)
[1] Griffith, op. cit., p. 172.   [2] Ibid., pp. 110–40.

or, as Ward put it, for 'spotless purity, voluntary poverty, extreme sensitiveness of conscience, rejoicing in shame, reproach, and suffering'.[1] They believed that neither Arnold nor any one else could secure these virtues under the system of independence which was a basic Public School characteristic. The uncontrolled boy is subject to grave 'spiritual dangers'. The character most subject to evil is he who with 'uninterrupted health and prosperity, and vigorous intellectual powers, devotes himself to congenial studies as the one pursuit of his life, without submitting himself to the special discipline suited to his case.'[2] Believing as they did, the Newmanites were strict authoritarians, desiring the control of Public School administration and of boys' activity by the Church.[3]

Of the liberal protestors against general vice and immorality Thackeray was the most vociferous and persistent. Most of his work dealt with a previous period, but in 1842 he published a scathing attack on contemporary Eton. Contrasting Henry VI's school with the Templemoyle Agricultural Seminary, he wrote that 'all the world is improving except the gentlemen', who still pay large sums to learn vice and little else, and who can only be kept in order by 'degrading personal punishment'. 'There are at this present writing five hundred boys at Eton, kicked, and licked, and bullied by another hundred—scrubbing shoes, running errands, making false concords and (as if that were a natural consequence) putting their posteriors on a block for Dr. Hawtrey to lash at; and still calling it education. They are proud of it—good heavens!—absolutely vain of it; as what dull barbarians are not proud of their dulness and barbarism? They call it the good old English system.'[4]

[1] Ward, *Ideal of a Christian Church*, p. 35.
[2] Ward, op. cit., p. 35. The failure to believe in an objective real conscience produces a destructive freedom and corrupts 'conscience in the true meaning of the word' into 'moral sense or taste'. 'Virtue is nothing more than the graceful in conduct,' not the dictate of a law-giver. (Newman, *Idea of a University*, Preface, pp. ix and 193.)
[3] Newman was, as we shall see later, at one and the same time an authoritarian and a believer in the freedoms of the old Public Schools. With Newman it was a question of rendering unto Caesar that which was Caesar's. As a believer in the free play of mind he was as much opposed to conformity as to moral licence.
[4] W. M. Thackeray, *Irish Sketch Book*, Illustrated Cabinet Edition, 2 vols., Boston, n.d., Vol. II, Chapter 5, p. 63.

Defence and Criticism: 1840–1860

Except for Thackeray's remarks and occasional objections to idleness and frivolity and lack of discipline expressed in private letters by William Johnson Cory, the only general attack on the social system was voiced by two dissatisfied introverts, James Anthony Froude and Lewis Carroll. Froude's anonymous *Shadows of the Clouds*, written as it was by a weak, delicate, and rather melodramatic young man about relatively unreformed Westminster, is as bitter a book as has been written about schools.[1] C. L. Dodgson went not to backward Westminster but to progressive Rugby. In 1855 he wrote a letter severely attacking the punishments for trifles and the inadequate discipline in the dormitories, which had disastrous effects on many small boys.[2]

As in earlier days, the centre of liberal and moral attack was the prefect system. To most of those who objected to fagging and boy government in the twenties and thirties, Arnold's reforms had proved satisfactory, but there were intransigents to whom independent monitorial rule was abhorrent in any form. In 1848 a reviewer of Creasy's book on Eton expressed his belief that fagging made 'tyrants of big boys, poor oppressed little bed-warmers, message-runners, ball-fetchers, and shoe-cleaners, of the younger ones'.[3] Six years later a *Times* leader launched an attack on the system as illustrated at Harrow, the reverberations of which spread far and wide. Vaughan had advised a boy to accept a monitorial whipping for answering back to a monitor at footer. The boy had received thirty-one such severe blows that he required medical attention. Though Vaughan had degraded the prefect, *The Times* was not satisfied and announced pontifically, 'We must now pronounce,

---

[1] Though much of what occurred was admittedly his own fault, Froude's book is nevertheless a severe indictment of the system that it describes. Froude was hated by his fellow collegers as much for his brains as for his weakness. Their cruelty drove him to lying and meanness as an escape, the worst result of a brutal system. Perverse boyhood then proceeded to hate him for the vices it had created; no one believed him, and even as a senior he was beaten by his equals. (Froude, *Shadows of the Clouds*, pp. 25 ff.)

[2] 'I cannot say,' he wrote, 'that I look back upon my life at a Public School with any sensations of pleasure or that any earthly considerations would induce me to go through my three years again.' (Stuart Dodgson Collingwood, *The Life and Letters of Lewis Carroll*, New York, 1899, p. 30.)

[3] *Prospective Review*, July 1848, p. 349.

without a moment's hesitation, that the monitorial system, as illustrated in the case before us, is entirely indefensible.'[1] In the controversy that followed this article, *The Times* found a number of supporters,[2] but, in contrast to what occurred in the similar affair at Winchester in 1829, the enemies of boy government found themselves hopelessly outnumbered by its friends.

As the fifties drew to a close criticism of Public Schools began to acquire a new aspect. The closer organization of school life with its more careful supervision, its over-emphasis of athletics, and its premium on conformity began to receive the attention before accorded exclusively to the cruelty and vice of the old loose system. In 1860, however, the new criticism was just in its infancy. Most of those who, like Frederick Harrison, Henry Sidgwick, and Principal Shairp felt the impact of conditions typical of the late fifties did not give expression to their resentment until after 1860. Fitz-James Stephen in his review of *Tom Brown's Schooldays* in 1858 was the only writer to discuss at any length the dangers implicit in the increasing emphasis on athletics. As we have seen, Stephen wrote, on the whole, as a conservative.[3] He did not like games because, as played in the fifties, they destroyed the freedom and thus the hardy independence that boys possessed in the older schools. 'The game is anything but a mere amusement'; it is 'something between a battle and a sacrifice'; sports 'are exercises and tasks, the performance of which is enforced by far stronger sanctions than any which the authorities of the school have it in their

[1] To make an older boy sacred is unfair to the younger boys, for 'hourly familiarity is not compatible with unfailing respect'. A boy has the right to supervision by a master, since the latter would not—this is in 1854—'have been playing football with the boys', and could therefore be respected. There ought to be more masters. (*The Times*, April 13th 1854, p. 9.)

[2] Including an old Etonian who considered the 'cruel and dangerous' prefect system an example of pounds before virtue. (*The Times*, April 29th 1854, p. 10.)

[3] The new criticism was by no means an exclusively left-wing movement. Libertarians and moralists were often joined in their pleas against oppressive supervision by dissatisfied lovers of the older Public School. Such was, for example, the Old Westminster who protested in 1858 that the 'flannel-waistcoat' element, which was afraid 'lest the boys should take cold', was destroying those fighting greens where bullies (who are always cowards) are beaten, and where stalwart hardy sons of Britain are made. (*The Times*, January 6th 1858, p. 10.)

power to apply'. A boy who does not play is a coward and a social outcast.[1] The result of this enforced discipline is the destruction of self-reliance. At the same time, Stephen is a liberal in his fear that athletics, by over-emphasizing the physical, will destroy interest in the mental.[2] Indeed, he accuses Arnold of having aided the overthrow of the intellectual by his exaggeration of the moral: Arnold's worries about moral childishness can, he believes, be laid to rest by encouraging intellectual variety.[3]

Though Stephen's was the only direct criticism of athleticism in the fifties, there was a silent protest of great interest growing up against it in the schools. Just as in the outside world poetic souls like Rossetti were warring against materialism and the crushing of individuality by escaping into a half-sensuous, half-mythical world of poetry, so in the schools those sensitive introverts who in Arnold's day might have been prigs working for the school, found asylum in these later days of manliness and conformity in a fruitless subjectivism, which might be sensual, aesthetic, religious, or all three. The best examples of this tendency are John Addington Symonds, William Mackworth Dolben, and William Johnson Cory.

Cory was in college at Eton from 1832 to 1842. While at school and afterwards, when he was an Eton master, he wrote a number of poems which reflect the feelings of an emotional weakling who turned to romantic friendship as an antidote to muscularity. Though the first edition of *Ionica*, published in 1858, was suppressed, presumably because the sensualness shone too patently through the romantic idealization, there are enough poems extant to serve as illustration of the growing preoccupation with 'Platonic' love of those whose temperaments revolted against Philistinism. One sample of Cory's art, which dealt almost exclusively with dead youths or tearful farewells to beloved friends, will indicate the nature of the poet's sentiments:

[1] *Edinburgh*, January 1858, p. 174. [2] Ibid., p. 193.
[3] Ibid, p. 181.

> You bid me lift my mean desires
> From faltering lips and fitful veins
> To sexless souls, ideal quires,
> Universal voices, wordless strains:
> My mind with fonder welcome owns
> One dear dear friend's remembered tones.[1]

Cory not only gloried in his own sentimental loves, but applauded those of his students at Eton. 'I have seen,' he wrote proudly, 'romantic, chivalrous friendships forming under my eye, to which I am almost admitted as a partner.'[2]

Digby Mackworth Dolben was an over-sensitive person who indulged not only in unhealthy romantic friendships, but in High Church ritualism as well. At Eton he wrote adoring poems to 'Archie', many of which he later burned when the supersensuous and beautiful object of his affections proved unworthy and neither supersensuous nor divine. Retreating from the world into religion, Dolben found his only relationship to Eton in the pleasing defiance of masters who objected to his activities.[3] After flirtations with Jesuit doctrines, which almost caused his expulsion, Dolben was finally confirmed at Eton. But he openly objected to the 'manly' brand of Christianity taught, and, along with eleven others, adhered to the doctrines of the High Church ritualists.

J. A. Symonds, though not as much of a misfit at Harrow as was Dolben at Eton, was also anything but the average healthy schoolboy. A mystic, full of brooding fancy, shy, weak, languid, morbidly self-conscious and neurotic, he hated exertion, rivalry, and noise. He disliked not only violent exercise and games of all kinds, but even the 'fat clay soil and pasture landscape of the country', and the cheap modern houses, dirty corridors, and ill-drained latrines.[4] He lived his real existence at school within himself,[5] only an occasional romantic friendship disturbing his dream life. Through one of his friends he was led, later on, to ritualism, which proved immensely attractive to his religious and

[1] William Johnson Cory, *Ionica*, London, 1891, pp. 5–6.
[2] Cory, *Letters*, p. 233.
[3] *Poems of Digby Mackworth Dolben*, Oxford, 1911, Introduction by Robert Bridges, pp. xxi ff., xxvi ff. He hated the school because it was 'full of mental temptations that you know nothing of'; it is impossible to be a saint there.
[4] Cf. Brown, *Symonds*, Vol. I, p. 76.   [5] Ibid., Vol. I, p. 72.

Defence and Criticism: 1840–1860

aesthetic nature. He and two friends 'donned surplices and tossed censers, arrayed altars in our studies, spent spare cash on execrable painted glass to dull our dingy windows, and illuminated crucifixes with gold dust and vermilion'.[1] When pictured against the background of Eton life these activities seem as pathetic as they are amusing. And Symonds was only one of the first of an unending line of British boys who were unfit for and revolted against being groomed for imperial service.

If there were still carpers who did not believe that all was for the best in the best of all possible school systems, the majority of Englishmen were well satisfied with the state of things moral and social in the Public Schools of the forties and fifties. Often their admiration was couched in the same terms and dealt with the same objects of praise as had previous eulogy. Most praise, however, represented the point of view of those moderates who were equally proud of the virtues of the older school and of the new morality, humanity, and efficiency.

The most fulsome general praise came, as was to be expected, from those with experience of the system. For to statements as to the virtues to be derived from Public School education, they were only too likely to add sentimental hymns to the joys of youth. Occasionally an old boy would confine himself to talk about 'the real spirit of gentlemen and the honour of the English character'[2] or the manliness, democracy and patriotism of his alma mater.[3] Usually, however, he gave free rein to his reminiscent emotions. If such books as Old Rugbaean's *Recollections of Rugby* and such articles as that by an Etonian in *Bentley's Miscellany* or that by an Old Carthusian in *Blackwood's* in 1840 have been more frequent since the sixties than before, the character of the sentimentality has not changed. *The Recollections of Rugby*, except for brief discussions of Arnold as an educator, already dealt with, is an attempt to relive for those who cannot return to Rugby the memories of the past. It frankly omits the

---

[1] Cf. Brown, *Symonds*, Vol. I, p. 80. [2] *The Times*, December 4th 1846, p. 6.
[3] Cf. Creasy, *Eton College*, pp. 64–69.

unpleasant, and it is quite shamelessly sentimental.[1] The article in *Bentley's* is even more maudlin. Surveying Eton, the author waxes eloquent over the great men whose 'impulses of ambition' were there first excited and who were there 'warmed with the flush of those glorious feelings' that made them famous. They come back to Eton to find 'how far preferable was the freshness of heart which accompanied the thoughtless schoolboy, to all the laurels which they had since reaped'. Since sentimentality and conservatism are ever akin, the author ends with praise for Eton's 'classic courts and happy faces, undisturbed by the desolating mania of reform, and the dangerous experiments of modern improvements'.[2] The Old Carthusian writes in much the same vein.[3] But it is worth noting that to him the masters as well as the boys and those Carthusian heroes of an age gone by, who are 'sureties for my good behaviour', are objects of love.

Sentimental praise of schools was not confined to the old boys among Rugbeians or Etonians or Carthusians, but occasionally found expression, as in earlier days, among those at school through school magazines. Of these publications Clough's *Rugby Magazine*, already discussed, and the *Eton School Magazine*, which existed from 1847 to 1848, are the most interesting. The *Eton School Magazine* is important

[1] In the following passage the author sums up the attitude of generations of old boys:
> 'Words can but imperfectly describe the feelings with which
> > "we revisit the hills where we sported,
> > The streams where we swam, and the fields where we fought"
> How many pleasant recollections are awakened at every step we take! what hosts of old associations crowd upon us as we see a well-known face! And what delightful reminiscences, which have long lain dormant, are stirred up within us as we gaze upon
> > "the wall whereon we tried our graving skill,
> > The very name we carved subsisting still,
> > The bench on which we sat while deep employed,
> > Though mangled, hacked, and hewed, not yet destroyed."'
(Old Rugbaean, *Recollections of Rugby*, p. 4.)

[2] *Bentley's Miscellany*, June 18th 1840, pp. 587–88, 592.

[3] *Blackwood's*, June 1840, pp. 779 ff., 'My Old School.' To him it is 'a positive duty' to hold his school and to cause it to be held, in honour'. 'I pity the man who does not love his old school.' The ties that bind him to his alma mater, hallowed by the past, are 'inferior in strength only to those of country and of blood'. In this alumnus' eyes Charterhouse is worthy of praise because it taught those 'lessons of open, honest, manly independence—of fighting one's way fairly and honourably, and boldly—which a public school only, can teach to a boy'. Schools may occasionally fail to produce scholars; they always 'make a gentleman'.

Defence and Criticism: 1840–1860

as the last Victorian school periodical worthy, from a literary standpoint of view, of being mentioned in the same breath with the *Etonian* or the *Microcosm*. Later an enlarged curriculum and organized athletics allowed no time for literary ventures such as Gladstone's or Praed's or Canning's. Moreover, the growing materialism seems to have stifled literary talent in all but the few, a sad and pointed commentary on what the Victorians called progress.

The *Eton School Magazine* presents some interesting contrasts to earlier Eton publications. It is, in the first place, far duller and less sophisticated than even the *Eton Miscellany*. For occasional sprightly imitation of eighteenth-century writers and comparatively adult comment on politics and scholarship has been substituted wearisome schoolboy platitudes about school and outside affairs. The didactic spirit of Victorianism has settled heavily on the pages of this last Public School literary effort. In the second place, it faithfully reflects in its point of view changes in the idea of a Public School that had taken place since Praed's day.

Though Eton is still sentimentally loved for its beauty, its joys, its uniqueness, the 'average superior station' of its membership and for the elegant verses and rowing feats of its future statesmen and heroes,[1] there is obviously a new spirit abroad in the land, a spirit that emanates from Rugby.[2] With a very un-Etonian reform gusto, the magazine fiercely attacked those who thought that 'the old system was the best; and [that] the only requisite to gain applause for any custom is, to show the antiquity of its origin'. There is no reason to lament the passing of Long Chamber, Montem, daily floggings; Eton, like the world, is progressing.[3] She

[1] Cf. *Eton School Magazine*, Eton, 1848, especially pp. 5, 9, 50, 54, 70.
[2] The editors consciously imitated the *Rugby Miscellany*.
[3] *Eton School Magazine*, p. 25. The editors are not so liberal in matters political or literary as they are in school affairs. Eton, unlike Rugby, was the home of authoritarian Toryism. The *Eton School Magazine* believed that a poet ought to be a monarchist, a religious poet, a traditionalist and an upholder of the existing order. Tennyson and the lake school with their simplicity and devotional spirit are preferable to Byron. Shelley was unpopular at Eton because he presumed to speculate without bowing to the 'authority of Revelation'. In politics the French Revolution of 1848 was characterized as an upheaval that made France 'a nation of anarchists and atheists', 'almost the lowest in the scale of civilized nations'. (Cf. *Eton School Magazine*, pp. 41, 95 ff., 177 ff.)

is acquiring a new religious and moral spirit which differentiates her from Eton of past days. It was, indeed, the chapel which now seemed to the editors of the *Eton Magazine* the symbol of Eton's meaning. 'I fancy, that when I shall have left Eton, pleasing as all my recollections of it will be, there will be none so delightful as those connected with our old chapel: any better thoughts or holier aspirations which may have sparkled among the wayward follies of my boyish career, will with it be recalled to mind, for it was there that they took their origin. . . . . I assert that *that* place, and *that* custom, calls forth many a fervent prayer from the most thoughtless of us.'[1]

If Public School men formed the main body of upholders of the system, there were a good many outsiders in the forties and fifties who contributed to the eulogy, often very fulsome, of upper-class social and moral education. Dickens, for example, 'took occasion' in 1858 'to declare his belief that there were no institutions in England so socially liberal as its public schools, and that there was nowhere in the country so complete an absence of servility to mere rank, position, or riches. "A boy there, is always what his abilities or his personal qualities make him . . . of the frank, free, manly, independent spirit preserved in our public schools, I apprehend there can be no kind of question." '[2]

Among numerous other writings by outsiders,[3] only Disraeli's description of Eton in *Coningsby* (1842) deserves

[1] *Eton School Magazine*, p. 9.
[2] Forster, *Life of Dickens*, Vol. II, p. 280. Dickens surely had a Public School as reformed by Arnold in mind in his picture of Dr. Strong's school in *David Copperfield*. Dr. Strong always trusted his boys and was 'the idol of the whole school'. 'We all felt that we had a part in the management of the place, and in sustaining its character and dignity. Hence, we soon became warmly attached to it. . . . We had noble games out of hours, and plenty of liberty.' (Cf. *David Copperfield*, New Century Library, London, 1900, p. 222.)
[3] The *Prospective Review*, very hostile to schools in many ways, could write that 'There is a certain spirit of manly confidence, of fresh, fearless self-respect, engendered in the hearts of boys, brought up in the heaving waves of a public school, which has to all men a great charm. (*Prospective Review*, July 1848, p. 349.) The Frenchman, Montalembert, found that Public Schools, on account of the 'moderate freedom' that they give, produce manly boys, and are thus the bulwark of national strength and liberty. (*Edinburgh Review*, April 1856, p. 582.) The German Wiese was an enthusiastic admirer of the freedom and authority of the English system as reformed by Arnold, and felt that what few faults it possessed were 'in the abuse and fallings away from the original system' not 'in that system itself'. (Wiese, *German Letters*, p. 5.)

special attention. Disraeli knew very little about Eton and his picture is about as life-like as a faded tintype. What makes it worthy of careful study is its reflection of the educational ideals of one who, more than any single Englishman, is responsible for transferring into practical politics the ideas of upper-class paternalism and of imperialism which have dominated Tory thought ever since. In Disraeli the Burkian-Coleridgean conception of the organic growth of a nation and its institutions, which took a liberal direction in Arnold and Hughes and Stanley, became conservative and nationalistic. The aristocracy as the embodiment of English ideals and the preserver of England's medieval institutions was to revive its ancient function of guardian of the poor and spreader of light to the uncivilized world.

Believing as he did in the aristocracy and in old institutions, Disraeli naturally found Eton appealing. Moreover, since he was an outsider gifted with the Jew's romantic temperament, he saw England's great Public School in an even more glamorous light than did her most ardent son. To the future Lord Beaconsfield Eton became the ideal training school for the ideal aristocrat who was to lead the British nation to domestic happiness and foreign conquest.

For the most part it is the old conception of a Public School that Disraeli has idealized as a background and inspiration for young Coningsby. As stated in Disraeli's glowing and ornate phrases, Eton education consists in a free life among equals[1] permeated by aged loveliness and patterned by customs derived from the consecrated past.[2] In the shades

[1] Those 'right people' over whose personalities the snobbish Disraeli throws such a mantle of glamour. Though a thorough snob, Disraeli claims, it may be added, that money or family do not count at Eton. From its superior height Eton can even allow sons of manufacturers to come and mix with its gilded youth. So young Millbank (supposed to be Gladstone), whose father had opinions 'of a very democratic bent' and 'disapproved of the system of education pursued there' not only came to Eton, but actually joined Coningsby's set, despite his father's insistence that he 'avoid the slightest semblance of courting the affections or society of any member of the falsely held superior class'. (Benjamin Disraeli, *Coningsby*, Everyman's Edition, 1928, p. 35.)

[2] Disraeli has given one of the most colourful invocations to Eton that has ever been written: 'That delicious plain, studded with every creation of graceful culture; hamlet and hill, and grange; garden and grove, and park; that castle-place, grey with glorious ages; those antique spires hoar with faith and wisdom, the chapel and the college; that river winding through the shady meads; the sunny glade and the solemn avenue; the room in the dame's house

of Eton young aristocrats sport happily all the day and night, sharpening their talons for the battle of life at the expense of masters, or engaging in nobly beautiful traditional ceremonies such as Montem, in which 'five hundred of the youth of England sparkling with health, high spirits and fancy dresses' marched to Salt Hill.[1] Above all they cement friendships.[2] The only worry of this group of 'right people' is that there might be a 'Reform Bill for Eton,' which would interfere with the happy manly life of England's best.[3]

What Coningsby derived from Eton was the traditional capability for leadership. He had practised by being the leader at school, and no 'power of manhood in passionate intenseness . . . can rival that which is exercised by the idolised chieftain of a great public school . . . that's fame, that's power; real, unquestioned, undoubted, catholic.' When, with 'expression' sad and 'serious', he left his beloved alma mater, he had been formed into the ideal captain of those Tory young Englanders of Disraeli's, who were dissatisfied with the lack of principles in Peel's 'conservative principles' and were ready to follow Disraeli down the road of medieval paternalism.[4] If Eton had in no ordinary sense educated Coningsby, she had provided the background, the atmosphere, the arena for his education.

Most of the praise of Public Schools so far recorded has been fairly general, and indeed most writers contented

where we first order our own breakfast and first feel we are free; the stirring multitude, the energetic groups, the individual mind that leads, conquers, controls; the emulation and the affection; the noble strife and the tender sentiment; the daring exploit and the dashing scrape; the passion that pervades our life, and breathes in everything, from the aspiring study to the inspiring sport—oh! what hereafter can spur the brain and touch the heart like this; can give us a world so deeply and variously interesting; a life so full of quick and bright excitement—passed in a scene so fair!' (Disraeli, *Coningsby*, p. 11.)

[1] Disraeli, *Coningsby*, p. 49.

[2] On this subject Disraeli waxes rhapsodic. 'At school, friendship is a passion. It entrances the being; it tears the soul. All loves of after life can never bring its rapture, or its wretchedness, no bliss so absorbing, no pangs of jealousy or despair so crushing and so keen! What tenderness and what devotion; what illimitable confidence; infinite revelations of inmost thoughts, . . . are confined in that simple phrase—a schoolboy's friendship! 'Tis some indefinite recollection of these mystic passages of their young emotion, that makes grey-haired men mourn over the memory of their schoolboy days. It is a spell that can soften the acerbity of political warfare, and with its witchery can call forth a sigh even amid the callous bustle of fashionable saloons.' (Disraeli, *Coningsby*, p. 36.)

[3] Ibid., pp. 26 ff.   [4] Ibid., p. 86.

Defence and Criticism: 1840–1860   389

themselves with eulogy of the system as a whole. A good many, however, focused their remarks upon the prefect system, partly because it was the chief specific means of moral education in a Public School and partly because, since it was the central feature of school training, and subject to dramatic abuse, it was, as we have seen, the object of the most severe attack. As reformed by Arnold the system of boy government appealed not only to conservative old boys but to masters and to many liberals as well. For, as controlled by a modern head master it was supposed to serve not only the ancient function of teaching gentlemen who were their superiors but the new one of preventing bullying and the tyranny of force. Thus historians like Creasy and head masters like Moberly and Vaughan were in the forties and fifties ardent supporters of the system, for to them it was the producer of order and of the 'character of an English Christian gentleman'.[1] Even liberals like T. H. Green supported Vaughan in his controversy with *The Times* in 1854. Green, whose strong sense of duty and sympathetic understanding of the weak had made him a fine prefect in the Arnoldian tradition when he was at Rugby under Goulburn, wrote to his father in 1854: 'The spirit of the age, raving against everything that sounds like oppression, seems likely to establish a worse tyranny in public schools, as everywhere else; for it is impossible for bullying to be stopped except by praepostors.'[2]

If most defenders of the prefect system preferred the new Arnoldian model, there were, judging from a curious pamphlet by a Harrow monitor, a few reactionaries who,

[1] Cf. Creasy, *Eton College*, p. 64; Thornton, *Harrow School*, p. 448; Moberly, *Letters to Heathcote*, pp. 8 ff., 104 ff.
[2] R. L. Nettleship, *Memoir of Thomas Hill Green*, London, 1906, pp. 6–7. Vaughan found support in many quarters for his stand. *Fraser's* (October 1854, pp. 401 ff.) claimed that the public was totally ignorant of the virtues of fagging and monitors. The sixth form, remodelled by Arnold and given responsibilities, was the only alternative to a spy system without freedom. Boys learn self-discipline and submission to authority through a fagging which was less tyrannical than it had been, and which often produced a fine relation between older and younger. A Rugbeian in *The Times* (April 15th 1854, p. 10) insisted that Arnold's monitorial system, with its controlled use of the birch and its right of appeal, was the best government possible; to abolish it would mean ending the 'great and distinctive feature of the English public school, its independent life and free development of character'. He adds, significantly, that to increase masters would lessen their income and thus lower their quality.

for patriotic or other reasons, wanted a return to the old uncontrolled kind of monitorial government. This old Harrovian disapproved not only of the Rugby system but of Vaughan himself because he was a Rugbeian. Harrow masters should be Harrovians. And monitors are not 'to be the mere tools of the head master', spies carrying out a master's orders, but a 'legitimate school authority' which can cane boys on 'their own responsibility'.[1]

D. THE CURRICULUM

If most Englishmen were relatively satisfied with the moral education given in Public Schools, there was not equal agreement about the intellectual training offered. After the battle of the thirties, there was a respite from controversy for a time, partly because Arnold and others had improved intellectual education and partly because change in the moral field absorbed attention. But the liberals never laid down their arms, and as the forties wore on they were joined by large groups of the middle classes who, under the stimulus of industrial needs, were not content with the complete anti-intellectualism of such as Hughes and with the tendencies in that direction championed by Carlyle.

Unfortunately the real issue of a truly liberal versus a narrow and outmoded education was faced as seldom as it had been in the thirties. Most of the liberals were liberal only in their desire for change in the curriculum; they either ignored the real ends of a liberal education entirely, or, under the stimulus of the new industrialism, perverted them to mean mere practical knowledge. Indirectly as a result of this there is even to-day a prejudice against useful knowledge as a means to an education that will broaden and stimulate the mind. Defenders of a purely literary education have been able successfully to contend, though without the shadow of proof, that they have a monopoly of the roads to true liberal goals. They have been able to ignore the obvious limitations involved in teaching only the classics in

---

[1] *A few words on the Monitorial System at Harrow*, by one who was once a Monitor, London (1854), pp. 3–8.

Defence and Criticism: 1840–1860

a nineteenth-century world and the still more obvious fact that boys at Public Schools were not learning even the classics in the broad sense that conservatives desired. Most conservatives clung tenaciously to all the features of the old system, even defending the making of Latin verses as a preparation for life.[1] If they allowed modern subjects like mathematics, history, and French into the curriculum, they were to take a very subordinate place.[2] They fought for an essentially classical curriculum, which they consciously and unalterably opposed to a system based on modern subjects. Such a system they identified with cram, competition and money getting.[3] In defence of the old curriculum all the time-worn justifications were brought forth. The classics, though not obviously useful, taught principles of logic,[4] and 'exertion, perseverance, and accuracy'.[5] They provided models of taste and were cultivators and discipliners of the mind.[6] Sir Robert Peel, who was one of the staunchest supporters of the classics, has well summed up the conservative position. Having shown that most great men in the 'arena of public competition' have been 'eminent for classical acquirements', and thus by implication that the classics are responsible for their success, he urges the upper classes 'to acquire those habits, and to cultivate those studies, which, at the same time that they are the highest solace and the most grateful relaxation from the cares of business and the world, are furnishing to him who takes delight in them new capacity for intellectual exertion, new stores of precious knowledge'.[7]

With one defender of the old order it is not possible to deal in such a summary manner. Though, like his contemporaries, Cardinal Newman was inclined to overlook the practical problems involved in making a system of instruction based

---

[1] Cf. *Fraser's*, September 1850, pp. 296–99; *Quarterly*, June 1855, p. 107; Moberly, *Letters to Heathcote*, p. 37.
[2] Cf. *Quarterly*, September 1855, p. 349; *Fraser's*, October 1854, p. 412. The *Quarterly* advocated a special professional education for those who needed it.
[3] Creasy, *Eton College*, p. 59; *Fraser's*, September 1850, p. 298.
[4] *Fraser's*, September 1847, p. 276.   [5] Moberly, *Letters to Heathcote*, p. 16.
[6] Creasy, op. cit., p. 59; *Quarterly*, June 1855, p. 107.
[7] *A Correct Report of the Speeches delivered by Sir Robert Peel on his Inauguration into the office of Lord Rector of the University of Glasgow, January 11, 1837*, London, 1837, pp. 24, 30.

on the classics function properly, and by implication to underrate the newer studies unnecessarily, he evolved a defence of the older Public School system which was far more than a narrow justification of the classics and which went much deeper into the question of the means and ends of a true liberal education than did any other ideas of the time.

His idea was truly catholic. Like Carlyle, and much more than the orthodox liberal leader Mill, he recognized the claims of the moral; at the same time his respect for the intellectual equalled that of Mill and exceeded that of Carlyle. Since to Newman the whole moral problem and its solution were above and distinct from the intellectual, he was able to champion mental stimulation and free thought without involving himself in the moral confusion which so hampered Arnold. Newman, like the most modern of progressives, saw that an education which did not aim at the cultivation of inquisitiveness and breadth of mind was not worthy of the name. Nevertheless, he was at one with the Public School theorists who laid such stress on mental discipline. Stimulus without rigorous training is unfruitful. 'Our desideratum is . . . the force, the steadiness, the comprehensiveness and the versatility of intellect.'[1] Like Creasy and others, he fought the tyranny of mere fact, the narrowly useful. Finally, Newman was no mere individualist, no believer in the omnipotence of personal judgment. What he aimed at and what many dissatisfied liberals are striving for to-day was a bond of union in a common culture, 'a characteristic tone of thought, a recognized standard of judgment'.[2] This common tone or idea which a community ought to embody must, however, be a growing and living conception, not one that has stagnated for lack of internal life and external stimulation.[3]

Newman felt that the Public Schools and the Oxford of the past provided in good part the kind of education that he desired. These 'public schools and colleges of England', 'with miserable deformities on the side of morals, with a

[1] Newman, *Idea of a University*, p. xvi.   [2] Ibid., p. 147.
[3] Cf. John Henry Cardinal Newman, *Rise and Progress of Universities*, London, 1873, pp. 234–35.

Defence and Criticism: 1840–1860

hollow profession of Christianity, and a heathen code of ethics,—I say, at least they can boast of a succession of heroes and statesmen, of literary men and philosophers, of men conspicuous for great natural virtues, for habits of business, for knowledge of life, for practical judgment, for cultivated tastes, for accomplishments, who have made England what it is,—able to subdue the earth, able to domineer over Catholics.'[1] That this should have been so, Newman realized, was not due to great teachers of the classics. The secret lay in the mere being together in a community. A Public School, 'which did little more than bring together first boys and then youths in large numbers', proved to be a better educational institution than a college with lecturers and examinations, because boys stimulated and learned from one another, and were 'moulded together' into an 'assemblage' with 'one tone and one character'.[2] Such an assemblage, according to Newman, 'will constitute a whole, it will embody a specific idea, it will represent a doctrine, it will administer a code of conduct, and it will furnish principles of thought and action. It will give birth to a living teaching, which in course of time will take the shape of a self-perpetuating tradition, or a *genius loci* . . . which haunts the home where it has been born, and which imbues and forms . . . every individual who is successfully brought under its shadow.'[3]

If Newman was far too sanguine in regard to actual conditions in the pre-Arnoldian school, he has admirably stated the ideal which animated the greatest of her early leaders. But as time went on the Public Schools ceased to be even theoretically the sort of places that Newman desired; his ideal of a liberal education was lost amid the raucous pleas for efficiency and knowledge that filled the nineteenth-century air.

When Wiese visited England in 1852, he found the attack on the classics in full swing, and he paraphrased typical English liberal opinion in the following words: 'Schools and

[1] Newman, *Idea of a University*, p. 146. [2] Ibid., p. 147.
[3] Ibid., p. 147.

Education are in a state of deep decay with us; schools for the people we scarcely possess at all; and what our young men learn in the higher schools and at the universities is out of all proportion to the time and money spent there; for what is it more than a . . . learning by rote, and the useless, or at least questionable faculty of making Latin verses? We must come to you, in Prussia, to learn how to organize schools.'[1] In other words, whatever its ideal virtues, the actual outcome of a classical training was highly unsatisfactory. At best boys learned to write Latin verse and to recite a few passages of Horace. They imbibed no classic literature, received no essential mental training, acquired no ability to write English, and, most important, derived no love of learning from their studies.[2]

If liberals were fairly well agreed as to the vices of the classical system, they were also in virtual accord as to the prime need in the way of reform. There must be new modern studies. Unfortunately, as suggested above, the new studies were usually advocated chiefly for their direct utilitarian value, not for their capacity to train or to stimulate the mind.

The radical reformers were the worst offenders in this respect. Thus a pamphlet written in 1839 laid all its emphasis on the contrast between practical necessity and a classical education, and insisted that the upper classes would lose the race with the lower classes for money and power if they did not acquire some of the latter's knowledge of commercial subjects.[3] Similarly, Griffith stressed the need for a commercial rather than a classical education as being more suited to an age of railways; he bitterly accused the

[1] Wiese, *German Letters*, p. 4.
[2] This was the argument of every opponent of the current system from *Punch* with its humorous reference to the fact that 'an education too exclusively classical has incapacitated [a certain Etonian] from writing English,' (*Punch*, January to June 1845, p. 232), to the serious Wiese who found that learning based on duty produced hatred of studying and made boys intellectually dependent and immature. (Wiese, op. cit., p. 99.)
[3] *Observations on the Present System of Education with Some Hints for its Improvement*, London, 1839, pp. 3 ff. The author of this article also insisted that the classics as currently taught were immoral, uninspiring, and fatal to love of learning.

Defence and Criticism: 1840–1860

clergy of defending the 'elegant imbecility' of the present system in order to keep the lower classes in submission.¹ Finally, the *Westminster Review* pleaded chiefly for a useful education. According to the *Westminster*, the French Revolution of 1848 has awakened 'a growing feeling among thoughtful men that some alteration is needed in our system of education'. 'How much longer are we to continue teaching nothing more than what was taught two or three centuries ago?' The 'circumstances of society have for a long time required' the classics to be supplemented by studies relating to the condition of men and the laws of nature, in a word, by science.²

Even some of the more moderate reformers gave the impression, by the emphasis in their attacks, of an exclusive interest in practical knowledge. Such is the effect of Thackeray's remarks before the students of the Templemoyle Agricultural Seminary. 'You are not fagged and flogged into Latin and Greek at the cost of two hundred pounds a year. Let those be the privileges of your youthful betters; meanwhile content yourselves with thinking that you *are* preparing for a profession while they are *not*; that you are learning something useful, while they, for the most part, are not: for after all, as a man grows old in the world, old and fat, cricket is discovered not to be any longer very advantageous to him.'³

Such also in part is the upshot of Whewell's reference to schools in *Of a Liberal Education*. Whewell realized the deeper needs of education, but he was so intent on destroying the monopoly of a narrow classical training that he seems to find virtue to reside in the mere acquisition of mathematics,

¹ Griffith, *Life and Adventures of George Wilson*, Preface and p. 15. Neither Griffith nor the author of the previously mentioned pamphlet were directly interested in the upper classes. The latter writer was, indeed, willing to let the Public Schools teach the classics. Griffith, it may be added, cared about Public Schools if not about the upper classes; as we have seen, he wanted the middle and lower classes to benefit by an education given at a Public School.
² *Westminster Review*, July 1850, pp. 393, 397.
³ Thackeray, *Irish Sketch Book*, Vol. II, Chapter 5, p. 61. And few Etonians read the classics after they leave school, though Peel often quotes classic poetry to astound the country gentlemen. 'Stout men in the bow-windows of clubs (for such young Etonians by time become) are not generally remarkable for a taste for Aeschylus.'

natural science, natural history, French, German, Italian, etc.[1]

On the other hand, there were a few liberals who saw the dangers that practical knowledge or indeed any mere knowledge for its own sake entailed. Wiese warned against the new competition and cram which resulted from the demands of an industrial age working on the universities and schools and to which the new subjects readily lent themselves.[2] Similarly, Dickens revolted against the cramming system, and his remarks are particularly interesting because he laid the blame for present conditions on the old studies, not on the new ones. In *Dombey and Son* he satirized a forcing system for the precocious. Dr. Blimber's school with its studies that 'went round like a mighty wheel', on which 'the young gentlemen were always stretched', is an exaggeration of what must often have occurred at Shrewsbury.[3] In *Bleak House* he directly attacked Public Schools and made a passionate plea for that variety and individual attention which alone could produce love of learning and intellectual independence. Richard Carstone 'had been eight years at a public school, and had learned, I understand, to make Latin verses of several sorts, in the most admirable manner. But I never heard that it had been anybody's business to find out what his natural bent was, or where his failing lay, or to adapt any kind of knowledge to *him*. *He* had been adapted to the verses, and had learned the art of making them to such perfection, that if he had remained at school until he was of age I suppose he could only have gone on making them over and over again, unless he had enlarged his education by forgetting how to do it.' Never having been guided or taught to think for himself, he never found his purpose in life. The trouble lay in the 'system which had addressed him in exactly the same manner as it had addressed hundreds of other boys, all varying in character and capacity'. 'I wonder,' Dickens added, 'whether the Latin

[1] William Whewell, *Of a Liberal Education*, London, 1850, Part II, Section 6, p. 63.
[2] Wiese, op. cit., p. 114.
[3] Charles Dickens, *Dombey and Son*, New Century Library, London, 1900, p. 175.

verses often ended in this, or whether Richard's was a solitary case'.[1]

But John Stuart Mill was the only liberal to take a positive stand which included the new subjects in an educational scheme with true liberal ends.[2] Within his self-imposed limits Mill's views, expressed in his *Inaugural Address* at St. Andrew's, were the broadest and most enlightened of his day.[3] His object, as he wrote later, was to tell of the 'various studies which belong to a liberal education, their uses and influences, and the mode in which they should be pursued to render their influences most beneficial. The position I took up . . . was, I think, calculated, not only to aid and stimulate the improvement which has happily commenced in the national institutions for higher education, but to diffuse juster ideas than we often find, even in highly educated men, on the conditions of the highest mental cultivation.'[4]

Mill's contention was that the classics and science could exist side by side if taught properly. In the *Autobiography* he cites—rather amusingly, since he was so exceptional—his own education as a proof of 'how much more than is commonly supposed may be taught, and well taught, in those early years which, in the common modes of what is called instruction, are little better than wasted.'[5] In the *Inaugural Address* he asked, '. . . is the human mind's capacity to learn, measured by that of Eton and Westminster to teach? I should prefer to see these reformers pointing their attacks

[1] Quoted in James L. Hughes, *Dickens as an Educator*, New York, 1903, p. 129.
[2] To Mill, because of his belief in the importance of environment, inherited from his father's associational psychology, education had always been the great hope of the world. But until his *Inaugural Address* at St. Andrews in 1867 his thoughts had been directed towards the education of the poor.
[3] Unlike Carlyle and Newman, Mill felt that intellectual, not moral and religious education was the business of the schools. His own education had been almost entirely intellectual and private. It had been the discipline of analysis, which tended to make of him a 'reasoning machine'. (*Autobiography*, p. 76.) He saw, when it was almost too late, that his emotions had been stifled, and that he had missed a good deal by not being allowed to mix with other boys. 'The deficiencies in my education were principally in the things which boys learn from being turned out to shift for themselves, and from being brought together in large numbers': viz. bodily skill and practical doing. (Mill, *Autobiography*, pp. 24–6, and *Inaugural address*, delivered to the University of St. Andrews, February 1st 1867, Boston, n.d., pp. 15 ff.)
[4] Mill, *Autobiography*, pp. 216–17. [5] Ibid., p. 1.

against the shameful inefficiency of the schools, public and private, which pretend to teach these two languages and do not.' The 'greater part of the English classical schools . . . are . . . mere shams'. Schools reform more slowly than governments and churches, 'for there is the great preliminary difficulty of fashioning the instruments: of teaching the teachers'.[1] He advised the reading of the classics before the grammar; then there would be time for science too. It would be disastrous if in an increasingly complicated world men could learn only one minute subject. French, German, and history are necessary as well as the classics and science, but they must be done out of school, as must political economy and sociology.

Along with his desire for a broad curriculum, Mill saw the danger of mere content, mere memory work and cram. 'Education makes a man a more intelligent shoemaker, if that be his occupation, but not by teaching him how to make shoes; it does so by the mental exercise it gives, and the habits its impresses'.[2] Classics will discipline the intellect by their regularity and complication, and rob a boy of self-sufficiency by their breadth. Science will give the method of judging truth, the experimental method. Mathematics will teach reasoning.

[1] Mill, *Inaugural Address*, p. 6.   [2] Ibid., p. 4.

CONCLUSION

In 1860 the smouldering embers of mid-Victorian criticism were kindled into a blaze by the publication of three letters to the *Cornhill Magazine* which abused in no measured terms the whole structure of Public School education. These letters initiated a controversy, extending over the next six or seven years, comparable in intensity to the outburst of the early thirties. Moreover, they were indirectly responsible for the creation in 1861 of a Parliamentary Commission to investigate conditions in the nine schools denominated 'Public', the first thoroughgoing interference with Public School independence to which those institutions had been subject. In 1864 this Commission submitted a lengthy report to Parliament, and, on the basis of this report, significant permanent changes in Public School organization and practice were eventually made. Thus the sixties, like the thirties, were a high point in the story of Public School development, a period both of culmination and of rebirth. They offer, therefore, a convenient spot at which to halt this narrative and to survey briefly the ground that we have already traversed. What significant configurations do we observe as we take a bird's-eye view of the terrain across which we have travelled?

The most obvious pattern that emerges from a consideration of Public School history is the evolutionary character of school growth. In certain respects, as we have seen, schools did not change at all. The Public School system at the time of the Public School Commission, no less than in the reign of Elizabeth, consisted of a number of highly individualized institutions which looked for guidance to their own pasts, taught chiefly the classics, relied for discipline largely on flogging, and, through being miniature worlds, imbued their pupils with self-reliance and group solidarity. At the same time schools were radically different in 1382 and in 1860. By the middle of Victoria's reign the scattered handful of semi-charitable institutions which represented the Public

School system in the sixteenth century had become a vast network of upper-class schools. Other subjects except the classics had been introduced, other disciplines except flogging initiated. A moral and religious revival had occurred, and the beginnings of a preoccupation with organized athletics were perceptible. The Victorian school, unlike its sixteenth-century predecessor, was primarily a mint for the coining of Empire builders. What evolutionary growth has meant is that reform has been gradual rather than revolutionary and has entertained a tremendous respect for forms inherited from the past. Even Arnold, the most radical reformer of the system, had to work slowly and to retain the structure of the prefect system and of boy life in general at the same time that he was modifying their meaning.

To characterize the nature of Public School growth in this manner implies nothing in regard to the causes of that growth. Romantic interpreters of school history have, however, extended the evolutionary conception to imply a causal no less than a descriptive pattern. They have contended that schools were living organisms developing in terms of some innate mystical principle. Such a view is tenable only if one persists in viewing Public School history in artificial isolation from its environment. To break down that isolation has been the chief function of the study of Public School literature which these pages have contained. Public Schools have, as we have seen, had a profound effect on many literary men such as Clough and Hughes and Matthew Arnold. Conversely, the written word in the hands of a Sydney Smith or a Stanley has exerted considerable direct influence on upper-class education. But more important from our present point of view, literature has been the chief reflector of general historic ideas and motivations, and thus the gateway to a perception of the relationship between education and society. This relationship, one discovers after an examination of Public School criticism, is exceedingly close, so close, indeed, that Public School evolution is ultimately understandable only in terms of it. More precisely, the history of Public Schools seems most satisfactorily explained when viewed as the expression in education of the psychological, economic, and other forces that determined general and especially upper-class behaviour.

This seems to have been true from the very beginning, though it has not been possible to provide much substantiating evidence for the early centuries. Yet William of Wykeham and the sixteenth-century school founders no less than eighteenth-century schoolmasters appear in the light of history to have been the mere servants of the age. Medieval education necessarily served the Church; sixteenth-century Eton and Harrow inevitably reflected Renaissance ideals and practice; the eighteenth-century Public Schools were, among other things, the product of the class divisions, the scepticism, the brutality of the time, and the conservatism and *esprit de corps* of the aristocracy. As we enter the nineteenth century the relationship between society and education can be more explicitly observed. The schools were, as we have seen, difficult to change chiefly because the upper classes were, for psychological and political reasons, attached to the past *per se*, and satisfied with the traditionalism, the independence from the State, the class character, the narrow classical training, and above all the free boy life with its escapades and its inculcation of manliness and patriotism which schools exhibited. At the same time new social classes with new needs and thus a new philosophy were beginning to take an interest in Public Schools. Chiefly for psychological reasons they objected to school immorality; for political and other reasons they fought the idea of schools as closed upper-class preserves; for economic reasons they attacked the intellectual fare which schools offered. Gradually—again with the aid of historical forces—these ideas began to influence the older ruling classes. As a result, through the instrumentality of Arnold and others, the new ideas found their way into the schools in the thirties. But their victory was only possible at the cost of compromise with the old order; neither extreme liberalism nor extreme reaction ever found embodiment in school practice. The Public Schools were as successful in fighting off ideas definitely uncongenial to the classes which supported them as they were unsuccessful in rejecting those that were vital to such groups. After Arnold's day new forces, industrialism and imperialism, began to dominate the political and economic scene. In the schools they produced, on the one hand, a retreat from liberalism and ethical idealism; on the other, they furthered the growth of athleticism and, with the aid of the older liberalism, created a demand for curricular and governmental reform which was to reach at least partial fulfilment in the sixties.

Thus it is evident that Public School history has been inextricably interwoven with the general economic and social development of the British upper classes. Moreover, it would seem that the relationship between schools and society has been of a special and more or less consistent character. On the one hand, Public Schools have always responded, despite their inherent conservatism, to the pressure of historic forces. On the other hand, they have always, except at brief and rare moments, been the followers rather than the initiators of new social movements. At most periods in history their system of education has been an accurate if tardy barometer of the needs and desires of the British upper classes. The Public Schools have never served as effective instruments for remodelling society along lines not definitely anticipated by the dominant ideas of the age.

In a second volume we plan to continue the study of the relationship between school and society from the days of the Public School Commission in the sixties, through the relative calm of the seventies and eighties and the iconoclasm of the pre-War and War years, to the troubled times in which we are now living. Those seventy-five years have witnessed a greater complexity of ideas and pressures and more rapid and bewildering changes than probably any period of similar length in English history. How have current ideas and forces manifested themselves in Public School criticism? What has been the nature of Public School response? Has upper-class education continued to reflect the temper of the age or has it broken significantly with dominant tendencies? These are the crucial questions which a study of the late Victorian and twentieth-century Public School must attempt to answer if, out of the story of the past, we may hope to attain insight into the story of the future.

BIBLIOGRAPHY

BOOKS AND PAMPHLETS

Ackermann, R., *The History of the Colleges of Winchester, Eton, and Westminster, with the Charter-House, the Schools of St. Paul's, Merchant Taylors, Harrow, and Rugby, and the Free School of Christ's Hospital*, London, 1816.

Ainger, Arthur Campbell, *Memories of Eton Sixty Years Ago*, London, 1917.

Arbuthnot, Sir Alexander J., *Memories of Rugby and India*, London, 1910.

Archer, R. L., *Secondary Education in the Nineteenth Century*, Cambridge, 1921.

Arnold, Matthew, *Letters*, collected and arranged by George W. E. Russell, 2 vols., New York, 1895.

Arnold, Matthew, *The Letters of, to Arthur Hugh Clough*, edited with an introductory study by Howard Forster Lowry, London and New York, 1932.

Arnold, Thomas, *Introductory Lectures on Modern History*, New York, 1845.

Arnold, Thomas, *The Miscellaneous Works of*, New York, 1845.

Arnold, Thomas, *Sermons Preached in the Chapel of Rugby School, with an Address before Confirmation*, New York, 1846.

Arnold, Thomas, *Sermons Preached mostly in the Chapel of Rugby School* called *Christian Life, its Course, its Hindrances, and its Helps*, London, 1841.

Arnold, Thomas, M.A., *Passages in a Wandering Life*, London, 1900.

Arnould, Sir Joseph, *Life of Thomas, First Lord Denman*, 2 vols., New York, 1874.

Ascham, Roger, *The Scholemaster*, edited from the texts of the first two editions by John E. B. Mayor; Memoir by Hartley Coleridge, London, 1911.

Ballantine, Mr. Serjeant (William), *Some Experiences of a Barrister's Life*, London, 1883.

Barker, Ernest, *National Character and the Factors in its Formation*, New York, 1927.

Barker, G. F. Russell, *Memoirs of Richard Busby, D.D.*, (1606–95). With some account of Westminster School in the Seventeenth Century, London, 1895.

Barrow, Rev. William, *An Essay on Education, in which are particularly considered the merits and the defects of the Discipline and Instruction in our Academies*, 2 vols., London, 1802.

Benson, Arthur Christopher, *Fasti Etonenses, A Biographical History of Eton*, Eton, 1899.

Bentham, Jeremy, *Chrestomathia, Being a collection of papers, explanatory of the Design of an Institution proposed to be set on foot under the name of the Chrestomathic Day School or Chrestomathic School for the Extension of the new system of instruction to the higher branches of learning, for the use of the Middling and Higher Ranks in Life* (first published in 1816). *Works of Jeremy Bentham*, by John Bowring, Vol. 8, Edinburgh, 1843.

Boswell, James, *Life of Samuel Johnson*, edited by Augustine Birrell, 6 vols., New York, 1906.

Bowdler, Thomas, *Memoir of the late John Bowdler, Esq.*, London, 1825.

Bowles, W. L., *Vindiciae Wykehamicae, or a Vindication of Winchester College in a Letter to Henry Brougham*, London, 1818.

Bradby, G. F., *The Brontës and other Essays*, London, 1932.

Bradley, A. G., Champneys, A. C., Baines, J. W., *A History of Marlborough College During fifty Years from its Foundation to the Present Time*, London, 1893.

Brandl, Alois, *Samuel Taylor Coleridge and the English Romantic School* (English Edition by Lady Eastlake), London, 1887.

Brinsley-Richards, J., *Seven Years at Eton, 1857–1864*, London, 1883.

Brock, Rev. Wm., *A Biographical Sketch of Sir Henry Havelock*, London, 1859.

Brooke, Henry, *The Fool of Quality*, Introduction by Rev. W. P. Strickland, 2 vols., New York, 1860.

Brougham, Henry, *A Letter to Sir Samuel Romilly from, upon the abuse of charities*, London, 1818.

Brougham, Henry, *Practical Observations on Popular Education*, Boston, 1826.

Brougham, Henry, *The Speech of, in the House of Commons, May 8, 1818, on the Education of the Poor and Charitable Abuses*, London, 1818.

Brown, Horatio, F., *John Addington Symonds, A Biography compiled from his papers and correspondence*, 2 vols., London, 1895.

Bibliography 407

Browning, Oscar, *Aspects of Education. Monographs of the Industrial Education Association*, Vol. 1, No. 5, New York, 1888.
Browning, Oscar, *An Introduction to the History of Educational Theories*, New York, 1886.
Browning, Oscar, *Memories of Sixty Years at Eton, Cambridge and Elsewhere*, London, 1910.
Bulwer, Sir Henry Lytton, *The Life of Henry John Temple, Viscount Palmerston*. Vol. I, Philadelphia, 1871.
Burke, Edmund, *Reflections on the French Revolution*, Vol. III of the *Writings and Speeches of Edmund Burke*, Boston, 1901.
Butler, Samuel, *The Life and Letters of Dr. Samuel Butler*, 2 vols., London, 1896.
Butler, Samuel, *The Way of all Flesh*, The Modern Library, New York, n.d.
Byron, Lord, *Hours of Idleness*, from *The Poetical Works of*, New York, 1868.

Carlisle, Nicholas, *A Concise Description of the Endowed Grammar Schools in England and Wales*, London, 1818.
Carlyle, Thomas, *Corn Law Rhymes*, Vol. III of *Critical and Miscellaneous Essays*, 4 vols., Boston, 1861.
Carlyle, Thomas, *Inaugural Address at Edinburgh University*, Vol. 29 of Centenary Edition of *The Works of Thomas Carlyle*, London, 1899.
Carlyle, Thomas, *Latter Day Pamphlets*, Vol. 5 of the Ashburton Edition of Thomas Carlyle's *Works*, London, 1885.
Carlyle, Thomas, *Letters of, to John Stuart Mill, etc.*, edited by Alexander Carlyle, London, 1923.
Carlyle, Thomas, *The Life of John Sterling. The Works of Thomas Carlyle*, v., The World's Classics, London, 1907.
Carlyle, Thomas, *Sartor Resartus*, Vol. I, Centenary Edition, London, 1899.
Carlyle, Thomas, *Shooting Niagara*, Vol. 30, Centenary Edition, London, 1899.
Chesterfield, 4th Earl of, *The Letters of Philip Dormer Stanhope*, Edited by Bonamy Dobrée, 6 vols., 1932.
Chesterfield, 4th Earl of, *Letters to his Son*, with topical headings and a special introduction by Oliver A. G. Leigh, 2 vols., New York, 1925.
Clarke, Charles, *The Beauclercs, Father and Son*, New York, 1866.
Clarke, Rev. Liscombe, *A Letter to H. Brougham in Reply to the Strictures on Winchester College contained in his Letter to Sir Samuel Romilly*, London, 1818.

Clough, Arthur Hugh, *Poems and Prose Remains*, 2 vols., with a selection from his letters and a memoir edited by his wife, London, 1869.
Cole, G. D. H., *The Life of William Cobbett*, London, 1924.
Coleridge, Arthur Duke, *Eton in the Forties, by an old Colleger*, London, 1896.
Coleridge, Samuel Taylor, *Biographia Literaria*, 2 vols., New York, 1847.
Coleridge, Samuel Taylor, *Specimens of the Table Talk of*, 2 vols., New York, 1835.
Collingwood, Stuart Dodgson, *The Life and Letters of Lewis Carroll*, New York, 1899.
Collins, William, *The Poems of*, edited with an introductory study by Edmund Blunden, London, 1929.
(Collins, W. L.) *The Public Schools, Winchester, Westminster, Shrewsbury, Harrow, Rugby*, Edinburgh, 1867.
Colvin, Sidney, *Landor*, New York, 1881.
Cook, A. K., *About Winchester College*, London, 1917.
Corbin, John, *School Boy Life in England, An American View*, New York, 1898.
Cory, William Johnson, *Extracts from the Letters and Journals of*, selected and arranged by Francis Warre Cornish, Oxford, 1897.
Cory, William Johnson, *Ionica*, London, 1891.
Cowper, William, *The Letters of*, edited by J. G. Frazer, 2 vols., London, 1912.
Cowper, William, *Tirocinium, The Poems of Cowper*, Vol. II of the Aldine Edition of the *British Poets*, London, 1843.
Crabbe, George, *The Life and Poetical Works of*, by his son, London, 1901.
Creasy, Sir Edward, *Memories of Eminent Etonians*, London, 1876.
Creasy, E. S., *Some Account of the Foundation of Eton College, and of the Past and Present Condition of the School*, London, 1848.
Cross, Wilbur L., *The History of Henry Fielding*, New Haven, 1918.
Cumberland, Richard, *Memories of*, written by himself, Philadelphia, 1856.
A Cyclopedia of Education, edited by Paul Monroe, New York, 1913.

Darwin, Charles, *His Life told in an Autobiographical Chapter and in a selected series of Published Letters*, edited by his son, Francis Darwin, New York, 1893.
Davidson, Randall Thomas, Benham, William, *Life of Archibald Campbell Tait*, 2 vols., London, 1891.

Davies, Gerald S., *Charterhouse in London*, London, 1921.
Day, Thomas, *The History of Sandford and Merton*, corrected and revised by Cecil Hartley, London, n.d.
Defoe, Daniel, *The Compleat English Gentleman*, edited by Karl D. Bülbring, London, 1890.
De Quincey, Thomas, *Autobiographic Sketches*, Vol. II of *The Works of Thomas De Quincey*, New York, 1876.
De Quincey, Thomas, *Education of Boys in Large Numbers*, Vol. 14 of *The Collected Writings of Thomas De Quincey*, Edition of David Masson, London, 1897.
Dickens, Charles, *Dombey and Son, David Copperfield; The Works of Charles Dickens*, New Century Library, London, 1900.
Dickens, Charles (edit.), *Life of Charles James Mathews*, New York, 1879.
Disraeli, Benjamin, *Coningsby*, Everyman's Edition, London and Toronto, 1928.
Dolben, Digby Mackworth, *Poems of*, edited with a memoir by Robert Bridges, Oxford, 1911.
Doyle, Sir Francis Hastings, *Reminiscences and Opinions*, London, 1886.
Drinkwater, John, *Pepys, his Life and Character*, London, 1930.
Dryden, John, *The Dramatic Works*, edited by Montagu Summers, 6 vols., London, 1931.

Edgeworth, Maria, *The Parents' Assistant*, London, 1897.
Edgeworth, Maria, and Edgeworth, Richard Lovell, *Practical Education*, London, 1798.
Edgeworth, Richard Lovell, *Memoirs of*, begun by himself and concluded by his daughter, Maria Edgeworth, 2 vols., London, 1820.
An Enquiry into the Melancholy Circumstances of Great Britain, London, 1740(?)
The Eton Abuses Considered in a letter to the author of Some Remarks on the Present Studies and Management of Eton School, London, 1834.
The Eton System of Education Vindicated: and its Capabilities of Improvement Considered, in reply to some recent Publications, London, 1834.
Etonensis, A Few Words in Reply to Some Remarks on the Present Studies and Management of Eton School, London, 1834.
An Etonian, *Reminiscences of Eton*, Chichester, 1831.
Everett, Charles Warren, *The Education of Jeremy Bentham*, New York, 1931.

Farrar, Reginald, *The Life of Frederick William Farrar*, New York, 1904.
Fichte, Johann Gottlieb, *Addresses to the German Nation*, translated by R. F. Jones and G. H. Turnbull, Chicago, 1922.
Field, Rev. William, *Memoirs of the Life, Writings and Opinions of the Rev. Samuel Parr*, 2 vols., London, 1828.
Fielding, Henry, *The Adventures of Joseph Andrews*, Vol. I of *The Works of Henry Fielding*, edited by G. H. Maynadier, Boston, n.d.
Findlay, J. J., *Arnold of Rugby, His School Life and Contributions to Education*, Cambridge, 1897.
Fitch, Sir Joshua, *Thomas and Matthew Arnold and their influence on English Education*, New York, 1897.
Forshall, Frederic H., *Westminster School. Past and Present*, London, 1884.
Forster, John, *The Life of Charles Dickens*, 2 vols., London, 1904.
Fowler, Thomas, *Shaftesbury and Hutcheson*, New York, 1883.
Fox, Charles James, *Memorials and Correspondence of*, edited by Lord John Russell, London, 1853.
Fremantle, Rev. W. R., *Memoir of the Rev. Spencer Thornton*, London, 1850.
Frere, John Hookham, *the Works of*, Vol. I. Memoir by the Right Honourable Sir Bartle Frere, London, 1874.
(Froude, James Anthony) Zeta, *Shadows of the Clouds*, London, 1847.

Gambier-Parry, Major, *Annals of an Eton House*, London, 1907.
Gaskell, Charles Milnes, *Records of an Eton Schoolboy*, privately printed, 1883.
Gibbon, Edward, *The Autobiography*, London and Toronto, Everyman's Edition, 1923.
Gignilliat, George Warren, Jr., *The Author of Sandford and Merton, A Life of Thomas Day, Esq.*, New York, 1932.
Gladstone, Wm. Ewart, *The Gladstone Papers*, London, 1903.
Gladstone, Wm. Ewart, *Arthur Henry Hallam*, Boston, 1898.
Gleig, G. R., *The Life of Arthur, Duke of Wellington*, London, 1865.
Godwin, William, *The Enquirer*, Edinburgh, 1823.
Gosse, Edmund, *Gray (English Men of Letters)*, London, 1906.
Gosse, Edmund, *The Life of Algernon Charles Swinburne*, London, 1917.
Graham, Edward, *The Harrow Life of Henry Montagu Butler, D.D.*, London, 1920.

Bibliography 411

Graves, Frank Pierrepont, *Great Educators of Three Centuries*, New York, 1912.
Gray (Thomas) *The Correspondence of, Walpole, West, and Ashton, 1734–1771*, by Paget Toynbee, 2 vols., Oxford, 1915.
Gray, Thomas, *Ode on a Distant Prospect of Eton College, The Golden Treasury*, London, 1923.
Great Public Schools, Eton, Harrow, Charterhouse, Cheltenham, Rugby, Clifton, Westminster, Marlborough, Haileybury, Winchester, various authors, London, n.d.
Gregory, Sir William, *An Autobiography*, edited by Lady (Augusta) Gregory, London, 1894.
Grier, Rev. R. M., *John Allen, Vicar of Prees and Archdeacon of Salop;* a memoir by his son-in-law, London, 1889.
Griffith, George, *The Life and Adventures of George Wilson, a Foundation Scholar*, London, 1854.
Gwynn, Stephen, *The Life of Horace Walpole*, Boston, 1932.

Halévy, Élie, *A History of the English People in 1815*, New York, 1924.
Haller, William, *The Early Life of Robert Southey, 1774–1803*, New York, 1917.
Hare, Augustus J. C., *Biographical Sketches*, London, 1895.
Hare, Augustus J. C., *Memorials of a Quiet Life*, 2 vols., London, 1872.
Hare, Augustus J. C., *The Story of My Life*, 2 vols., New York, 1896.
Harrison, Frederic, *Autobiographic Memoirs*, 2 vols., London, 1911.
(Hewlett, Rev. Joseph James) *Peter Priggins, The College Scout*, edited by Theodore Hook, Paris, 1841.
Hicks, W. R., *The School in English and German Fiction*, London, 1933.
(Hill, Matthew Davenport), *Plans for the Government and Liberal Instruction of Boys in Large Numbers; as Practised at Hazelwood School* (first published in 1822), London, 1894.
Hill, Sir Rowland, Hill, George Birkbeck, *The Life of Sir Rowland Hill*, 2 vols., London, 1880.
The History of a Schoolboy, London, 1787.
A History of Shrewsbury School, from the Blakeway MSS., and many other sources, Shrewsbury, 1889.
Hodder, Edwin, *The Life and Work of the 7th Earl of Shaftesbury*, 3 vols., London, 1888.
Hodgson, James T., *Memoir of the Rev. Francis Hodgson*, 2 vols., London, 1878.

Hogg, Thomas Jefferson, *The Life of Percy Bysshe Shelley*, 2 vols., London, 1858.
Holland, Lady Saba, *A Memoir of the Reverend Sydney Smith*, edited by Mrs. Sarah Austin, London, 1855.
(Holt), *A Letter to the Right Hon. Sir Wm. Scott . . . in answer to Mr. Brougham's Letter to Sir Samuel Romilly.*
Hook, Theodore, *Gilbert Gurney*, 3 vols., London, 1836.
Hoole, Charles, *A New Discovery of the old Art of Teaching School*, Syracuse, New York, 1912 (1660).
How, F. D., *Six Great Schoolmasters (Hawtrey, Moberly, Vaughan, Kennedy, Temple, Bradley)*, London, 1904.
Howson, Edmund M., and Warner, George Townsend, *Harrow School*, London, 1898.
Hughes, James L., *Dickens as an Educator*, New York, 1903.
Hughes, Thomas, *The Manliness of Christ*, New York, 1880.
Hughes, Thomas, *Memoir of a Brother*, London, 1873.
(Hughes, Thomas) *Tom Brown's School-days*, by an Old Boy, New York, 1928.
Hunt, Leigh, *Autobiography*, edited by Roger Ingpen, 2 vols., New York, 1903.

Jones, Henry Festing, *Samuel Butler, A Memoir*, 2 vols., 1919.
Josephson, Matthew, *Jean-Jacques Rousseau*, New York, 1931.

Kaye, John William, *The Life and Correspondence of Charles, Lord Metcalfe*, 2 vols., London, 1858.
Keppel, George Thomas, Earl of Albemarle, *Fifty Years of My Life*, New York, 1876.
Kinglake, A. W., *Eothen*, Edinburgh, 1896.
Knight, Charles, *Passages of a Working Life*, 3 vols., London, 1864.
Knight, William, *Principal Shairp and His Friends*, London, 1888.
Knox, Vicesimus, *Essays Moral and Literary*, 2 vols., New York, 1793.
Knox, Vicesimus, *Liberal Education or a Practical Treatise on the Methods of Acquiring Useful and Polite Learning*, 2 vols., London, 1789 (1781).
Knox, Vicesimus, *Winter Evenings, or Lucubrations on Life and Letters*, 2 vols., London, 1790.

Lafourcade, Georges, *Swinburne, A Literary Biography*, London, 1932.
Lake, Katherine, *Memorials of William Charles Lake, Dean of Durham*, London, 1901.

Bibliography 413

Lamb, Charles, *The Essays of Elia, Letters*, Vols. 1, 2, 6, 7, of *The Works of Charles and Mary Lamb*, edited by E. V. Lucas, New York, 1905.

Lang, Andrew, *Life, Letters, and Diaries of Sir Stafford Northcote, First Earl of Iddesleigh*, Edinburgh, 1891.

Laughton, John Knox, *Memoirs of the Life and Correspondence of Henry Reeve*, 2 vols., London, 1898.

Leach, Arthur F., *A History of Winchester College*, New York, 1899.

Leach, Arthur F., *The Schools of Medieval England*, London, 1915.

The Legacy of an Etonian, edited by Robert Nolands, Cambridge, 1846.

A Very Short Letter from One Old Westminster to Another touching some Matters connected with their School, London, 1829.

Letters from a Nobleman to his Son, during the Period of his Education at Eton and Oxford, 2 vols., London, 1810.

Locke, John, *Some Thoughts Concerning Education*, with introduction and notes by Rev. Canon Daniel, M.A., London, (1895 (?)).

Lubbock, Alfred, *Memories of Eton and Etonians*, London, 1899.

Lyte, H. C. Maxwell, *A History of Eton College, 1440–1875*, London, 1875.

Lytton, the Earl of, *Life of Edward Bulwer*, 2 vols., London, 1913.

Lytton, the Right Hon. Lord, *England and the English*, London, 1874 (1833).

McDonnell, Michael F. J., *A History of St. Paul's School*, London, 1909.

Macready, W. C., *Reminiscences*, edited by Sir Frederick Pollock, London, 1875.

Maitland, Frederic William, *The Life and Letters of Leslie Stephen*, New York, 1906.

Malet, Sir Alexander, *Some Account of the System of Fagging at Winchester School with Remarks and a Correspondence with Dr. Williams, Head Master of that Public School on the late Expulsions Thence for Resistance to the Authority of the Praefects*, London, (1828(?)).

Malleson, Colonel D. B., *The Life of Warren Hastings*, London, 1894.

(Mansfield, R. B.), *School Life at Winchester College or the Reminiscences of a Winchester Junior*, London, 1866.

Markham, Captain, F., *Recollections of a Town Boy at Westminster, 1849–1855*, London, 1903.

Martineau, James, *Essays, Reviews and Addresses*, Vol. I, London, 1890.
Masson, David, *The Life of John Milton*, 6 vols., London, 1881.
Melville, Lewis, *William Makepeace Thackeray, A Biography*, 2 vols., London, 1910.
Merivale, Charles, *Autobiography of Dean Merivale, with selections from his correspondence*, edited by his daughter Judith Anne Merivale, London, 1899.
Mill, John Stuart, *Autobiography of*, with preface by John Jacob Coss, New York, 1924.
Mill, John Stuart, *Dissertations and Discussions*, Vol. I, Boston, 1865.
Mill, John Stuart, *Inaugural Address Delivered to the University of St. Andrews, Feb. 1st, 1867*, Boston (1867).
Milman, Arthur, *Henry Hart Milman, D.D.*, London, 1900.
Milton, John, *On Education, Prose Works of John Milton*, London, 1835.
Minchin, J. G. Cotton, *Old Harrow Days*, London, 1898.
Minchin, J. G. Cotton, *Our Public Schools, Their Influence on English History, Charterhouse, Eton, Harrow, Merchant Taylors', Rugby, St. Paul's, Westminster, Winchester*, London, 1901.
Moberly, George, *Five Short Letters to Sir William Heathcote on the Studies and Discipline of Public Schools*, London, 1861.
A Few Words on the Monitorial System at Harrow by one who was once a Monitor, London (1854).
Monroe, Paul, *A Text-Book in the History of Education*, New York, 1918.
Moore, Thomas, *The Life of Lord Byron* from the *Works of Lord Byron, with his Letters and Journals and his Life*, 17 vols., London, 1833.
Moore, Thomas, *Memoirs of the Life of Richard Brinsley Sheridan*, Philadelphia, 1825.
Morley, John, *The Life of William Ewart Gladstone*, 3 vols. in 2, New York, 1911.
Moultrie, John, *The Dream of Life*, London, 1843.
Mozley, Rev. T., *Reminiscences Chiefly of Towns, Villages, and Schools*, 2 vols., London, 1885.

Neff, Emery, *Carlyle*, New York, 1932.
Nesbitt, George L., *Benthamite Reviewing, The First Twelve Years of the Westminster Review, 1824–1836*, New York, 1934.
Nettleship, R. L., *Memoir of Thomas Hill Green*, London, 1906 (1888).

Bibliography   415

Newman, John Henry Cardinal, *The Idea of a University*, London, 1919 (1852).
Newman, John Henry Cardinal, *Rise and Progress of Universities*, London, 1873 (1854).
Norwood, Cyril, Hope, Arthur H., *The Higher Education of Boys in England*, London, 1909.

Observations on the Present System of Education with Some Hints for its Improvement, London, 1839.
Old Etonian, *A Letter to Sir Alexander Malet in reference to his pamphlet touching the late expulsions from Winchester School with a word in passing to the Editor of the Literary Gazette* (1829(?)).
An Old Rugbaean, *Recollections of Rugby*, London, 1848.
Old Wykehamists, *Winchester College, 1393–1893*, published in commemoration of the 500th anniversary of the opening of the college, London, 1893.
Osborne, James Insley, *Arthur Hugh Clough*, London, 1919.
Overton, John Henry, and Wordsworth, Elizabeth, *Christopher Wordsworth, 1807–1885*, London, 1890.
Owen, Robert, *A New View of Society or Essays on the Principle of the Formation of the Human Character and the Application of the Principle*, London, 1813.

Palmer, Roundell (Earle of Selbourne), *Memorials, Part Family and Personal, 1766–1785*, Vol. I, London, 1896.
A Parent, *Some Remarks on the Present Studies and Management oj Eton School*, London, 1834.
Parkin, George R., *Edward Thring, Head Master of Uppingham School, Life, Diary and Letters*, London, 1900.
Parry, A. W., M.A., *Education in England in the Middle Ages*, London, 1920.
Peake, Richard Brinsley, *Memoirs of the Colman Family*, 2 vols., London, 1841.
Pearson, Charles Henry, *Memorials by Himself, His Wife, and His Friends*, edited by William Stebbing, New York, 1900.
Peck, Walter Edwin, *Shelley, His Life and Work*, 2 vols., Boston 1927.
Peel, Sir Robert, *A Correct Report of the Speeches delivered by, on his inauguration into the office of Lord Rector of the University of Glasgow, January 11, 1830*, London, 1837.
Peel, Sir Robert, *. . . from his Private Papers*, edited by Charles Stuart Parker, 3 vols., London, 1891.

Pepys, Samuel, *The Diary of*, edited, with additions, by Henry B. Wheatley, 8 vols., London, 1893.
Pestalozzi's *Leonard and Gertrude*, translated and abridged by Eva Channing, Boston, 1885.
Praed, Winthrop Mackworth, *Poems*, with a memoir by the Rev. Derwent Coleridge, 2 vols., London, 1864.
Prothero, Rowland E., *The Life and Correspondence of Arthur Penrhyn Stanley*, 2 vols., London, 1894.
Public Education. Consisting of Three Tracts, reprinted from the *Edinburgh Review* (Sydney Smith), *The Classical Journal, The Pamphleteer*. (Also contains W. Vincent's *Defence of Public Schools*), London, 1817.
Purcell, Edmund Sheridan, *Life of Cardinal Manning*, 2 vols., London, 1896.

Quick, Robert, *Essays on Educational Reformers*, London, 1890 (1868).

Reid, T. Wemyss, *Life of the Right Honourable William Edward Forster*, 2 vols., London, 1888.
Remarks on the Rev. Dr. Vincent's Defence of Public Education, with an attempt to state fairly the Question whether the Religious Instruction and Moral Conduct of the Rising Generation, are sufficiently provided for, and effectually secured in our Schools and Universities. By a layman, London, 1802.
Rennell, Thomas, Master of the Temple, *A Sermon preached in the Cathedral Church of St. Paul, London, on Thursday, June 6, 1799, being the time of the Yearly Meeting of the Children Educated in the Charity Schools in and about the Cities of London and Westminster*, London, 1799.
Report of Her Majesty's Commissioners Appointed to Inquire into the Revenues and Management of Certain Colleges and Schools and the Studies pursued and Instruction Given therein. (Report is in 4 vols., and appears as Vols. 5 and 6 of *Reports from Commissioners* for 1864), London, 1864.
Third Report from the Select Committee on the Education of the Lower Orders, Reports from Committees, Session, 27 January–10 June, 1818. Vol. IV.
Ruville, Albert von, *William Pitt, Earl of Chatham*, translated by H. J. Chaytor, 3 vols., New York, 1907.
Robinson, Henry Crabb, *Diary, Reminiscences, and Correspondence*, 3 vols., London, 1869.
Rouse, W. H. D., *A History of Rugby School*, New York, 1898.

Bibliography 417

Rousseau, J.-J., *Emile or Education*, translated by Barbara Foxley, Everyman's Library, London and Toronto, 1930.
Rowcroft, Charles, *Confessions of an Etonian*, 3 vols., London, 1852.
Russell, Bertrand, *Education and the Good Life*, New York, 1926.

Salt, Henry S., *Memories of Bygone Eton*, London, 1928.
Sargeaunt, John, *Annals of Westminster School*, London, 1898.
S[idgwick], A[rthur] and S[idgwick], E. M., *Henry Sidgwick, A Memoir*, London, 1906.
Smith, Adam, *An Inquiry into the Nature and Causes of the Wealth of Nations*, Vol. II, Everyman's Library, London and Toronto, 1931.
Smith, Goldwin, *Cowper (English Men of Letters)*, London, (1880).
Smollett, Tobias, *The Adventures of Peregrine Pickle, from the Works of Tobias Smollett*, edited by George Saintsbury, London, n.d.
Southey, Robert, *The Life and Correspondence of*, edited by his son, the Rev. Charles Cuthbert Southey, New York, 1855.
Southey, Robert, *The Life of the Rev. Andrew Bell*, 3 vols., London, 1844.
Southey, Robert, *Selections from the Letters of*, by John Wood Warter, 4 vols., London, 1856.
Stanley, Arthur Penrhyn, *The Life and Correspondence of Thomas Arnold, D.D.*, New York, 1846.
Stephen, Leslie, *The Life of Sir James Fitzjames Stephen*, London, 1895.
Stephens, W. R. W., *The Life and Letters of Walter Farquhar Hook*, 2 vols., London, 1879.
Stephens, W. R. W., *A Memoir of the Right Hon. William Page Wood, Baron Hatherley*, 2 vols., London, 1883.
Strachey, Lytton, *Eminent Victorians*, London, 1918.
Swift, Jonathan, *Essay on Modern Education in Volume XI of the Prose Works of Jonathan Swift*, edited by Temple Scott, London, 1907.

Tawney, R. H., *Religion and the Rise of Capitalism*, London, 1926.
Teignmouth, The Right Hon. Lord, *Memoirs of the Life, Writings, and Correspondence of Sir William Jones*, 2 vols., London, 1835.
Thackeray, Francis St. John, *Memoir of Edward Craven Hawtrey*, London, 1896.
Thackeray, William Makepeace, *The English Humourists of the Eighteenth Century*, Edited by George Saintsbury, London, n.d.

Thackeray, William Makepeace, *Irish Sketch Book*, Illustrated Cabinet Edition, 2 vols., Boston, n.d.
(Thackeray, William Makepeace), *Men's Wives*, by G. Fitz-Boodle, edited by George Saintsbury, London, n.d.
Thackeray, William Makepeace *The Newcomes*, edited with an introduction by George Saintsbury, London, n.d.
Thackeray, William Makepeace, *The History of Pendennis*, edited by George Saintsbury, London, n.d.
Thackeray, William Makepeace, 'Punch in the East,' from *Miscellaneous Contributions to Punch*, 1843-1854, edited by George Saintsbury, London, n.d.
Thackeray, William Makepeace, *The Roundabout Papers*, London, 1907.
Thirlwall, Connop, *Letters Literary and Theological*, edited by J. J. Peronne, London, 1881.
Thomas, W., *Le Poète Edward Young, 1683-1765*, Paris, 1901.
Thompson, Henry L., *Henry George Liddell, D.D., Dean of Christ Church, Oxford, A Memoir*, London, 1899.
Thornton, Percy M., *Harrow School and its Surroundings*, London, 1885.
Timbs, John, *School-Days of Eminent Men*, London, n.d.
Trench, Rev. Francis, *A Few Notes from Past Life, 1818-1832*, Oxford, 1862.
Trollope, Anthony, *An Autobiography*, with an introduction by Michael Sadler, (The World Classics), London, 1923 (1883).
Trollope, Anthony, *Orley Farm*, London, 1871.
Trollope, Thomas Adolphus, *What I Remember*, Vol. I, London, 1887.
Trotter, Captain L. I., *The Life of the Marquis of Dalhousie*, London, 1889.
(Tucker, William Hill) *Eton of Old or Eighty Years Since, 1811-1822, by an old colleger*, London, 1892.
Tucker, William Hill, *Memoir of the Life and Episcopate of G. A. Selwyn*, Vol. I, New York, 1879.
Tupper, Martin Farquhar, *My Life as an Author*, London, 1886.

Vincent, William, D.D., *A Defence of Public Education, Addressed to the Most Revered the Lord Bishop of Meath*, London, 1802.
Vindication of the Enquiry into Charitable Abuses with an Exposure of the Misrepresentation contained in the Quarterly Review, London, 1819.

Bibliography 419

Walker, William Sidney, *The Poetical Remains of*, edited with a memoir by J. Moultrie, London, 1852.
Walpole, Horace, Fourth Earl of Orford, *The Letters of*, edited by Mrs. Paget Toynbee, 16 vols., Oxford, 1903.
Walpole, Spencer, *The Life of Lord John Russell*, 2 vols., London, 1889.
Ward, Wilfred, *William George Ward and the Oxford Movement*, London, 1889.
Ward, Rev. W. G., *The Ideal of a Christian Church*, London, 1844.
(Westmacott, Charles Malloy) Blackmantle, Bernard, *The English Spy*, 2 vols., London, 1825.
Whewell, William, *Of a Liberal Education*, London, 1850.
Whitridge, Arnold, *Dr. Arnold of Rugby*, with an introduction by Sir Michael Sadler, New York, 1928.
Wiese, L., *German Letters on English Education*, translated by W. D. Arnold, London, 1854.
Wilberforce, Robert Isaac, *Life of William Wilberforce*, 5 vols., London, 1838.
Wilkins, Harold, T., *Great English Schools*, London, 1925.
Wilkinson, Rev. C. Allix, *Reminiscences of Eton*, London, 1888.
Wilkinson, Tate, *Memoirs of His Own Life*, 4 vols., York, 1790.
Williams, Mrs. E., *The Life and Letters of Rowland Williams, D.D.*, 2 vols., London, 1874.
Williams, Isaac, *The Autobiography of*, edited by the Ven. Sir George Prevost, London, 1892.
Wilson, David Alec., *Carlyle*, 5 vols., London, 1923-9.
Wilson, Professor (John), *Noctes Ambrosianae*, Vols. II and III, Edinburgh, 1855.
Wood, Norman, *The Reformation and English Education*, London, 1931.
Wordsworth, Charles, *Annals of My Early Life, 1806-46*, London, 1891.
Wordsworth, Charles, *Christian Boyhood at a public school; a collection of sermons and lectures delivered at Winchester College*, 2 vols., London, 1846.
Wordsworth, William, *The Prelude*, from *The Complete Poetical, Works of William Wordsworth*, Cambridge Edition, Cambridge, 1904.
Wright, Ernest Hunter, *The Meaning of Rousseau*, London, 1929.

Yonge, Charlotte Mary, *Life of John Coleridge Patteson*, 2 vols. London, 1874.

PERIODICALS

Bentley's Miscellany, V, June 1840, *A Day at Eton*, by Edward Jesse.
Blackwood's Magazine, May 1825, June 1840, *My Old School*.
British and Foreign Review, I, October 1835, *Education of the Aristocracy*.

Edinburgh Review, November 1812, *Musae Edinenses*; XXX, September 1818; XXI, March 1819; LI, April 1830, *Public Schools of England—Eton*; LIII, March 1831, *Public Schools of England—Westminster and Eton*; LXXVI, January 1843, *The Late Dr. Arnold*; LXXXI, January 1845, *Life and Correspondence of Dr. Arnold*; CIII, April 1856, *French Judgments of England*; CVII, January 1858, *Tom Brown's Schooldays*.
The Eton School Magazine, consisting of original papers of miscellaneous literary character in prose and verse. The entire production of Eton boys of the present day, 1847-8.
The Etonian, 3 vols., London, 1823.

The Flagellant, signed Robert Southey, London, 1792.
Fortnightly Review, XCV, April 1911, *The Arnolds: A Study in Heredity*.
Fraser's Magazine, XXVI, August 1842, *My Life and Times*, by Nimrod; XXXVI, September 1847, *A Defence of a Classical Education*; XLII, September 1850, *Eminentl Etonians* (Review); L, October 1854, *Our Public Schools —their Discipline and Instruction*.

Gentleman's Magazine, June 1813, *Recollections of Christ's Hospital* (Charles Lamb).
Good Words, October 1895, *Rugby and Oxford, 1830–1850*, by W. C. Lake.
The Literary Gazette and Journal of Belles Lettres, Arts, Sciences, etc., November 22nd 1828.

The Microcosm, a periodical work, Windsor, 1788, signed Gregory Griffin.

The Nation and Athenaeum, November 1, 1930, 'Fagging,' by James Herbert.

The New Monthly Magazine, VII, 1823; XIII, 1824, *Recollections of Eton*, XIV, 1825, by Thomas Campbell; XIX, 1827, *Recollections of a Public School*; XXV, 1829, *School Discipline*; XLVIII, October 1836, *Eton Revisited*; LII, January 1838, *Education for the Upper Classes*.

The New Statesman, May 17, 1930.

The Nineteenth Century, XV, March 1884, *My Schooldays from 1830 to 1840*, by G. G. Bradley.

The North British Review, XXVIII, February 1858, *Arnold and his School*.

The Parents' Review, November, December 1895, January, March, April 1896, *Memories of Arnold and Rugby 60 Years Ago by a Member of the School in 1835, 1836, 1837*.

Prospective Review: IV, July 1848, *Eton College*, VIII, April 1852, *German Letters on English Education*.

Punch, January–June 1845, January–June 1854.

Quarterly Journal of Education, V, January 1833, *Westminster School*; VII, January 1834, *English Boarding Schools*; VIII, October 1834, *The Endowed Schools of England, Eton School*; IX, January 1835, *Harrow School, Flogging and Fagging at Winchester*; X, July 1835, *On the Discipline of Large Boarding Schools*.

Quarterly Review, V, May 1811, *State of the Established Church;* VII, June 1812, *Tales of Fashionable Life*, by Miss Edgeworth; VIII, December 1812, *Electa Tentamina*; XIV, October 1815, *Tweddell's Remains*; XIX, July 1818, *Mr. Brougham—Education Committee*; XXXIX, January 1829, *Elementary Education*; XLIV, January 1831, *Moore's Life of Byron*; LII, August 1834, *Eton School—Education in England*; LXX, September 1842, *The Orestes of Aeschylus* (S. Butler); LXXIV, October 1844, *Stanley's Life of Arnold*; XCVII, June 1855, *Memoirs of Sydney Smith*; XCVII, September 1855, *School Sermons*; CII, October 1857, *Rugby Reminiscences*.

The Rugby Magazine, July 1835 to July 1837, 2 vols., London, 1837.

The Spectator, LXVIII, June 18, 1892, *Dr. Arnold after Fifty Years*.

The Spectator (Addison and Steele's), 8 vols., Boston, 1872, Nos. 157, 160, 313, 337.

Temple Bar, LXVII, February 1883, *Mr. Gladstone's Schooldays*, by James Brinsley Richards.

The Times, September 11, 1818; November 26, 1823; March 2, 1825; February 25, 1833; May 4, 15, 16, 1833; January 2, 1836; February 24, 1845; March 3, 1845; December 4, 1846; April 13, 15, 29, 1854; August 29, 1854; January 6, 1858; August 12, 1858; October 13, 1927; May 10, 1930.

Westminster Review, I, January 1824, *Education*; IV, July 1825, VIII, April 1828, *Scientific Education of the Upper Classes*; X, January 1829, *System of Fagging*; XXII, January 1835, *The Effect of Endowments*; XXIII, October 1835, *English Aristocratic Education*; XXXIX, February 1843, *Dr. Arnold*; XLII, December 1844, *Life and Correspondence of Thomas Arnold, D.D.*, LIII, July 1850, *Classical Education*.

INDEX

Ainger, Arthur, 369, 370, 371
Albemarle, George Thomas Keppel, Lord, 152n., 184
Allen, John, 152n., 182n., 198
Arbuthnot, Sir Alexander, 302, 324
Arnold, Matthew, 24, 261, 275, 288, 289, 301, 308, 313, 315, 326, 367, 400
  and Thomas Arnold (of Rugby), 317–23
Arnold, Thomas (of Rugby), xix, 6, 11, 18, 33, 40, 71, 72, 83, 84, 85, 86, 88, 93, 97n., 108, 111, 155, 158, 168, 169, 170, 192, 196, 199, 205, 213, 216n., 218, 219, 223, 224, 225, 227, 231, 232, 233, 234, 288, 289, 316, 375, 381, 386n., 387, 389, 390, 392, 400, 401
  causes of success, 236
  character, 242–5
  criticism of, 275–6, 292–300
  educational ideals, 248–61
  educational methods, 261–75
  influence on disciples, 240, 300–33
  influence on other schools, 240–2, 275–81, 285–7, 334–71
  interpretation of by disciples, 308–19, 329–33
  life, 245–8
  measure of success, 237–40
Arnold, Thomas (brother of Matthew Arnold), 315, 319, 378, 383
Ascham, Roger, 32, 60–1
Athletics and Athleticism:
  Arnold's views on, 276, 280
  criticism of 1840–60, 380–3
  in early nineteenth century, 217n., 218, 231
  in eighteenth century, 39–40, 64, 85
  in forties and fifties, 336–8, 340, 346, 351–2, 354, 369–71, 400, 402
  and Hughes, 332–3
  praise of 1840–60, 299
  at Rugby under Arnold, 305, 306, 310, 326, 329
Authoritarianism:
  and Arnold, 243, 244, 248, 249, 256, 294
  and Carlyle, 201, 202
  and liberal-conservatives, 192–4

Authoritarianism—*contd.*
  and liberals, 130, 166
  and middle classes, 128
  and Public School masters, 31, 106
  and reactionaries, 119–20, 153, 166, 378
  and upper classes, 101, 106, 185

Ballantine, William, 164n.
Barrow, William, 171, 175, 176, 179, 181, 182
Bell-Lancaster Monitorial System, 74, 86, 139n., 147, 148n., 169, 225
Bentham, Jeremy, 77, 123, 147, 148, 152n., 164n., 176n., 226, 293
Benthamites:
  and Arnold, 259
  and the education of the poor, 138n., 148n.
  general ideas, 127
  and opponents, 199
  and Public School government, 138
  and Public School intellectual education, 147–50
Bentley's Miscellany, 383–4
Blackwood's Magazine, 138n., 383–4
Bowdler, John, 163, 167n., 251
Bowles, William Lisle, 140, 142, 172
Bowyer, James, 87, 126n., 164n.
Bradley, George Granville, 275, 295, 296, 302n., 339, 340, 347, 351
British and Foreign Review, 205, 209, 211, 212
Brooke, Henry, 134
Brougham, Henry (Lord Brougham and Vaux), 108, 132, 133n., 135, 136, 137, 139, 142, 148n., 156, 167, 168, 374
Browning, Oscar, 9, 26n., 27, 29, 124, 370n., 371n.
Buildings and Grounds:
  beauty of, 54, 101, 385, 387
  and health, 360–2
  inspiration of, 55, 110–14, 263, 387
Burke, Edmund, 101–2, 107, 109, 113, 122, 126n., 174, 194, 195, 247, 263, 387
Busby, Richard, 12, 18, 23, 29, 32, 33, 48, 63, 86, 88, 229, 230, 268
Butler, George, 74, 79, 81, 82, 177n., 226

424   Public Schools and British Opinion

Butler, Henry Montagu, 335, 344n., 345n.
Butler, Samuel, 234, 241, 353, 354
Butler, Samuel (of Shrewsbury), xix, 19, 74, 78, 81n., 82, 84, 86, 88, 143n., 160n., 162n., 175, 223, 224, 225, 226, 227, 236, 237, 241, 266, 268, 353, 354n., 364, 365
  work at Shrewsbury, 228–34
Byron, George Gordon, Lord, 19, 45n., 76, 81, 87, 93, 94, 109, 126n., 175n., 177, 180, 187, 198, 268, 300, 319, 341, 385n.

Campbell, Thomas, 145, 146n., 166
Canning, George, 109, 172, 174, 179, 189, 216n., 385
Carlisle, Nicholas, 135
Carlyle, Thomas, 194–9, 238, 244, 245, 247, 250, 258, 259, 265, 268, 288, 290, 316, 390, 392, 397n.
  educational ideas, 200–3
Carroll, Lewis, 379
Charterhouse School, xvii, 53, 63, 95, 112, 114, 135, 147n., 153n., 162n., 164, 165, 177n., 198, 334, 348, 383
  in early nineteenth century, 73–87
  in eighteenth century, 5–43
  in the forties and fifties, 360–2
  under Russell, 224–8
Cheltenham School, xviii., 334, 346, 347, 350n., 360
Chesterfield, Philip Dormer Stanhope, Lord, 49, 50, 63–4, 155n., 192
Christ's Hospital, xviiin., 10n., 17, 87, 152n.
Church and the Public Schools:
  and Arnold, 265
  and churchmen, 106, 119–21
  and Coleridge, 195
  High Church attack on, 374, 378
  liberal attack on, 138
  relations between, 6, 7, 8, 11, 12, 13, 369, 401
  See religion in the Public Schools
Clarke, Liscombe, 140, 141, 176
Class Feeling in the Public Schools:
  and Arnold, 256–7, 265, 268, 276–81
  as a conservative force, xviii, 104, 106, 119, 364
  criticism of, 64, 128, 134, 207, 376
  existence of, 25, 52, 53n., 77–8, 81, 85, 94, 99, 350, 363, 371

Class Feeling etc.—*contd.*
  and Hughes, 328
  praise or denial of, 52, 141, 179, 185, 191, 383, 386, 387–8
  production of by schools, 45–6, 178, 191
  as reason for patronizing schools, 20, 51, 66, 77, 79, 104, 128
Classics:
  and Arnold (Matthew), 321
  and Arnold (Thomas), 247, 250, 260, 266, 269–70
  and Butler, 230, 232–3
  criticism of, 56–60, 145–50, 202–3, 210–2, 393–8
  in eighteenth century, 26–30
  at Eton in the fifties, 365–6
  and a gentleman's education, 21–2
  and Humanism, 25–6
  and Kennedy, 353
  and the lower classes, 24
  and Moberly, 360
  praise of, 106, 173–9, 210, 390–3
Clifton College, 334, 346, 347
Clough, Arthur Hugh, 238, 239, 240, 261, 275, 279, 280, 286, 295–6, 301, 308, 312, 317, 318, 319, 320, 321, 323, 326, 384, 400
  and Arnold, 309–17
Cobbett, William, 133, 134, 138n., 146
Coleridge, Arthur Duke, 100, 363, 366, 367
Coleridge, Edward, 367, 368
Coleridge, Samuel Taylor, 87, 117, 126n., 164n., 165, 181n., 194–9, 204, 246, 247, 263, 327, 352, 374, 375, 387
Collins, William, 47, 52
Colman, George (the elder), 49
Colman, George (the younger), 53n.
Conservatives and Conservatism:
  post-Arnoldian (the new conservatism):
    and Arnold, 293–300
    forces and ideas, 287–92
    growth of in forties and fifties, 287–8, 372
    and Hughes, 325, 332
    meaning of, 287–8
    praise of Public Schools by, 383–93
    in schools of forties and fifties, 333–71
  pre-Arnoldian:
    and Arnold, 237, 246, 248–9, 253, 258–60, 261–4

Index 425

Conservatives etc.—*contd.*
class motives of, 103–7, 119, 178, 182, 183–4, 186, 288, 292
criticism by liberals of, 14, 20, 136, 203–4
criticism of schools by, 380
decline of in the thirties, 200
educational philosophy of, 105–6, 173–4, 211–2, 223, 287–8
and governors and masters, 14, 223
and Hughes, 329
individual motives of, 92–103
and liberal-conservatism, 192–3
meaning of, 92
and middle classes, 128, 287
persistence of, in fifties, 287
political philosophy of, 101–2
praise of Public Schools by, 105–7, 139–43, 172–91, 383–93
and reactionaries, 119
and romantic attachment, 107–16
Cory, William Johnson, 367, 379, 381–2
Cotton, George Edward, 302n., 335, 336, 340, 346, 347, 348, 349–52
Cowley, Abraham, 48
Cowper, William, 34, 43–4, 45, 49, 51, 52n., 54, 60, 63–4, 66–7, 71, 77, 84, 152n., 154, 169, 188n.
Crabbe, George, 157n.
Creasy, Sir Edward, 369n., 379, 383, 389, 391, 392
Cumberland, Richard, 44n., 49

Dalhousie, James Ramsay, Lord, 112, 191
Darwin, Charles, 118, 143n., 175n.
Day, Thomas, 43n., 61, 63, 134, 155
Defoe, Daniel, 21, 22, 31, 48, 57
Denman, Thomas, Lord, 111, 115
De Quincey, Thomas, 141, 152n., 168, 187, 190, 218n.
Dickens, Charles, 265, 293, 368, 372, 386, 396–7
Differences between Public Schools, 3, 4, 8, 9, 17, 73–5, 338, 399
Disraeli, Benjamin (Lord Beaconsfield), 196, 199, 265, 290, 386–8
Dolben, William Mackworth, 381, 382
Doyle, Sir Francis Hastings, 298
Drury, Joseph, 19, 40, 81, 87, 177, 228, 233n.
Dryden, John, 18, 48

Edgeworth, Maria, 126, 146, 147, 155, 166, 168, 169, 176
Edgeworth, Richard Lovell, 126, 146, 147, 155, 167, 168, 169
Edinburgh Review, 14, 136, 137, 155, 156, 168, 183, 208, 209, 210, 211, 214, 218n., 294, 334n.
Education, Intellectual, in the Public Schools:
condition and effect of:
under Arnold, 240, 243, 250, 260, 265–6, 268–70, 276, 277, 281, 295, 302–33
under Butler, 230, 232–3
in early nineteenth century, 79, 86–8, 90, 125, 144n., 174–6
in eighteenth century, 25–30, 31, 33
in forties and fifties, 334–71
under Russell, 225
summary, 400–1
criticism of, 55–62, 129–31, 132–3, 143–50, 167, 194, 202, 207–13, 288, 381, 393–8
praise of, 47–50, 105–7, 111, 117, 172–9, 182–3, 288, 390–3
See classics, masters, modern studies, tutorial system
Education of the Lower Classes, 133n., 137n., 148n., 264–5
Education, Medieval:
and the Church, 7n.
disciplinary theory of, 30
of gentlemen, 20, 36
in the Public Schools, 25
Education, Moral, in the Public Schools:
condition and effect of:
under Arnold, 238, 240, 249–56, 259, 266–7, 270–4, 276–81, 302–33
under Butler, 230–1
in early nineteenth century, 76, 77, 82–4, 86, 88, 89, 97n., 99, 103, 117n., 125, 151n., 160n., 161n., 164n., 178
in eighteenth century, 30–46
in forties and fifties, 292, 334–71
under Russell, 223
summary, 400–1
criticism of, 59–65, 117, 119–21, 129–31, 151–70, 172, 193, 194, 197, 203, 213–19, 251, 288, 377–83
praise of, 50–5, 105–7, 111, 117, 119–21, 141, 179–91, 288, 292–300, 383–90

Education, Moral, etc.—*contd.*
  See athletics, buildings, class feeling, friendships, happiness, masters, prefect-fagging system, religion, traditions
Eton College, xvii, 48, 49n., 51, 52, 53, 54–5, 62n., 63, 65, 93, 94, 96, 99n., 100, 101, 103, 107, 108, 110, 111, 113, 114, 115, 126n., 134, 135, 138, 147, 152n., 153n., 154, 155n., 161, 162n., 173, 174, 175n., 176, 177, 179, 180, 185, 187, 189, 190, 198, 203, 204, 206, 208, 209, 211, 212, 214, 215, 216, 217n., 218, 223, 228, 230, 232, 233n., 242, 263, 266, 269, 287, 291, 293, 297, 298, 299, 338, 342, 343, 347, 350, 360n., 374n., 378, 379, 381–3, 383–8, 397, 401
  in early nineteenth century, 73–90
  in eighteenth century, 4–44
  under Hawtrey, 360–71
Eton Miscellany, 174, 385
Eton School Magazine, 384–6
Etonian, 93, 173, 174, 385
Evangelicalism, 120–1, 153–4, 161–3, 198, 199, 249–50, 251, 252, 347
  See reactionaries

Farrar, Frederick W., 345n., 352
Fichte, Johann Gottlieb, 127n., 196, 197, 201
Fielding, Henry, 49, 51, 53, 61, 62, 63
Forces influencing Public School History and Criticism:
  and Arnold, 236
  and Butler, 229
  in early nineteenth century, 90–131, 144, 145, 178, 182, 183–4, 192–9, 207, 212–13
  in eighteenth century, 6, 8, 20–5
  in forties and fifties, 279–81, 286–92, 372
  and Russell, 225
  summary of, 400–3
  See conservatives, liberal-conservatives, liberals, reactionaries
Forster, John, 292
Foundationers at the Public Schools:
  condition of, 4–6, 7, 8, 10–1, 15–6, 24, 29, 37, 78, 214, 348 n., 363–5
  criticism treatment of, 134–7, 206, 376–7
  See membership
Fox, Charles James, 43, 174

Fraser's Magazine, 78, 88, 117n., 188n., 189, 389n., 391
French Revolution:
  and conservatives, 182–3
  and English thought, 123, 125–7
  and Hazelwood, 169
  and liberals, 164
  and reactionaries, 162
  and school rebellions, 79–82
Frere, Bartle, 188
Frere, John Hookham, 179, 189
Friendships in Public Schools, 52, 55, 98, 110, 117n., 180, 181n., 381–3, 388n.
Froude, James Anthony, 362, 373, 379

Gabell, Henry Dison, 80, 82, 243, 245n., 270
Gaskell, Charles Milnes, 93n., 152n., 174
Gentleman:
  meaning of, at Renaissance, 20–1
  medieval education of, 36
  seventeenth century education of, 21
Germany and the Public Schools:
  and Arnold, 247
  and liberal-conservatives, 194–8
  and liberals, 218n.
Gibbon, Edward, 49, 51–2, 61, 63–4, 126n.
Gladstone, William Ewart, 28, 87, 88, 89, 90n., 93n., 109, 141, 162n., 174, 176n., 180, 182n., 198, 288, 322, 364, 368, 385, 387n.
Goddard, William Stanley, 18, 40, 73, 80–1, 84, 86, 243
Godwin, William, 125, 126n., 146, 175n., 187, 188
Goethe, Johann Wolfgang, 194, 198, 201, 247, 293
Goodall, Joseph, 15, 87, 89, 365
Government of the Public Schools:
  and Arnold, 238, 259, 264–5, 268
  and Butler, 229
  and conservatism, 14, 24, 34, 80, 92, 106, 223
  criticism of, 66, 129–30, 132–8, 194, 203–6, 373–5
  in eighteenth century, 7, 11–3, 15–6
  in forties and fifties, 359, 361–4
  praise of, 106, 139–41
Gray, Thomas, 44, 47, 53, 55, 66, 77, 96, 117n.
Green, Thomas Hill, 389

Index

Griffith, George, 375, 376–7, 394–5

Haileybury School, 334, 346, 347
Hallam, Arthur Henry, 93n., 94, 141, 174, 180, 366
Happiness of Boys in Public Schools:
 as conservative force, 52–5, 93, 95, 97–9, 179–81, 383–6, 386–8
 denial of, 117, 215, 257
 and romantic attachment, 109
Hare, Augustus J. C., 80, 84, 237, 345n.
Harrison, Frederic, 346n., 380
Harrow School, xvii, 52, 93n., 94, 98, 103, 107, 111, 112, 128n., 133n., 134, 151n., 154, 161, 162n., 176, 179, 181, 191, 198, 199, 202, 206, 212, 231, 233n., 240, 242, 269, 287, 297, 302–3, 318, 334, 347, 352–3, 355n., 360n., 379, 382, 389–90, 401
 in early nineteenth century, 73–87
 in eighteenth century, 5–44
 under Vaughan, 341–6
Hastings, Warren, 40, 49
Hatherley, William Page Wood, Lord, 81, 187n.
Havelock, Sir Henry, 87, 182n., 198, 243
Hawtrey, John, 79, 87, 154, 223, 228, 233n., 300, 360n., 364–6, 367, 378
Hazelwood School, 147, 168–70
Heath, Benjamin, 19, 40, 87
Hewlett, Joseph James, 153n., 227
High Church Reaction (Oxford Movement), 196n., 241n., 246, 287, 289, 293, 308, 316, 339, 343, 357, 374, 377–8, 382
Hill, Mathew Davenport, 147, 168–70, 218n., 227
Hill, Sir Rowland, 147, 168–70, 218n., 227, 262
Hill, Thomas Wright, 147, 168–70, 227
Hodgson, Francis, 154, 365, 366n.
Hook, Theodore, 117n., 153n., 226
Hook, Walter Farquhar, 117n., 152n.
Hoole, Charles, 32
Hughes, Thomas, xviii, 239, 273, 286, 299, 301, 303, 309, 336, 351, 352, 373, 387, 390, 400
 Tom Brown's Schooldays, 324–33
Humanitarianism, 62, 67, 118, 128n., 130, 165, 215n., 225, 226, 256–8, 281, 287, 334
 See liberals
Huxley, Thomas Henry, 212

Imperialism and the Public Schools, 45, 105, 191, 276, 280, 290–2, 327, 368, 400, 402
Industrialism and the Public Schools, 65, 104, 207, 213, 290, 327, 334, 390, 402
Inertia as a conservative force, xviii, 100
Interrelations of the Public Schools, 6, 76, 230, 240, 334–71

James, Thomas, 14n., 19, 82, 85, 86, 87–8, 144, 176n., 230, 231, 240
Johnson, Samuel, 50, 242

Keate, John, 33, 74, 75, 81, 82, 85, 97n., 177, 182, 215n., 226, 231, 267n., 270, 298, 349, 364, 366, 371
 work at Eton, 88–90
Kennedy, Benjamin Hall, 230, 231, 232n., 233, 234, 286, 341n., 346, 352–5
Kinglake, A. W., 89
King's College, Cambridge, 7, 10, 11, 13, 15, 209, 365
Kingsley, Charles, 199, 326, 327, 328, 331, 332, 352
Knox, Vicesimus, 154, 155, 160, 161, 171, 178, 179, 182

Lake, William Charles, 293–4, 295, 296, 301, 302–3, 305, 306, 310, 317, 324, 339
Lamb, Charles, 10n., 87, 152n., 181n.
Landor, Walter Savage, 88n., 164n., 176n.
Liberal-Conservatives and Liberal-Conservatism:
 and Arnold, 192, 248, 292–4
 and Carlyle, 200–1
 and Farrar, 352
 and Germany, 194–8
 and Hughes, 327–8, 332–3
 and Maurice and Kingsley, 327
 meaning of, 192
 motives of, 207
 philosophy of, 192–3, 210–2
 and Public Schools, 193–4, 200, 203–19
 and religious revival, 198–9
 and upper classes in forties, 287
Liberals and Liberalism:
 and Arnold (Matthew), 322
 and Arnold (Thomas), 237, 242, 243, 246, 248–9, 256–8, 268, 276–81
 and Butler, 229, 234

Liberals and Liberalism—*contd.*
  class motives of, 121–2, 127–9, 145, 207, 286
  criticism of Public Schools by, 57–9, 67, 129–31, 132–9, 144–50, 155–60, 164–6, 166–70, 200, 203–19, 373–7, 378–81, 393–8
  decline of, in forties, 287, 288, 289
  educational ideas of, 123, 146, 147, 149–50, 166, 167–70, 210–12, 226
  and Hughes, 328
  individual motives of, 117–18
  and liberal-conservatives, 192–3
  political ideas of, 122–3
  in the Public Schools of the forties and fifties, 287, 292–4, 334–71
  and reactionaries, 120
  and Russell, 225
  and Stanley, 308
Libertarianism:
  and Arnold, 248–9, 255, 258–61, 280, 294
  and eighteenth-century critics, 62
  and Hazelwood, 169
  and liberal-conservatives, 192–3
  and liberals, 122, 152, 159, 164, 165, 212
  and middle classes, 128
  and reactionaries, 120
  and upper classes, 39, 79n., 106, 185
Liddell, Henry George, 226, 361–2
Lily, William, 25, 26n.
Literary Gazette, 159
Locke, John, 18, 22, 31, 43, 50, 51, 56, 66, 67, 123, 124, 125n., 146, 179, 253
  educational theories, 57–9, 61, 62–3
Long Chamber at Eton, 78, 99n., 100, 198, 363–5, 385
Longley, Charles Thomas, 228, 233n. 341–2
Lower Classes:
  admission of, to Public Schools, 5, 8, 9–11, 15, 20–5
  influence of, on Public Schools, 138n., 144n., 145, 207
  opinions on admission of, 133–7, 141–3
  treatment of, in Public Schools, 78
  See education of lower classes, foundationers, membership
Lubbock, Alfred, 370, 371
Lyon, John, 5, 24, 30, 32, 39, 41
Lytton, Edward Bulwer-Lytton, Lord, 204, 207, 208, 210, 211, 212, 214, 215, 218n.

Macready, William Charles, 152n.
Malet, Sir Alexander, 158–9
Manning, Henry Edward, 93n., 98, 162, 198
Marlborough College, xvii, 242, 302n., 318, 334, 346, 347, 348–52, 361
Martineau, James, 239, 246, 292
Masters in the Public Schools:
  conservatism of, 34, 92–3, 106–7
  criticism of (general), 119–20, 144, 145, 160–6, 210, 214
  criticism of relations to boys, 130–1, 158–60, 166–8, 210, 215n., 216, 217, 218
  praise of, 47–8, 86–7, 177, 384
  question of increase in numbers of, 145, 161, 209, 218, 362, 365
  reformers among, 86–9, 223–81, 338–71
  relations to boys, 32–3, 37, 39–41, 62, 75, 78–82, 83–4, 86, 88, 89, 160n., 227, 230–1, 245, 267, 272–3, 277–81, 336, 366, 371
  relations to governing bodies, 11, 12
  selection of, 14, 34, 360
  and upper classes, 105, 111
  See Arnold, Butler, education intellectual, education moral, etc.
Mathews, Charles, 164n.
Maurice, Frederick Dennison, 326–7, 352
Membership of the Public Schools:
  criticism of, 66, 129–30, 132, 133–6, 206–7, 376–7
  nature of:
    and Arnold, 264–5, 268
    in early nineteenth century, 73–4
    in eighteenth century, 8, 15, 16–25, 66
    in the forties and fifties, 350, 355, 363
    question of founders' intentions, 9–11
  summary, 401
  praise of, 104, 117, 119, 128, 141–3
  size of, 17, 73, 74, 100, 103n., 226, 228, 238, 287, 341, 348, 360, 364
Merchant Taylors School, xviin., 25n., 38, 164n.
Merivale, Charles, 27, 83, 160n.
Metcalfe, Charles, 87, 93n.
Microcosm, 93, 174, 177, 185, 189, 190, 312, 385

Index

Middle Classes:
  and Arnold, 243
  criticism of Public Schools in eighteenth century, 61, 64, 67
  and Hazelwood, 168
  and liberal-conservatism, 192–3, 198 200
  and liberalism, 121–31, 401
  and new conservatism, 288–92
  and new schools, 347
  and reaction, 119–21
  and reform in forties and fifties, 287–9
  and reform of Shrewsbury and Charterhouse, 224–6, 228, 232
  relations to Public Schools in early nineteenth century, 73–4, 77, 78, 97
  relations to Public Schools in eighteenth century, 5, 6, 9, 10, 20–1
  and useful knowledge, 57, 211–12, 390–1
Mill, John Stuart, 123, 204, 212, 374–5, 392, 397–8
Milman, Henry Hart, 89, 93n.
Milton, John, 31, 48, 51, 59, 60, 123
Moberly, George, 74, 285, 286, 334, 356–60, 362, 389, 391
Modern Studies:
  advocacy of, 26n., 57–9, 145, 150, 210–12, 390, 394–8
  and Arnold, 268–9
  introduction of, 354, 365, 366, 400
Montem, 38, 155n., 365, 385, 388
More, Hannah, 154, 155
Moultrie, John, 93n., 114, 153n., 174, 180, 185
Mozley, Thomas, 75, 77, 226
Mulcaster, Richard, 25, 32

National Institutions, Public Schools as, xv, xvii, 11, 65–6, 71, 75, 76, 110, 140
New College, Oxford, 7, 11, 13, 15, 360
Newman, John Henry, 196n., 308, 374, 377, 378n., 391–3, 397n.
New Monthly, 108, 117n., 145, 147n., 157, 166, 209, 216, 218n.
Nicoll, John, 18, 29, 33n., 44n., 48, 49, 63, 74
Nimrod (James Apperley), 78, 88, 117n., 188n., 189, 373
North British Review, 298
Northcote, Sir Stafford (Lord Iddesleigh), 367, 368

Oppidans (Commoners, Non-Foundationers, Paying Students, etc.) 8
  See membership
Organic Growth, xvi, 3, 8, 35, 101–2, 122–3, 355, 387, 399–400
Oundle School, 15
Owen, Robert, 133, 148n., 199

Palmerston, Henry John Temple, Lord, 182n., 198, 288, 343n.
Pamphlets and Books, Anonymous:
  An Enquiry into the Melancholy Circumstances of Great Britain, 57
  Eton Abuses Considered, etc., 208, 209, 210, 211, 214, 215, 217n., 218n.
  Eton System Vindicated, etc., 110, 139, 142, 177, 179, 210
  Etonensis, A few Words in Reply to Some Remarks, etc., 140, 176, 177, 209, 210
  Etonian, Reminiscences of Eton, 85, 373
  History of a Schoolboy, 154
  Legacy of an Etonian, 89
  A Very Short Letter from One Old Westminster, etc., 110, 142, 177, 180
  A Letter to Sir Alexander Malet, etc. (Old Etonian), 186, 189
  A Letter to the Rt. Hon. Sir Wm. Scott, etc. (Holt), 116, 141, 142
  Letters from a Nobleman to his Son, etc., 144, 183
  Observations on the Present System of Education, etc., 394
  Public Education, 103, 144, 173, 181, 188, 191
  Recollections of Rugby (Old Rugbaean), 302, 324, 373, 383–4
  Some Remarks on the Present Studies and Management of Eton School (A Parent), 204, 209, 217n.
  Vindication of the Enquiry into Parliamentary Abuses, 108, 136–7, 140, 143
  A Few Words on the Monitorial System at Harrow, 390
Parr, Samuel, 81, 82, 86, 87, 160n., 176
Patteson, John Coleridge, 368, 369
Pearson, Charles Henry, 297, 298, 299, 339, 340, 351n.
Peel, Sir Robert, 137n., 177n., 182n., 198, 243, 343, 388, 391
Pepys, Samuel, 48, 53

Pestalozzi, Johann Heinrich, 56n., 126n., 196, 201, 218n.
Pitt, William (Lord Chatham), 48, 49n., 61, 63, 174
Praed, Winthrop Mackworth, 87, 93n., 94, 110, 115, 174, 178, 180, 366, 385
Prefect-fagging System:
  and Arnold, 239, 266, 267, 272–3, 277
  in early nineteenth century, 80, 81, 82–4, 88
  in eighteenth century, 40–2, 63
  opinions of, 117, 130–1, 157, 158–60, 167–8, 170, 185–91, 207, 214, 215, 216, 217, 225, 226, 231, 305, 379–80, 389–90
  in forties and fifties, 342, 343, 349, 354, 356, 358, 362, 368
Professional Classes and the Public Schools, 9, 20–2, 73–4, 77, 228, 268
Prospective Review, 371n., 376, 379, 386n.
Public School Commission, xviin., xix, 10, 286, 335, 340n., 351, 355, 360, 361, 375, 399, 402
Public Schools, definition of, xvii, 3
  See education intellectual, education moral, Eton, Harrow, etc., forces influencing, government, membership
Punch, 335, 394n.

Quarterly Journal of Education, 205–7, 209, 211, 216–8, 266
Quarterly Review, 104n., 139, 140–1, 142, 145n., 160, 172, 173, 176, 177, 178, 179, 183, 184, 187, 189, 206, 207, 208, 209, 210, 211, 214, 217, 228, 233n., 293, 299, 304, 327, 391

Reactionaries and Reaction:
  and Arnold, 248, 249–56, 401
  criticism of Public Schools, 153–4, 161–4, 374, 377–8
  in early nineteenth century, 116, 118–21
  and liberal-conservatives, 192–3
  and middle classes, 128
  motives of, 178
  and the thirties, 200
Realism, Educational Theory of, 25n., 56, 57
Rebellions in Public Schools, 33, 79–82, 231, 349

Religion in the Public Schools:
  and Arnold, 248–53, 256–7, 266–7, 271, 293–300
  criticism of, 119–20, 130–1, 161–3, 214, 217, 377–8
  in early nineteenth century, 161n.
  in eighteenth century, 30, 33–4
  in forties and fifties, 336, 337, 344, 356–8, 369
  political purpose of, 183
  and the religious revival, 198, 199, 287, 289, 345
  and ritualism, 382–3
  upper class feeling about, 105, 386
Renaissance and the Public Schools, 5, 10n., 401
  and democracy, 23
  and idea of a gentleman, 20
  and the classics, 25–30
Rennell, Thomas, 161–3
Romantic Attachment, xvi, xviii, 53–4, 66, 71, 107–16, 118, 207, 264, 278, 372–3, 383–8
Romantic Movement and the Public Schools, 96–7, 101, 107, 109, 120, 291
Rossall School, 334, 346
Roundell, Charles S., 341n.
Rousseau, Jean Jacques, 31, 56n., 58, 96, 97, 109, 126, 127n., 133, 146, 197n., 255
  educational theories, 124–5
Rowcroft, Charles, 160n., 187, 190, 373
Rugby Magazine, 312–13, 384
Rugby School, xvii, 108, 114, 117n., 151n., 152n., 170n., 179, 192, 199n., 219, 223, 230, 233, 234, 285, 289, 293, 295, 297, 298, 301, 338, 342, 344, 345, 346, 347, 348, 349, 351, 356, 359, 360n., 362, 364, 366, 373, 379, 383, 384, 385, 390
  Arnold at, 237–81
  Arnold's disciples at, 302–33
  in early nineteenth century, 72–88
  in eighteenth century, 3–37
  in forties and fifties, 338–41
Russell, Bertrand, 31, 276, 277, 280
Russell, John (of Charterhouse), xix, 74, 84, 86, 138n., 147n., 153, 165, 223, 224, 230, 232, 236
  work at Charterhouse, 224–8
Russell, John Russell, Lord, 160n., 189, 288

St. Paul's School, xviin., 25n., 32, 38, 48, 164n., 334

Index

Savile, Sir Henry, 17n, 27n.
Scott, Sir Walter, 101, 102, 175n.
Selborne, Roundell Palmer, Lord, 76, 83, 99, 151n.
Select Commtitee on the Education of the ower Orders (1818), 15–6, 132, 135–7, 139–41
Selwyn, George Augustus, 90n., 177, 368
Sentimentalism, 54–5, 66, 90n., 95–9, 117n., 177, 208, 372–3, 383–4, 386–8
Shaftesbury, Anthony Ashley Cooper Lord, 293, 340n.
Shelley, Percy Bysshe, 94, 117, 126n., 153n., 164n., 175n., 300, 313, 370, 385n.
Sheridan, Richard Brinsley, 87
Sheriffe, Lawrence, 5
Shrewsbury School, xvii, 118, 162n., 223, 224n., 334, 341n., 396
  Butler at, 228–35
  in early nineteenth century, 73–88
  in eighteenth century, 3–24
  Kennedy at, 352–5
Sidgwick, Henry, 334, 340, 380
Smith, Adam, 66, 67, 123, 132–3, 134, 146, 205, 374
Smith, Goldwin, 341n.
Smith, Southwood, 150
Smith, Sydney, xviii, 103n., 117, 144, 155–6, 157, 161, 166, 167, 168, 400
Smollett, Tobias, 43, 61–2, 63
Southey, Robert, 126n., 139n., 157, 160, 164, 165, 167–8, 181n., 188
Spectator (Addison and Steele's), 50n., 51, 59, 60, 61–2
Spectator, 261
Stanley, Arthur Penrhyn, 199, 236, 238, 239, 240, 246, 247, 251, 253, 258, 268, 274, 275, 279, 285, 286, 293, 298, 301, 302, 303, 310, 311, 315, 317, 318, 319, 320, 323, 324, 326, 330, 331, 339, 343, 344, 345, 362, 387, 400
  and Arnold, 304–9
State and the Public Schools:
  and Arnold (Matthew), 322
  and Arnold (Thomas), 223n., 264–5,
  and Butler, 223n., 229
  and liberals, 122, 130–1, 132–3, 134, 136, 204–6, 374–5
  relations between, 6, 7, 8, 11, 12, 223, 401

Steele, Richard, 32, 48, 53, 61–2, 63, 119, 120
Stephen, James Fitzjames, 299, 318, 331, 380–1
Stephen, Leslie, 299, 363
Strachey, Lytton, 242, 243, 246, 257n., 266, 269, 276, 277, 280, 314n., 342, 353
Sumner, Robert, 19, 87
Sutton, Thomas, 5, 6, 10
Swift, Jonathon, 21, 22, 50, 60
Swinburne, Algernon Charles, 370
Sydney, Sir Philip, 23, 37
Symonds, John Addington, 346n., 381, 382–3

Tait, Archibald Campbell, 302n., 338–9
Thackeray, Thomas, 18, 19, 87
Thackeray, William Makepeace, 8, 53n., 77, 83, 95, 109, 115, 117n., 152n., 153n., 164, 165–6, 177n., 178, 180, 184, 226, 227, 368, 372–3, 378, 395
Thirlwall, Connop, 154, 199
Thornton, Spencer, 252
Thring, Edward, 30, 33, 223n., 362n., 363n., 367
The Times, 136, 151n., 156, 185, 206, 237, 343, 361, 372, 373, 379–80, 383, 389
Traditions and Traditionalism:
  and Arnold, 261–4, 272, 301
  and Butler, 229–30
  criticism of, 129–30, 216, 375
  and Hughes, 328
  in post-Arnoldian school, 345, 349, 350–1, 355, 359, 360, 363–4
  praise of, 119, 171, 173, 300, 384, 387–8
  in pre-Arnoldian school, 3, 8, 9, 14, 33, 34, 36, 38–42, 56, 75, 76, 80, 101–3, 223, 399–401
  and romantic attachment, 110, 111–14
  and Russell, 227–8
Trench, Francis, 79
Trollope, Anthony, 25n., 78, 94, 117, 134n., 143n., 153n., 188n.
Trollope, Thomas Adolphus, 78, 83, 134n., 153n., 162n., 184, 187n.
Tucker, William Hill, 78, 81, 89, 190, 365n.
Tupper, Martin Farquhar, 162n., 165, 226, 227
Tutorial System at Public Schools, 27, 88, 209n., 214, 366
Tweddell, John, 184, 187

Udall, Nicholas, 17, 25, 32
Universities and the Public Schools, 6, 7, 11, 13, 25, 137, 365
Upper Classes:
  and Arnold, 264
  conservatism of, 92–3, 103–6
  criticism of their predominance in Public Schools, 207, 376
  criticism of Public Schools by, 119–21
  and education of the poor, 149n.
  and liberal-conservatism, 192–9, 200, 207, 286–7
  and middle classes, 72, 121, 128
  and new conservatism, 287–92
  in the Public Schools, xv, xvii, 10, 18, 19, 20, 21–3, 66, 73–5, 77–8, 281, 401
  traditions of, 36, 37
Uppingham School, 15, 346, 362n.

Vaughan, Charles James, 74, 286, 301, 305, 310, 317, 334n., 335, 341, 351, 352, 379, 389, 390
  and Arnold, 302–3
  work at Harrow, 343–6
Vincent, William, 161–2, 182

Walpole, Horace (Lord Orford), 43, 47, 53, 54–5, 66, 77
Ward, William George, 81, 83, 84, 158, 316, 339, 374, 377, 378
Wellesley, Richard Wellesley, Lord, 111, 115
Wellington, Arthur Wellesley, Duke of, 94, 226, 257
Wellington School, 346
Westmacott, Charles Mallory, 180
Westminster College, xvii, 48, 49, 51, 53n., 54, 63, 64, 101, 110, 126n., 134, 135, 138, 148, 152n., 161,

Westminster College—*contd.*
  164, 181n., 198, 216n., 242, 295, 334, 360n., 379, 397
  in early nineteenth century, 73–8
  in eighteenth century, 4–43
  in forties and fifties, 360–2
Westminster Review, 98–9, 108, 110n., 139, 147, 148–50, 158–9, 205, 207, 211, 215, 256, 293, 374, 395
Whewell, William, 395–6
Wiese, Leopold, 297n., 335, 372, 386n., 393, 394n., 396
Wilberforce, William, 163
Wilkinson, C. Allix, 89
Wilkinson, Tate, 61
William of Wykeham, 4, 6, 10, 30, 32, 33, 37, 39, 41, 42, 241, 355, 357, 401
Williams, David, 16, 81, 84, 158
Williams, Isaac, 93n., 98, 176n., 182n., 198, 243
Williams, Rowland, 99n., 152n., 182n., 198
Wilson, John (Christopher North), 149n.
Winchester College, xvii, 48, 54, 62, 63, 65, 134, 135, 141, 147, 152n., 156, 158, 162n., 168, 170, 172, 176, 206, 237, 241, 242, 243, 246, 263, 285, 287, 297, 317, 342, 380
  in early nineteenth century, 73–86
  in eighteenth century, 4–43
  in forties and fifties, 355–60
Wordsworth, Charles, 85, 93n., 98, 198, 237, 285n., 356–9, 360n.
Wordsworth, Christopher, 82, 286, 341–3
Wordsworth, William, 96–7, 246, 285n.

Young, Edward, 54